CLINICA   E
WITH IN

The Wiley Series in

CLINICAL PSYCHOLOGY

J. Mark G. Williams
(Series Editor)

School of Psychology, University of Wales, Bangor, UK

William Yule (Editor)	Post-Traumatic Stress Disorders: Concepts and Therapy
Nicholas Tarrier Adrian Wells Gillian Haddock (Editors)	Treating Complex Cases: The Cognitive Behavioural Therapy Approach
Michael Bruch Frank W. Bond (Editors)	Beyond Diagnosis: Case Formulation Approaches in CBT
Martin Herbert	Clinical Child Psychology (second edition)
Eric Emerson Chris Hatton Jo Bromley Amanda Caine (Editors)	Clinical Psychology and People with Intellectual Disabilities
J. Mark G. Williams Fraser N. Watts Colin MacLeod Andrew Mathews	Cognitive Psychology and Emotional Disorders (second edition)
Phil Mollon	Multiple Selves, Multiple Voices: Working with Trauma, Violation and Dissociation
Paul Chadwick, Max Birchwood and Peter Trower	Cognitive Therapy for Delusions, Voices and Paranoia
Peter Sturmey	Functional Analysis in Clinical Psychology
	Further titles in preparation: *A list of earlier titles in the series follows the index*

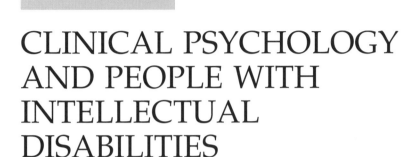

CLINICAL PSYCHOLOGY AND PEOPLE WITH INTELLECTUAL DISABILITIES

Eric Emerson and Chris Hatton,
Hester Adrian Research Centre, University of Manchester, and Lancashire Clinical Psychology Training Course, UK

Jo Bromley
South Manchester University Hospitals NHS Trust, Manchester, UK

Amanda Caine
Rochdale HealthCare NHS Trust, UK

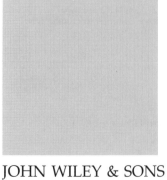

JOHN WILEY & SONS
Chichester · New York · Weinheim · Brisbane · Singapore · Toronto

Other Wiley Editorial Offices

John Wiley & Sons Inc., 111 River Street, Hoboken, NJ 07030, USA

Jossey-Bass, 989 Market Street, San Francisco, CA 94103-1741, USA

Wiley-VCH Verlag GmbH, Boschstr. 12, D-69469 Weinheim, Germany

John Wiley & Sons Australia Ltd, 33 Park Road, Milton, Queensland 4064, Australia

John Wiley & Sons (Asia) Pte Ltd, 2 Clementi Loop #02-01, Jin Xing Distripark, Singapore 129809

John Wiley & Sons (Canada) Ltd, 22 Worcester Road, Etobicoke, Ontario M9W 1L1

Wiley also publishes its books in a variety of electronic formats. Some content that appears in print may not be available in electronic books.

Library of Congress Cataloging-in-Publication Data

Clinical psychology and people with intellectual disabilities / Eric Emerson . . . [et. al.].
      p. cm. — (The Wiley series in clinical psychology)
    Includes bibliographical references and index.
    ISBN 0–471–96783–1 (cloth). — ISBN 0–471–97662–8 (pkb : alk. paper)
    1. Mentally handicapped—Mental health. 2. Mentally handicapped—Psychology. 3. Mentally handicapped—Counselling of. I. Emerson, Eric. II. Series.
    [DNLM: 1. Mentally Disabled Persons—psychology. 2. Mental Retardation—complications. 3. Mental Disorders—therapy. 4. Psychology. Clinical—methods. WM 300 C641 1998]
    RC451.4.M47C5   1998
    616.89—dc21
    DNLM/DLC
    for Library of Congress   98–33515
                                              CIP

British Library Cataloguing in Publication Data
A catalogue record for this book is available from the British Library

ISBN 0–471–96783–1 (cased)
ISBN 0–471–97662–8 (paper)

Phototypeset in 10/12pt Times from the authors' disks by Intype London Ltd
Printed and bound in Great Britain by Biddles Ltd, Guildford and King's Lynn
This book is printed on acid-free paper responsibly manufactured from sustainable forestatry, in which at least two trees are planted for each one used for paper production.

CONTENTS

ABOUT THE EDITORS

Eric Emerson is Professor of Clinical Psychology in Intellectual Disability at the Hester Adrian Research Centre, University of Manchester and Clinical Tutor on the Lancashire D Clin Psych Course. He qualified as a clinical psychologist in 1978, is a Fellow of the British Psychological Society and has worked as a clinical psychologist in the UK and Canada. Over the last decade he has been particularly involved in research and development in the area of challenging behaviours shown by people with intellectual disabilities.

Chris Hatton is a Research Fellow at the Hester Adrian Research Centre, University of Manchester, and Research Tutor on the Lancashire D Clin Psych Course. He has been involved in research and development covering a wide range of issues, including service quality and quality of life in residential services, stress and morale, and ethnic issues in service provision.

Jo Bromley qualified as a clinical psychologist in 1995. She is currently working with children with intellectual disabilities and their families at the Duchess of York Children's Hospital in South Manchester and is involved in teaching and supervision on the Clin Psy D course at the University of Manchester. Previously, she was involved in research relating to challenging behaviours shown by children and adults with intellectual disabilities.

Amanda Caine qualified as a clinical psychologist in 1981. She has worked as a clinical psychologist primarily with children and adults with intellectual disabilities. Since 1983 she has been involved in teaching and supervision on the Clin Psy D course at the University of Manchester. She is currently Consultant Clinical Psychologist with the Rochdale Healthcare NHS Trust. She has been involved in research and development on a range of issues, including ethnic issues in service provision, mental health issues and the use of psychotropic medication.

LIST OF CONTRIBUTORS

Jo Bromley
Carol Kendrick Unit, Duchess of York Children's Hospital, Nell Lane, West Didsbury, Manchester M20 2LR, UK

Amanda Caine
Department of Clinical Psychology, Birch Hill Hospital, Rochdale OL12 9BQ, UK

Sue Candy
Learning Disability Service, Plymouth Community Services NHS Trust, Westbourne Unit, Scott Hospital, Beacon Park Road, Plymouth PL2 2PQ, UK

Isabel C.H. Clare
Lifespan Healthcare NHS Trust, Douglas House, 18b Trumpington Road, Cambridge CB2 2AH, UK

John Clements
Applied Psychology Services, Crewes Place, Crewes Lane, Warlingham, Surrey CR3 9NS, UK

Christine Emerson
School Psychological Service, Education Department, PO Box 33, Northgate House, Halifax HX1 1UN, UK

Eric Emerson
Hester Adrian Research Centre, University of Manchester, Manchester M13 9PL, UK

Chris Hatton
Hester Adrian Research Centre, University of Manchester, Manchester M13 9PL, UK

Anthony Holland
Lifespan Healthcare NHS Trust, Douglas House, 18b Trumpington Road, Cambridge CB2 2AH, UK

Judith McBrien
Learning Disability Service, Plymouth Community Services NHS Trust, Westbourne Unit, Scott Hospital, Beacon Park Road, Plymouth PL2 2PQ, UK

Sue McGaw
Trecare (NHS) Trust, 57 Pydar Street, Truro, Cornwall TR1 2SS, UK

Jude Moss
Community Learning Disability Team, 102 Manchester Road, Chorlton, Manchester M21, UK

Glynis H. Murphy
Tizard Centre, University of Kent at Canterbury, Canterbury, Kent CT2 7LZ, UK

Helen Prosser
Hester Adrian Research Centre, University of Manchester, Manchester M13 9PL, UK

Bob Remington
Psychology Department, University of Southampton, Highfield, Southampton SO9 5NH, UK

Steve Turner
Hester Adrian Research Centre, University of Manchester, Manchester M13 9PL, UK

SERIES PREFACE

The Wiley Series in Clinical Psychology aims to provide a comprehensive set of texts covering the application of psychological science to the problems of mental health and disability. The field of intellectual disability continues to be one in which psychology has the role as the major contributor: in understanding the nature of the problems to be addressed, and in designing and delivering interventions.

Because of the complexity of the field, it has been important for psychologists to study individual aspects of such disability in great depth. By contrast, the authors of this book take a broad view. What can a psychological understanding contribute across the entire range of issues raised when someone has such a disability? Starting from basic issues of epidemiology and cause, and from descriptions of the basic psychological disabilities, they consider issues raised when mental health problems co-occur, when sexual abuse is alleged, and when a person's behaviour is found to challenge the resources of the people or services that surround him or her. They examine the family context, and how to address it; the organisational context and how to understand and work within it (including its legal aspects). Finally, they consider health promotion issues, and how to work with communities to take proper account of the increased risk of physical, mental and lifestyle problems that may occur in people with such disabilities.

This is a truly comprehensive text, written out of both rich clinical experience and an extensive academic knowledge of the area. It will be an invaluable guide for both students and practitioners in the field extending far beyond the clinical psychology perspective in which the book is grounded. With guides for further reading at the end of each chapter in addition to a comprehensive reference list, this will be an important source book for many years to come.

J. Mark G. Williams

Series Editor

PREFACE

This book has grown out of our attempts to prepare trainee Clinical Psychologists to work with people with intellectual disabilities. Some time ago, frustration at not being able to recommend a single relatively comprehensive practically oriented text led, seemingly quite naturally, to discussion about what such a text would contain and speculation about possible contributors. Before too long we found ourselves in possession of a proposal and then a little later a contract. The time from contract to manuscript, however, took a little longer.

Our main aim has been to produce a text that trainee Clinical Psychologists (and others in similar situations) would find practically useful in their work with people with intellectual disabilities—not as a comprehensive step-by-step 'how to do it' book, rather as a source of ideas and techniques that, taken together, would help provide a framework for guiding work with individuals, families and organisations. We also hope that the book will have wider appeal in providing an update for practising psychologists and an insight into current psychological approaches for other professionals.

We have no delusions, however, about the comprehensiveness of this book. People with intellectual disabilities are remarkably diverse. The work undertaken with them by Clinical Psychologists and other supporting professionals is likely to explore many avenues not covered in the following pages. We do hope, however, that we have managed to give some useful guidance on the main areas of clinical practice.

There are, of course, many people to thank for their support in helping us translate our initial idea into the reality of the book you are holding: Michael Coombs and Lesley Valerio at Wiley for their considerable patience; our partners and friends for their forbearance; the numerous people who have provided encouragement over the years; and, last but not least, our many contributors for delivering their chapters (more or less) on time!

Eric Emerson
Chris Hatton
Jo Bromley
Amanda Caine

18 June 1998

PART I

Setting the Scene

Chapter 1

INTRODUCTION

Eric Emerson*, Amanda Caine**, Jo Bromley† and Chris Hatton*

The aim of this book is to provide a resource for clinical psychologists working with people with intellectual disabilities, as well as other professionals who are providing services within a psychological framework. In this introductory chapter we will discuss some of the basic principles which we believe should *always* underlie the support provided by psychologists to people with intellectual disabilities. Following that, we will provide a brief overview of the organisation and content of the rest of the book.

BASIC PRINCIPLES

In the following sections we will suggest that, wherever possible, psychological support provided to people with intellectual disabilities should be:

❏ Socially valid.
❏ Functionally based.
❏ Constructional.

In discussing these issues we will also address various aspects of 'formulation', briefly outline some ways to evaluate the impact of your intervention, and provide a framework to guide the selection of specific interventions. In this chapter we will be using the term 'intervention' very broadly to cover any aspect of a clinical psychologist's work which is intended to have either a direct or an indirect impact on the life of a person with intellectual disabilities. This means that 'interventions', as

*Hester Adrian Research Centre, Manchester; **Rochdale Healthcare NHS Trust; †South Manchester University Hospitals NHS Trust, UK

Clinical Psychology and People with Intellectual Disabilities. Edited by E. Emerson, C. Hatton, J. Bromley and A. Caine.
© 1998 John Wiley & Sons Ltd.

discussed in this chapter, include such diverse activities as individual and group therapy (of any 'school'), determining a person's or his/her family's eligibility for services, and assessing the reliability of a suspect's confession obtained at time of police interview.

Interventions should be socially valid

The concept of social validity originated within applied behaviour analysis in response to the apparent failure of services to implement behavioural procedures which had been 'demonstrated' to be clinically effective (Wolf, 1978). It provides a framework which, we believe, is equally applicable to considering the aims and process of all forms of intervention. An intervention which is socially valid should:

❑ Address a socially significant problem.
❑ In a manner which is acceptable to the main constituencies involved.
❑ Result in socially important outcomes or effects (Kazdin & Matson, 1981; Schwartz & Baer, 1991; Wolf, 1978).

Formulation: what is socially significant?

The first requirement of social validity (that our intervention should address a socially significant problem) may, at first sight, appear straight forward. Aren't challenging behaviours, mental health problems, law breaking, etc. 'socially significant problems'? Of course they are. It is important, however, that we keep in mind that a 'socially significant problem' is a social construction reflecting cultural norms and expectations and the 'meaning' which is ascribed to the behaviour of members of identifiable social groups. Take, for example, self-injury through slapping yourself on the cheek, smoking and long-distance running: three forms of repetitive behaviour which carry with them a certain probability of self-inflicted health risks. Clearly, the extent to which these three behaviours are seen as legitimate targets for intervention can not be simply explained by either a sober assessment of real risk (cheek slapping is probably the least 'risky' of the three) or knowledge of underlying factors (cheek slapping and long-distance running may both be main tained, in part, by the release of β-endorphin). However, cheek slapping by someone with an intellectual disability is often seen as a legitimate target for intervention, smoking is becoming more so but, to date at least, the number of people referred to a clinical psychologists for treatment of their 'obsessional' running is very small indeed.

So, before accepting a referral as a 'socially significant problem' (and consequently a legitimate concern for a clinical psychologist) we need to be clear about such issues as whether the person's behaviour or psychological state is primarily a problem for the person him/herself, significant others in his/her life and/or the social institutions (e.g. health and social care agencies) which impinge upon them.

Often, of course, such 'problems' are multi-faceted. There is a real risk, however, within health care professions that, by simply focusing on the behaviour of the person who 'presents' with the problem, we omit other equally (if not more) important aspects of the 'problem'. Take, for example, the issue of aggression, the 'social significance' of which is clearly multi-faceted. These facets include:

❑ Injuries to significant others which directly result from the person's aggression.
❑ Injuries to the user and significant others which result from carers 'managing' episodes of aggression (Spreat et al., 1986).
❑ Carers and care staff experiencing feelings of anger and annoyance in response to episodes of aggression (Bromley & Emerson, 1995).
❑ High levels of stress in families and among care staff (Bersani & Heifitz, 1985; Quine & Pahl, 1985).
❑ Families giving up care and seeking a residential placement for their son or daughter (Tausig, 1985).
❑ Impaired development of social relationships (Anderson et al., 1992).
❑ Reduced access to community-based activities and generic health services (Emerson et al., 1997; Hill & Bruininks, 1984).
❑ Institutionalisation (Borthwick-Duffy et al., 1987).
❑ Social and material deprivation (Emerson et al., 1992).
❑ Inappropriate treatment (Singh & Repp, 1989).
❑ Abuse (e.g. Rusch, Hall & Griffin, 1986).

Indeed, for many people with intellectual disabilities who are frequently or seriously aggressive towards others, the 'problem' is not so much what they do, but what is done to them. As a result, a socially valid intervention will need to address (and make a difference to) the various aspects of the 'problem', which may involve intervening to change the behaviour of the person and those around them. In many instances interventions will need to specifically target some of the *secondary processes* by which people become socially handicapped by their psychological problems (e.g. enhancing the practical and emotional coping strategies used by care staff).

As we noted above, the social significance of the 'problems' faced by people with intellectual disabilities is, of course, determined by personal and social values about the role of people with intellectual disabilities in society and the legitimate and appropriate aims of educational, health and social care services. Over the past three decades the values under pinning most educational, health and social care agencies for people with intellectual disabilities have been powerfully influenced by the linked ideas of *self-determination, inclusion* and *quality of life.*

Historically, people with intellectual disabilities have often been viewed as being incapable of taking responsibility for their lives or of even having a legitimate role in contributing to decisions made about them. In many respects, people with intellectual disabilities have commonly been viewed as 'eternal children' who have no significant role to play in the adult world (cf. Wolfensberger, 1975). These notions are gradually giving way in Europe, North America and Australasia and being replaced by a view which proclaims the full citizenship of people with intellectual disabilities (cf. United Nations, 1971 *Declaration of the General and Specific Rights of the Mentally Retarded*; Ward, 1995). These changes have been reflected in many areas, including: the growth of the self-advocacy move ment (e.g. Sanderson, 1995); the increasing involvement of people with intellectual disabilities in training (e.g. Wright, 1995), quality assurance (e.g. Allen, 1995) and service provision (e.g. Whittaker, 1995); the development of person-centred approaches to planning and provision (e.g. O'Brien, 1987); the development of procedures for enabling people with severe and complex disabilities to exercise choice (Lancioni, O'Reilly & Emerson, 1996); and the recognition of the importance of user control and choice in clinical practice (cf. Bannerman et al., 1990). The issue of self-determination and the importance of establishing a 'therapeutic alliance' between the psychologist and people with intellectual disabilities will be taken up in later chapters.

In addition to an increasing focus on self-determination, choice and empowerment the vast majority of contemporary educational, health and social care agencies for people with intellectual disabilities have an expressed commitment to the ideas of the integration or inclusion of people with intellectual disabilities in mainstream society (see Chapter 4). The rationales behind these aims are to be found in the influential concepts of normalisation and social role valorization (Emerson, 1992; O'Brien & Tyne, 1981; Nirje, 1969; Perrin & Nirje, 1985; Wolfensberger, 1972, 1980, 1983; Wolfensberger & Thomas, 1983). These ideas are most commonly operationalised in current health and social care services for people with intellectual disabilities in terms of O'Brien's (1987) five 'service accomplishments':

❑ Ensuring that service users are *present* in the community by supporting their actual physical presence in the same neighbourhoods, schools, work places, shops, recreation facilities, and churches as ordinary citizens.

❑ Ensuring that service users are supported in *making choices* about their lives by encouraging people to understand their situation and the options they face, and to act in their own interest, both in small everyday matters and in such important issues as who to live with and what type of work to do.

❑ Developing the *competence* of service users by developing skills and attributes that are functional and meaningful in natural community environments and relationships, (i.e. skills and attributes which significantly decrease a person's dependency or develop personal characteristics that other people value).

❑ Enhancing the *respect* afforded to service users by developing and maintaining a positive reputation for people who use the service by ensuring that the choice of activities, locations, forms of dress and use of language promote the perception of people with disabilities as developing citizens.

❑ Ensuring that service users *participate* in the life of the community by supporting people's natural relationships with their families, neighbours and co-workers and, when necessary, widening each individual's network of personal relationships to include an increasing number of people.

The acceptability of intervention procedures

The second component of social validity suggests that interventions should address the socially significant problem in a manner which is acceptable to the main constituencies involved (e.g. people with intellectual disabilities, significant others in their lives, paid carers, professionals and managers employed within support services).

While apparently straightforward, the acceptability (or not) of intervention procedures has generated much controversy over recent years in relation to the use of 'aversive' behavioural procedures to help people overcome their challenging behaviours (see Chapter 8). Indeed, many thousands of words have been written on the acceptability (or not) of using such procedures. Opinions have ranged from suggesting that to use 'aversive' procedures may be the most ethically appropriate course of action in certain situations (Van Houten et al., 1988), to a 'call to action' to Amnesty International to investigate the use of such procedures as a form of torture (Weiss, 1992).

The central issue of this rather confused debate has been defining the conditions under which it may be justified or acceptable to use of a set of procedures of a given level of intrusiveness or aversiveness. This is of central importance to the issue of social validity, since concerns about procedural acceptability may, at times, need to be balanced against the social significance of the outcomes of intervention (see below). This not just an academic argument, as meta-analyses of the behavioural literature do suggest that more intrusive interventions *are* more effective in suppressing challenging behaviour (Didden, Duker & Korzilius, 1997; Scotti et al., 1991).

A number of aspects of an intervention are likely to influence its 'acceptability' among the wide range of stakeholders involved in the intervention process. All of these are likely to be important considerations in their own right. Indeed, we suggest using the following nine questions (see Figure 1.1), as a basis for *documenting* the likely acceptability of any proposed intervention.

When running through the checklist, keep the following points in mind:

❑ Many approaches to intervention may involve some degree of psychological distress. Psychotherapy can be uncomfortable at times. Gentle Teaching (McGee et al., 1987) is likely to be stressful for people who are uncomfortable with close personal contact.

❑ Similarly, virtually all approaches will involve some (if only implicit) restrictions on the user's autonomy or freedom of movement. At a minimum these are likely to involve being around the 'therapist' at certain times. Other approaches (e.g. rewarding appropriate behaviour) implicitly involve restricting the person's free access to rewards (otherwise they wouldn't be rewarding).

❑ Mis-match between the beliefs of stakeholders and the basis for the intervention often leads to inconsistent or failed implementation. If, for example, a family are convinced that their son's overactivity is due to additives in their diet, they may be less than enthusiastic about your proposed 'positive parenting' programme! In such cases it may be necessary to undertake a significant amount of groundwork in helping people to test out their beliefs before giving your suggestions a try.

❑ Don't forget that norms of decency and acceptability vary between and within social groups. What is acceptable for (primarily) young, white middle-class women clinical psychologists may not be acceptable to a devout Muslim family, a retired colonel or a family struggling in poverty.

❑ Costs and opportunity costs are important. Health care rationing is (and will continue to be) a reality for us all. The time and energy invested in your proposed intervention could be used in other ways (opportunity costs). It is important that you think about these things (rather than just leaving it up to the accountants).

Figure 1.1 Dimensions of treatment acceptability

1. What level of pain or psychological distress will the person experience?
2. What restrictions will be placed on the person's autonomy or freedom of movement?
3. To what extent does the intervention match the beliefs of stakeholders about the reasons underlying the problem?
4. Does the intervention transgress any social norms of acceptability and decency?
5. What evidence is available about the likely effectiveness of intervention?
6. What evidence is available about the likely 'side-effects' of intervention?
7. What effort will be required from carers to implement the intervention?
8. What will the intervention cost?
9. What are the opportunity costs of the intervention?

Achieving socially important outcomes

The final component of determining the social validity of any approach to intervention is that it *results in socially important outcomes or effects*. In our discussion of problem formulation (above) we drew attention to the importance of taking a broad perspective when considering the 'social significance' of the problem. One consequence of adopting such an approach is that it demands that 'interventions' should be selected on the basis of their having predictable (positive) effects on the many facets of the presenting problem.

Information pertinent to judging the likely impact of interventions can be drawn from two complementary sources. First, in some areas significant amounts of research have been conducted into the impact of certain approaches to intervention on the problems faced by people with intellectual disabilities. Thus, for example, the effectiveness of behavioural approaches in helping people with intellectual disabilities overcome 'challenging behaviours' has been reasonably well researched (see Didden, Duker & Korzilius, 1997; Emerson, 1995; Scotti et al., 1991). In contrast, other approaches, for example the use of cognitive-behavioural approaches with people with intellectual disabilities, has as yet received little scientific attention (Stenfert Kroese, Dagnan & Loumidus, 1997).

Where evidence arising from scientific evaluations is available, it should play a central role in clinical decisions regarding the selection of intervention approaches. Indeed, to reject a relatively 'proven' approach in favour of an approach for which little or no substantive evidence exists is unprofessional, unethical and would to be difficult to justify in a court of law.

Given the importance we attach to attending to the 'evidence-base' which should underlie clinical practice, we have sought to clearly distinguish within the remainder of the book between statements supported by scientific evidence and statements or suggestions based on consensual notions of 'good practice'. All too often, however, the scientific 'evidence-base' may be found wanting in specific situations. Thus, for example, the extensive research which addressed the effectiveness of behavioural approaches in helping people with intellectual disabilities overcome 'challenging behaviours' has very little to say about such key issues as either the long-term or social impact of interventions (cf. Emerson, 1995).

In such situations the importance of adopting a 'scientist-practitioner' approach (cf. Marzillier & Hall, 1992) becomes paramount. This approach to clinical practice is characterised by five key stages:

❑ First, *the formulation of the problem faced by the person with intellectual disabilities should reflect contemporary scientific knowledge about the psychological processes which may underlie or be implicated in the presenting situation.* That is, a coherent model needs to be constructed which has face validity in accounting for the person's problem. Such a model should be consistent with: (1) current models or theories about the types of psychological mechanisms which may underlie or be involved in the expression of the problem faced by the person; (2) the information about the person's problem as far as they are known. Thus, for example, the severe self-injurious behaviour shown by a person with severe intellectual disabilities may initially be formulated as a possible example of operant behaviour maintained by a process of negative reinforcement involving escape from 'aversive' social contact (see Chapter 8).

❑ Second, *an attempt is made to test hypotheses generated from this model empirically.* This may involve the collection of additional descriptive information during subsequent 'assessments' or undertaking functional (experimental) analyses (see Chapter 8).

❑ Third, *the model accounting for the person's problems is reviewed and, if necessary, revised in light of the information collected.*

❑ Fourth, *an intervention is selected based on (1) the model accounting for the person's problems and (2) scientific evidence regarding the effectiveness of different interventions in addressing outcomes of importance.*

❑ Finally, *a scientifically valid approach is taken to evaluating the outcomes of the intervention.*

By now you probably will not be surprised when we suggest that evaluating outcomes involves more than just measuring changes in the frequency of specific 'problem' behaviours or changes in the severity of 'dysfunctional' states. If the 'social significance' of the problems faced by a person with intellectual disabilities and mental health problems includes potentially losing his/her home and job and avoidance by all and sundry, then these are the types of outcomes we need to monitor in order to judge the impact of our intervention. For example, if our intervention reduced the self-injurious behaviour of a young woman with severe intellectual disabilities by 75%, would we consider it a success if, even at that lower rate, she lost her home and her sight?

Evans and Meyer (1985) have argued the case for expanding the way we evaluate the impact of interventions to include the assessment of 'meaningful outcomes' (see also Emerson, 1995; Horner, 1991; Meyer & Evans, 1989, 1993; Meyer & Janney, 1989). When applied to challenging behaviour, this would include the assessment of change in:

❏ The challenging behaviours shown by the person.
❏ Replacement skills and behaviours, including, for example, the development of self-control strategies to support behaviour change and the development of alternative communicative responses.
❏ Procedures for managing the person's challenging behaviour, including use of medication, restraint and crisis management techniques.
❏ The physical consequences of the person's challenging behaviour, such as trauma, skin irritations (e.g. Iwata et al., 1990).
❏ The restrictiveness of the person's residential and vocational placement.
❏ Broader aspects of the person's quality of life, including physical and social integration, personal life satisfaction, affect and the range of choices available to the individual (e.g. Schalock, 1996).
❏ The quality of life of carers.
❏ The perceived significance of the person's challenging behaviour by others (e.g. family, staff, public).

It is only practicable, of course, to evaluate a certain number of outcomes. In selecting which outcomes to measure, you need to be confident that there is a plausible association between the person's difficulties and potential outcomes. For example, it may be tempting to judge the effectiveness of an intervention to reduce self-injury in terms of changes in the person's participation in community-based activities. This would be OK as long as his/her self-injury did, in fact, act as a significant barrier to participation. While such a relationship may be assumed to operate in general, in specific instances other factors (e.g. physical isolation of the setting; service policies, resources and orientation) may be much more important.

Possible approaches to measuring various outcomes are suggested in Figure 1.2.

Figure 1.2   Assessing socially significant intervention outcomes of intervention

Potential benefits to the person

Development and/or increased/more appropriate use of skills	Direct observation Diaries Structured interview with person/informants
Increased and/or more appropriate social contact with co-residents/workers and care staff	Direct observation Diaries Structured interview with person/informants
Increased participation in domestic, vocational and recreational community-based activities	Direct observation Diaries Structured interview with person/informants
Increased and/or more appropriate social contact with non-disabled peers, family and acquaintances	Diaries Structured interview with person/informants
Reductions in rate, duration, intensity of challenging behaviour and/or unwanted psychological states Reductions in injuries received	Observational methods (see *Journal of Applied Behavior Analysis*, 1967 onwards) Self-completed questionnaires (see Chapter 12) Structured interview with person and/or informants Analysis of incident reports Medical inspection Analysis of hospital/medical contacts 'Blind' rating of photographs Rating scales Structured interview with person and/or informants
Reduced use or restrictive management practices	Analysis of medication records Recording of time spent in restraint/seclusion Analysis of records detailing restriction of liberty Analysis of risk taking policies for person
Increased personal life satisfaction	Ratings/observation of positive affect Structured interview with person/informants

Potential risks/costs to person

Psychological or physical distress caused by intervention procedure	Observation of negative affect (e.g. negative vocalisations, screaming, escape)
Restrictions imposed on lifestyle by intervention on procedure	Analysis of programme documentation (e.g. restriction of free access to positive reinforcers, restriction of movement due to requirement to attend therapeutic activities)
Replacement of challenging behaviour with other/ new challenging behaviours	Observational methods (see *Journal of Applied Behavior Analysis*, 1967 onwards) Structured interview with person and/or informants
Reduced participation and/or social contacts	See above

Potential benefits to others	
Reductions in injuries received	Medical inspection Analysis of hospital/medical contacts 'Blind' rating of photographs Rating scales Structured interview with person and/or informants
Increased participation in domestic, vocational and recreational community-based activities	See above
Increased and/or more appropriate social contact with co-residents/workers and care staff	See above
Increased and/or more appropriate social contact with non-disabled peers, family and acquaintances	See above
Increased personal life satisfaction	See above Rating of stress Formal measures of quality of life
Potential risks/costs to others	
Injuries received as a result of intervention process	See above
Psychological distress caused by intervention process	Structured interview
Restrictions on liberty imposed by intervention process	See above
Financial costs resulting from intervention process	Analysis of programme documentation Structured interview
Reduction in participation, social relationships, etc.	See above

From Emerson (1995), with permission.

Intervention should be person-centred and functionally-based

It seems a truism to suggest that intervention should be person-centred. What else could such interventions be? The rather uncomfortable answer to this question is that, all too often, our approach to intervention seems to be symptom-based, illness-based or (challenging) behaviour-based. The more we get involved in trying to understand the nature of the person's specific difficulty that we have been asked to help with, the easier it seems to become for us to loose sight of the person.

It is important, however, that we do not completely individualise the 'problem'. People are enmeshed in social systems and institutions. Indeed, the person (and the problem with which he/she is faced) can only be understood when he/she is seen in his/her social context. This is particularly important for people with intellectual disabilities who lack the power and ability to exercise control over social institutions. As a result, we will often need to 'intervene' at the level of the social systems and institutions surrounding the person.

By being 'functionally-based' we mean that *the selection or design of approaches to intervention should reflect knowledge of the factors underlying the person's difficulties*. Again, while such a statement appears stunningly obvious and is central to the scientist-practitioner model discussed above, it has not been reflected in the 'cook book' mentality which dominated clinical practice for many years.

For example, behavioural practice has, until relatively recently, paid little attention to the processes underlying the challenging behaviours shown by people with intellectual disabilities. Instead, 'behaviour modification':

> . . . relied largely on the use of potent reinforcers or punishers to override the reinforcement contingencies or biologic processes that maintained problem behavior. The treatments were effective, but they were often artificial, conspicuous, difficult to implement for long periods of time, and deemed unacceptable by some caregivers (Mace & Roberts, 1993, p. 113).

Similarly, the prescription of psychoactive drugs to people with intellectual disabilities has paid scant attention to the neurobiological processes involved in any challenging behaviours or mental health problems with which they present (Baumeister & Sevin, 1990).

The importance of adopting a functional approach is simply illustrated by considering the use of time-out procedures. *Time-out* is a punitive behavioural procedure in which the person's opportunity to access positive reinforcers is removed or reduced for a set period following the occurrence of a target behaviour. This may involve the brief seclusion of the person in a barren environment, removal to a less stimulating part of the current setting or the withdrawal of potentially positively reinforcing activities or events from the vicinity of the person.

The logic of such a procedure is that, by arranging the person's environment to ensure that occurrence of challenging behaviour reliably results in *reduced* opportunity for reinforcement, the challenging behaviour should become less frequent over time and eventually disappear. Indeed, this is the most likely outcome if time-out is used with a person whose challenging behaviour is maintained by positive reinforcement (e.g. their challenging behaviour elicits the attention of carers). But what would happen if the person's challenging behaviour was maintained by the (negatively) reinforcing consequences of the escaping from a task they found aversive? In this case, application of a typical 'time-out' procedure would *guarantee* that each episode of the challenging behaviour continued to be (negatively) reinforced by arranging for the contingent removal of aversive materials and/or attention (e.g. teacher demands). At best such an intervention would be ineffective, at worst it could lead to a significant strengthening of the behaviour (cf. Durand et al., 1989; Solnick, Rincorer & Peterson, 1977).

The main implication of adopting a functionally-based approach is that it places much greater emphasis on the assessment process. It also alters the purpose of assessment from describing what the person does to also understanding why they do it.

Intervention should be constructional

In general, approaches to intervention can be placed within one of two categories.

Pathological approaches focus on the elimination of behaviours (e.g. self-injury) or states (e.g. anxiety, distress). As Israel Goldiamond pointed out, 'Such approaches often consider the problem in terms of a pathology which, regardless of how it was established, or developed, or is maintained, is to be eliminated' (Goldiamond, 1974, p. 14).

He contrasted this with what he termed a *constructional approach*; an orientation 'whose solution to problems is the construction of repertoires (or their reinstatement or transfer to new situations) rather than the elimination of repertoires' (Goldiamond, 1974, p. 14). In other words, the aim of a constructional approach is to help the person to develop new (more appropriate) ways of acting, rather than simply to eliminate a problem.

For example, suppose you have been asked to help a young woman with intellectual disabilities who tended to respond aggressively when her job coach corrected her while learning a new task. A pathological approach would pose the question: how can we stop her being aggressive? In contrast, a constructional approach would pose the question: how should she respond to similar situations in the future? So, while the pathological approach is concerned with the *elimination* of aggression, the constructional approach is concerned with the *establishment* of more appropriate ways of acting in the situations which evoke aggression.

There are two main reasons for adopting a constructional approach. First, they offer some safeguard against the abuse of therapeutic power. The early years of 'behaviour modification' were quite rightly criticised for their reliance on pathological approaches, whose main aim was the elimination of troublesome behaviour. Winnet and Winkler (1972) characterised these aims succinctly in their review of the application of behavioural techniques in educational settings: 'Be still, be quiet, be docile'. Second, all interventions *must* involve a constructional component. We cannot just eliminate behaviours; something will take their place. Behaviour is a dynamic process and (like nature) abhors a vacuum. Pathological approaches leave the issue of what will take the place of the person's difficulties to chance. A constructional intervention addresses it directly.

The value of adopting a constructional approach was illustrated in a recent study by Sprague and Horner (1992). They evaluated the impact of a pathological intervention (reprimand and very brief physical restraint) and a constructional intervention (prompting to ask for help in response to difficult tasks) on the aggression and tantrums shown by a 15 year-old boy with intellectual disabilities. Assessment had indicated that his challenging behaviours served the function of eliciting his teacher's help when presented with a difficult task. The two interventions were applied in sequence to his aggression. While the pathological intervention reduced his aggression, other problem behaviours (head and body shaking, screaming, hitting objects and putting his hands to his face) all increased so that, overall, there was no change in the overall rate of challenging behaviours. The constructional intervention eliminated all problem behaviours.

There may, of course, be situations in which it is easier and simpler to adopt a pathological approach. Occasionally, a person's difficulties may only occur in response to a particular situation which is not itself of any intrinsic value (e.g. travelling to college by one particular route; Kennedy & Itkonen, 1993). Simply avoiding that situation (i.e. by travelling by a different route) may not be constructional, but is likely to be the least intrusive and most effective option. It is likely, however, that such examples are relatively rare and that pathological approaches should be considered the exception rather than the rule.

A framework for selecting interventions

The issues we have discussed so far in this chapter provide a basis for a framework for selecting interventions or deciding whether a specific intervention is justified. Meinhold and Mulick (1990) suggest that this should involve a four-stage process:

1. Identify the problem.
2. Conduct a feasibility assessment of potential solutions.
3. Assess the potential risks, costs and benefits of possible solutions (and of inaction).
4. Make a decision.

Identify the problem

As we have seen, the 'problem' faced by many of the people with intellectual disabilities who you will be working with needs to be conceptualised broadly (i.e. beyond the specific reason for referral), but remain specific to the life of that particular person. Challenging behaviours, for example, are challenging because of the significant social costs and financial costs to the person him/herself, to carers and to other family members, co-residents and co-workers, care staff and agencies responsible for the purchase and provision of health and welfare services.

Conduct a feasibility assessment of potential solutions

Potential solutions to the problem (intervention strategies) need to be feasible. Usually this means that they need to be practically feasible. That is, the human and other resources necessary for the successful implementation of the approach need to be identified and compared with what is actually available. Advocating solutions which are not practicably feasible is equivalent to advocating inaction. Two key aspects of any feasibility analysis will be:

❏ To examine critically whether *you* possess the skills required to appropriately design and implement the intervention under consideration;
❏ To determine the level of supervision *you* will require during the intervention and whether such supervision is likely to be available.

Assess the potential risks, costs and benefits of possible solutions (and of inaction)

Once you have identified potential feasible solutions, you need to consider the possible risks, costs and benefits of these solutions—along with the potential risks, costs and benefits of doing nothing. Figure 1.2 provides a guide to some of the aspects of risks, costs and benefits which it may be important to consider.

Make a decision

The final stage in the process involves the weighing up of the risks, costs and benefits of:

❑ The potential courses of action.
❑ The 'default' option of inaction.

Obviously, this will be a complex process with different stakeholders in the intervention process placing different weights on the importance of the various possible outcomes. Normally, of course, the person him/herself would play a major role in this process by giving consent to a treatment selected out of a range of proffered options. Situations in which the user of services is defined as legally incompetent raise some complex problems regarding issues of consent (see Chapter 5).

AN OVERVIEW OF THE BOOK

The book comprises three main sections.

PART ONE contains six chapters which present and discuss issues of general importance to many areas of clinical practice. Chapters 2 ('Causes and Epidemiology' by Chris Hatton) and 3 ('Development, Cognition and Performance' by John Clements) address the essential nature of intellectual disability in relation to its definition, causes, manifestation and consequences. The information contained in these chapters highlights not only the social construction of intellectual disabilities, but also the importance of taking into account the very real impairments and problems faced by people with intellectual disabilities in our clinical practice. Chapters 4 ('Service Provision' by Amanda Caine, Chris Hatton & Chris Emerson) and 5 ('Common Legal Issues in Clinical Practice' by Tony Holland) describe some of the institutional and legal structures that shape clinical practice. Knowledge of such issues provides an essential underpinning for the professional practice of clinical psychology (Division of Clinical Psychology, 1995). Chapters 6 ('Interviewing People with Intellectual Disability' by Helen Prosser & Jo Bromley) and 7 ('Assessment' by Eric Emerson) discuss general issues involved in working in partnership with people with intellectual disabilities during problem formulation, assessment and intervention.

PART TWO contains six chapters which provide more specific guidance relating to clinical practice in six areas. Each of these chapters begins with a brief overview of the area followed by more practical advice on assessment, intervention and problem solving when working with people with challenging behaviour (Chapter 8 by Eric Emerson); people who have or are considered at risk of offending (Chapter 9 by Isabel Clare & Glynis Murphy); people who have been sexually abused (Chapter 10 by Jude Moss); parents who have intellectual disabilities (Chapter 11 by Sue McGaw); people with intellectual disabilities who also have mental health problems (Chapter 12 by Amanda Caine & Chris Hatton); and people who have communication problems (Chapter 13 by Bob Remington).

PART THREE contains three chapters which address issues involved at working at different 'levels': with families (Chapter 14 by Jo Bromley); with organisations (Chapter 15 by Judith McBrien & Sue Candy); and with communities (Chapter 16 by Steve Turner & Chris Hatton).

It is our sincere hope that clinical psychologists (and particularly those at the beginnings of their careers) will find the information contained within this book useful when working with people with intellectual disabilities. In our own terms we hope that it is a socially valid intervention. We are confident that it addresses a socially significant problem. We hope that it does so in a way acceptable to the main parties involved. And we hope that it has an impact.

FURTHER READING

Division of Clinical Psychology (1995). *Professional Practice Guidelines.* British Psychological Society: Leicester.

Chapter 2

INTELLECTUAL DISABILITIES— EPIDEMIOLOGY AND CAUSES

*Chris Hatton**

INTRODUCTION

This chapter will briefly outline some of the major issues concerning the epidemiology and causes of intellectual disabilities, and their importance in planning and delivering services.

Epidemiology has been defined as 'the study of the distribution and determinants of health, disease, and disorder in human populations' (Fryers, 1993), and is of fundamental importance for service planning. Quite simply, to provide a needs-led service you have to know how many people with intellectual disabilities there are, what services they are likely to need, and whether there will be any changes in the need for services in the future. While epidemiology operates at the level of population needs rather than individual needs, it is crucial when looking at the coverage of current services and considering service developments.

Considering the causes or aetiology of intellectual disabilities is also important, both for planning purposes and for working with individuals (Luckasson et al., 1992). The combination of biomedical, social, behavioural and educational causes of intellectual disabilities can have profound implications for prevention, treatment and management pro- grammes.

However, determining the epidemiology and causes of intellectual dis- abilities is at best an inexact science. As 'intellectual disability' is socially constructed, what it means, how it is measured, and therefore who counts as having an 'intellectual disability' has varied over time (Trent, 1995; Wright & Digby, 1996). For example, from medieval times until the end

*Hester Adrian Research Centre, Manchester, UK

Clinical Psychology and People with Intellectual Disabilities. Edited by E. Emerson, C. Hatton, J. Bromley and A. Caine.
© 1998 John Wiley & Sons Ltd.

Figure 2.1 Epidemiology in practice 1—Asian people with intellectual disabilities and service provision

A recent project across two UK local authority areas attempted to identify all Asian people with intellectual disabilities, whether or not they were known to specialist services (Azmi et al., 1996a, b). This project found that there were substantial numbers of Asian adults with intellectual disabilities who were not known to specialist services, and that Asian people with intellectual disabilities were less likely to use residential and respite services compared to their white counterparts. Furthermore, a high prevalence of Asian children with intellectual disabilities were found in special schools which, taking into account the relatively young age profile of the UK Asian population, would lead to a doubling of the numbers of Asian adults with intellectual disabilities in the next decade.

Local services used this information to address obvious gaps in service coverage, attempt to increase awareness of specialist services in the Asian communities, improve communication between services and Asian families, and attempt to provide services which would meet the needs of Asian users and their families. Service planners could also use this information to plan for an increased Asian population in adult specialist services over the next decade.

of the nineteenth century, parents, professionals and the courts conceptualised 'intellectual disability' in terms of deficits in what would now be called 'adaptive behaviour', and it is only in the twentieth century that a professionally driven conceptualisation of 'intellectual disabilities' as a deficit in intelligence has predominated (Wright & Digby, 1996). Definitions of 'intellectual disability' also vary across countries (Fernald, 1995), according to a whole host of ideological, political, economic and cultural factors (Fryers, 1993). Therefore, before looking more closely at the literature concerning epidemiology and causes, we must first look at how people are currently classified as having an 'intellectual disability'.

CLASSIFICATION

As mentioned above, 'intellectual disability' is socially constructed. The classification system used will determine who counts as having an 'intellectual disability', with obvious consequences when considering the epidemiology and causes of intellectual disability.

The AAMR definition and classification system

The most comprehensive and widely accepted definition and classification system has been devised by the American Association on Mental Retardation (AAMR). The most recent revision of this classification was in 1992 (Luckasson et al., 1992), presented in Figure 2.2.

There are some important elements of this definition that are worth noting.

> ... substantial limitations in present functioning ...

Mental retardation is defined as a fundamental difficulty in learning and performing certain daily life skills. There must be a substantial limitation in conceptual, practical and social intelligence, which are specifically affected in mental retardation. Other areas (e.g. health, temperament) may not be.

> ... significantly subaverage intellectual functioning ...

This is defined as an IQ standard score of approximately 70–75 or below (approx. 2 standard deviations below the mean), based on assessment that includes one or more individually administered general intelligence tests. These data should be reviewed by a multidisciplinary team and validated with additional evaluative information.

> ... with related limitations in two or more of the following adaptive skill areas ...

Intellectual functioning alone is insufficient to classify someone as having mental retardation. In addition, there must be significant limitations in adaptive skills (i.e., the skills to cope successfully with the daily tasks of living). The concept of adaptive behaviour is linked to what skills would be appropriate for a person's age.

Figure 2.2   AAMR 1992 Definition of 'Mental Retardation'

Mental retardation refers to substantial limitations in present functioning.

It is characterized by significantly subaverage intellectual functioning, existing concurrently with related limitations in two or more of the following adaptive skill areas:

- Communication
- Self-care
- Home living
- Social skills
- Community use
- Self-direction
- Health and safety
- Functional academics
- Leisure
- Work

Mental retardation manifests before age 18.

... manifests before age 18 ...

The 18th birthday approximates the age when individuals in this (i.e., US, but also UK) society typically assume adult roles. In other societies, a different age criterion might be more appropriate.

Further issues in classification

The AAMR definition and classification system outlined above represents the leading edge of current thinking in this area. However, there are a number of issues regarding classification which are likely to arise when working in services for people with intellectual disabilities.

Levels of intellectual disability

Although the 1992 AAMR classification system does not define levels of intellectual disability, the concept of different degrees of severity of intellectual disability is in almost universal usage. These classifications are based on standardised IQ scores, although consideration should also be given to adaptive behaviour when making a judgement about level of intellectual disability.

Once again, the IQ scores used to define different levels of intellectual disability vary over time and between different classificatory systems, but a widely used system is that of the International Classification of Diseases (or ICD), produced by the World Health Organisation (see Figure 2.3).

For many purposes (such as epidemiological studies), all people with IQ < 50 are classified as people with severe intellectual disabilities.

Cultural and linguistic diversity

As 'intellectual disability' is socially constructed, cultural and linguistic diversity must be taken into account when deciding whether a person has intellectual disabilities. Issues here include the validity of conducting IQ tests on individuals from different ethnic and linguistic groups, and also the consideration of what behaviours are appropriate for different cultures.

Present functioning

The classification system outlined here (in common with others) focuses on the present functioning on the individual. 'Intellectual disability' is

Figure 2.3 Level of intellectual disability (ICD-10 classification)	
IQ	
Mild	50–70
Moderate	35–49
Severe	20–34
Profound	< 20

not necessarily a life-long trait or condition, and depending on people's circumstances and responses to them they may not be regarded as having intellectual disabilities throughout their lives (see also Chapter 3). Indeed, many people with mild intellectual disabilities have only intermittent and time-limited contact with services, usually to assist at times of crisis.

Classification in service settings

The AAMR classification outlined above is to a great extent a gold standard. In existing services, decisions about whether a person has intellectual disabilities do not involve assessments at the above level of detail or specificity. Also, because such assessments are made by professionals within services, decisions about whether a person has intellectual disabilities are frequently influenced by the availability of services and the professional's judgement of what is in the best interests of the individual. Many factors can impact upon this decision; financial, political, ideological, administrative.

> Classification is the end point in a complex interaction between social, economic, political and organizational factors (Richardson & Koller, 1985).

Consequently, there may be people within intellectual disability services who would not meet the above criteria (e.g., people who were institution alised many years ago). It is also likely that there are people not in contact with intellectual disability services who do meet the above criteria.

Services are increasingly developing eligibility criteria to decide who is eligible for intellectual disability services and to 'prioritise' (i.e., ration) service provision. These eligibility criteria vary widely between different services, and use widely different methods of assessment.

EPIDEMIOLOGY

As the previous discussion will have made clear, people with intellectual disabilities are a very diverse group, with widely different characteristics and needs. The social construction of intellectual disability and consequent problems in identifying a person as having an intellectual disability make it difficult, if not impossible, to produce definitive epidemiological figures for this group (Fryers, 1993; Richardson & Koller, 1985). The general epidemiological literature generally has two ways of counting the number of people with a particular disorder in a given population, *incidence* and *prevalence* (see Figure 2.4).

Incidence

The study of the incidence of a disorder can answer important questions for service planners. For example, several studies have demonstrated that improvements in neonatal health services have resulted in an increase in the birth and survival rates of very low birthweight children, a widely established risk factor for intellectual disability (Louhiala, 1995). However, these improvements in health care have also resulted in fewer surviving children developing intellectual disabilities, meaning that the number of very low birthweight children with intellectual disabilities does not appear to be increasing (Kitchen et. al., 1992). Similarly, debates about the efficacy of prenatal screening for Down's syndrome, although fundamentally ethical in nature (Glover & Glover, 1996), will also partly depend on incidence data regarding changes in the birth rates of people with Down's syndrome (Steele, 1993).

While determining the incidence of specific, easily identifiable conditions such as Down's syndrome may be possible, attempting to determine the incidence of intellectual disability as a whole is difficult, if not impossible, for a number of reasons.

First, establishing a diagnosis of intellectual disability for all babies at or soon after birth is impossible. This is important because many children are not classified as having intellectual disabilities until later in childhood (these would therefore have to be counted retrospectively). It is also important because many babies with more severe disorders are still-born or die soon after birth, before any assessment of intellectual functioning is possible.

Figure 2.4   Definitions of incidence and prevalence (Richardson & Koller, 1985)

Incidence refers to the number of new cases of a disorder arising in a population in a stated period of time.

Prevalence is the number of cases, old and new, existing in a population at a given point in time or over a specified period.

Second, many disorders causing severe intellectual disability are biomedical, and are the result of genetic, prenatal or perinatal factors. To establish the true incidence of these disorders would include counting every conception, including the large number of conceptions spontaneously aborted due to the severity of the disorders. Although the establishment of prenatal genetic testing makes it possible to carry out incidence studies of genetically determined disorders, this clearly does not account for all people with intellectual disabilities, and the majority of genetic abnormalities do not necessarily result in intellectual disability (Dykens, 1995).

Although incidence studies for intellectual disability generally have not been conducted, incidence information for specific disorders associated with or causing intellectual disability will be discussed in the causes section below.

Prevalence

Studying the prevalence of intellectual disability is fundamental to developing needs-led services. Prevalence studies have been used to examine the number and changing needs of people with intellectual disabilities over time (Martindale et al., 1988), to identify particular subgroups with high needs (Azmi et al., 1996), and to examine shortfalls in service provision (McGrother et al., 1993).

There have been a number of studies attempting to determine the prevalence of people with intellectual disabilities (see Fryers, 1993; McLaren & Bryson, 1987; Richardson & Koller, 1985; for reviews). The studies that have been conducted report a wide range of prevalence rates, due to a range of methodological factors. These include:

❑ *Sampling method.* Studies which use total population samples, and assess all members of a population for intellectual disability, typically report higher prevalence rates than studies using administratively defined populations (i.e., those currently using services for people with intellectual disabilities or those known to services).

❑ *Classification criteria.* As discussed earlier, classification systems for deciding whether a person has an intellectual disability vary over time and across different geographical areas, and different researchers have used more or less stringent criteria for classifying people with intellectual disabilities.

❑ *Assessment method.* Clearly, the method used to assess intellectual disability will influence the prevalence rate found. Reliance on IQ alone tends to result in higher prevalence rates than those using IQ and

adaptive behaviour assessment methods (assuming a normal distribution, one would expect approximately 3% of the population to score
below 70 on a standardised IQ test). Other factors, such as the skills
of the professional conducting the assessment and the language and
culture of people being tested (and those doing the testing) will all
influence the prevalence rate reported.

Because there are a number of issues involved when viewing prevalence
studies; studies will be broken down into those considering prevalence
across the life-span; and those considering the prevalence of people with
mild (i.e., IQ 50 or 55 to 70) or severe (i.e., IQ < 50 or 55) intellectual
disabilities.

People with mild intellectual disabilities

European and North American studies (see Fryers, 1993; McLaren &
Bryson, 1987; Richardson & Koller, 1985) report the following findings
(for various reasons, some studies in Asian countries report quite different findings, see Kuo-Tai, 1988, Yaqoob et al., 1995):

❏ General prevalence rates (i.e., across all ages) of mild intellectual
  disabilities between *3.7 to 5.9 per 1,000*, with total population studies
  reporting higher prevalence rates than studies using administratively
  defined populations (i.e., those known to services).
❏ More males with mild intellectual disabilities than females (ratio
  approx. 1.6:1).
❏ An increase in the apparent prevalence of mild intellectual disabilities
  throughout the school years, followed by a sharp drop around the
  school leaving age.
❏ A disproportionate number of people with mild intellectual disabilities
  come from disadvantaged socio-economic backgrounds.

However, these findings are of limited validity, and illustrate clearly the
complex processes involved in the classification of people as having
intellectual disabilities. This is particularly true of people with mild intellectual disabilities, where the disability rarely has a clear cause. Particular
problems with the validity of these studies include:

❏ The rise in prevalence throughout the childhood years reflects the
  gradual classification of more children as having a mild intellectual
  disability throughout childhood and adolescence. This may be dependent on administrative and financial factors, and also the services
  available for children with mild intellectual disabilities.
❏ The sharp drop in apparent prevalence at school leaving age illustrates
  the methodological problems in using administratively defined popu-

lations. After leaving school, many adolescents classified as having mild intellectual disabilities do not use adult services for people with intellectual disabilities, resulting in an apparently sharp drop in prevalence. This suggests a considerable underestimation of the prevalence of mild intellectual disabilities in the adult years.

❏ The greater number of males with mild intellectual disabilities compared to females appears to be largely due to a greater likelihood of males being labelled as having an intellectual disability, possibly due to different sex-role expectations for males and females. However, it is worth noting that X-chromosome-linked genetic disorders (see causes below) could account for some of this discrepancy.

People with severe intellectual disabilities

European and North American studies (see Fryers, 1993; McLaren & Bryson, 1987; Richardson & Koller, 1985) report the following findings (again, findings from some Asian countries may be different; see Kuo-Tai, 1988; Yaqoob et al., 1995):

❏ General prevalence rates (i.e. across all ages) of severe intellectual disabilities between *3 to 4 per 1,000*, with total population studies reporting higher prevalence rates (e.g., 6.3 per 1,000) than studies using administratively defined populations.

❏ Some studies report little difference in prevalence between males and females, others report a higher prevalence in males.

❏ An increase in the apparent prevalence of severe intellectual disabilities throughout the school years, with little if any reduction at school-leaving age.

❏ People with severe intellectual disabilities are from a range of socio-economic backgrounds.

For people with severe intellectual disabilities, the classification of intellectual disability is usually more definite, and can occur earlier than for people with mild intellectual disabilities. Also, more people with severe intellectual disabilities have associated disorders or specific biomedical causes, resulting in parents from a range of socio-economic backgrounds having a child with severe intellectual disabilities. Finally, children with severe intellectual disabilities are likely to continue receiving services after leaving school. All these factors increase the validity of prevalence studies involving people with severe intellectual disabilities.

UK trends—prevalence and service need

When considering the service needs of people with intellectual disabilities in the UK, three issues stand out when considering future service developments:

❑ In the UK at least, prevalence rates of severe intellectual disabilities at birth reached a peak in the mid 1960s, followed by a slight decrease to the mid 1970s and possibly another more recent increase (Fryers, 1993; Martindale et al., 1988). Partly due to the general 'baby boom', there is also a high prevalence of people with less mild and moderate intellectual disabilities between the ages of 30 and 40. As these two cohorts of people are now at an age where many require residential services, the need for residential services is set to increase over the next decade (Parrott et al., 1997); this despite a substantial current shortfall in residential places (Emerson & Hatton, 1996a). These trends are represented in Figure 2.5 below, which presents age-specific prevalence rates for people with intellectual disabilities in Sheffield.

❑ In common with other European and North American countries, the life expectancy of people with intellectual disabilities is increasing dramatically, although the life expectancy of people with intellectual disabilities is still lower than that of the general population (Carter & Jancar, 1983; Strauss & Eyman, 1996). This is resulting in an increased demand for services generally, and also an increasing demand for services associated with dementia.

❑ There is some evidence (Azmi et al., 1996; see also Yaqoob et al., 1995) of much higher prevalence rates of intellectual disability for children in some Asian communities in the UK. If this increased prevalence continues, the need for services directed to Asian people with intellectual disabilities will dramatically increase in the next 10 years.

Disorders and conditions associated with intellectual disabilities

When planning and developing services, it is important to know the likelihood of the person with intellectual disabilities having disorders that may interact with their disability. A range of disorders have been found in addition to a person's intellectual disability. While the number of additional disorders a person is likely to have increases with the severity of the intellectual disability, the type of additional disorders reported does not seem to vary significantly across the range of intellectual disabilities (McLaren & Bryson, 1987). The wide variation in prevalence rates for associated disorders reflect a wide range of methodological, classification, and assessment differences across studies, and therefore should not be treated as definitive.

The most common disorders or conditions associated with intellectual disabilities include:

❑ *Epilepsy.* Between 15% and 30% of people with intellectual disabilities have been reported to have epilepsy (McLaren & Bryson, 1987).

❑ *Cerebral palsy / other motor impairments.* Reported in 20–30% of people with intellectual disabilities (McLaren & Bryson, 1987).

❑ *Sensory impairments.* Reported in 10–33% of people with intellectual disabilities, although studies using clinical criteria for sensory impairments report much higher rates than studies using functional criteria (Hatton & Emerson, 1995; McLaren & Bryson, 1987).

❑ *Challenging behaviour.* Reported in 6–14% of people with intellectual disabilities, although there are widely different criteria for determining and measuring challenging behaviour (Emerson, 1995; McLaren & Bryson, 1987).

❑ *Psychiatric disorders.* Due to difficulties in accurately identifying psychiatric disorders in people with intellectual disabilities, the range of prevalence rates reported are particularly wide (10–71%; Borthwick-Duffy, 1994; McLaren & Bryson, 1987), although studies using more stringent psychiatric criteria tend to report rates of psychiatric disorders (around 15–20%) similar to that of the general population.

Figure 2.5   Age-specific prevalence rates (per 1,000) for people with mild, moderate and severe intellectual disabilities in Sheffield at 1 January 1995

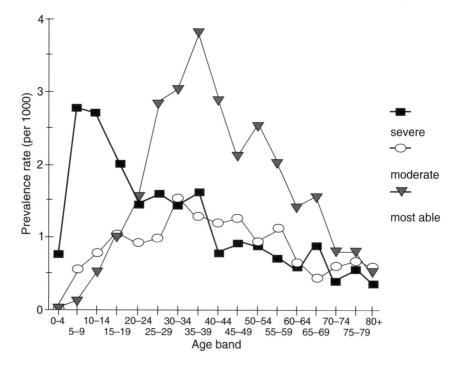

CAUSES OF INTELLECTUAL DISABILITY

Understanding the causes of a person's intellectual disability can have a potentially crucial impact on prevention, treatment and management

---

Figure 2.6   Epidemiology in practice 2—predicting future demand for residential services

While it is currently estimated that there is a shortfall of around 20,000–25,000 residential places for people with intellectual disabilities in the UK (Emerson & Hatton, 1996b), little is known about whether the demand for residential services is set to increase or decrease in the foreseeable future. Evidence from the Sheffield Case Register (Parrott et al., 1997) suggests that over the next decade there will be a substantial increase in demand for residential places over the next ten years. First, due to improvements in health care in the past 20 years, an increasing number of children with severe and complex disabilities are surviving through to adulthood. The number of children surviving to young adulthood, when they are typically placed in residential services, is set to increase substantially in the next ten years. Second, associated with the general 'baby boom', there are increased numbers of adults with mild to moderate intellectual disabilities in the 25–40 age group. Over the next 10–15 years, as their carers age, the demand for residential services for this group will also rise substantially. Taking into account mortality rates, it is estimated that there will be a 7.8% increase in demand for residential places between 1996 and 2001, and a further 4.5% increase between 2001 and 2006. Clearly, an increase in the resources allocated to intellectual disability services is required if this increased demand (let alone the current shortfall) is to be met.

---

programmes for that individual. The 'new genetics' (Dykens, 1995; Emerson & Hatton, 1996b; Plomin et al., 1997) is driving much of the research attempting to link genetic 'causes' to treatment and management.

First, the prospect of 'gene therapy' is rapidly advancing. For example, Duchenne Muscular Dystrophy, an X-gene linked genetic disorder resulting in mild intellectual disabilities and death by the age of 20, may soon become treatable by introducing 'therapeutic' DNA into the foetus (Dunckley, Piper & Dickson, 1995). Since this and other single enzyme disorders (most amenable to gene therapy) may cause severe intellectual disability in up to 20 per cent of people with severe intellectual disabilities, future advances in gene therapy may have a significant impact on this group of people.

Second, understanding the cause of a person's intellectual disability may also have implications for management programmes. One well-known example is Phenylketonuria, a deficit in metabolising a particular protein which causes severe intellectual disabilities if untreated. However, such intellectual disabilities can be completely avoided by a diet low in the protein phenylalanine. The 'new genetics' has also introduced the concept of the 'behavioural phenotype' (Berney, 1997; Dykens, 1995; Emerson & Hatton, 1996b; Hodapp & Dykens, 1994; Plomin et al., 1997). This concept proposes that the genetic basis of syndromes which lead to intellectual disabilities may be reflected in people showing common behavioural as well as physical characteristics. For example, self-injurious behaviour is much more likely in people with Lesch-Nyhan syndrome and Rett syndrome; and people with Fragile-X syndrome are more likely to be overactive and show attention deficits and stereotyped behaviour (Harris, 1992), with obvious consequences for educational and behaviour management programmes. However, some caution needs to be expressed regarding the behavioural phenotype approach. Correspondences between genetic syndrome and particular behaviours are rarely perfect; many people with the genetic syndrome do not show the behaviour and many people without the genetic syndrome do show the behaviour. There is a danger that self-fulfilling prophecies may occur within services (e.g., if a person has a particular genetic syndrome, then particular behaviours are inevitable and not amenable to intervention). It also raises the spectre of a new eugenics, with pre-natal genetic testing for a wide range of genetic 'disorders'. These and other ethical and social dimensions of the 'new genetics' have yet to be fully debated (Emerson & Hatton, 1996b).

As might be expected from the previous discussions concerning classification and epidemiology, determining the causes of intellectual disability is a complex and inexact process, particularly for people with mild intellectual disabilities. Consequently, the following discussion will focus largely on people with severe intellectual disabilities, as the aetiology of people with mild intellectual disabilities is largely unknown (McLaren & Bryson, 1987; Matilainen et al., 1995).

Generally, studies estimate that for people with severe intellectual disabilities, aetiology is unknown for between 20 and 40% of cases (McLaren & Bryson, 1987), although figures in recent studies are at the lower end of this range (Matilainen et al., 1995; Wellesley, Hockey & Stanley, 1991). For people with mild intellectual disabilities, aetiology is unknown for a somewhat higher 45% to 62% of cases (McLaren & Bryson, 1987; Matilainen et al., 1995; Wellesley, Hockey & Stanley, 1991).

For perhaps the majority of people, the determinants of intellectual disability will involve a complex interaction between biomedical, social, behavioural and educational factors. These factors may influence the individual at the prenatal, perinatal, and postnatal stages of life (Luckasson et al., 1992).

Prenatal causes

Overall, studies estimate that 2–40% of cases of severe intellectual disability can be accounted for by chromosomal disorders, and that a further 20–30% of cases accounted for by other prenatal factors, such as single gene disorders, multi-factorial/polygenetic causes and environmental effects (McLaren & Bryson, 1987; Matilainen et al., 1995; Wellesley, Hockey & Stanley, 1991). For people with mild intellectual disabilities, only 4% to 10% of cases are generally accounted for by chromosomal disorders (McLaren & Bryson, 1987, Matilainen et al., 1995), although some studies report figures as high as 19% (Gostason et al., 1991), with a further 11% to 23% of cases assumed to be due to other prenatal causes (McLaren & Bryson, 1987; Matilainen et al., 1995).

Biomedical factors

Prenatal biomedical factors potentially determining intellectual disability include chromosomal disorders, single gene disorders and other syndrome disorders (Luckasson et al., 1992, provide a comprehensive list of potential aetiologies). A textbook on medical genetics, such as Connor and Ferguson-Smith (1993) or Plomin et al. (1997), provide useful explanations of basic genetics principles, together with information on the incidence, clinical features, aetiology and recurrence risk of various common chromosomal and single-gene disorders. Advances in medical genetics are being made at a rapid pace, with an increasing number of genetic abnormalities and associated syndromes being identified. However, the identification of new genetic and chromosomal abnormalities is unlikely to account for the majority of cases of currently unknown aetiology (McLaren & Bryson, 1987).

Chromosomal disorders. These account for between 20% and 40% of all live births of people with severe intellectual disabilities. This range of estimates possibly reflect differences across studies in the availability of amniocentesis and genetic screening, and differences in maternal age (McLaren & Bryson, 1987). The majority of conceptions with chromosomal disorders spontaneously abort (Connor & Ferguson-Smith, 1993).

By far the most common chromosomal disorder associated with intellectual disability is Down's syndrome (Trisomy 21, where a person has an extra chromosome-21). Approximately 1 in 700 live births have Trisomy 21, and almost all people with Down's syndrome have an additional intellectual disability to some degree. People with Down's syndrome are at risk for congenital heart problems, thyroid problems, epilepsy, immunological deficiencies, vision and hearing loss, and reduced lifespan with early-onset dementia (Moss & Turner, 1995). Other less common chromosomal disorders are listed in Figure 2.7.

Single gene disorders. In recent years, there has been increasing interest in Fragile-X syndrome, which occurs largely (but not exclusively) in males, and has been claimed to be the most common hereditary cause of intellectual disability, although not all males and only one third of females with Fragile-X syndrome show intellectual disability to any degree (Hagerman & Cronister, 1991). Estimates of the frequency of Fragile-X vary considerably; for males estimates range from 1 in 1,100 to 1 in 2,500; for females 1 in 1,700 to 1 in 5,000 (Moss & Turner, 1995). Common (although not conclusive) indicators of Fragile-X include an elongated face with large ears, and enlarged testes in males. Other single-gene disorders associated with intellectual disabilities are listed in Figure 2.7.

Other syndrome disorders. There are a wide range of other relatively rare biomedical syndromes that may have a prenatal causal effect on later intellectual disabilities. These often have a genetic basis in that they are the result of dominant or recessive genes, but they may also have a polygenetic basis, and vary widely in the severity of the effect. These include neurofibromatosis, tuberous sclerosis, myotonic dystrophy, craniosynostosis syndromes, and inborn errors of metabolism. Other prenatal biomedical causes of intellectual disabilities may not be associated with genetic disorders, but may be the result of disorders of brain formation at the prenatal stage. Spina bifida is probably the most well known of this group of disorders (Connor & Ferguson-Smith, 1993; Stern, 1985).

Environmental factors

Whilst the importance of prenatal environmental effects has long been recognised, assessing the degree of their causal influence on the later development of intellectual disabilities has still to be conclusively determined. Studies have produced a wide range of estimates for the number of cases attributable to the prenatal environment (0.7–11.2% for people with severe intellectual disabilities; 8.2–8.8% for people with mild intellectual disabilities; McLaren and Bryson, 1987; Matilainen et al., 1995). Factors here include maternal malnutrition and ingestion of drugs and toxins during pregnancy (e.g. fetal alcohol syndrome), maternal diseases during pregnancy, and irradiation during pregnancy, although the relative impact of these factors in influencing intellectual disability is unknown (Berg, 1985, McLaren & Bryson, 1987).

Perinatal causes

Overall, studies estimate that approximately 10% of cases of severe intellectual disability are due to perinatal causes. Figures for mild intellectual disability are more variable, ranging from 1% to 19% of cases (McLaren & Bryson 1987; Matilainen et al., 1995; Wellesley, Hockey & Stanley, 1991).

Biomedical factors

Intra-uterine infections are the most common biomedical perinatal cause of intellectual disabilities, accounting for 2% to 6% of people with severe intellectual disabilities, and only 1% of people with mild intellectual disabilities. Such infections include cytomegalovirus, which causes an inflammation of brain tissue, toxoplasmosis, which destroys brain tissue, rubella, which can have a large number of effects, neonatal herpes, which can affect the central nervous system, and bacterial meningitis (Berg, 1985; McLaren & Bryson, 1987).

Environmental factors

The most common perinatal cause of severe intellectual disability is asphyxia (lack of oxygen; or hypoxia and ischaemia), with 4% to 8% of people with severe intellectual disability suffering asphyxia during birth. The figures for asphyxia in people with mild intellectual disabilities vary widely, from 5% to 19%. Another common cause of intellectual disability is premature birth of the child (3–5% of people with severe intellectual disabilities; figures for people with mild intellectual disabilities unknown). Other perinatal traumas that may result in intellectual disability include haemorrhaging in the brain due to abnormal labour and/ or delivery, premature birth, and umbilical cord accidents (Berg, 1985; McLaren & Bryson, 1987; Stern, 1985).

Postnatal causes

Very little is known about the relative impact of postnatal factors on the development of intellectual disabilities. Studies of people with severe intellectual disabilities report a wide range of estimates (1–13%) of people influenced by postnatal factors (McLaren & Bryson, 1987; Matilainen et al., 1995; Wellesley, Hockey & Stanley, 1991). For people with mild intellectual disabilities, there has been a common assumption that environmental factors, particularly those associated with socio-economic disadvantage, were the predominant causal factor, although these links are usually inferred rather than demonstrated (Clarke, 1985; McLaren & Bryson, 1987).

Biomedical factors

There are a wide range of postnatal biomedical factors that may impact upon the development of intellectual disability, although estimates of their prevalence are as yet unavailable. Such factors include infections (e.g. encephalitis, meningitis), diseases affecting the central nervous system, degenerative disorders (e.g. Rett syndrome, Friedrich's ataxia and basal ganglia disorders), and epilepsy and related disorders (Berg, 1985, Connor & Ferguson-Smith, 1993; Stern, 1985).

Environmental factors

Again, a wide range of environmental factors, probably in a multifactorial fashion, can influence the development of intellectual disabilities. Head injuries, various toxic disorders (e.g., high levels of lead or mercury, dehydration, hypoglycemia) and malnutrition can all cause intellectual disabilities. Environmental deprivation, such as psychosocial disadvantage, child abuse and neglect, and chronic social/sensory deprivation, have all been hypothesised to influence the development of intellectual disability, although the relative impact they have compared to other factors is largely unknown (Berg, 1985; Clarke, 1985; Stern, 1985).

CONCLUSIONS

As the above outline has hopefully demonstrated, understanding the epidemiology and causes of intellectual disabilities is important for developing needs-led services, and developing prevention, treatment and management programmes for people with intellectual disabilities. As 'intellectual disability' is socially constructed and subject to variations in definition and identification, studying the epidemiology and causes of intellectual disability is an at best inexact science. Despite these variations, it is becoming clear that there are substantial numbers of people with intellectual disabilities who require a variety of services, and that demand for services is likely to increase rather than decrease in the immediate future. Research concerning the causes of intellectual

Figure 2.7   Genetic disorders associated with intellectual disabilities

Name and syndrome name		Birth prevalence	Associated features
Chromosomal disorders			
Trisomy 21	Down's syndrome	1 in 700 (related to maternal age)	Almost all some intellectual disability Most survive well into adulthood; some evidence of accelerated ageing
Trisomy 18	Edward's syndrome	1 in 3,000	All have severe intellectual disability 10% survive to age one year
Trisomy 13	Patau's syndrome	1 in 5,000	All severe intellectual disability seizures 18% survive to age one year
15q–(Maternal)	Angelman syndrome	1 in 20,000	Generally moderate intellectual disability Also known as:
15q–(Paternal)	Prader–Willi syndrome	1 in 10,000	Almost all some intellectual disability. Short stature, over-eating
7p–	Williams syndrome	1 in 25,000	Almost all some intellectual disability by later childhood
5p–	Cri-du-chat syndrome	Very rare	Half show severe intellectual disability
Klinefelter syndrome (XXXY)		1 in 1,000 males	Some reduction in verbal skills, severe intellectual disability uncommon
Other very rare chromosomal disorders include Trisomy 8, 9p+ and 4p–			
Single gene disorders			
Fragile-X syndrome (X-linked)		1 in 1,100–2,500 for males 1 in 1,700–5,000 for females	Some degree of intellectual disability in most males; one third of females
Lesch–Nyhan syndrome (X-linked)		1 in 20,000 males	Almost all severe intellectual disability. All show severe self-injury, usually hand and lip biting
Duchenne's muscular dystrophy		1 in 3,500 males	Variable effect on intellectual ability: Verbal skills more impaired. Progressive muscle wastage, almost all die before age 20
Phenylketonuria		1 in 10,000	Untreated, some severe intellectual disability

Data from Connor & Ferguson-Smith, 1993; Fryers & Russell, 1997; McLaren & Bryson, 1987; Plomin et al., 1997.

disabilities is developing more sophisticated methods of identifying potential causes of intellectual disability, tracking their behavioural effects, and therefore suggesting new methods for prevention, treatment and management.

FURTHER READING

Clarke, A.M., Clarke, A.D.B., & Berg, J.M. (eds) (1985). *Mental Deficiency: The Changing Outlook* (4th edn). Methuen: London.

Connor, J.M., & Ferguson-Smith, M.A. (1993). *Essential Medical Genetics (4th edn)*. Oxford: Blackwell.

Fryers, T. (1993). Epidemiological thinking in mental retardation: Issues in taxonomy and population frequency. In *International Review of Research in Mental Retardation*: Volume 19 (ed. N.W. Bray). Academic Press: San Diego.

Luckasson, R., Coulter, D.L., Polloway, E.A., Reiss, S., Schalock, R.L., Snell, M.E., Spitalnik, D.M., & Stark, J.A. (1992). *Mental Retardation: Definition, Classification, and Systems of Supports* (9th edition). American Association on Mental Retardation: Washington DC.

McLaren, J., & Bryson, S.E. (1987). Review of recent epidemiological studies of mental retardation: prevalence, associated disorders, and etiology. *American Journal of Mental Retardation* **92**, 243–254.

Chapter 3

DEVELOPMENT, COGNITION AND PERFORMANCE

*John Clements**

INTRODUCTION

To qualify as intellectually disabled there are two key exams to pass. The first one is cognitive—performance on an IQ test well below the average, such performance held to reflect underlying difficulties in processing information, problem solving and learning from experience (see also Chapter 2). The second is a practicum—functioning in everyday life which is markedly different from what is expected from others of a similar age. There is a relationship between these areas, but the determinants of performance in each area differ to some extent—social functioning is not entirely predicted by IQ scores.

The aims of the present chapter are to summarise what is known about:

❏ The social constructions of intellectual disability.
❏ Specific components of the information-processing system whose functioning might explain some of the observed differences in learning and performance.
❏ The patterns of change over time in cognitive and social functioning and the factors which influence such change.

SOCIAL CONSTRUCTIONS OF INTELLECTUAL DISABILITY

Some would question the whole validity of the concept 'intellectual disability'. Sociological perspectives on 'deviance' suggest that the real

*Applied Psychology Services, Warlingham, Surrey, UK

Clinical Psychology and People with Intellectual Disabilities. Edited by E. Emerson, C. Hatton, J. Bromley and A. Caine.
© 1998 John Wiley & Sons Ltd.

origins of performance differences lie in the social constructions made by powerful groups of those who are different and powerless ('deviant'). The deviant are identified, excluded and allocated resourcing that is deficient in quantity and quality. Negative attitudes and expectations form around those labelled, adding further to the likelihood of poor performance (the self-fulfilling prophecy).

From a quite different perspective, radical behaviourism also challenges concepts of disability and impairment—performance differences reflect differences in reinforcement history and other environmental inputs. Structure the environment correctly and the differences will disappear, to put the argument in its extreme form.

The most common construction of intellectual disability, however, reflects a more positivist view of the world. There is such a 'thing' as intellectual disability. It is a long-term characteristic of individuals. The intellectual differences so identified reflect real differences in underlying cognitive processes. These processes are determined by damage to the central nervous system of biological or early environmental origin. Environmental inputs can influence performance, but within the limits set by the underlying impairments.

Disability, pathology and difference—a personal view

Population performance on IQ tests is normally distributed (by design) and there are large individual differences in social functioning. The standards expected of any member of society are culture-bound—the demands placed upon individuals will vary over time and from society to society. All individuals require support from others throughout their lives. The cut-off point at which some people are declared disabled is therefore relative. It is a social judgement to which a scientific element is added (IQ testing, adaptive behaviour assessment). It is made as a matter of social policy, to organise the response of society to a group of people who are observably different in a socially significant way.

In most Western societies such a judgement is made in terms of pathology. The individuals are judged disabled, impaired, deficient, defective (the terms change over time). This is often supported by research showing that the social differences can be accompanied by biological differences (interestingly, the same line of argument is not applied to the other end of the scale—gifted as pathology?).

Pathologising leads to a number of problems. At the level of fact we know little about the 'normal' by which the other is judged 'defective'— our understanding of human information processing and learning at both the cognitive and biological levels is relatively crude. At the level of social implication, pathologising is akin to identifying the problem as one of disease. The thrust of social policy will then be to eliminate the problem by intervening with the individuals affected—ideally, to find a way of boosting functioning, if not to segregate the contaminated and try to prevent affected individuals being born or surviving. If a reliable way of lifting performance into the acceptable band width is not found, the other options are likely to predominate (and have done so repeatedly from an historical perspective on social policy).

The alternative to pathologising is to consider the issue one of difference rather than disability. This would acknowledge the continuous distribution of individual competences, interdependence and biological variability as part of the human condition. Indeed, such a stance would celebrate such diversity. The thrust of social policy becomes how to include all members of society in that society. This will of course mean assistance for all members to gain the maximum quality of life possible in the circumstances. However, the emphasis upon diversity and inclusion lays an equal responsibility on society to adapt to and to accommodate those differences, to create a more open, less prejudiced and discriminatory society. Intervention at the societal level becomes as important as intervention at the individual level.

These are complex and emotionally charged issues. However, it may be important for the reader to understand that the author of this chapter is trying to advance his own understanding of the concepts of difference and inclusion; and to find ways of thinking and working that reject traditional notions of disability and impairment. This will affect both the content of the chapter and the language used. However, every attempt will be made to represent the current state of knowledge in the areas that the chapter is to cover. It is thus hoped that the substance of the chapter will be relevant to all its readers, whether or not they share the author's stance.

UNDERSTANDING PERSONAL FUNCTIONING

Cognitive perspectives

Explaining low IQ

Cognitive research in the field of intellectual differences has a long history (see Clements, 1987). Much of the earlier work sought to identify the factors underlying observed differences in IQ scores. One focus was on whether the development of those identified as intellectually disabled was like normal development (same stages and sequence) going slowly, or whether it was qualitatively different, marked by deviant features. While there was considerable support for the delay model, it was equally clear that there were large individual differences within the population administratively defined as intellectually disabled. Rates of development could vary across domains of cognitive functioning—there were many different profiles. There could be anomalies in development, e.g., unusual characteristics of language development such as echolalia, restricted social usage of language skills. There could be specific cognitive disorders in the context of general delay, where functioning was much less than would be predicted by overall IQ—e.g. specific difficulties in acquiring language, specific difficulties in developing social understanding. No single characterisation of intellectual disability proved tenable.

Another focus of the earlier cognitive research was investigation of specific, discrete elements in the cognitive system whose functioning might explain the more general intellectual differences, e.g. attentional or memory differences. This is a large literature with few replicated findings and certainly no support for the general notion that intellectual differences could be explained by the functioning of highly specific elements in the cognitive system. However, a number of findings did emerge with some consistency, findings that related to IQ, not mental age. These included:

❏ Difficulties in holding and slowness at analysing information at the first level of input (sensory registration).
❏ Difficulties in discovering which were the relevant aspects to attend to in problem-solving situations.
❏ Difficulties in applying strategies that would help learning, even when those strategies were potentially available, e.g. clustering items in list-learning tasks.

There was a large volume of research on memory but no unequivocal findings of limited capacity linked to IQ (as opposed to developmental level/ mental age).

This earlier work also produced findings that act as a clear reminder that performance is not just determined by cognitive variables—e.g., prolonged failure on discrimination tasks leading to subsequent failure on tasks which had previously been solved. Likewise, growing up with disability and rejection inducing expectations of failure, avoidance of new or difficult tasks, reliance upon others to solve problems. Motivational variables have an impact upon cognitive functioning! This reinforces the message from the huge behavioural literature on skills development that performance is as much a function of environmental as it is of cognitive variables.

Subsequent cognitive research has tended to focus upon cognitive systems rather than individual components and to seek to explain specific areas of functioning rather than low IQ.

Cognitive systems and specific performance differences

The language system.   People identified as intellectually disabled are vulnerable to a wide range of specific language and communication disorders. These disorders can be found in those who achieve higher scores on IQ tests but are more common in those scoring below 70. There are a large number of specific difficulties and patterns, with impact upon expression and comprehension and the syntactic, semantic and pragmatic elements in the communication system (Clements, 1987). This is a vitally important area to identify, as early communicative functioning correlates with later social development (Bailey, Philips & Rutter, 1996) and communication difficulties correlate with the development of challenging behaviours (see Chapters 8, 9, 10 and 13).

However, even for those who do not experience specific communication disorders, many show slower development of verbal skills compared to development in other areas. The profound significance of this has really not been explored. It may link to one of the few generalised findings noted earlier about problems in the use of strategies in problem-solving situations. It may link to the oft-remarked difficulties in generalisation of learning. It may have important implications for intervention.

Specific communication difficulties/disorders are seen as biological in origin and in need of specialised interventions. There have been many exciting developments in terms of augmentative systems of communication. However, the needs of those who develop communications skills without specific help may be overlooked. Research has shown how the sheer quantity of verbal input, as well as certain qualitative characteristics, that young children receive makes a huge difference to the sophistication of the language system that develops. Work on social and cognitive development, to be discussed later, illustrates how particular types of language interaction make a difference to the development of social understanding and internal controls (Hay, 1994; Dunn, 1996). Yet there is every reason to believe that children identified as disabled may receive a quite restricted verbal input.

Thus, the role of the symbolic communication system is profound in terms of both intellectual and social functioning and a number of diverse needs in this area will be present for people identified as intellectually disabled.

Executive function. 'Executive function' refers to a system important for many areas of problem solving (see Pennington & Ozonoff, 1996). Key processes involved are strategic planning, working memory, selection of task-relevant information, inhibition of task-irrelevant information, and inhibition of previously emitted but inappropriate responding. People with executive function difficulties find it hard to tackle problems in an organised way, perseverate on irrelevant or incorrect responses, find it hard to organise information in time (sequential processing). These difficulties will be more evident in problem-solving situations rather than in familiar tasks and routines. These difficulties have been associated with damage to the frontal areas of the brain and the associated systems which project extensively to and from the frontal areas. Damage in these brain areas can also impact upon movement and affect
—over/under activity, lack of initiative, low emotional responsiveness. Damage in childhood seems to produce effects similar to damage in adulthood.

There has been much interest in whether these kinds of difficulties are present in a range of developmental difficulties. Pennington and Ozonoff's review indicates that specific problems in executive functioning (not explained by developmental level or level of intellectual functioning) can be found in attention deficit hyperactivity disorder and autism but not in conduct disorder and Tourette's syndrome. The link with autism is of particular interest, not just because of how executive function problems might explain the behavioural manifestations of autism, but also because of the link between autism and IQ less than 70. A number of those identified as intellectually disabled will also be diagnosable along the autistic continuum. A number will also be diagnosable as having attention deficit hyperactivity disorder. These individuals may therefore experience disruption to new learning because of executive function problems.

This generates some interesting speculations. If the problems outlined above are present from early in life, then the impact upon learning and motivation must be profound. It must make the acquisition of knowledge and skills very difficult and be very discouraging. It would make it hard to focus attention on to relevant stimuli, hard to keep in mind what one is trying to do, hard to inhibit irrelevant responses, even though at a more general level one would understand the tasks at hand.

Although there is little hard evidence in this area, Dunn (1996) cites work by Meins and Russell as suggesting a link between executive capacity and the quality of attachment in young children. It also seems likely that the outcome of the experience of executive difficulties would be a person who acquired fewer skills than one might otherwise expect and someone who understood more than they could reveal through their everyday behaviour. Many readers may well feel that they know people who present in these kinds of ways.

Theory of mind (social cognition).   Autism research is again the source of a major development in cognitive perspectives upon those who behave differently. The work on theory of mind (see Happe, 1994) has shown that people with autism can have specific difficulties in grasping that other people have knowledge and beliefs that are different to their own; and that they have great difficulty in sensing other people's feelings and inferring emotions from facial expressions or linking situations to emotions. The problem lies in extracting socially important information from available inputs, and the research is careful to demonstrate that these problems are not explained by overall IQ or developmental level. Although the research initially showed that problems in social cognition were exclusive to those diagnosed autistic, subsequent research has identified similar problems in people with different diagnostic labels, e.g. those with conduct disorders (Bailey, Philips & Rutter, 1996). Given that a number of people with IQs below 70 can also be labelled autistic and conduct-disordered, the significance of this research for understanding the needs of those who are intellectually different cannot be underestimated. Social cognition problems will interfere radically with the acquisition of social relating skills and raise the likelihood of behaving in ways that others find unacceptable.

And a few more things besides . . .   There are many other areas of knowledge relevant to constructing a cognitive view of the intellectual differences with which this chapter is concerned. It is clear from the educational field that there are information-processing problems in a wide range of specific domains—reading, mathematics, spelling. The field of cerebral palsy has illustrated how serious motor problems can mask intellectual functioning but also the correlate with the presence of specific difficulties in the perceptual domain. Some of the recent discussions in autism have suggested major disturbances in the domain of motor control, which serve to interfere with social functioning and conceal true knowledge and understanding (Hill & Leary, 1993). Rourke (1995, cited in Bailey, Philips & Rutter, 1996) has talked of right hemisphere non-verbal learning disability marked by good verbal IQ, poor academic performance, clumsiness, impaired pragmatic and social functioning and specific problems with mathematics.

In summary, therefore, recent cognitive research suggests that:

❑ Whilst some functioning reflects slow but normal processing and development in all areas, there can be a range of domain-specific

processing difficulties (e.g. language, social, perceptual, reading, mathematical).
❑ Particular difficulties have been explored in social cognition and executive functioning with other interesting ideas about non-verbal learning disabilities and the impact of movement control problems upon more general functioning.
❑ There can be problems at the strategic level—how to problem-solve, how to extract higher order concepts.
❑ There remains the possibility of problems in specific components of the information-processing system (e.g. working memory).

The challenge of the new cognition is twofold. First, it is necessary to develop assessment tools that more adequately represent cognitive functioning and individual differences. In the long run this is a formidable undertaking as it will require the development of norm- and criterion-referenced instruments. However, a start can be made with the judicious use of the normative assessments already available, combined with qualitative data collection on people functioning in their everyday lives. Out of this a picture can be assembled of what information is processed, to what degree, and how it is used. This in turn leads on to the second challenge: to develop remedial and compensatory interventions that enable people to know more and to control more in their lives.

The role of affective characteristics

Individual functioning is determined by a wide range of factors, both intra-individual and environmental. Significant intra-individual contributions come from the cognitive and affective domains. The term 'affect' is used broadly to refer to arousal levels, personality factors, deprivation states and specific, time-limited emotional moods and states. The environment, of course, has a huge role to play in generating affects of all kinds, but the emphasis in this section is upon personal characteristics which show some stability across time and environments.

Attention deficit disorder is thought currently to involve a problem of under-arousal. Given the interference with concentration, learning and social behaviour that is part of this syndrome, it may provide a useful perspective upon the functioning of some people who experience generalised difficulties in learning. Individual differences in personality will also influence the ease with which certain kinds of learning occur—e.g. the learning of social inhibitions. Personality has been a neglected area in the field of intellectual differences despite some early studies demonstrating, for example, that extroverts respond better to material incentives, introverts to performance targets. Earlier reference was made to the impact upon behavioural style of growing up with intellectual disabilities—people becoming less willing to try new things, take risks, more likely to seek support/direction; or, alternatively, becoming more socially withdrawn, less trusting, less accepting of help.

These more global concepts of personality, motivation and behavioural style will have a significant effect upon both what is learned and the conditions most likely to promote development, but as yet have received scant attention in the academic study of intellectual differences. The measurement of these variables could be relatively straightforward, given the volume of general research in this area.

The more fluctuating variables of mood and emotional state do tend to be incorporated into current formulations of behavioural difficulties (see Chapters 8 and 9). However, it is clear that such variables are active from early childhood and may thus have an important impact upon development over time. High anxiety levels may inhibit learning, as may low mood and social avoidance. These may be direct effects and may also operate indirectly, as when they are implicated in major behavioural difficulties, such as aggression and self-injury, which limit social engagement and learning opportunities. While everyone experiences these affects on occasion, some people may be constitutionally vulnerable to them or to extremes of expression ('emotionality').

The role of affect in autism is also a relatively neglected domain in the academic literature, compared to clinical experience. Many people with autism will have unusual interests and joys which need to be respected. Some seem to experience a strong bias to negative emotions, often experienced with great intensity—huge arousal surges of uncertain meaning, sustained low mood and powerful anger. Such experiences can be observed across the ability range. They may be present from early in life and may also become very prominent in adolescence/young adulthood. They are often implicated in major behavioural difficulties and in the disruption of the learning process. Their precise nature and meaning are in need of much greater exploration.

There will also be important interactions between the above variables and environmental factors. Links have been hypothesised between child temperament and parenting style, which may determine the degree to which impulse control and social understanding develop. While identifying current affective variables will be relevant to immediate assistance work, identifying vulnerabilities could have a key role in preventative work.

PERSONAL FUNCTIONING OVER TIME

The paths along which individual development proceeds over time are many and varied. This section will try to summarise what is known about the factors that promote or inhibit development.

Environmental influences

The environment can accelerate development in a number of ways. At the macro level the opportunities that are offered and the general quality of life can influence both IQ scores and social competence for people identified as intellectually different.

Within child development research it is also clear that family interaction (quantity and quality) affects later intellectual and social performance, both at a general level and in terms of more specific variables, such as the development of language, social cognition and self-control. For example, parental practices which include explaining reasons for distress, firm boundaries but the avoidance of punitiveness, encouragement to help others and tolerance of dependency tend to promote in the child understanding of others and internalising of controls. Explanations about feelings, reasons and mental states may be particularly influential when embedded in play, comforting and joking, rather than being used exclusively during behaviour-controlling interchanges (Hay, 1994; Dunn, 1996). The sheer frequency of speaking, the size of the vocabulary used and the way language is used in problem solving and explanation, the amount of encouragement and support offered as opposed to criticism, can influence cognitive functioning (Hart & Risley, 1995). While these are findings from 'normal' development and cannot be directly extrapolated to the development of people that are identified as disabled, the findings raise some very exciting issues about the role of the everyday environment in promoting cognitive growth. Certainly, any possibility of enhancing the development of social cognition, self-control and the internalisation of values should be taken particularly seriously, as these areas relate strongly to prosocial behaviours. Given the significance of challenging behaviour in development and service provision (see Chapters 4, 8 and 9), this raises some important research questions in terms of both prevention and remediation.

Controversy has raged over the role of structured early intervention. Educational interventions in the preschool years with 'disadvantaged' children, at risk for scoring later IQ below 70, demonstrated boosting effects on IQ in the early school years. Whilst the IQ gains were often lost later, effects upon attainment and cognitive functions such as expectations and social competence held up into adult life. The impact of early intervention with children having more recognisable developmental disabilities has tended to demonstrate enhancement of performance at the time but with no long-term effects upon overall intellectual functioning. The exception to this is the work of Ivar Lovaas, showing that intensive preschool intervention with children diagnosed autistic will yield, for a proportion, impacts upon intellectual and social functioning that make them indistinguishable from others of a similar age. The impacts carry through to adult life. These are controversial claims but are backed by some research findings and are not to be dismissed (Emerson, 1996). The implications for service provision are profound.

At a less controversial level, it is quite clear that environments that offer structured approaches to teaching and skill development will enhance social competence more than those that simply leave people to their own devices or simply offer opportunities without structured support.

As they can help, so also can environments hinder development. Environments that offer people poor quality relationships and few opportunities will damage both intellectual and social functioning. Life events (losses and changes) and trauma can also disrupt the developmental trajectory. Their effects upon emotional well-being and cognitive functioning (e.g. self esteem) may lead to regression in social functioning and inhibition of the capacity to learn. These effects may be short- or long-term.

Individual influences

Although less well researched, behaviours and characteristics of individuals will influence their developmental trajectory. General IQ remains a significant predictor of learning and unaided social functioning amongst people whose scores fall in the range below 70. Verbal abilities also have an impact, with those who develop good communication skills attaining better social functioning and less likely to develop challenging behaviours under current service arrangements (Bailey, Philips & Rutter, 1996). The presence of severe challenging behaviours can itself impact upon development and performance. The effects can be direct—the behaviours disrupt the learning process. They can be indirect—the response of others may lead to the exclusion of those who challenge from opportunities and experiences; or to the use of drugs or other restraints which may interfere with development (see also Chapter 8).

Individuals who score below 70 may also have additional difficulties which disrupt the developmental process—sensory difficulties or functional difficulties such as attention problems. Less obvious are the effects of temperament and personality referred to earlier.

One might include as an individual variable the notion of age and stage of development. The question of early intervention has already been discussed and it is often felt that there is greater plasticity in the 0–5 age range, with intervention at this point having more widespread and longer-lasting effects. However, some studies have shown IQ gains in adult life. Certainly from a clinical perspective many people growing up with disabilities do seem to flower during their early adult lives. This raises the intriguing possibility that more intense intervention post-school might yield cognitive gains as well as the skill gains that can accrue through much of the lifespan with the right kind of support.

There is finally the question of individual choice. Individuals may choose to avail themselves of opportunities . . . or not. Individuals may choose courses of action which to others seem damaging—exploitative relation ships, dangerous sexual practices, dropping out of education, use of drugs, staying fat. The work of Robert Edgerton, documenting the lives chosen by people identified as intellectually disabled, is a poignant reminder of the real choices people make when offered real lives. Their choices may not conform to the *Diktat* that human beings should live lives which enable them to fulfil the potential that others perceive (Edgerton, 1989).

Biological influences

Like other sources of influence, biological factors can help or hinder development. Diet can impact in a number of ways. As noted in Chapter 3, metabolic difficulties such as phenylketonuria will reduce intellectual functioning and early diagnosis and treatment by a diet will prevent this. There is, in addition, some evidence that adults who have been already damaged by phenylketonuria may benefit from the diet in terms of social functioning.

In the field of autism there is theorising about the role of metabolic difficulties as a source of brain neurotransmitter malfunction and consequent behavioural functioning that generates the label 'autism'. There are some encouraging findings on the impact of gluten- and casein-free diets on the social functioning of some individuals (Shattock, 1995). Controversy continues around the role of additives in determining social and intellectual functioning. While the general application of specific diets cannot be justified, some individuals may experience greater well-being and function better with diets that exclude specific substances to which they are sensitive.

The role of drugs is as controversial as that of diets. While there is no evidence that drugs can enhance intellectual functioning, they may impact upon emotional well-being (anxiety, depression) or cognitive interference (hallucinations) and thereby promote social functioning. But drugs can also inflict damage. Major tranquillisers such as chlorproma zine may interfere with learning or inflict irreversible damage upon motor and sensory systems. They can sometimes pose a threat to life itself. Toxins such as lead can damage the nervous system, although this risk has been reduced in many places by the removal of lead from paint, petrol and water pipes.

Some behaviours such as self-injury may impact biologically. They can lead to additional brain damage or sensory impairment (e.g. loss of vision) which in turn impact upon development over time. Disease processes will likewise influence functioning. Early onset degenerative disorders such as lipid storage diseases may dramatically alter the rate of development or lead to loss of earlier gains made. People with Down's syndrome are vulnerable to the brain pathology associated with Alzheimer's disease. This neuropathology develops in early to mid-adult life but only a proportion of people with Down's syndrome actually show functional deterioration. This seems most likely after the age of 40 but it must be stressed that it does not affect all people with Down's syndrome and may affect others without Down's syndrome (Zigman et al., 1993).

There are also phenomena which markedly impair development and which at the time of writing are not well understood but are assumed to be biological. In Rett's syndrome, apparently normal development in girls is followed by catastrophic loss of skills such as mobility, speech and social relating, subsequent to which further development occurs at a very slow rate (at the time of writing the cause is thought to be genetic). This pattern may also be evident in others—the development of some children with autism is unremarkable at first, with a rather sharp diversion on to a more typical autistic track around the age of 18 months to 2 years (loss of speech and social relating skills are the things noted). Not all children later diagnosed as autistic show this pattern.

In summary, therefore:

❑ The influences over a person's developmental trajectory will include environmental, individual and biological factors (promoters and inhibitors in each domain). From a practical perspective it is important to establish whether an individual's living environments contain the elements most likely to promote development and well-being.

❑ Key environmental enhancers include positive relationships, learning and experience opportunities, structured help for skill acquisition and perhaps specific styles of relating.

❑ It seems likely that there are interactions between environmental and individual factors such as temperament and age. Temperament is likely to influence how much structure is required (more for the more impulsive) and how much arousal to evoke at learning points (less for the more sensitive). In terms of age, the two leading candidates for positive synergy are the preschool period and early adult life.

❏ The biological factors identified are primarily inhibitors and intervention rests upon compensatory strategies such as diet.

From the perspective of those paid to provide services to people identified as intellectually disabled, all the above indicates the need to assess the current environmental, individual and biological factors influencing development; and to identify the environmental and biological arrangements that will maximise personal well-being and development. However, personal well-being and development are not the only contributors to social functioning, a point that is sometimes missed when there is over-emphasis upon the concept of independence for people identified as disabled.

DEVELOPMENT AND INCLUSION

Human beings do not function independently, they function interdependently. The interdependence is of many sorts. We may rely upon others to do the things that we cannot do or choose not to do for ourselves, we may rely upon others for social-emotional support, for material support, for information. It is therefore misleading to suggest that the key to social functioning is personal independence—gaining skills has its role but so too does the availability and accessibility of supports.

Thus, any consideration of 'performance' must look not just at how the knowledge and skills of the individual can be increased but at how environments can be constructed to support inclusion. This has both ideological and technological components. At the ideological level work is needed to move towards a more open society, one in which those who are different can experience acceptance and value rather than rejection and denigration. The development, cognition and performance of people regarded as intellectually disabled is a political as well as a psychological issue.

At the technological level there are a number of ways in which support may be offered to enhance inclusion. Personal assistance will be extremely important—e.g. physical support, using comprehensible language, pausing to give people time to speak, offering encouragement to support perseverance, doing something for someone that he/she cannot do for him/herself. Technical assistance may include mobility aids, communication aids, putting information into other media (e.g. visual rather than verbal) to aid comprehension. Material resources will also have a role to play—most people with disabilities are poor, and poverty may set far more limits on social functioning than disability. Resources may be enhanced by improving access to employment, raising benefits, improving access to home ownership by mortgage schemes sensitive to the problems faced by those on low incomes.

Whilst practice abounds with examples of ways to enhance inclusion, research in this area is very limited. It is no coincidence that research work is dominated by how to change the competence of individuals regarded as intellectually disabled. This reveals the unspoken assumption that to be included in society one has to pass a competence test. It is this assumption that needs to be challenged.

RECOMMENDED FURTHER READING

Hay, D.F. (1994). Prosocial development. *Journal of Child Psychology and Psychiatry*, **35**, 29–72.

Pennington, B.F., & Ozonoff, S. (1996). Executive functions and developmental psychopathology. *Journal of Child Psychology and Psychiatry*, **37**, 51–88.

Kroese, B., Dagnan, D., & Loumides, K. (eds) (1997). *Cognitive Behaviour Therapy for People with Learning Disabilities*. Routledge: London.

Chapter 4

SERVICE PROVISION

Amanda Caine*, Chris Hatton** and Chris Emerson[†]

INTRODUCTION

People with intellectual disabilities receive assistance from many agencies throughout their lives. Different services attempt to meet a variety of needs and have separate statutory responsibilities. Thus, clinical psychologists and other professionals working with people with intellectual disabilities need to have some understanding of this complex system of service provision.

The current complexities of service provision for people with intellectual disabilities are the result of many factors, including changing legislation, changing service practices and wider changes in society. Therefore, to understand the life stories of individuals with intellectual disabilities, to work effectively within current service structures, and to plan better services for the future, a basic understanding of three factors is required:

❑ An understanding of the historical development of services for people with intellectual disabilities.
❑ An understanding of the policy and legislative frameworks within which services operate and people with intellectual disabilities live.
❑ An understanding of the current pattern of service provision for people with intellectual disabilities.

This chapter aims to provide a brief overview of these three areas with specific reference to working with people with intellectual disabilities; more general overviews concerning issues in health and social care are available elsewhere (e.g. Kat, 1995).

*Rochdale Healthcare NHS Trust, UK ** Hester Adrian Research Centre, Manchester; [†]Calderdale School Psychological Service

Clinical Psychology and People with Intellectual Disabilities. Edited by E. Emerson, C. Hatton, J. Bromley and A. Caine.
© 1998 John Wiley & Sons Ltd.

A BRIEF HISTORY OF SERVICE PROVISION

A historical perspective is useful in a number of ways. It reinforces the notion that 'intellectual disability' is socially constructed and, in a climate where claims are often made about marvellous new ways of providing radically new services, it can provide a sobering perspective with which to evaluate such claims.

We are often told a particular story of the development of services for people with intellectual disabilities. This story often starts with the grim old Victorian institution and recounts a tale of heroic attempts to move away from it towards radically better services for people with intellectual disabilities (e.g. Bradley & Knoll, 1995). While clearly a comforting view of history for professionals, there are considerable doubts about the accuracy of this progressive view (Trent, 1995; Wright & Digby, 1996). This section will present a brief, non-heroic history of service provision for people with intellectual disabilities in the UK.

Before the institution: the poor laws and 'community care'

The period from medieval times to the nineteenth century is often viewed as radically different from today, either a golden age or an era of neglect. However, the continuities between this period and today's era of 'community care' are perhaps as notable as the differences. From medieval times through to the late nineteenth century, the legal system distinguished between 'lunacy' (acquired and punctuated by 'lucid intervals') and 'idiocy' (congenital and irreversible) (Andrews, 1996; Neugebauer, 1996; Rushton, 1996). In practice, the classification of 'idiocy' was dependent on a number of pragmatic factors. People would only come to the attention of the courts or poor law administrators if they needed financial support, usually triggered by family life-cycle crises or disruptive behaviour on the part of the person with 'idiocy' (Andrews, 1996; Rushton, 1996).

The responses of poor law administrators to 'idiocy' varied widely, although incarceration in asylums (many of which excluded 'idiots') or workhouses was rare. Poor law relief was instead directed towards providing basic necessities, often for a limited period of time. Such relief could be directed towards family members who would otherwise struggle to support the person, same-sex 'keepers' or 'nurses', who provided lodgings and care for the person (Andrews, 1996; Rushton, 1996), or to the person him/herself to enable him/her to live independently.

Institutions as social reform: the Victorian era

The reasons for the rise in institutions for people with intellectual disabilities are complex, unclear and hotly debated (see Scheerenberger, 1983; Trent, 1995; Wright & Digby, 1996). Increasingly urban, industrial ised societies, with their associated changes in family structures and household economies, changing conceptions of 'idiocy', and the Victorian penchant for social reform all combined to create fertile ground for the rise of the institution in the late nineteenth century.

Victorian society, by demanding an increasingly educated workforce (universal elementary education was introduced in the 1890s) and increasingly requiring families to live in urban settings, both increased the visibility of people with intellectual disabilities and reconstituted them as a social problem. For example, parents increasingly cited poor educational performance as a major factor precipitating admission to institutions throughout the nineteenth century (Wright, 1996).

Implicit in the notion that 'idiots' were ineducable was a re-conceptualisation of 'idiocy' based on John Locke's distinction between madness (right reasoning from wrong principles) and idiocy (lack of reasoning ability). This formulation placed 'idiots' at the wrong end of a spectrum of general reasoning ability and, as reasoning ability was claimed to be the defining characteristic of humanity, led to 'idiots' being considered as not fully human (Goodey, 1996). Here were born several conceptions of people with intellectual disabilities still widespread today; lacking in intelligence; qualitatively different from other people; and less than human.

As with institutions for 'lunatics' (Porter, 1990; Scull, 1993), the first institutions for 'idiots' were founded on the basis of a new optimism about the possibilities of teaching skills to people formerly regarded as incurable (Gladstone, 1996). The first specialised institutions, run by voluntary agencies, were designed to take in 'idiot' children for a maximum of five years and train them to become productive members of society. However, only a small number of 'idiots' were considered to be likely to benefit from such regimes.

Early optimism surrounding specialist institutions was not borne out in practice; stories of spectacular success were not repeated, and children tended to remain in institutions much longer than their allotted five years. By 1881 only 3% of the 29,542 institutionalised 'idiots' were in specialist 'idiot asylums' (Rose, 1985; cited in Gladstone, 1996); with an approximately equal number of pauper 'idiots' estimated to live outside institutions of any kind (Gelband, 1979; cited in Gladstone, 1996).

Institutions provided by state agencies were different in size, ethos and character from the earlier voluntary 'idiot asylums' and did not select on the basis of likely trainability. They were much larger, with advocates of large institutions citing advantages such as rapidly increasing demand, economies of scale, and increasing precision of classification for the purposes of education, training and treatment. Indeed, to keep costs low, many 'idiot asylums' encouraged the retention of adult 'idiots' within the institution, to carry out necessary work at minimal cost (Gladstone, 1996). This resulted in an ethos of permanent containment and regimented routines necessary to ensure the smooth running of the institution (Gladstone, 1996; Jackson, 1996).

Private problem to social threat: the early twentieth century

By the end of the nineteenth century a rise in the number of people classified as 'idiots' was apparent. Debates continue concerning how much of this rise was 'real' (see Day & Jancar, 1991; Race, 1995; Ryan, 1987). While improved living conditions and health care throughout the nineteenth century may have contributed to an actual rise in the number of people with intellectual disabilities, due to increased survival rates among severely disabled infants and improvements in longevity, social factors appeared to be the major fuel for the increased demand for institutional places, including changing demands on families and expanding conceptions of 'idiocy'.

Several strands of thought around this time converged to reconceptualise the 'idiot' as a threat to society. First, the increasingly influential medical profession began to conceptualise 'idiocy' as an organic disease, with a concomitant pessimism about training or 'cure' and a reinforcement of the idea of 'idiots' as qualitatively different from the rest of society. Second, the eugenics movement claimed that social ills, including poverty, crime and 'immoral' sexual behaviour, were caused by people of inferior genetic stock. Furthermore, according to eugenicists, human traits were heritable. Therefore, people of inferior genetic stock (including 'idiots') should not be allowed to have children, ensuring that inferior genes would not be passed on to future generations. Third, educationalists and psychologists developed the theory of unified intelligence, which in its IQ test form could be used as an impeccably 'scientific' method for classifying people as being mentally deficient at a young age, and placing them in segregated institutions. Mental deficiency was an expanded administrative definition which included 'idiots', 'imbeciles' and the 'feeble-minded'. Through the use of terms such as 'moral imbecility', many people engaging in behaviour unacceptable to Edwardian sensibilities, such as drunkenness or 'immoral' sexual behaviour, were brought under the umbrella definition of 'mental deficiency' (Cox, 1996; Jackson, 1996).

The permanent segregation of people with 'mental deficiency' now became an explicit goal for institutions (Jackson, 1996), a stark contrast to the early Victorian aims of training and re-integration into society. It was argued that this would result in a great saving of money to the community at large, while protecting society from people with 'mental deficiency' and also protecting people with 'mental deficiency' from themselves and society (Jackson, 1996).

The Royal Commission on the Care and Control of the Feeble-Minded (1904–1908) was in part a response to this changed atmosphere, and recommended the setting up of an expanded nationwide network of permanent, segregated institutions (or 'colonies') for people with 'mental deficiency'. The Mental Deficiency Act of 1913 went part of the way towards trying to achieve this goal. These colonies were to be controlled by Boards of Control of local authorities, who had wide-ranging powers both to admit people to institutions and to detain them once they were institutionalised (Digby, 1996; Race, 1995; Ryan, 1987). However, the Act failed to provide adequate new resources for local authorities, leading to its uneven and incomplete implementation (Digby, 1996; Thomson, 1996).

Although local authorities undoubtedly used the Act as a framework for the social control of 'undesirables', their response to people classified as 'mentally deficient' was not inevitably the placement of people in permanent, segregated 'colonies' or specialist institutions (Cox, 1996; Thomson, 1996). In addition to enabling the institutionalisation of people with 'mental deficiency', the 1913 Act also allowed for local authorities to place people with 'mental deficiency' under 'supervision' with their families, or under 'guardianship' with a range of service providers (Thomson, 1996), which sometimes included their families. Families were also supported by newly opened 'occupation centres', which provided activities during the day for people with 'mental deficiency' (Thomson, 1996).

The NHS and community care

The setting up of the welfare state in the UK after the Second World War provided a framework for services which is still present today. The 1944 Education Act, for example, led to the establishment of a number of special schools for children with intellectual disabilities, although the terms of the Act also excluded children with severe disabilities who were deemed to be 'ineducable', an exclusion only overturned in 1970 legislation. The establishment of the National Health Service (NHS) in 1948 also brought all institutions under the aegis of the health service, an arbitrary decision but one with long-term consequences. As institutions became hospitals, so people with intellectual disabilities became patients with health problems.

The number of people with intellectual disabilities in institutions rose to a peak of approximately 60,000–64,000 in the 1950s and 1960s, although another 35,000–40,000 people were living outside institutions under care or guardianship orders at this time (Felce, 1996; Race, 1995). At around this time doubts were voiced about whether the institution was a desirable place for people with intellectual disabilities to live. First, many of the claims made by eugenicists, for example about the heritability of intelligence, had been discredited by the 1950s. and a gradual shift in social mores meant that people with intellectual disabilities became seen as less of a threat to society. Second, a renewed interest in the rights of individuals after the Second World War led to increasing calls for people with intellectual disabilities to enjoy the same civil rights as other citizens (see Emerson, 1992).

An increasing body of evidence began to emerge that institutions were clearly not the best possible option for people with intellectual disabilities. Research proliferated demonstrating the debilitating effect of institutions on child development in general and the development of people with intellectual disabilities in particular. Some of this research suggested that people with intellectual disabilities previously thought to be 'ineducable' could develop their skills with appropriate education and support; the kind of education and support that was not provided in institutions. Furthermore these alternatives seemed to provide a much better social and material environment than that provided by large, barren institutions. Finally, and possibly most damagingly, there were a series of scandals concerning hospitals for people with intellectual disabilities, starting with the Committee of Enquiry into Ely Hospital in 1969, which castigated the ill-treatment meted out by staff on their patients (see Mittler & Sinason, 1996; Race, 1995).

Thus, throughout the 1960s alternatives to institutionalisation were firmly on the agenda. At the level of 'high politics', the Seebohm Report of 1968 (enacted in 1970) recommended the setting up of social services departments in local authorities to provide a more pro-active, comprehensive and integrated service for families and individuals requiring help, including people with intellectual disabilities living outside institutions. The White Paper of 1971, *Better Services for the Mentally Handicapped*, advocated a massive increase in community-based services for people with intellectual disabilities and a consequent reduction in hospital places, although the White Paper stopped some way short of proposing total hospital closure. From this point, children became increasingly less likely to be admitted to mental handicap hospitals, and some adults began to leave, at first to relatively large (approximately 20-place) community-based units or hostels (see Felce, 1996; Race, 1995).

This equivocal stance gradually changed throughout the 1970s and 1980s, with Government-sponsored committees, such as the Jay Committee, becoming increasingly influenced by the ideas of normalisation as they were promoted in the UK (Emerson, 1992; King's Fund, 1980; O'Brien & Tyne, 1981; Wolfensberger, 1972). These principles (see the Introduction for more information) emphasised the integration of people with intellectual disabilities into local communities. In the UK the means adopted to achieve these ends focused on moving people with intellectual disabilities out of hospitals into ordinary houses, on the assumption that if institutional environments created institutional behaviour, it followed that 'ordinary' environments would create more valued, 'ordinary' behaviour.

After the demonstrated success of pilot projects providing 'ordinary life' services to people with severe and profound intellectual disabilities (see Felce, 1989; Lowe & de Paiva, 1991), the implementation of 'ordinary living' services became more widespread throughout the UK, although there is evidence that 'ordinary living' services are geographically patchy and by no means the dominant model of residential provision (Emerson & Hatton, 1996b, 1997). In line with developments in North America, Australasia and Scandinavia, the number of people with intellectual disabilities living in institutions fell sharply throughout the 1980s (Emerson et al., 1996; Hatton et al., 1995), with the number of hospital places approximately halving between 1980 and 1992 (Emerson & Hatton, 1994). Day services in the form of day centres (first named 'adult training centres', where industrial work was carried out for little money; later re-named 'social education centres', where the ostensible aims were educative) also expanded during this period, as did family support services such as respite and domiciliary care (Gray, 1996; Stalker, 1996).

There are currently profound debates concerning the future of services for people with intellectual disabilities, following the implementation of community care in the early 1990s. In the areas of residential services (Emerson & Hatton, 1996b; Hatton & Emerson, 1996; Mental Health Foundation, 1996), day services (Mental Health Foundation, 1996; Wertheimer, 1996) and family support services (Stalker, 1996), it is apparent that current service provision, while in some areas an improvement on previous service provision, is falling short of the 'ordinary life' principles supposedly underlying these services. Normalisation principles around raising the status of people with intellectual disabilities as a group are being replaced by notions of individual rights or empowerment (Ramcharan et al., 1997), reflected in the growth of self-advocacy (Mental Health Foundation, 1996; Whitaker, 1996) and rhetoric concerning 'person-centred planning', where the person with intellectual disabilities ostensibly has total control over the support she/he uses (O'Brien & Lovett, 1992).

These ideas are feeding into current service developments in the UK around supported living (Simons, 1995), innovative forms of family support (Stalker, 1996) and changing day services, including supported employment (Wertheimer, 1996), although the extent to which these service changes will result in socially significant changes in the lives of people with intellectual disabilities has yet to be tested. Furthermore, the extent to which such services can be implemented, given scant resources and an increasing population of people with intellectual disabilities, is highly debatable, and there are currently lobbying groups arguing that the 'failure' of community care should result in the expansion of rural 'village' communities based on the sites of old mental handicap hospitals (Cox & Pearson, 1995). The effects of these debates on future services for people with intellectual disabilities is, as yet, unclear.

POLICY CONTEXT

National policy

There are several pieces of legislation which determine current service provision. These are often statements of good intentions and are rarely accompanied by extra resources. As a result, the intentions of legislation are not always translated into practice.

National policy relating to people with intellectual disabilities is now fairly explicit and has widespread support. The 1990 NHS and Community Care Act and associated guidance on issues such as care management provides much of the over-arching legislative and organisational framework within which services are commissioned and provided. This legislation is backed up by various policy statements. There are two dedicated policy documents for services to adults with intellectual disabilities: *Health Services for Adults with Learning Disabilities* (Department of Health, 1992c), and *Social Care for Adults with Learning Disabilities* (Department of Health, 1992a). Others include those arising from the *Health of the Nation* framework (see Chapter 16) and the 'Mansell Report', which sets out a framework for people who challenge and/or have additional mental health needs (see Chapters 8, 9 and 12). Some of the main aspects to highlight from these sources are that:

❑ People with intellectual disabilities, and their families where appropriate, should be central to the assessment and planning of their services.
❑ Services should be planned on an individual basis.
❑ Whilst there is a range of acceptable living arrangements, all should be 'outward-looking, closely associated with the general community and limited in size'.
❑ People with intellectual disabilities should be enabled to access generic services (including health services) as far as possible, but with the back-up of specialist skills and resources.

National policy is clear on the expectation that services involve users in a broad range of issues. There is now a wide breadth of experience across the country on effective, non-tokenistic approaches to achieve this, varying from direct involvement in assessment and individual planning through to involvement in wider strategic issues. Discussion as to why this approach is important and some descriptions about effective approaches can be found in the report of the Mental Health Foundation's Committee of Inquiry (Mental Health Foundation, 1996). Organisational structures should enable service users and advocates to have an impact on debates about the future style and direction of services in a way that is beyond the token user in a planning group. This will often necessitate organisations changing the way in which they operate and consult if tokenism is to be avoided.

Current legislation

The following section will describe some key features of current legislation (see also Chapter 5).

The National Health Service & Community Care Act 1990 (with effect from April 1993).

Nationally, there are six key objectives for community care:

1. To promote domiciliary, day and respite care services to enable people to live in their own homes wherever it is feasible and sensible.
2. To make practical support for carers a high priority.
3. To provide community care on the basis of careful assessment of individuals' needs and the co-ordination of services by the agencies involved.
4. To work closely with the voluntary and independent sector in providing a comprehensive, high quality service.

5. To clarify who is responsible for what and to ensure that we all account for our performance.
6. To secure better value for taxpayers' and community charge payers' money.

Under this legislation certain agencies have responsibility to assess needs for services, specify what services are required and commission an appropriate organisation to provide them (see Roberts & Griffiths, 1993).

The Education Act, 1981

The Act placed a duty on Local Education Authorities (LEAs) to assess and determine appropriate provision for pupils with special educational needs through a formal assessment procedure and the issuing of a Statement of Special Educational needs. It was expected that statements would be required for approximately 2% of the school population which would include children with intellectual disabilities (termed severe and complex learning difficulties in the educational system). If necessary, the statement could be in place throughout the school life of the child, but would discontinue when the child left school (generally at 19 years of age for pupils with intellectual disabilities). The intention of the Act was to meet these special needs in mainstream schools as far as possible, provided that three conditions are met as follows:

1. The child can receive at the school specified the special education which is necessary to meet his/her individual needs.
2. The education of other children in the school must not be adversely affected.
3. The local education authority's resources are used efficiently.

The Education Reform Act, 1988

This Act set in place the National Curriculum. All pupils in maintained schools, including those with special educational needs, are expected to follow the National Curriculum. There are, however, arrangements (Circular No. 15/89) to enable head teachers, where necessary, to modify or disapply any aspect of the National Curriculum arrangements for a particular child. The Act also established local management of schools (known as LMS) with delegated budgets, and also enabled schools to seek grant-maintained status.

The Children Act, 1989

The Act is intended to bring together and clarify all previous legislation regarding children's welfare. It therefore covers a wide range of issues and has 108 sections. Section 1 is the cornerstone of the Act and makes it clear that the child's welfare is of paramount consideration. Thus, the child's welfare is the decisive issue. The Act also emphasises parental responsibility and defines this as all the rights, duties, powers and authority which by law a parent of a child has. Further sections of the Act cover various orders concerning child care, local authority support for children and families, care and supervision orders, protection of children, community homes, voluntary homes and voluntary organisations, registered children's homes, private arrangements for fostering children, child minding and day care for young children, and finally the supervisory functions and responsibilities of the Secretary of State. The Act defines 'children in need' quite broadly and includes children with disabilities.

The Education Act, 1993 (Part III)

This piece of legislation was an attempt to build on the framework of the 1981 Act in order to overcome some of the problems which had become apparent. These included education authorities taking too long to carry out statutory assessments and producing too many statements, and a lack of recognition of a continuum of need, with the broader band of pupils with special needs (estimated at approximately 18% of the school population) failing to receive additional support as resources were targeted almost entirely at those with statements (approximately 2%). An independent Special Educational Needs (SEN) Tribunal was established to consider parent's appeals against LEA decisions. The 1993 Act places duties on local authorities and schools to identify, assess, record, meet and review special educational needs, involving a five-stage model of need, and to establish a Special Needs Register in every mainstream school. It imposes a time limit on the statutory assessment procedure and a duty on the Local Authority to conduct an annual review for pupils with Statements and to prepare a Transition Plan at the first review after the child's 14th birthday. Other agencies must contribute to the formal assessment and to the reviews. Detailed directions regarding the implementation of the SEN legislation are contained in the Code of Practice, to which all LEAs and schools must have regard.

The Education Act, 1996 (Part IV)

This Act incorporated and replaced the 1993 Act and all other previous special educational needs legislation. The 1996 Act is the legislation to which LEAs and schools must currently have regard.

Educational legislation in Northern Ireland

Legislation in Northern Ireland closely mirrors that in England and Wales. For instance, the Education Reform Act (Northern Ireland Order), 1989, is very similar to the Education Act, 1988. The Education Act (Northern Ireland Order), 1996, establishes special needs legislation in line with that in place in England and Wales.

Educational legislation in Scotland

The main body of legislation governing provision for special educational needs in Scotland is contained in the Education (Scotland) Act, 1980, amended by the Education (Scotland) Act, 1981. Children with the most significant difficulties undergo a process called Recording (similar to statementing) and are issued with a Record of Need. Instead of a transition plan, children must have a Future Needs Assessment produced 9 months before they leave school (see below).

Organisational roles and responsibilities

Recent legislative changes have increased the need for close inter-agency working, whilst creating uncertainty and tensions amongst key agencies. The roles and responsibilities of different agencies, together with current issues affecting these roles and responsibilities, will be briefly discussed below.

Services for children

Local authorities have a duty to:

❑ Safeguard and promote the welfare of children within their area who are in need.
❑ So far as is consistent with that duty, to promote the upbringing of such children by their families, by providing a range and level of services appropriate to those children's needs.
❑ Establish and maintain a register of children with a disability, and

introduce the concept of children in need (of whom only a small proportion may also have special educational needs).

Healthcare provision

The NHS has a responsibility for ensuring that people's health needs are assessed and treated quickly, effectively and in the least intrusive manner possible. The Department of Health (1995b) states that good practice is now acknowledged to require health authorities, GP fundholders and NHS trusts to be working together to ensure that:

❑ Contracts for general health services meet the needs of people with intellectual disabilities.
❑ Where additional help and support is needed, to enable people to access these services, and that this is contracted for and provided.
❑ There are adequate links to GPs and the primary health care team, and that they have sufficient knowledge about service options.
❑ Regular screening and checks are undertaken across the full range of health matters.
❑ Hospital and community health services develop the skills and knowledge to provide services to people with intellectual disabilities.

Joint commissioning

Joint commissioning (between health and social services) of services for people with intellectual disabilities is now regarded as desirable, if not essential. The Department of Health guidance on the topic sets out various approaches, whilst not being prescriptive on how it should be developed. Across the country, the rhetoric of joint commissioning is greater than the reality. The most common approach being developed for adult services is that of the Social Services Department taking on a lead purchasing function following a transfer of the bulk of District Health Authority funds. Social Services even more naturally take the lead in children's services, given their obligations under the Children Act. This approach requires the Health Authority to be very clear about the specific 'healthcare' services it will continue to commission, and for there to be clear working links between health care professionals and the care management processes. Both these elements are frequently lacking from joint commissioning arrangements.

National policies often result in contradictory imperatives for different statutory organisations, such as to simultaneously collaborate and compete with each other, and to be engaged in prevention work while simultaneously prioritising short-term waiting lists. Such contradictory imperatives are often exacerbated by different organisational cultures across agencies, which influence the way in which they work and the speed at which change is made. These difficulties need to be addressed if joint commissioning is to have any impact on the services received by people with intellectual disabilities and their carers (Hattersley, 1995).

Continuing NHS care

National policy states that, where it is thought that continuing NHS care might be appropriate, then ' . . . multi-professional assessment and consultation with parents and carers are necessary to determine whether the services they need can only be provided by the NHS or whether other alternatives would be more appropriate and cost effective'. The continuing care guidance offers a potential framework for health and local authorities to agree its appropriate role, although this guidance explicitly states that it does not replace other policy documents.

Primary Care Services

The White paper the New NHS Modern and Dependable (November 1997) replaces GP fundholders with larger Primary Care (commissioning) Groups serving natural populations of approximately 100,000. Primary Care Groups are fundamentally about improving the health of the population they serve. They will provide a direct means by which GPs (and their primary care team) and community nurses, working in co-operation with other health and social care professionals, will lead the process of securing appropriate, high-quality care for local people. One purpose of these groups is to better integrate primary and community health services and work more closely with social services on both planning and delivery (Health Service Circular HSC 1998/065). These groups will be established in April 1998.

NHS trusts as providers of social care

There is a continuing debate regarding the appropriateness of NHS trusts providing 'social care' in the community. Legislation enables this to take place, provided that the legal powers being used by the health authority and NHS trust are not those relating to the provision of 'health care'. Most commonly this involves a S28A (Section 28) transfer of funds being made through the local authority, and the trust then using its income-generation powers (Department of Health, 1992b). However, in many parts of the country some or all of the commissioning agencies and NHS trusts have taken the view that it is inappropriate for a healthcare provider to become substantially involved in non-healthcare provision.

Care management

National policy is clear that services should be based on the assessed needs and wishes of individuals, rather than individuals being fitted into pre-planned services. This represents a fundamental shift of the attitudes and approaches taken by most organisations. Local authorities have been given the lead role in this, through Children Act requirement for children and through the assessment process for adults. However, NHS trusts are required to contribute to these processes and must therefore have sufficient funds to do so. Current trends in care management are moving towards 'person-centred' assessment and planning, where systems focus on developing the positive aspects of a person's life and abilities. One consequence of this approach is that people are likely to receive services from a wide range of providers, including non-professional or 'natural' supports, rather than be dependent upon one organisation for all aspects of their needs (Department of Health & Social Services Inspectorate, 1991).

Future directions in policy?

The major planks of community care policy are likely to remain the same. Guidance on implementation, however, is constantly changing (e.g. with three relevant guidance papers published in December 1997 alone). It is likely that there will be an increasing emphasis on monitoring and audit activity at local and national levels. As there is an increasing emphasis on the contribution of evidence-based purchasing in order to increase clinical effectiveness (Kat, 1995), it is possible that there will be a similar shift in focus in community care, towards a more informed approach to commissioning.

SERVICE PROVISION—THE CURRENT PICTURE

Services for people with intellectual disabilities are in a state of flux, with many innovative services springing up and many not-so-innovative services being given innovative new labels. Given this changing picture, any typology of service 'models' is likely to be incomplete and somewhat reductionist. Nevertheless, such a typology can be useful in illustrating the range and extent of services currently existing in the UK.

Services for children

Pre-school services

Children with severe intellectual disabilities are likely to be referred to child development units run by NHS Trusts. There they are likely to undergo a multi-professional assessment involving some or all of the following—paediatrician, speech and language therapist, clinical psychologist, educational psychologist, occupational therapist, physiotherapist, specialist teacher and social worker. Health services have a responsibility to inform the local authority of any child under the age of five whom they consider likely to have special educational needs.

Many areas have a Portage scheme in place which may be managed and or funded by education, health or social services. Such schemes employ specialist workers who set up structured programmes with parents to help the child develop specific skills.

Education services

In some education authorities, substantial numbers of children receive segregated education in a range of special schools which may include schools for children with moderate learning difficulties. In other authorities most children, including many children with severe learning difficulties, will now be in mainstream schools. The nature of integration may range from children with severe learning difficulties being based in a specialist unit or classroom attached to a mainstream school with opportunities for social integration, through to full integration, where a child with severe learning disabilities follows an individual differentiated curriculum within a mainstream classroom alongside his/her non- handicapped peers. Research evidence (see Farrell, 1997, for a review) suggests that integration is both more common and more successful for younger and more able children with severe learning difficulties who do not present challenging behaviour. The effects of integration for other groups is more equivocal, particularly in the areas of meaningful social integration with non-disabled peers.

Family support services

The most common form of family support service for families with a school-age child is respite care, now becoming known as short-term breaks (Robinson, 1996; Russell, 1996). These are services where children spent one or more nights away from their family, in a staffed unit or with other families in family-link schemes. Only a minority of families with a child with intellectual disabilities use such services, however. Families from ethnic minorities, families with a child with complex needs and low-income families are less likely to use such services (Robinson, 1996). Other, less widespread, family support services include befriending schemes, where a 'befriender' goes out with the child from his/her home for a day or an evening, and 'sitting' schemes, where a person stays in the house with the child for an evening while the carers go out (Robinson, 1996).

Services for adults

Residential services

Accurate information concerning the number and characteristics of residential services for people with intellectual disabilities in the UK is currently lacking, although some general trends are apparent. First, it is clear that there is a current shortfall of approximately 25,000 residential places for people with intellectual disabilities (Emerson & Hatton, 1996b; Mental Health Foundation, 1996), with epidemiological trends (see Chapter 2) driving an increase in demand for residential places of approximately 12% over the next decade (Parrott et al., 1997). It is also worth noting that residential services are geographically patchy across the UK, with different regions and local authorities providing very different numbers and types of residential places (Emerson & Hatton, 1996b, 1997). Second, partly due to Community Care legislation, voluntary and private sector residential services are rapidly expanding, with concomitant reductions in health and social services residential provision. Third, there are substantial inequalities of access to residential services, with tentative evidence suggesting that Afro-Caribbean men are much more likely to access residential services, and people from other minority ethnic groups are much less likely to do so (Emerson & Hatton, 1996b). Finally, it is worth noting that, although substantial attention has been paid to residential services, approximately half of all adults with intellectual disabilities live with their families (Evans et al., 1994; Mental Health Foundation, 1996). Taking these trends into account, current major models of residential provision include:

Mental handicap hospitals.   NHS-managed, segregated, usually large (50+ places) and located in rural or semi-rural areas, with numbers continuing to fall rapidly (Emerson & Hatton, 1994; 1996b). As people with more skills have tended to leave hospitals earlier, mental handicap hospitals currently contain a high proportion of people with complex needs. Extensive research suggests that mental handicap hospitals are of poor quality and provide a materially and socially impoverished lifestyle to their residents (Emerson & Hatton, 1994; Hatton & Emerson, 1996).

Village or residential communities. Managed by voluntary or private sector, very diverse in physical characteristics and outlook, prototypically large (50+ places) and rural, but can be smaller and urban, with numbers probably stable. These communities are sometimes guided by spiritual or religious values, and tend to offer services to people with more skills and fewer complex needs. There is almost no information regarding the quality of residential or village communities or the lifestyle they offer to residents (Hatton & Emerson, 1996).

Hostels. Usually managed by social services, less often by health or independent sector services, segregated, medium-sized (10–25 places), can be purpose-built or converted large houses, and located in urban settings, with numbers probably falling. Research evidence suggests that hostels are of substantially higher quality than institutions, but they fall some way short of ordinary life principles (Emerson & Hatton, 1994; Hatton & Emerson, 1996).

Group homes or staffed houses. Historically managed by health and social services, but there is a continuing transfer to the independent sector, segregated, relatively small (2–8 places), usually 'ordinary' houses (sometimes with conversions) in urban locations, with numbers probably rising. Staffed housing services can successfully support people with complex needs. Research evidence suggests that staffed houses are generally of higher quality than hostels and mental handicap hospitals and offer a more independent and valued lifestyle to residents. However, in some respects (especially poverty and choice) staffed housing services still fall short of 'ordinary life' principles or normative social standards, and also vary widely in their quality, with some houses offering a lifestyle similar to that offered by institutions (Emerson & Hatton, 1994; Hatton & Emerson, 1996).

Supported living. A number of diverse approaches to providing residential supports to people with intellectual disabilities can be subsumed under this label. The basic principles of supported living include the separation of housing and support, person-centred planning, and the use of 'natural' supports (see Howard, 1996, and Simons, 1995, for more details; Hatton, 1996, for a commentary). Prototypically, this involves a person living alone as a named tenant in an ordinary flat or house, although it could also involve life-sharing arrangements (where a person shares a flat with a person or family without intellectual disabilities).

This sector appears to be small but expanding. It is claimed that supported living services can successfully support all people with intellectual disabilities, although there is as yet no research evidence concerning the lifestyle afforded by supported living beyond individual success stories (Simons, 1995).

Independent living.   By definition, this 'model' involves people with considerable skills living independently, except for some support by social workers. People living independently usually live in urban, rented accommodation. There is little research evidence concerning independent living (see Flynn, 1989; Hatton & Emerson, 1996), although that which exists suggests that the positive and valued aspects of independent living are often accompanied by poverty, unemployment and victimisation by people in local communities.

Specialist residential services.   There are a number of residential services which specialise in providing support to people grouped on the basis of particular characteristics or needs. These usually involve people with complex needs, such as offenders, people with challenging behaviour, people with multiple disabilities and people with mental health problems, where routine residential services are perceived to be absent or inadequate. Specialist services come in a range of sizes, locations, philosophies and managing agencies, although a substantial proportion are managed by health and voluntary sector providers. There is no available evidence concerning the number of people in such services, although it is probable that this sector is expanding. Research evidence tends to focus on specific examples of such services (e.g. Clare & Murphy, 1993; Hatton, Emerson & Kiernan, 1995; Mansell, 1994), with varying results.

Day services

As with residential services for people with intellectual disabilities, the purpose and usefulness of predominant patterns of day service provision are increasingly being called into question (Mental Health Foundation, 1996; Wertheimer, 1996). For at least the past 20 years, the purpose-built social services day centre has been the dominant form of day service, with over 200,000 adults with intellectual disabilities using them to some degree (Department of Health Statistics Office, 1995). Here, adults are typically brought to centres in segregated transport between the hours of 9.30 a.m. and 4.00 p.m., Monday to Friday. The extent, range and quality of activities offered by day centres vary greatly (Mental Health Foundation, 1996), and questions are increasingly being asked about the day opportunities which can be offered in segregated buildings

(Wertheimer, 1996). On normalization and integrationist grounds (not to mention the potential cash saving), there is an argument to move away from building-based services to more flexible daytime support, where individual support workers spend time with people with intellectual disabilities outside their home, enjoying a range of activities in integrated community settings.

On this model, adults with intellectual disabilities can experience the range of further education, work and leisure activities experienced by people in society generally. Further education schemes for people with intellectual disabilities do exist, but are geographically patchy, often unclear in their purpose, and are under considerable resource pressure at present (Mental Health Foundation, 1996). Supported living schemes, where adults with intellectual disabilities are employed with support and training from job coaches, are increasing, although complexities regarding benefit and prevailing economic conditions often make the provision of full-time jobs for people with intellectual disabilities problematic (Wertheimer, 1996).

Family and individual support services

In addition to residential and day services, there is a range of services which aim to provide additional support to carers, individuals with intellectual disabilities, or both simultaneously.

As with family support services for children, there is a range of respite (or short-term break) services provided for families containing an adult with intellectual disabilities. The most common form of respite service is provided in specialist respite units (Flynn et al., 1995); however, such services are variable in the quality of experience they offer for users and are less likely to be used by families from ethnic minorities (Azmi et al., 1996a,b). Other types of long-standing short-term breaks include domiciliary services (often called 'sitting' or 'befriending' services) and holidays for users (often organised through social services day centres). More recently, there has been an expansion in short-term family place ments, which are thought to provide a better experience for users and to be more accessible to people from ethnic minorities (Orlik, Robinson & Russell, 1991). However, the need to provide a better short-term break experience for users has to be balanced against the wish of carers to have reliable respite services with trained staff (Stalker & Robinson, 1994).

Community-based professional support is also available to people with intellectual disabilities and their carers. This support is usually in the form of multi-disciplinary community-based community learning disability teams, which can include input from clinical psychology, psychiatry, nursing, speech therapy, occupational therapy, social work and other professions. Such teams vary widely in terms of their size, professional membership and purpose, with some evidence that they have contributed towards the establishment of more co-ordinated services focused on the needs of individuals (Brown & Wistow, 1990; McGrath & Humphreys, 1988). However, the tensions of multi-disciplinary working can reduce the efficacy of community support teams. In addition to these general teams, specialist challenging behaviour teams, designed to provide additional support to individuals, services and families, have expanded considerably in recent years, although evidence for the efficacy of these teams is somewhat equivocal (Emerson et al., 1996).

Advocacy

Although often not conceptualised as a service, advocacy schemes including people with intellectual disabilities do exist, although they are geographically patchy and often somewhat marginal within service structures, operating on small and unstable budgets. Citizen advocacy aims to provide additional (usually non-professional) support to a person with intellectual disabilities, to help people to express their views and to ensure that people's rights and aspirations are respected. Self-advocacy (a somewhat curious term) aims to encourage self-determination and political action, on both an individual and a group level, by people with intellectual disabilities. The most widespread self-advocacy organisation in the UK is People First, which is beginning to be consulted and involved in the processes of service planning and provision and quality assurance.

CONCLUSIONS—WHAT ABOUT THE USERS?

The ministerial foreword to the White Paper *Caring for People* (Department of Health, 1989) was explicit that its proposals '... will give people a much better opportunity to secure the services they need and will stimulate public agencies to tailor services to individual's needs. This offers the prospect of a better deal for people who need care and for those who provide care. Our aim is to promote choice as well as independence' (Department of Health, 1989). However, an independent review of initial monitoring and evaluation identified an imbalance: the bulk of such activity had been concerned with organisational structures, systems and processes, rather than with outcomes for service users and carers, which lay at the heart of the White Paper's overt policy objectives (Henwood & Wistow, 1994). This remains the case and few local authorities or health services are yet attempting to use improved outcomes for users and carers systematically as the main criteria against which their services are judged.

There seems to have been relatively little change in services for users and carers since the advent of the NHS & Community Care Act, and the traditional range of domiciliary, day and institutional provision still prevails. Indeed, the main planks of community care, particularly at a time when resources for people with intellectual disabilities are unlikely to increase, can be seen as a return to the philosophy of care underlying the Poor Laws of 250 years ago. It remains to be seen whether services will change radically in form in the foreseeable future and, if they do, whether they will result in similarly radical improvements in the lives of people with intellectual disabilities.

FURTHER READING

Mental Health Foundation (1996). *Building Expectations: Opportunities and Services for People with a Learning Disability.* Mental Health Foundation: London.

Mittler, P., & Sinason, V. (eds) (1996). *Changing Policy and Practice for People with Learning Disabilities.* Cassell Education: London.

People First (1992). *Oi! It's My Assessment.* People First: London.

Roberts, G., & Griffiths, A. (1993). *What Can We Do? The Legal Framework of Community Care Services for Adults with Learning Disabilities.* MENCAP/National Development Team: Manchester.

Wright, D., & Digby, A. (eds) (1996). *From Idiocy to Mental Deficiency: Historical Perspectives on People with Learning Disabilities.* Routledge: London.

Chapter 5

COMMON LEGAL ISSUES IN CLINICAL PRACTICE

*Anthony Holland**

INTRODUCTION

When working with adults with intellectual disabilities clinical situations can arise where a knowledge of the law can be crucial in helping to inform decision making. A comprehensive understanding of the relevant aspects of law and how it applies to people with intellectual disabilities is outside the remit of this chapter and legal texts should be consulted (see Cooper & Vernon, 1996). However, it is essential that those working in services for and with adults with intellectual disabilities have a broad conceptual understanding of the relevant law as well as a specific knowledge of more defined areas of law, such as the *Mental Health Act 1983*. This is important for several reasons. First, the law relates to questions of individual rights, the duties and powers of services and the process whereby decisions can be made concerning adults who may not be able to make decisions for themselves. Second, it provides guidance with respect to our role as professionals and/or carers, and the responsibilities we have in terms of a duty of care and how that is balanced with respect to risk. Third, people with intellectual disabilities may engage in offending behaviour and in this context may be vulnerable and have special needs (see also Chapter 9). Finally, it is important to appreciate the lessons of history with respect to the use and abuse of legal powers. For example, in the past, the use of the *Mental Deficiency Act 1913* had a very negative outcome and perpetuated a model of care which would now be seen as both inappropriate and abusive. However, the 1971 Education Act ensured that children previously considered 'uneducable'

*Department of Psychiatry, University of Cambridge, and Lifespan Healthcare NHS Trust, UK

Clinical Psychology and People with Intellectual Disabilities. Edited by E. Emerson, C. Hatton, J. Bromley and A. Caine.
© 1998 John Wiley & Sons Ltd.

received special schooling by placing a statutory responsibility on Local Education Authorities to provide education (see also Chapter 4).

Definitions

When it comes to clinical practice, and also to legislation, the use of 'labels' is a necessary part of the process. Clinicians need to be able to impart information in a meaningful way and legislation needs to refer to those it is aiming to help. It is therefore important to define what is meant by the 'label(s)' being used and to ensure that their use is for the benefit of those to whom it refers. Both within the UK and internationally there a number of different terms which are commonly used ('mental retardation', 'learning disability', 'learning difficulties', 'intellectual disability', 'developmental disability'). 'Learning disabilities' is the generally accepted term in the UK. In this book 'intellectual disability' is used. Whatever the term used, it needs to be recognised that this group of people are extremely heterogeneous. Although they have in common a history of early developmental delay, a delay in or a failure to acquire basic living and social skills and a significant intellectual impairment, they differ in terms of the extent and nature of their intellectual impairment and resultant intellectual disabilities, the presence or not of physical and/or sensory impairments and disabilities and in terms of their personalities and backgrounds (see also Chapter 3). This term 'intellectual disability' refers to both those people with profound and multiple disabilities in need of 24-hour support, and those whose basic day-to-day skills are adequate but who were identified at school as having mild generalised intellectual difficulties, and as adults continue to have difficulty with the more complex skills required for adult life. Given the extremes represented by this one term it is likely that not only will there be very different needs, but the extent to which individuals will be able to take responsibility for their lives and make decisions for themselves will vary considerably (see Murphy & Clare, 1995).

This chapter attempts to provide a conceptual framework to help think about the way the law may be helpful and what our responsibilities are, and to discuss some specific situations where the law and knowledge of it is important. The focus of the chapter is clinical, and specific clinical situations are discussed where legal issues may be of particular importance and where a legal perspective may help in decision making. Outlined below are three areas in which those working in health and social care services may face difficult dilemmas, yet are expected to make decisions, some of which may be against the wishes of the person him/herself and/or his/her family. They are:

❑ Decision making by adults with intellectual disabilities and the balance between risk and an adult's right to autonomy.
❑ The management of suspected abuse or neglect of people with intellectual disabilities living in the community.
❑ Suspected offending behaviour by a person with a intellectual disability and the special provisions in law if someone with an intellectual disability is arrested for an alleged offence.

HISTORICAL BACKGROUND

There have been remarkable changes and advances in the recognition of the rights of minority groups, such as those with disability, particularly through the United Nations Conventions and Declarations. Cooper and Vernon (1996) have succinctly summarised the roles of different generations of rights from the 'civil and political', to the 'economic, social and cultural' and the more recent 'development' rights. These different 'generations' of rights, starting with the *Universal Declaration of Human Rights* (Secretary General, UN, 1948), include a statement of the basic rights to life, as well as the rights to freedom of opinion, to a fair trial, and to freedom from torture, slavery and violence. They are followed by rights reflecting quality of life, including working in favourable conditions, an adequate standard of living, the best possible mental and physical health, education, and the right to enjoy the benefits of cultural freedom and scientific progress. These should be enjoyed by all without discrimination. Finally, the more complex and contested areas include the rights to peace and security, economic autonomy, and to development itself. These concepts are outlined in greater detail in subsequent Covenants that have a legal standing in those countries where they have been accepted (e.g. *International Covenant on Civil and Political Rights* and the *International Covenant on Economic, Social and Cultural Rights*; Secretary General, UN, 1976a,b). Subsequently, the specific issues concerning people with 'mental retardation' (General Assembly, UN, 1971) or with disabilities (General Assembly, UN, 1975) have been addressed through 'declarations'. Essentially these 'declarations' outline certain principles that have been agreed by the member states of the United Nations. These include statements relating to having, as far as meaningfully possible, the same rights as others, to security, to a decent standard of living, to freedom from exploitation and abuse, etc. Both declarations have much in common and are also concerned with issues as diverse as the right of access to necessary and appropriate treatment and the right meaningful employment. In 1993 the General Assembly of the UN adopted the standard rules on the equalisation of opportunities for persons with disabilities. This followed the above declarations and covenants and the experience gained during the United Nations Decade of Disabled Persons (General Assembly, UN, 1994).

Whilst the United Nations provides the relatively recent and international perspective, the UK has its own history, and England and Wales has one legal system and Scotland another. Historically, a distinction had been made between those with impairments present from childhood (now referred to as 'intellectual disability') and those whose mental disability is acquired later in life (mental illness). Later different Acts of Parliament (e.g. *Mental Deficiency Act 1913; Lunacy Act 1890*) were enacted to meet the needs of these two groups of people.

The passing of the *Mental Deficiency Act 1913* was influenced by the beliefs of the eugenics movement and their concerns about the effects on society as a whole of people considered 'feeble-minded' or 'moral imbeciles' and, e.g. in both Europe and the USA, sterilization without consent took place. The definitions of the various 'labels' used in the Act were imprecise and the behaviour of individuals was a major determining factor as to whether someone met the specific criteria and could or could not be detained. The 'colonies', which rapidly expanded at that time, became hospitals with the establishment of the National Health Service in 1948. This policy in the UK of segregation and institutionalisation was officially reversed with the publication of the 1971 White Paper, *Better Services for the Mentally Handicapped* (Department of Health, 1971).

Mental health legislation and the treatment of people with mental disorder was extensively reviewed by the Percy Commission and resulted in a new approach leading to the *Mental Health Act (MHA) 1959*. The advent of effective medications had changed the outlook for people with serious and debilitating mental illnesses such as schizophrenia, depression or manic depressive psychosis. The principle was also established that people in need of treatment, because of a mental disorder, should have the option of informal admission and not have to be admitted compulsorily, as had previously been the case. However, the new MHA (1959) continued to enable compulsory admission for assessment or treatment of a mental disorder to take place if considered necessary. It was recognised that mental illness, in particular, may affect a person's ability to make judgements and that he/she, when mentally unwell, may be at risk of suicide or of harming others. In addition, treatment was now possible and, because of its potential beneficial effects, should be given compulsory if necessary. The Act therefore continued to give social workers, psychiatrists and the Courts the power, under certain circumstances, to detain people with a range of mental disorders in hospital for treatment. The 1959 MHA was superseded by the 1983 MHA, which included changes in definitions and powers of appeal. This is discussed in greater detail below.

It is now widely accepted that people with intellectual disabilities should live in community settings and the concept of normalisation (see Chapter 1) has helped people to radically re-think the way support is provided (Brown & Smith, 1992). Recently in the UK there have been considerable legislative changes, particularly the passing in 1990 of the *NHS and Community Care Act*, as well as specific disability legislation. The effect of the former was to create the split between social and health care purchasers (commissioners), on the one hand, and social and specialist healthcare providers, on the other. The purchasers or commissioners are responsible for ensuring that appropriate services are developed and provided. This Act has placed a statutory duty on social services to undertake 'needs-led assessments' for those with special needs. It is this assessment that is the route into social care provision but not necessarily the guarantee that individual needs will be met. In the case of people with intellectual disabilities, the complexity of need is such that there should be a close partnership between purchasers and providers, and between health and social services to ensure that relevant services and expertise are available (see also Chapter 4). It is in the context of these changes, which have led to care in the community, and there being a greater emphasis on individual choice and other changes in society, that issues of a clinical/legal nature have to be considered.

LEGALLY SIGNIFICANT DECISIONS IN CLINICAL PRACTICE

People with intellectual disabilities live in a variety of registered and unregistered social care settings with differing levels and quality of support and different philosophies of care. They will be registered with general practitioners and in addition may see staff working in multidisciplinary community health teams, who become involved at the request of persons with intellectual disability themselves, their families, other carers or general practitioners. In this context, issues around consent and the responsibility of carers and clinicians can be crucial. Outlined below are examples of situations in which (a) the results of clinical decisions made may be clearly against the expressed wish of the person; and/or (b) the person does not have the capacity to understand the situation and therefore cannot either consent or withhold his/her consent.

Figure 5.1   Mr P

Mr P is aged 46. He lives with his widowed mother and attends a work experience programme for people with intellectual disabilities. He is able to make his wishes known with difficulty because of his limited speech, although he can use some signs to indicate his views. He has always indicated he wanted to continue to live at home with his mother. However, recently he has become increasingly distressed and has been mumbling to himself about death. He has lost weight and is sleeping poorly. He now says he wants to leave home. In conversation he says his mother does not love him any more, something she says is certainly not true. What should the response be to him wanting to leave home? Can he be prevented from leaving home and if so, how?

Figure 5.2   Ms S

Ms S is aged 19 and has recently left her local special school and now attends an adult education course at her local college. She was diagnosed as having Prader–Willi Syndrome when aged 5 years. The severe tendency to over-eat, which results in severe obesity, has been managed by her parents by keeping tight control on her access to food. Now she is more independent and has her own money she has been obtaining extra food and her weight has increased by 15 kilograms in three months. She is now severely obese and is suffering from physical complications. She does not accept she has a problem. Her parents are concerned that she might die. Can her access to her benefits and her food be controlled? Can and should her over-eating be stopped—if so, how?

Figure 5.3   Mr T

Mr T is now aged 23 and lives in a housing association flat with an hour each day of support. He has Asperger's syndrome and has filled his flat with magazines on his favourite subject, model trains. He has difficulty planning and organising his life and spends money meant for food on magazines. He has severe debts. Recently he has being going to a 'friend's' house where he obtains money to buy more magazines. There is increasing concern that he is being sexually abused. What responsibilities do services have under these circumstances? How might he be protected from abuse?

Figure 5.4   Mr R

Mr R is aged 32 and lives at a group home run by a local branch of a voluntary organisation. He has a moderate intellectual disability. Returning home one evening he tells the care staff that he has set a fire at a local college. He has a history of setting fires in the past and also has periods when he becomes irritable and threatening. He has adequate living skills but he easily wanders into potentially risky situations and has been assaulted himself. He is described as being easily led. Should the staff inform the police? If the police are involved what else do the staff need to consider?

Decision making by people with intellectual disabilities

In England and Wales, case law has established the absolute right of individuals aged 18 years or over to make decisions for themselves, even if the outcome of such a decision may appear to others to be potentially deleterious (see Gunn, 1994). The actual decision an individual makes is influenced by the particular circumstances and his/her perception of the risks and benefits of the various possible courses of action, in the context of his/her particular moral, cultural and family background and experiences. In addition, we live within a society with both unwritten and written rules (laws) which, if transgressed, may result in an adverse outcome. However, the right to autonomy is only meaningful if the person has the ability to make the decision in question, is aware of the relevant facts and is not under duress when arriving at a decision. Adults may, through reason of mental disability (e.g. because of a intellectual disability, dementia, severe mental illness or head injury), be unable to make particular decisions for themselves. At present in England and Wales there is no power for others to make decisions, such as to consent to a particular course of action (e.g. to have specific medical treatment), on behalf of that person. Neither the family nor paid carers can legally consent in his/her place; instead, the process outlined by the House of Lords in the case of *Re: F* applies. The action taken by, for example, the health professional, in the case of health treatment, has to be in the person's best interest and has to be necessary. This is not the same as 'consent' but rather is the basis for a defence for that particular course of action if it were to be challenged later. In unusual cases involving a healthcare decision which is neither a necessity nor an emergency, such as a sterilisation, a Court ruling as to whether such a course of action is lawful is normally expected (British Medical Association and the Law Society, 1995).

One extreme example where the 'patient' clearly lacks capacity is in the case of someone who is unconscious following a road traffic accident. Under these circumstances, if urgent medical treatment were required, there would be a duty to undertake such treatment even though the person was unable to consent. If time allowed it would be good practice to consult close relatives but they would not be able to consent on behalf of the unconscious adult. Where such decisions can become more complex is where the person him/herself may be able to express an opinion about a particular decision but his/her ability to make that decision is in question.

The capacity of a person with a mental disability to make specific decisions is therefore a key issue in determining the outcome of the decision making process. There is now increasing guidance available about the determination of capacity, such as that provided by the British Medical Association and Law Society (1995). The main legal test to date has been referred to as the 'Eastman' test and concerned a man detained in a maximum-security hospital with a diagnosis of paranoid schizophrenia. He was advised that he needed an amputation of a gangrenous foot but refused to consent to this. To operate without the individual's consent would have been an assault unless, by reason of his mental illness, he was considered unable to make that particular decision. If that had been the case the common law would apply and the treating doctor could have proceeded, defending his/her decision on the grounds that such a course of action was in the best interest of the person concerned. Dr Nigel Eastman, an expert witness, proposed that the following questions needed to be asked when considering the validity of the individual's choice.

❑ Did he comprehend and retain the treatment information?
❑ Did he believe that it was relevant to him?
❑ Could he weigh it in balance and arrive at a choice?

In this particular case, the Court was of the opinion that the person did have the capacity to make that particular decision, and therefore the fact he would not consent to the operation must be respected. It would have been unlawful for the operation to take place. Other advice broadly makes the same points, focusing not on the outcome of a decision, but instead on the questions pertaining to the person's understanding of what was being asked of him/her and whether he/she were able to arrive at a reasoned decision. In assessing capacity the proposals in 'Who Decides? 1997' (Lord Chancellor's Department) go a step further. It is argued that, where time permits, the past and present feelings of the person concerned should be considered and he/she should be encouraged to participate in the process. The views of other appropriate persons should also be obtained. These might include not only family and other carers but health professionals, such as clinical psychologists.

Autonomy versus responsibility of care

The focus of the discussion on decision-making by people who may not be able to make decisions for themselves tends to centre on the making of healthcare decisions. However, the same issues apply in day-to-day life. Families and other carers are making decisions all the time on behalf of people with intellectual disabilities. These may include when the person should get up or go to bed, what clothes the person should wear, what they should eat, when and where they should go out and so on. The extent to which the person him/herself is involved will vary according to the patience and philosophy of the carers, the extent of the person's ability to consider the issues and communicate a choice, and the complexity of the decision being asked of him/her. Dilemmas may arise when, for example, someone with an intellectual disability makes a 'choice' which can be seen by others as being associated with a significant risk of harm, abuse or neglect.

In considering the clinical scenarios outlined earlier, a crucial part of the assessment process will be to determine the capacity of that person to make that particular decision. Is he/she aware of the risks of a particular course of action? How serious are the likely consequences? Does he/she have the ability to take part in the decision-making process and would he/she accept a 'safer' compromise? Carers may wish to involve psychologists and others in the community health team for people with intellectual disabilities in advising about such issues (Murphy & Clare, 1995). The person's advocate may also be involved. Documenting the outcome of a particular course of action and the reasons for it is important. For example, the decision not to take a person out when he/she is in a confused state following a seizure, and if necessary locking the door temporarily, may well be a very sensible decision. The person whilst confused is very likely to get hurt and may not be able to understand the risk he/she is taking. However, when the confusion has reduced he/she may very well be able to make that particular decision and be able to go out safely.

Much of the time, family members and other carers make such decisions without being aware of the significance of them. It is obvious to them that the person with a severe intellectual disability cannot go out by him/herself and clearly it would be irresponsible of them to let him/her do so. The issues become more significant if the group home concerned is poorly resourced and/or the attitude of the staff is such that the person virtually never goes out and the doors of the house are locked from the inside much of the time. The legality of this *de facto* detention has been questioned by Gunn (1997) and he has argued that such 'detention' should not take place without a legal framework, such as that of the MHA, in place. This is problematic because of the requirements of the MHA (see below). In response to Gunn's paper, it has been argued that care staff have a responsibility to make a reasoned and written case if door-locking is being used regularly and that steps should be taken urgently to improve the situation (Holland, 1997).

Adults with intellectual disabilities at risk of abuse or neglect

People with intellectual disabilities may lead very dependent lives, may require intimate care and be unable to describe their experiences or likes and dislikes. The fact that both physical and sexual abuse occurs is beyond doubt, even if the exact scale is difficult to establish. Hospital scandals in which physical and/or psychological abuse clearly took place have been reported (e.g. Ely Hospital, Ashworth Special Hospital), as has abuse in community settings (e.g. recent Buckinghamshire Court Case). More recently, the extent of sexual abuse has become apparent (Brown, Stein & Turk, 1995). However, there are a number of major difficulties which can contribute to an unsatisfactory outcome. In the first instance, abuse has to be suspected; second, it may be difficult to collect sufficient evidence to proceed with criminal charges; and finally, depending on where he/she living, there may be limited powers available to remove someone from an alleged abusive environment.

The difficulties faced in one particular situation were well illustrated in the case of Beverely Lewis (Fennell, 1989). She had a severe intellectual disability and was cared for by her mother, who probably had a serious mental illness. The concern was that she had died as a result of neglect. The post mortem reported the presence of chronic rubella encephalitis, which might also have accounted for her general decline, and pneumonia and a lung abscess as the cause of death. It was argued at the time that, as she was an adult, there were no legal powers (i.e. equivalent of an emergency protection order, as is the case in the present Children's Act) to remove her from the family home against her mother's wishes. In retrospect, the question of legal powers to act could be disputed and there were definitely powers which could have been used to ensure that the mother's suspected mental illness was assessed and treated (i.e. the MHA). However, the difficulty is that, quite rightfully, people are cautious about such a major course of action, and it may be very hard to know just how serious the neglect and/or abuse is until the person dies. In addition, there is a fear that a too authoritarian approach may upset the delicate balance which may have been established between the family carer and supporting professionals.

There are common factors to the other 'risk' scenarios outlined earlier. It is clearly essential to bring together as much knowledge as possible. The agencies involved are likely to be social services, health (GP and intellectual disability services) and the criminal justice agencies. Legal advice may well be required. Hopefully, time is available to try to engage with the parties concerned, the presence or not of neglect or abuse established and the situation resolved. Whilst there is no public law framework for intervening in some situations and criminal proceedings may flounder due to lack of evidence, there are powers which may helpful. These include the facts that social care homes have to be registered, that the registration officers have the right to make announced and unannounced visits and can withdraw registration, that an approved social worker can seek a warrant from a Magistrates' Court to gain entry to premises and remove a person to a place of safety for up to 72 hours (Section 135, MHA), and that the police may also seek a warrant if criminal behaviour is suspected. There is also the power of Guardianship included in the MHA (see below). The potential value of a Guardianship Order in these circumstances is that it can determine where someone should live. The problem with such an Order is that it requires the consent of the nearest relative (unless a Court agrees that he/she should be removed from that role) and does not give the power to remove someone from one place and take him/her to the designated place. In many cases people with intellectual disabilities do not meet the criteria for one of the four named mental disorders and therefore guardianship cannot apply. However, Guardianship Orders should be considered in these circumstances. There is also Section 47 of the *National Assistance Act 1948*, which is primarily concerned with public health issues concerning elderly people living in unhygienic conditions, and is rarely used and inappropriate for this type of situation.

If the situation cannot be resolved and there remain serious concerns, the following need to be considered: the person's capacity to appreciate that he/she has a choice and whether he/she is being intimidated by carers; whether criminal proceedings against alleged perpetrators of the abuse are possible or not, and whether the powers of the police or social worker (under the MHA) would be helpful.'

Conclusions

Whatever the scenario, the decision to intervene or not may be a very real dilemma. One of the values of multidisciplinary work is not only the different skills available but that these decisions can be shared. In some cases, if the person's ability to make a particular decision is clearly limited and the outcome of either making or not making that particular decision is potentially serious, then intervention may take place without consent using the common law defence. In other situations it may be necessary to look for acceptable compromises and to monitor the situation closely, and in others the use of the MHA may be applicable. For example, in some situations where further assessment and treatment of a person's mental disorder is being considered, or the person with an intellectual disability may have committed an offence, then the MHA may be helpful. In such situations, social care providers and specialist health teams should document the reasons for their decisions and regularly review the outcome. This is the process that should be followed, for example, with Mr S and Mr T (Figures 5.2 and 5.3).

MENTAL HEALTH ACT, 1983

Mental health legislation has evolved significantly since the days of the *Mental Deficiency Act*. However, such legislation is still viewed with considerable suspicion and the use of 'Sections' frequently misunderstood and seen as a last resort. This should not be the case. Such legislation can have an important place in often complex and difficult clinical situations. Its use should be for a clear and defined purpose and should, as far as it is possible to judge, result in a positive outcome in the longer term.

The basic thinking behind the 1959 and 1983 MHAs was that, whilst consent to treatment and if necessary voluntary admission to hospital for treatment of a mental disorder is to be preferred, the very nature of some forms of mental disorder is such that they affect a person's judgement and treatment without consent may be justified. Such a course of action (i.e. admission to hospital and/or giving medication without consent) would be false imprisonment and/or assault without the provision of the MHA to make that course of action legal. Rightfully, the powers of the MHA are limited and carefully defined. Although they include the option of a Guardianship Order for people living in the community, they are heavily focused towards detention in hospital settings (see below).

Under the MHA the powers to treat without consent are limited to the treatment of mental disorder (e.g. mental illness) and not physical illnesses. Treatment of the latter, in the absence of consent, is undertaken on the basis of common law in the person's best interest (see above). Outlined below are some of the key issues, but when in doubt frequent consultation of the MHA, its Code of Practice (1993) and reference manuals (Jones, 1996) are strongly recommended.

Use of the MHA

The MHA consists of ten Parts each concerned with different matters relating to people who have, or may have, a mental disorder. Each Part is further sub-divided into Sections and it is these that are frequently referred to when the MHA is used (e.g. Section 3, 37, etc.). The matters covered by the MHA include detention in hospital (or registered mental nursing home) for assessment or treatment of a mental disorder, Guardianship Orders in community settings, criminal proceedings when the person concerned may have a mental disorder, consent to treatment for mental disorder, rights of appeal to Mental Health Review Tribunals (MHRT), the management of the property and affairs of people with a mental disorder (Court of Protection) and other matters including, for example, the right to after-care when discharged from hospital.

Central to understanding the use of the MHA is an understanding of the term 'mental disorder'. This is defined in the MHA as follows:

❏ Mental illness.
❏ Arrested or incomplete development of mind.
❏ Psychopathic disorder.
❏ Any other disorder or disability of mind.

For certain sections in the MHA, 'mental disorder' is more tightly defined as:

❏ Mental illness.
❏ Psychopathic disorder.
❏ Mental impairment.
❏ Severe mental impairment.

'Mental illness' is taken to be a specific disorder defined in such texts as the International Classification of Mental Disorders (ICD-10) or the American Diagnostic and Statistical Manual (DSM-IV). 'Mental impairment' is defined in the MHA as follows:

> A state of arrested or incomplete development of mind (not amounting to severe mental impairment) which includes significant impairment of intelligence and social functioning and is associated with abnormally aggressive or seriously irresponsible conduct on the part of the person concerned.

In deciding whether the MHA can and should be used, a series of questions needs to be asked. The exact nature of these questions will depend on the section of the MHA being considered. These include the following. Does the person concerned meet criteria for mental disorder as defined in the MHA? Is he/she in need of assessment and/or treatment for his/her mental disorder? Is compulsory detention in hospital necessary because of the 'nature and degree' of his/her mental disorder and for the 'person's health or safety' and/or for the 'protection of other people'? People with intellectual disabilities can be said to have 'arrested and incomplete development of mind'. They may also suffer from an additional mental illness. For the criteria to be met for mental impairment there has to be a history of developmental delay together with evidence of a significant intellectual and social impairment. What is 'significant' is not defined but there should be reliable evidence of an IQ usually of 75 or below, and evidence from the history, or on assessment, of impaired social and/or living skills. As stated earlier in the chapter, these are the standard criteria for 'intellectual disabilities' but in the case of mental impairment there must also be evidence of behavioural difficulties (see Mental Health Act Code of Practice, 1993).

In the case of Mr P (Figure 5.1), the history suggests the possibility that he is developing an additional mental illness over and above any intellectual disability. Detailed assessment, ideally at his home, should clarify this. However, if he insists on leaving home, his health is at risk and there are concerns about his safety, the use of Section 2 of the MHA may well be justified. This is for 28 days and provides the opportunity to assess him in a hospital setting and commence treatment for his depression or other mental illness if it were shown to be present. If further time in hospital were considered necessary but he was unwilling to stay, Section 3 may be required. The criteria required for this are stricter. In both cases he has the right of appeal to a Mental Health Review Tribunal (MHRT) and under these circumstances he should be legally represented. The process of compulsory admission to hospital requires that an approved social worker (ASW) makes an application and that the application is supported by two medical recommendations (usually a psychiatrist and a doctor who knows the person well, e.g. the GP). The outcome of this process is that the reasons for the apparent change in the person are identified, a treatment strategy is developed and there is time to develop the necessary support and after-care.

Civil Sections (as opposed to hospital orders imposed by Courts) enabling assessment and/or treatment to take place (e.g. Sections 2 and 3) cannot be renewed once the person has returned to the community and has improved sufficiently that he/she no longer needs to be in hospital. If legal safeguards are required, a Guardianship Order might be considered. This can only be used if the person has one of the four specific mental disorders listed above. It requires the approval of the nearest relative and the agreement of the Social Services, who usually act as Guardian. A Guardianship Order has limited powers but does require that a person lives in a particular place and allows access to key personnel. Its main strength is that it provides a framework for supporting people who may be vulnerable but who are able to live relatively independent lives. The difficulties in supporting Mr T (Figure 5.3) may possibly be helped using a Guardianship Order in the context of helping to manage his life in a less risky manner.

Part III of the MHA is concerned with those who have or may have a mental disorder and are charged or convicted of offences. In this context, the MHA can be used to admit someone to a hospital for assessment or treatment. Such a course of action can have definite benefits but careful consideration needs to be given to the positive and negative aspects of such a course of action. This is covered in more detail below.

Treatment, consent and after-care when detained under the MHA

The focus of the main civil and hospital orders (e.g. Sections 2, 3, 37 and 38) are to enable lawful detention in hospital for assessment and/or treatment of mental disorder because it is of a 'nature or degree' to warrant detention, the individual's health may be at risk, or he/she may be a risk to others, and it is necessary for him/her to be detained in hospital to receive treatment. In this context, under Section 58 specific treatment can be given for the mental disorder, even if the person is not willing to consent or is unable to consent. In practice this, primarily refers to the use of medication to treat severe depression, mania or severe psychotic illnesses. Such treatment has to be directed by the named 'responsible medical officer (RMO)', must be clearly stipulated, and requires consent or a second medical opinion (e.g. to continue medication after three months without consent; ECT). With rarely used and potentially controversial treatments, both consent and the agreement of a second approved doctor is required (e.g. neurosurgical treatment of a mental disorder, implantation of anti-libidinal medication). Whilst the reasons for this can be understood, it has been argued that it denies potentially valuable treatment to those who cannot consent by reason of their mental disability. Such situations are rare but illustrate the ethical and clinical dilemmas which can occur, primarily when treating people with intractable mental illness.

'Treatment' in the MHA is broadly defined and includes nursing care and would also include psychological treatment strategies. In practice, most treatments (particularly psychological treatments), other than giving medication, require at least the assent of the person concerned and are unlikely to be effective without co-operation. Whilst the use of the MHA for acutely mentally ill people can be valuable, its use in the case of people with intellectual disability requires greater consideration. If the person is also mentally ill it may be of value, or if there is uncertainty as to the reasons for the offending or problematic behaviour, admission for assessment and then for treatment may have its place, but only if there is a clear and established longer-term strategy.

There are important legal safeguards enshrined in the MHA. These include the right to appeal to a MHRT, the visits of the Mental Health Act Commission to see those who are detained, and the responsibilities placed on the RMO with respect to second opinions. A further important factor is the right to 'after-care'. Social and/or health services have a duty to provide appropriate after-care for those who are or who have recently been subject to detention. Detention in hospital is only of value if it helps to address certain important clinical issues that ultimately enable the person concerned to live successfully in an appropriate community setting. In the case of people with intellectual disability, the quality and extent of 'after-care' may be the critical factor determining success or not. Quality after-care should therefore be clearly established with the help of Section 117.

Conclusions

It is a significant and major decision to use the MHA to limit an individual's freedom or to force him/her to have treatment to which he/she is not consenting. The fact that a MHA exists at all is an acknowledgement that mental disorders can affect a person's judgement and lead to suicide and other behaviours that the person would not normally have engaged in when mentally well. Whilst it may meet the needs of those with acute mental illness, it is less satisfactory for those with other forms of mental disorder covered in the Act. However, there are occasions when its use can provide the opportunity to help resolve a serious and potentially risky situation. The use of a Section to detain someone in hospital is a serious decision and the power to appeal an important safeguard against potential injustice.

OFFENDING BY PEOPLE WITH INTELLECTUAL DISABILITIES

Chapter 9 by Clare and Murphy will consider the main issues with respect to offending behaviour and assessment, management and treatment of such behaviour. If a person with an intellectual disability is alleged to have offended, there are a number of potential dilemmas which need to be faced. There is a general wish to protect people with intellectual disability from the criminal justice process, but this course of action does not allow the facts of the case to be properly investigated by the experts (i.e. the police), the alleged perpetrator may not have the benefits of the case being heard by a jury, and the rights of the victim may also not be met. The concern is that summary justice can occur and individuals held in *de facto* detention (see Gunn, 1997), or detained under a civil section of the MHA but without the due process of law. In contrast, however, the criminal justice process is likely to be traumatic and people with intellectual disabilities may be particularly vulnerable and open to abuse and at risk in settings such as police cells or prisons. They may not understand what is being asked of them and find Court proceedings both threatening and incomprehensible. Past miscarriages of justice have also highlighted the potential vulnerability of people with intellectual disabilities when being interrogated. It is also recognised that people with intellectual disabilities may not be able to understand the legal process and may not have been aware that what they were alleged to have done was wrong. For these reasons there are now legal safeguards which help to minimise these concerns.

The decision to advise the Court to take a different cause of action than would otherwise have been the case because a person has a possible mental disorder is not always straightforward. There are different points in the criminal justice process at which reports might be requested and where diversion from the criminal justice system might take place (Murphy & Holland, 1993). When the person is clearly mentally ill and suffering from abnormal mental beliefs (e.g. delusions) and/or abnormal mental experiences (e.g. auditory hallucinations), then rapid admission to hospital may well be indicated. However, this course of action has its limitations, particularly when there is no specific treatment likely to result in a significant and sustained improvement. Those Acts of Parliament that are particularly relevant to people with intellectual disabilities suspected of offending are outlined below.

Police and Criminal Evidence Act (PACE) 1984

At the time of arrest the police inform the suspect of his/her rights. This is in the form of the 'Caution' and the 'Notice to Detained Persons', which gives details of legal rights, e.g. to consult a solicitor. If the police have reason to believe that a person has a mental disorder or intellectual disability, they should arrange for a third party to be present (appropriate adult), usually a carer or social worker. This person has the responsibility to advise the person, to observe that the interview is being conducted fairly and to facilitate communication. If these guidelines are not adhered to, the defence can ask the judge at the time of the trial to rule that part of the evidence, e.g. a confession, be ruled inadmissible. The defence may well seek expert advice as to the person's intellectual ability, suggest ibility and the reliability of interview evidence. Psychologists and psychiatrists may well be asked to advise the defence lawyers about the reliability of confession and other evidence obtained at time of police interview. The intellectual ability, comprehension, suggestibility and potential acquiescence of a person with an intellectual disability in the context of police interrogation may require thorough evaluation. Clare, Gudjonsson & Harari (in press) have demonstrated that the current version of the Caution is poorly understood, even by the general population. The potential for people to incriminate themselves inadvertently is therefore considerable. For this reason it is important for services to ensure that people with intellectual disabilities, whose behaviour is such that they may well come into contact with the criminal justice system, are helped to be made aware of what should happen and who should be with them if such an occasion were to arise.

Criminal Procedure (Insanity) Act 1964 (amended 1991)

This Act of Parliament was intended to protect those recognised as being 'unfit to plead', by reason of disability, from the distress of trial. Under the original Act those found unfit to plead or not guilty by reason of insanity had to be detained indefinitely in hospital without trial and therefore without the facts of the case being determined. The person may, of course, have been innocent of the offence and there have been cases in which people have been detained for long periods of time. For those who were mentally ill at the time, treatment may well result in them becoming fit to plead and therefore a trial could take place. However, for those found unfit due to 'arrested or incomplete development of mind', the likelihood of marked change is small. Furthermore, the criteria for being unfit were such that many, regardless of intellectual level, could be considered unfit. The problems created by the original Act led to the use of 'unfit to plead' being avoided if at all possible. The Act was amended as a result of a Private Member's Bill in 1991. It is now possible for a trial of the facts to take place and if found unfit to plead, the person will not automatically be detained in hospital. A range of options are available to the Court, from the use of hospital orders to discharge. Expert evidence, such as psychological evidence, may be called to guide the Court as to whether the person concerned understands the concept of being 'guilty' or 'not guilty', can follow the proceedings in Court and can instruct his/her lawyers. The amended Act has the advantage that the question of fitness to plead is assessed by one jury and the facts of the case by another. If the facts are proven the Court can determine sentence, perhaps following further expert evidence. The circumstances are then similar to those which pertain when the use of the MHA is being considered when a person with a mental disorder has been convicted of a crime (see below).

Mental Health Act 1983 and Hospital Orders

As described earlier, the MHA offers the possibility of diverting people who have or may have a mental disorder from custody in the criminal justice system to hospital for the purposes of assessment and/or treatment. This is undertaken through the use of 'hospital orders', which are similar to the civil orders of the MHA, but are imposed by the Courts following expert evidence. The task of services on these occasions is to try and understand the reasons for the offending behaviour which has been alleged, to support the person through the criminal justice process and to advise the Courts as to possible sentence if convicted. If assessment in hospital is indicated, either before or after conviction, Sections 35, 36 and 38 can be used. The advantage of such assessment is that it enables a more complete picture to be established and for advice to be given to the Court which is well-informed. As with anyone else, the Court has a range of sentencing options (e.g. fine, Probation Order, imprisonment) as well as other possible options (e.g. admission to hospital using a hospital order, Section 37 Guardianship Order, Probation Order with condition of treatment). For a hospital order (Section 37) or Section 37 Guardianship Order to be used, specific criteria have to be met which are similar to those used with civil orders (see use of the MHA). In the case of very serious offences, a Crown Court may also wish to impose a Section 41 order which places major restrictions on leave and discharge. When a Section 41 has been imposed the power to grant leave and to discharge, along with other responsibilities, lies with the Home Office.

In the case of Mr R (Figure 5.4), the involvement of the police has the advantage of the facts being properly investigated, the 'suspect' has the right to legal representation, and it gives the opportunity for the Court to consider various possible courses of action. This may include the use of a Probation Order or a period of assessment in hospital (e.g. Section 35) to determine whether treatment in hospital under a Section 37 is both possible (i.e. necessary criteria are met) and appropriate (i.e. there are treatment strategies which may diminish the risk of re-offending).

Conclusions

When a person with intellectual disabilities is alleged to have offended, or is convicted of an offence, this may provide an opportunity to under take a more detailed assessment so that management strategies can be put in place which may reduce the risk of future offending (see Chapter 9 by Clare & Murphy). However, people with intellectual disabilities may be vulnerable in such a situation and legal representation and an appreciation of the various safeguards outlined above is important.

SUMMARY AND CONCLUSIONS

There is a broad range of international, European and national laws and guidelines which are very significant for people with intellectual disabilities. In England and Wales the common law provides the basic framework whereby decisions can be made on behalf of adults who may not able to make particular decisions for themselves. This includes decisions about day-to-day life as well as decisions relating to healthcare. Care staff and those working in clinical services need to consider the issue of 'capacity', as it is this which may be critical in helping to resolve the question of an adult's right to self-determination versus the protection of those who are vulnerable from undue risk.

Mental health legislation has changed and developed and, although the potential for inappropriate use is always present, there are particular criteria which need to be met if it is to be used, and there are also checks and balances. For those detained in hospital there is a right to appeal to MHRTs, and under these circumstances legal representation is crucial. The present MHA can provide an important mechanism for ensuring that a person with an intellectual disability and/or other mental disorders can receive a thorough assessment and, if appropriate, treatment. Where an offence has taken place, the use of Probation Orders, assessment and/or treatment Sections under the MHA can provide the basis for beginning to resolve complex and difficult problems and developing an appropriate network of support for the person concerned. Under these circumstances, admission to hospital is but the starting point for the development of a comprehensive package of care in a community setting. The recent case (*L vs Bornewood NHS Trust*), which is subject to an appeal hearing at present by the House of Lords, has highlighted the use of the MHA if hospital admission is considered and the person is without capacity. One crucial argument put forward was that the MHA carries with it rights to appeal which are particularly important when someone cannot make decisions for themselves. This whole question is the subject of a proposed new Bill (Who Decides?).

Some decisions that have to be made when working with people with intellectual disabilities present as major dilemmas. There are not always clearly right or wrong answers. This is well illustrated in the continuing tension between the right to self-autonomy and the need to protect people from risk if, because of mental disability, they are unable to make that judgement for themselves. No one discipline has the body of knowledge that allows sound decisions to be made. Multi-disciplinary work is essential.

ACKNOWLEDGEMENTS

My thanks to Robbie Patterson for her administrative help and to Isabel Clare and Kay Beaumont for their advice during the preparation of this chapter.

RECOMMENDED FURTHER READING

British Medical Association and the Law Society (1995). *Assessment of Mental Capacity: Guidance for Doctors and Lawyers*. British Medical Association: London.

Cooper, J., & Vernon, S. (1996). *Disability and the Law*. Jessica Kingsley: London.

Murphy, G.H., & Clare, I.C.H. (1995). Adults' capacity to make decisions affecting the person: psychologists' contribution. In *Handbook of Psychology in Legal Contexts* (eds R. Bull & D. Carson). Wiley: Chichester.

PART II

Clinical Skills

Chapter 6

INTERVIEWING PEOPLE WITH INTELLECTUAL DISABILITIES

Helen Prosser* and Jo Bromley**

INTRODUCTION

In the wake of social role valorization (see Chapter 1) there is now a recognition that people with intellectual disabilities should be accorded the right and opportunity to articulate their needs and express their opinions on issues which concern them. There are certainly many practical benefits to interviewing people with intellectual disabilities themselves, rather than just relying on the views of carers or of an interested third party. Primarily, one maximises the likelihood of obtaining valid information about such persons' psychological sense of well-being, their physical and mental health, their needs and problems, their family and social relationships, and their satisfaction with the services they receive. As a consequence:

❏ Clients are more likely to receive the help or treatment they need promptly.
❏ The knowledge and skills of health professionals are effectively put to use.
❏ Clients are supported more successfully as their capacity for making choices about how they would like to live is enhanced.
❏ Client satisfaction is increased.

Since health care studies with the general population have shown that patient satisfaction is an important determinant of patients' compliance with treatment (Ley & Llewelyn, 1995), effective interviewing may also lead to improved compliance with beneficial treatment regimes.

Typically, people with intellectual disabilities often experience difficulty

*Hester Adrian Research Centre, Manchester; **South Manchester University Hospitals NHS Trust, UK

Clinical Psychology and People with Intellectual Disabilities. Edited by E. Emerson, C. Hatton, J. Bromley and A. Caine.
© 1998 John Wiley & Sons Ltd.

in describing subjective feelings and internal emotional states. Consequently, subjective feelings and mood changes, or specific mental health symptoms such as depressive ideas, are much harder to detect in someone with limited expressive language skills, often resulting in over-emphasis on observable behavioural signs (see also Chapters 10 and 12). However, the amount of reliable and valid information you get from the person him/herself is potentially much greater than talking to a third party alone. A third party is useful in describing observable behaviours, but he/she may not be aware of a person's underlying needs and emotional feelings and are likely to be unreliable sources on attitudes and subjective issues such as client satisfaction, or a client's experience of pain. Whilst information from a key informant is essential, relying solely on third party accounts runs the risk of ignoring a vital source of information.

Talking to both an informant and the person with intellectual disabilities him/herself can therefore give a much greater insight into a person's behaviour. Recent research using the Psychiatric Assessment Schedule for Adults with Developmental Disability (PAS-ADD), a semi-structured clinical interview designed specifically for use with people with intellectual disabilities, has shown that interviewing both the respondent (client) and a key informant (carer) is essential for sensitive detection of psychiatric problems in people with intellectual disabilities. For comprehensive assessment, the interview is conducted once with the respondent and once with a key informant. Using the PAS-ADD with a population of people with mild and moderate intellectual disabilities known to psychiatric services, it was shown that the psychiatric problems of 35.2% of people would not have been detected if the person with intellectual disability him/herself had not been interviewed (Moss et al., 1996a, b).

Most of the principles involved in interviewing people with intellectual disabilities are straightforward enough and are not fundamentally different from those applicable to interviewing children or adults in the general population. The ground rules and foundations for good practice that you already know from your general training on communication are equally applicable when interviewing people with intellectual disabilities, and it is important to remain aware of the skills you already possess (refer to Shea, 1988, for further reading).

However, because of cognitive disability and frequently associated limited communication skills, obtaining views or information from people with intellectual disabilities does pose particular difficulties. One such difficulty is that of response bias and, in particular, the proclivity of people with intellectual disabilities to acquiesce, especially to closed 'Yes' or 'No' questions (Sigelman et al., 1981). Acquiescence is when the respondent gives an affirmative reply to contradictory prompts, i.e. replies 'Yes' to both of the questions, 'Are you happy?' and 'Are you sad?', or when a person agrees with whatever statement has been given. The reasons that people are thought to acquiesce are basically due to two factors, impaired cognitive development and social desirability (Shaw & Budd, 1982). Acquiescence is more common when the question is not understood or when respondents do not know how to answer it, although it is can also be a way of seeking social approval. For example, the respondent may reply 'Yes' even when he/she understands the question, but replies 'Yes' because he/she believes that a negative or other answer will displease the interviewer, and/or the respondent will be looked upon unfavourably by the interviewer. Research by Sigelman et al. (1981) suggest that acquiescence is negatively correlated with IQ scores.

However, minimising acquiescence and obtaining valid responses from people both with and without intellectual disabilities can be optimised by adopting particular interviewing techniques. Studies have shown how an interviewer's behaviour and the content and form of the interview, in the specific type of questions asked and the wording used, can directly determine the client's ability to respond validly. If inappropriate interviewing techniques are used, co-operation and reliable and valid information are threatened (Heal & Sigelman, 1995; Schuman & Presser, 1977; Shaw & Budd, 1982; Sigelman et al., 1981). This chapter offers practical advice and guidance on developing effective communication and interviewing techniques in order to obtain valid and reliable information from people with intellectual disabilities in the course of regular clinical work, issues specifically related to forensic interviewing are covered in Chapter 9.

SETTING CONDITIONS

As with any clinical session, an interview with a person with intellectual disabilities is best conducted in private in order to safeguard confidentiality. There are, however, some situations in which a third party may be present, such as when the person with intellectual disability specifically requests it or if the respondent has communication problems that he/she requires help with. The interviewee may have difficulties with pronunciation, for example; English might not be his/her first language or he/she may prefer a non-verbal form of communication, such as Makaton, with which the interviewer might not be familiar. In these cases, a third party may act as an interpreter and may be helpful in avoiding any misunderstandings. However, the person accompanying the respondent should be asked to refrain from commenting or offering information, and should only participate in the interview if directly asked to do so in order not to bias the respondent's information.

Putting the person at his/her ease and enhancing confidence is always a priority and should be attended to throughout the interview. The general advice is that interviews should be natural, unobtrusive and unthreatening interactions. It is important that the respondent does not feel that he/she is under scrutiny and for the interviewer to be sensitive to the clients' problems; and to try and minimise feelings of nervousness, anxiety or agitation to produce a relaxed, informal, conversational atmosphere. It may be more helpful to conduct the interview in a setting that is familiar for the interviewee such as his/her place of work, day centre, or a local health centre. In an ideal world it is also helpful to spend some time with the interviewee before the interview starts, perhaps working alongside him/her or making an informal visit before a formal interview begins.

OPENING THE INTERVIEW

The attitude of anyone being interviewed, whether or not he/she has an intellectual disability, is likely to be determined by his/her expectations of the interaction. People with intellectual disabilities may have had negative experiences in the past and they may be worried that something will happen to them as a result of the interview, such as returning to an institution, changing residence, being given medication, or changing day care arrangements. People are likely to be concerned that information may be passed on to someone else and are probably less likely to be compliant if they are worried about the consequences of disclosing information. It can therefore be very helpful to start by explaining what you intend to do with the information you are hoping to get from your interview and to be clear about the bounds of confidentiality. If you can, take time to explain:

- ❑ What the purpose of the interview is.
- ❑ What questions will be asked.
- ❑ Who and what the information is for.
- ❑ Why the information is important.
- ❑ How long the interview will take.
- ❑ The limits on the interview's confidentiality.

In order to check whether the person has understood the purpose of the interview you can ask her/him to explain it back. It might also be important to take some time to reassure the respondent that there are no 'right' or 'wrong' answers and that she/he need not answer any questions he/she does not wish to.

After introducing the session, it is advisable to begin with relatively easy questions such as, 'Do you go to a day centre?', 'Where do you live?', or 'Do you have family living nearby?'. Respondents can usually accurately reply to these questions and this strategy makes respondents less anxious and more confident about their ability to respond appropriately, develops a rapport between interviewer and respondent, and gives the respondent practice at answering. Potentially more probing and sensitive questions are best asked during the middle or towards the end of the interview, when the respondent is more confident and feels more relaxed, to capitalise on the rapport that has been built up. Various studies have shown that if respondents perceive themselves as incompetent and unable to answer questions they are more likely to be open to suggestibility (see Bull, 1995), so the ordering of questions is an important issue. If people can be put at their ease and made to feel competent at the start of an interview, their own views are likely to be elicited and the information is likely to be more valid.

THE CONTENT OF THE INTERVIEW

The type of questions asked and the phrasing and wording of questions are important elements of effective interviewing. When working with people with intellectual disabilities, the clinician must have an understanding of the cognitive ability of the individual and adapt his/her questioning accordingly. The expressive and receptive language skills of people with intellectual disabilities vary widely but it is useful to bear in mind that all individuals have a much greater understanding of language and the meaning of words than they regularly use (see also Chapter 13). Someone with mild intellectual disabilities may have very good expressive verbal skills and respond appropriately to simple open-ended questions. On the other hand, someone with moderate intellectual disabilities may need more prompting and so respond better to closed-type questions, with the interviewer using cross-questioning techniques as a means of assessing validity. A discussion of these various questioning styles is given below.

Open questions

When starting the interview, it is a good idea to begin with an open question as this gives the respondent free rein to describe the situation as he/she sees it. For example, if you were interested in finding out about someone's feelings about his/her current residential placement, you might start by asking an open question such as, 'Tell me about your home?' or 'What is it like to live where you do?'. Even if you feel the respondent is rambling off the point, it is often those problems or symptoms which are spontaneously mentioned that are more convincing than those elicited only by direct and closed questioning, such as 'Do you have any problems with your flat mate?'. This type of question only requires an answer of 'Yes' or 'No' and does not require or necessarily encourage the respondent to elaborate. A surprising amount of accurate and relevant information can often be obtained by letting the person tell her/his own story, with the questioner only interjecting occasionally, such as 'Can you tell me more about that?' or 'Can you explain what you mean by . . .?'. By starting an interview in this way, one also gains more idea of the person's linguistic or communicative abilities and can then target questions more appropriately, and the issue of acquiescence can be side-stepped. As such it could be argued that open-ended questions yield more valid answers than closed question, as there is less chance of someone giving a forced or expected answer.

However, although open questions are good ice-breakers and can provide very valuable information, they are often difficult for someone with intellectual disabilities to answer as they require quite a high level of cognitive and communicative skill. As such, open-ended questions achieve a lower response rate than closed questions, and are thus limited in their usefulness (Sigelman et al., 1982).

Closed questions

Yes/no questions

Since there is more of a risk that a respondent will acquiesce when presented with a closed yes–no question such as 'Are you usually happy?' or 'Do you have any friends?', the interviewer must pay close attention to monitoring the validity of clients' responses to such questions. This can be done through additional probing and cross-questioning techniques or by seeking external validation from other sources. These methods allow inconsistencies to be assessed and the fullest answers possible obtained.

For example, if one wanted to find out about attitudes towards and satisfaction with current residential accommodation, the interviewer might ask, 'Do you like living here?' followed by 'Would you rather live elsewhere?'. In addition to this, item-reversal techniques provide a check on the validity of the respondent's answers to closed questions. For instance, a closed question such as, 'Are you happy?' can be followed by its reverse question, 'Are you sad?' further into the interview. Obviously, the answers to each should not be contradictory.

Multiple-choice questions

With multiple-choice questions, it is worth noting that respondents may experience difficulty in remembering a choice of replies and some have a tendency to echo the last phrase of an interviewer. Multiple-choice questions can also create tension and confusion as sometimes it is difficult for the respondent to understand what is really being asked.

However, multiple-choice questions may still be used appropriately if the interviewer takes time to explore whether the person can under stand the question or if the question is supported by visual or written scales that might make it easier for the person to understand (see section on self-report measures, below).

Either/or questions

Better than both multiple choice questions and yes–no questions are either–or questions. These offer a choice of no more than two responses. They are still susceptible to response bias in that people with intellectual disabilities do have a tendency to favour the latter of the two options. However, Sigelman et al. (1981) found that oppositely worded either–or questions generated responses that were more consistent than answers to oppositely worded yes–no questions. In their study, 43.9% of the target group contradicted themselves by saying 'Yes' to opposite yes–no questions, whilst only 13% contradicted themselves by picking out the second option of an either–or question and only 2% chose the first option twice. As a general rule, if you are using either–or questions and the respondent echoes or repeats the last part of a question, further clarification is called for and it should be regarded as a request for help with understanding the question.

When there is no alternative to a closed question, the answer should be followed up with a request for an example. To assess someone's understanding of actual words and concepts that are used in the interview, questions may be framed so as to allow the subject to reply by giving examples, rather than a definition, e.g. 'What do you do when you are in a bad mood?', or 'How do you show that you are happy?'. Open statements such as, 'Tell me more about this?' are very useful in order to clarify and validate responses to closed questions. There is also no reason why pictures cannot be used to enhance understanding. It is interesting to note that when Sigelman and colleagues tried replacing verbal either–or questions with pictorial ones, more respondents were able to answer the pictorial than the verbal questions and fewer people contradicted themselves with the pictorial responses than with the verbal options.

Questions to avoid

What are the types of questions an interviewer might want to avoid when talking to someone with intellectual disabilities? One should be careful of using suggestive or leading questions. A common fault of poor interviewers is to distort the person's own story to fit their preconceptions. Try not to ask questions in such a way that you make it clear which answers you are expecting, e.g. 'You're not sleeping very well, are you?' or 'You don't get on well with your sister, do you?' Pre-hand knowledge or information from a third party may lead you to think you know what the answer to a question is going to be, but people often keep their innermost thoughts hidden. It is also important as an interviewer that you try not to challenge the respondent's answer (e.g. by saying, 'Do you really?' or 'Are you sure?') as this will only aggravate the problems of acquiescence and can hinder rather than help to clarify an issue.

In general, if you need to ask very direct questions, it is also more helpful if you are very specific. It is best to avoid very abstract questions and concepts, e.g. 'What is the extent of your problems?' or 'What do you expect to do in the future?'. This level of generality makes greater demands on the language abilities of respondents, requiring them to both respond to abstract terms and collate experience relevant to the issue in question and distil a summary position.

Appropriate vocabulary

Sophisticated vocabulary, difficult propositions and complex linguistics raise a respondent's intellectual demands and increase the probability that someone with intellectual disability will either not respond or respond inappropriately. If a person does not understand the question you are likely to get no response, an unintelligible response, an irrelevant response, a 'don't know', 'don't remember' or 'not sure' response, a refusal to answer or an inadequate response.

People with intellectual disabilities often do not know the meaning of words used by professionals. Therefore, questioning needs to be simple, often repetitive and carefully explained in order to keep the respondent's attention. To simplify questioning, the following are useful guidelines:

❏ Use short words and short sentences. Simplify a sentence if the person does not seem to understand it.

❏ Use single clause sentences. Questions such as, 'How well do you know and like the staff?' should be avoided, because they essentially contain two questions and might be quite difficult to follow. Try to introduce one idea at a time. Also, avoid subordinate clauses. 'When you are at the centre, on a Thursday, and Jill's there, do you get angry? is quite a long-winded and confusing question to understand.

❏ Use active verbs rather than passive ones. For example, 'Did you make the bed?' is easier to follow than 'Was the bed made by you?'.

❏ Use the present tense where possible. 'Are you upset?' is better than 'Have you been upset?'. It is appropriate, however, to use the present tense to introduce a concept, and then move to the past tense if you need to know more than the present, e.g. 'Were you upset before Christmas?'.

❏ Avoid questions regarding abstract consideration of future actions or attitudes, such as 'What do you expect to do in the future?'. Such questions are highly speculative and one might not get a very reliable answer. Stick with more concrete questions about the present or the past.

❏ Avoid double negatives, e.g. 'How do you not not hit him?'. Also, use 'Can you sit still?' rather than 'Can't you sit still?'

❏ Avoid jargon and unexplained technical terms.

❏ Use concrete descriptions and avoid figurative language. For example, it might be better to ask 'What is your job?' rather than 'What do you do for a living?'.

❏ Prepare your questions in advance with the above principles in mind. If you are using a written questionnaire, apply the Flesch formula (1948) to assess readability.

❏ Try to monitor your own speech for colloquialisms. How many times do you normally say 'You know', 'OK?', 'It's like . . .'? These kind of statements might detract the person from the real question you would like them to answer.

The two examples of interview questions below illustrate the value of the suggestions above. The first example is a question from the Schedule for Clinical Assessment in Neuropsychiatry (SCAN) (World Health Organization, 1994), a psychiatric interview used in the general population. In the second example the question seeks the same information, but has been adapted for use with someone with intellectual disabilities (Moss et al., 1996d).

SCAN: Do you have the feeling that you are being blamed or accused by others because of some action or lapse of deficiency that you yourself feel was blameworthy?
(How much of the time have you been free of the feelings?)
(How often have you had the feeling that you were blamed for something really serious?)

In this example, the main question is very precisely worded, but the vocabulary is very sophisticated and there are also two propositions within a single sentence—'Do you feel blamed by others?' and 'Is it because of a lapse or personal deficiency?'. In the first prompt, in brackets, somebody with intellectual disabilities would probably have difficulty in comprehending the abstract concept of 'being free of a feeling'. In the second prompt, the person is being asked two things— whether he/she feels blamed for something 'really serious' and if so, how often he/she feels like this. All of these linguistic complications raise the intellectual demands and increase the probability that a respondent with intellectual disability will either not respond or respond inappropriately.

In the following example, taken from the PAS–ADD, the question has been reworded to make it less linguistically demanding and thus more suitable to people with intellectual disabilities. The grammar has been simplified and the complex vocabulary replaced by more everyday words. The propositions have been broken down into separate simple probes. The essential nature of the question, however, is retained.

PAS-ADD: Do you think that you are blamed for something?
(Has anyone said that you have done something bad?)
(What do you think you have done?)
(Is it your fault?)
(Do you feel guilty?)
(Do other people say it's your fault?)
(Do you think you should be punished?)

Anchor events

Questions relating to time, number and frequency pose particular problems for people with intellectual disabilities. Accurate information regarding when events occurred and the time-course of problems is often essential but can be difficult to obtain from respondents with intellectual disabilities. One way to help the respondent to focus on time-course is to get him/her to think about an event the person can remember accurately which has occurred in the recent past. Such events may include his/her own birthday or a birthday of a close relative or friend, Christmas, Easter, parties, days out, etc.

Summarising

People with intellectual disability tend to have a relatively short span of attention. It is important, therefore, to recap and summarise what the respondent has said and also to ask whether what has been said has been understood. As with any interview, there are a number of benefits to doing this. It re-engages and focuses the respondent's attention, giving him/her an opportunity to add more detail. It also provides the respondent with the opportunity to concur with or refute the interviewer's interpretation of what has been said, which encourages validity.

Use of self-report measures

As part of your interview, you may want to include some kind of self-report measure to assess a particular area of the interviewee's subjective experience. In the last decade there have been a number of studies which have examined the use of self-report measures for people with intellectual disabilities. The types of measures that have been investigated include questionnaire studies (e.g. Reynolds & Baker, 1988), word or graphic rating scales (e.g. Lovett & Harris, 1987) and visual analogue scales or VASs (e.g. Dagnan & Ruddick, 1995). Felce and Perry (1995) provide a good review of the types of measures used for assessing the quality of life of people with intellectual disabilities.

In clinical practice there is nothing to stop an interviewer designing his/her own scale to access a certain opinion from a client with intellectual disabilities. However, there are a few points to consider. In general, when using a scale rather than a questionnaire, research by Levine (1985) suggests that three-point scales are easier for people with intellectual disabilities to use than four-point ones, as people tend to get the two middle points of the latter scales confused. The main problem with three-point scales, however, is that they limit a person's possible choice of responses, and sometimes suffer from ceiling effects. VASs which tend to have two anchor points marked out but no intermediate marks are often seen as a less restrictive alternative.

When using any self-report measure, it is important to check that it has been validated and that evidence is available to suggest the client can use the measure appropriately. Validity can be checked in a number of ways, e.g. clients' responses can be compared to carers' responses. As noted in the introduction, however, the views of clients and carers may differ and there is a danger of relying on carers' responses to validate clients' responses, particularly given the high turnover of carers in residential settings (Crocker et al., 1989), as carers are not always too familiar with their clients and may give misleading information.

An alternative method of assessing whether clients can use a self-report measure appropriately is by including some kind of training or assessment procedure into the measure itself. As part of an assessment of the quality of life of a group of people with intellectual disabilities, Cummins and his colleagues (see, for example, Cummins et al., in press) wanted to establish whether participants could use a VAS scale to indicate how important they thought certain activities were to them. Before showing participants the scale, Cummins asked each one to distinguish between smaller- and larger-sized blocks. If they could do this successfully, he then asked people to put the different blocks on the VAS, the largest at the top and the smallest at the bottom. Subsequently, he showed participants a VAS which had 'not important at all' at one end and 'very important' at the other and asked people to rate how important certain activities were for them by using this scale. If people could not distinguish the different-sized blocks or could not put them correctly on the scale, it was assumed that they could not use the scale in the correct way and would need to be asked the question in a different format.

The same procedure was used by Bromley, Emerson & Caine (in press) to establish whether people with mild and moderate intellectual disabilities could use a 'pain ruler' to indicate different degrees of pain intensity. The pain ruler in this study had 'no pain' at one end an 'lots and lots of pain' at the other. At the 'no pain' end the ruler was coloured white but it graduated through the red scale until it was a deep red at the other end. Participants in this study had to be able to distinguish between different sized blocks and place them correctly on the scale. They were then shown three photographs of a man and three of a woman displaying facial expressions of mild, moderate and severe pain. The photographs were shown one at a time and in a random order and participants had to use the scale to show how much pain they thought the person in the photograph was in. Participants were then shown a series of photographs of different types of simulated painful experiences. The photographs could be divided into seven categories corresponding to different types of pain (leg injury, cut, hit, hair pull, bite, foot injury and burn). Within each category there was one photograph of a more 'severe' pain and one of a 'mild' pain (e.g. the 'severe' cut showed someone having supposedly cut his finger very badly when cutting vegetables, the 'mild' cut was someone pricking her finger with a needle). Participants then had to rate how much pain they thought the person in the photograph was in, using the pain ruler—the rationale being that if they rated the 'severe' photograph as being consistently more painful than the 'mild' photograph, then this was evidence that they knew how to use the ruler effectively.

Results indicated that participants with intellectual disabilities did rate the more severe pain more highly than the milder pain in all of the pain categories. However, whilst the differences between the severe and mild ratings were statistically significant in all but one category (hit) at the first testing session, only two categories had a significant rating at the second time of testing. What seemed to happen was that, although participants still rated the 'severe' photographs higher than the 'mild' on the scale, their ratings of the 'mild' increased *per se* and they tended to use only the top half of the scale, a problem Cummins has also noted in his work. The difference between the 'severe' and 'mild' ratings was then not significant.

The kind of approach used in the above two studies follows the basic principles of task analysis and is representative of the type of strategy that is often used when teaching children with mild to severe intellectual disabilities (see e.g. Gable & Warren 1993). It is a useful contribution in terms of teaching people with intellectual disabilities how to use certain measures and/or checking if they can use certain scales appropriately. However, one must be careful not to *assume* that the ability to place blocks on a scale, which is quite a concrete task, is automatically indicative of the ability to use a scale for more abstract purposes, and it is helpful to be aware of the potential limitations of using these kind if scales.

Be creative!

Whilst the above guidelines should help you conduct an effective interview with someone with intellectual disabilities, it is worth remembering that each client is an individual and you may have to try more creative methods of engaging him/her in conversation than you would a member of the general population. There is nothing to stop you using drawings and photographs to help explain a certain concept or involve the person in the interview process. If the person feels more comfortable talking when walking it may be better to get to know the client and ask certain questions while out on a walk. Work out what questions you would like to ask the client and perhaps discuss with someone who knows him/her well how you might best access the client's views.

INTERVIEWING CARERS

This brings us to our final point; interviewing carers. Although we have noted the potential dangers of relying solely on third-party interviews, it is still important to see either a relative or someone who knows the respondent well in addition to the respondent him/herself. Carers may be able to give additional information or another view of a situation, as well as to validate the information told by respondents. For example, carers are sometimes better able to date the onset of illness accurately, especially if it was gradual, or remember dates of events that are likely to be important to the respondent (e.g. the death of a close relative). A relative or carer can also give a useful indication of how disabling an illness is or how a behaviour affects other people. Interviewing other carers also enables you to discern to what extent parents and carers are aware of the individuals' needs and problems. The caveat is that if the carer's and client's answers are different, one should not automatically assume the carer's view is the correct one.

Relatives, people with whom the respondent lives and care staff are all liable to have different information at their disposal. The respondent may be more likely to open up to his/her parent, and talk about things which it would be more difficult for a stranger to gain access to. On the other hand, a key worker may have access to information which parents do not see, so in some cases it may be appropriate to talk with more than one informant. Nevertheless, it is important that the informant is someone who has known the person well for some time and has regular contact with her/him, or is used to observing and communicating with the respondent in the particular environment relevant to your area of interest. If the identified client is able to give informed consent, his/her opinion should always be sought before other carers are interviewed and if possible one should check if there are any parts of your interview with the client that he/she would not like you to discuss.

FURTHER READING

Heal, L.W., & Sigelman, C.K. (1995). Response bias in interviews with individuals with limited mental ability. *Journal of Intellectual Disability Research*, **39**, 331–340.

Sigelman, C., Budd, E.C., Spaniel, C., & Schoenrock, C. (1981). When in doubt say yes: acquiescence in interviews with mentally retarded persons. *Mental Retardation*, **19**, 53–58.

Sigelman, C., Schoenrock, C., Spanhel, C., Hromas, S., Winer, J., Budd, E., & Martin, P. (1980). Surveying mentally retarded persons: responsiveness and response validity in three samples. *American Journal of Mental Deficiency,* **84**, 479–484.

Sigelman, C., Budd, E., Winer, J., Schoenrock, C., & Martin, P. (1982). Evaluating alternative techniques of questioning mentally retarded persons. *American Journal of Mental Deficiency,* **86**, 511–518.

Chapter 7

ASSESSMENT

Eric Emerson[*]

In this chapter we will discuss issues related to the general process of 'assessment'. More detailed discussion of particular aspects of assessment techniques and approaches are covered in the following chapters, which each describe a specific area of clinical practice.

Assessment, of course, it is not an end in itself. Most people do not particularly enjoy being assessed and many carers complain bitterly about the seemingly unending round of 'assessments' to which they and their son/daughter are subjected. Rather, assessment should be the process by which information is collected which will help to guide the design and implementation of constructional and socially valid interventions. This being the case, you will need to be very clear about:

❏ The aims of the assessment (including understanding the broader context in which the assessment is taking place).
❏ The most appropriate and efficient ways of achieving those aims.

THE AIMS OF ASSESSMENT

It may seem obvious, but the first step of all assessments is to clarify aims. This will, in turn require establishing:

❏ The essential reason(s) for undertaking the assessment (e.g. to develop an intervention programme to help someone overcome his/her challenging behaviour; to determine whether someone is eligible for a particular type of support; to determine an individual's competence in giving evidence in court).
❏ Who will act on the information provided by the assessment.

*Hester Adrian Research Centre, Manchester, UK

Clinical Psychology and People with Intellectual Disabilities. Edited by E. Emerson, C. Hatton, J. Bromley and A. Caine.

❏ The specific question(s) for which the assessment is to provide the answer(s).

As stated above, assessment is the process by which information is collected which will help guide the design and implementation of constructional and socially valid interventions. By interventions we include such 'systemic' interventions as gaining access to particular services (e.g. respite care), providing safeguards against exploitation, neglect or abuse (e.g. through determining the reliability of confession and other evidence obtained at time of police interview) as well as more traditional psychological interventions. Any of these 'interventions' are constructional if they involve the user developing more socially appropriate strategies to deal with life's problems. By socially valid, we mean interventions that: address a socially significant problem; in a manner acceptable to the main stakeholders involved; and result in socially significant outcomes. Both of these concepts are discussed at greater length in Chapter 1.

In some situations, the task of clarifying the essential purpose of the assessment may appear to be relatively straightforward (e.g. to determine whether someone is eligible for a service for people with intellectual disabilities). Often, however, this task is far from simple. Three types of problems are commonly encountered.

First, it is extremely unusual for a person with intellectual disabilities to refer him/herself to a clinical psychologist. Commonly, referral decisions are made by significant others (e.g. professionals, care staff, relatives), possibly without consulting or discussing this with the person him/herself. The first step in any referral, therefore, is to determine (wherever possible) the person's own understanding of the reason for referral, an issue which is discussed at greater length in Chapter 12.

Second, the nature of the 'problem' may have been incompletely conceptualised by the referring agency. Thus, for example, the explicit reasons for referrals are often non-constructional, being phrased in terms of eliminating troublesome behaviour (rather than replacing it with more appropriate behaviour). Similarly, the referring agency may have a somewhat limited view of what constitutes a 'socially significant problem'. For example, in the following chapter we point out that challenging behaviours often have wide-ranging personal and social consequences. These may include: impairing the health and/or quality of life of the person, those who care for him/her and those who live or work in close proximity; abuse; inappropriate treatment; exclusion; deprivation; and systematic neglect. If our interventions are to be socially valid, they must be judged not only against their impact in reducing the frequency, duration or intensity of the person's challenging behaviour, but also in ameliorating or preventing some of these broader physical and social consequences associated with challenging behaviour.

Third, many referrals contain hidden agendas (see Chapter 15). This may be particularly true for referrals related to the treatment of challenging behaviour. Here the 'real' underlying reasons for referral can commonly include enlisting the help of the clinical psychologist to document the extent of the challenge in order to (often unwittingly) support arguments for additional resources or the person's exclusion from their home, school or workplace.

In all situations it is important to *clarify* and *document*, as early as possible in the assessment process, the actual purpose of the assessment which *you* will be undertaking and to negotiate any changes between your aims and the requested reason for referral with the referring agency and, wherever possible, the person him/herself. This will help to minimise problems of misunderstanding about what you are trying to achieve and potential confusion about the sources and types of information you consider legitimate and relevant to answering the basic question(s) posed by the referring agency.

At the end of the day, the general questions underlying assessment often fall into one of three types:

❑ *Is* the person intellectually disabled? *Is* he/she clinically depressed?
❑ *Can* the person undertake a specific task or activity independently (e.g. give informed consent, clean tables at a cafe, travel independently)? What support would he/she need to complete the task successfully? *Can* this person express his/her choices and preferences?
❑ *Why* is the person acting in this challenging/difficult/problematic manner?

One way of clarifying the basic aims of the assessment is to ask the following two questions. *Who will do what* with the information generated by the assessment process? What information do they *actually need*? In addition to clarifying aims, asking these questions will also provide information which will be useful in selecting the most (cost) effective approaches to assessment.

This process of clarifying aims will also, of course, draw attention to the inherently 'political' nature of assessment. Assessment is not a neutral activity. Any assessment undertaken should at least contain the possibility of bringing about significant consequences for the person, significant others in their lives (and the assessing clinical psychologist). Being clear about these potential consequences is essential if clinical practice is to proceed within a professionally and ethically justifiable framework (cf: Division of Clinical Psychology, 1995).

Having identified the basic aim of the assessment, it is also important to specify the particular questions which your assessment will (and some times will not) address. While the overall aims will usually be related to bringing about positive change for someone with an intellectual disability, what specific questions will your assessment be able to address?

Often, the clinical psychologist may only be able to address certain aspects of the underlying question. Take, for example, the question '*Why* is this person showing severe self-injurious behaviour?'. While it may be appropriate for a clinical psychologist to attempt to determine what behavioural processes may underlie the person's self-injury, it is probably beyond their competence and resources to do more than simply draw attention to the potential roles of neurobiological factors. Again, to help ensure that all parties are aware of the process and likely outcomes of your assessment it is important to *clarify* and *document*, as early as possible in the assessment process, what specific questions you will be addressing and draw attention to potentially important questions which you are unlikely to be able to answer.

At the end of the day, you should be able to provide concise answers to each of the following questions for each assessment you undertake:

❏ Why is this question is being asked?
❏ To what purposes will the information be put?
❏ Who will use the information?
❏ Are the results of the assessment likely to be of practical benefit to the user?

If answering these questions is not straightforward, you probably are not justified in spending any further time and effort on that particular assessment! These questions will also help to shape the next stage of the assessment process: selecting particular methods or approaches to assessment.

THE PROCESS OF ASSESSMENT

Once you have clarified the aims and context of the assessment, the next step is to select the methods or approaches which will generate the information needed to answer the question. There are a number of questions to keep in mind when selecting approaches to assessment.

Will the approach give you the information you need?

What you need, of course, is information which is:

❑ Reliable.
❑ Valid.
❑ Answers questions pertinent to the aim of the assessment.

A brief note on psychometrics

Jacobson and Mulick (1996) provide a concise up to date general discussion of psychometrics in relation to intellectual disabilities. The psychometric properties of some approaches to assessment (e.g. many IQ tests, some scales of adaptive behaviours, some checklists of challenging behaviours) appear to have been reasonably well established. Even for these scales, however, two problems are likely to arise.

First, not all of these tests have been standardised on people with severe disabilities (e.g. many commonly used IQ tests). As a result, their use with people with more severe disabilities may involve a number of problems including marked inter- and intra-test variability (Evans, 1991). Second, the reliability of informant-based measures (e.g. scales of adaptive behaviours, checklists of challenging behaviours) is dependent on the characteristics of the test *and* the characteristics of the informants and the context in which they are working. Inter-informant reliability in one context (the original validation study) does not necessarily generalise to another (the context in which you are using them). So, for example, while the Motivation Assessment Scale (a scale designed to determine the functional significance of self-injurious behaviour; Durand & Crimmins, 1992) was reported to have acceptable levels of inter-informant reliability in its original validation, a recent study in the UK using experienced teaching staff indicated that levels of agreement were so poor as to make the scale unusable (Thompson & Emerson, 1995).

For many other tests or approaches to assessment, we simply do not have information on either the reliability or validity of the information they present. As a result, *wherever possible the reliability and validity of the information generated through your assessment process needs to be evaluated (rather than assumed).* This is standard practice in the use of observational procedures (see Suen & Ary, 1989). It needs to become standard practice when collecting informant-based information. This can often be approached quite simply by collecting and comparing information gained from:

❑ Several informants (reconciling areas of disagreement is often an interesting and worthwhile process in itself) or;

❏ Several approaches (e.g. checking out informant accounts of a person's abilities by spending time with the person yourself).

It is probably safe to assume, however, that information provided by care staff may be of questionable reliability and validity (see Chapter 6). As a result, when the accuracy of information is of paramount importance (e.g. when trying to understand why someone is showing challenging behaviour) it is nearly always advisable to check out informant accounts through additional, more detailed, assessment.

Types of assessment

As we mentioned above, the general questions underlying assessment often fall into one of three types:

❏ *Is* the person intellectually disabled?
❏ *Can* the person undertake a specific task or activity independently (e.g. give informed consent, clean tables at a cafe, travel independently)? What support would they need to complete the task successfully?
❏ *Why* is the person acting in this challenging/difficult/problematic manner?

The most common types of '*Is*' questions encountered in clinical practice are linked to well-established diagnostic or classificatory systems (e.g. *is* the person intellectually disabled/depressed/autistic?). Collecting the information to answer such questions will usually require the use of traditional norm-referenced approaches to assessment (e.g. the use of standardised IQ tests). A number of issues (beyond the issues relating to basic psychometrics mentioned in the preceding section) need to kept in mind when considering the use of and interpreting the results of such tests.

First, all such tests assume that the person in the test situation is performing to the best of his/her ability (Morgenstern & Klass, 1991). This assumption may be called into question when assessing people with intellectual disabilities. Evans (1991) suggests that people with intellectual disabilities may show much greater 'interest variability' and lower motivation to perform 'correctly' in formal testing situations. Thus, for example, pre-school children with disabilities show greater decrements in performance when tested by an unfamiliar adult than do non-disabled pre-school children (Fuchs et al., 1985; cited in Evans, 1991). Evans concludes:

The literature on what happens to performance when one deliberately reinforces test behaviour . . . indicates that, to the extent that the external reinforcement improves performance, it does so differentially. The more disadvantaged or disabled the subject, the greater the benefit. This suggests that the motivational and attributional sets for someone with severe disabilities cannot be assumed to be the same as for someone who understands the nature of the test and its personal implications (Evans, 1991, p. 31).

This does, of course, suggest that a 'truer' picture of the person's abilities may be gained by altering test procedures to systematically reinforce 'test-compliant' performance. The obvious drawback of such a course of action is that any modifications will violate the standard test procedures and, unless very clearly documented indeed, may lead to 'inexplicable' variations in test performance if the person is tested agin in the future using (different) procedures.

Second, as we have seen in Chapter 2, a significant proportion of people with intellectual disabilities will also have additional (although often unrecognised) sensory and physical impairments. The impact of such additional impairments in a formal test situation will inevitably be to reduce actual performance to below that of which the person is 'theoretically' capable.

Third, the vast majority of tests of intellectual or cognitive performance are, at least in part, culturally biased. As Evans (1991) suggests:

IQ tests, despite their supposedly measuring fundamental cognitive abilities, actually necessitate (and thus gauge) the sorts of academic knowledge and skills traditionally taught in mainstream school and fostered in the home environment of the dominant culture (Evans, 1991, p. 26).

Given that many people with intellectual disabilities will have had limited or no exposure to mainstream educational experiences, their performance on such tests may again fall below that of which they are 'theoretically' capable. This is, of course, likely to be an even greater problem for people with intellectual disabilities in minority ethnic and cultural groups. In such cases any intellectual impairments are likely to be compounded, not only by exclusion from mainstream education, but also by reduced exposure to 'the sorts of academic knowledge and skills traditionally fostered in the home environment of the dominant culture'.

Finally, as suggested in Chapter 3, the performance of people with intellectual disabilities in any situation may be affected by specific cognitive deficits as well as any 'general' impairment in overall cognitive abilities. Again, the impact of any specific cognitive deficits will be to reduce actual performance to below that of which the person is 'theoretically' capable.

Consideration of the above factors suggests that the performance of people with intellectual disabilities on norm-referenced tests standard-ised on the general population will need to be interpreted with great caution. Unfortunately, there are no hard and fast rules for determining the possible extent of under-achievement of a particular individual with intellectual disabilities on any specific test. As a result, it becomes essen-tial that the equivocal nature of the results of any formal testing procedures are clearly documented and communicated to referring agents.

Fortunately, the majority of questions underlying assessment are either 'can' (can the person undertake a specific task?) or 'why' (why is the person acting in this challenging/difficult/problematic manner?) questions.

'Can' questions are most appropriately answered through a process of 'functional assessment' (Browder, 1991; Cipani & Morrow, 1991; Gaylord-Ross & Browder, 1991). Cipani & Morrow (1991) identify four stages in undertaking a functional assessment:

❏ Conduct an 'ecological inventory' to identify the skills required by the person to function independently in important natural settings.
❏ Identify the skills which the person already possess.
❏ Identify and prioritise discrepancies between the skills needed and those already possessed.
❏ Identify possible adaptations to the tasks contained in the person's natural settings.

The basic aim of a functional assessment is to identify specific skills (to be learned) or adaptations (to be made) which will enable the person to function more independently in real world settings. In addition, a func-tional assessment may be of value in identifying particular learning strategies suited to the individual (Cipani & Morrow, 1991).

An ecological inventory should specify: (a) the nature of the setting (e.g. the living room in the person's home); (b) the activity (e.g. selecting, loading and playing a CD); (c) the skills required to undertake the activity (e.g. selects CD from shelf; walks over to CD player; presses open/close switch; checks tray is empty; (if applicable) removes CD from tray; removes selected CD from case; etc.). In effect, specifying the skills required by the activity is equivalent to undertaking a detailed 'task analysis' of the chosen activity.

The most appropriate way of identifying the skills which the person already possesses is through repeated direct observation in the person's actual setting at the time in which the activity would normally be per-formed. This will enable accurate information to be collected on: (a) what components of the task the person can complete independently; (b) any common or systematic errors the person is likely to make; (c) the levels and nature of assistance available in the setting (e.g. how staff typically support the person with the task); (d) what components of the task the person can complete with different degrees of assistance (e.g. with varying degrees of prompting). It is, of course, tempting at times to attempt to collect such information in either artificial environments or through third-party informants (e.g. by using one of the many checklists of adaptive behaviour; Widaman & McGrew, 1996). It should be recognised, however, that such 'short-cuts' run a significant risk of generating inaccurate information due to either the failure of skills to generalise to novel 'artificial' environments or to the poor observing/reporting skills of third parties. As a result, time 'saved' in the process of assessment may well be subsequently lost during intervention.

The third and fourth phases in conducting a functional assessment involve undertaking a 'discrepancy analysis' from which intervention priorities (skills to be learned, adaptations to be made) are determined. All things being equal, discrepancies should be addressed through skill development unless the task itself is *unnecessarily* complicated (i.e. more complicated than equivalent tasks undertaken by people without disabilities). There are at times, however, situations in which simple sustainable adaptations can be made to the task which can immediately promote independent action and will make the learning of complex skills redundant (e.g. colour-coding the person's favourite CDs rather than teaching recognition of the specific CD covers). Adaptations are likely to be appropriate when: (a) they do not involve grossly atypical modifications to natural environments (e.g. painted lines on the floor to mark the route to the bathroom are probably best avoided!); (b) they can be sustained across all or the majority of settings in which the task is encountered; (c) the time 'saved' (by not teaching a new skill) is used constructively.

The final (and quite common) types of assessment questions are '*why*' questions (usually '*why* is the person acting in this challenging/difficult/problematic manner?'). The attempt to answer such questions is, perhaps, central to the scientist-practitioner model, which is often seen as underlying the appropriate practice of clinical psychology (see Chapter 1). Rather confusingly, the process of attempting to answer 'why' questions has also been termed 'functional assessment' or 'functional analysis' (see Chapter 8). Answering 'why' questions involves five stages:

❑ Clarify exactly what it is that he/she does which is deemed problematic (e.g. how, where, how often, with what intensity, for how long does the person 'self-injure');
❑ Review the existing literature to generate a list of possible reasons

why people with intellectual disabilities may show such behaviours (e.g. existing evidence suggests that self-injurious behaviour may, among other things, be maintained by operant processes and/or β-endorphin activity).

❑ Review the information collected to date against these preliminary hypotheses and identify the types of information which could lead to the rejection of, or support of, particular hypotheses (e.g. self-injurious behaviour maintained by contingent escape from aversive educational activities should occur at a higher rate in situations in which such tasks are likely to be presented, and at a lower rate in situations in which such tasks are unlikely to be presented).

❑ Collect additional information (e.g. through naturalistic observations or systematic experimental analyses, see Chapter 8).

❑ Review the information collected to date against the remaining hypotheses.

In short, the process is identical to the process underlying much scientific enquiry and, as such, demands the same degree of precision and sophistication as well-conducted research.

Do I/we have the resources to implement it effectively? Is it cost-effective?

In practice there is often a trade-off to be made between accuracy of information, breadth of coverage, resources and the need for action. When trying to strike the right (most cost-effective) balance, it is useful to think about the consequences of the assessment either failing to come up with an answer or coming up with the wrong answer(s). Sometimes the consequences of 'getting it wrong' are not too damaging (e.g. temporarily delaying the acquisition of a new skill). At other times, the consequences could be critical (e.g. introducing an inappropriate intervention for life-threatening challenging behaviour). Clearly, the more critical the results, the greater the justification for investing additional time and energy to make sure you get it right.

Will it be credible to the people who need to use the information?

Finally, it is important to consider the likely credibility of the resulting information in the eyes of the people responsible for taking action. For example, the aim of assessment may be to determine whether somebody has an intellectual disability. It is highly likely that the people who want/need this information are going to be much more convinced by a conclusion based on formal IQ testing and a formal assessment of adaptive behaviour than one based on a qualitative holistic 'getting to know you' approach. The underlying aim of assessment is usually to bring about positive change for someone with an intellectual disability. Perusing avenues or activities which are not seen as credible by the people who are ultimately responsible for acting on the information is largely a waste of time.

FURTHER READING

Browder, D.M. (1991). *Assessment of Individuals with Severe Disabilities*. Paul H. Brookes: Baltimore, MD.

Hogg, J., & Raynes, N. (1986). *Assessment in Mental Handicap*, Croom Helm: London.

PART III

Clinical Issues

Chapter 8

WORKING WITH PEOPLE WITH CHALLENGING BEHAVIOUR

*Eric Emerson**

INTRODUCTION

In this chapter we will provide guidelines for working with people with challenging behaviour. As we will see, challenging behaviours are shown by a wide variety of people and come in many forms. To make our task more manageable (and to minimise overlap with the following chapters) we will focus in this chapter on aggressive, disruptive and self-injurious behaviours shown by people with *severe* intellectual disabilities. Virtually all the work which has been undertaken in this area is behavioural (see Emerson, 1995, for a review of the relevant research). This will be reflected in the prominence given to behavioural models of challenging behaviour and behavioural approaches to assessment and intervention. This does not mean that we believe other approaches are invalid, simply that, to date, there is insufficient evidence to support their use in an 'evidence-based' NHS.

Definitions

Challenging behaviour refers to 'culturally abnormal behaviour of such an intensity, frequency or duration that the physical safety of the person or others is likely to be placed in serious jeopardy, or behaviour which is likely to seriously limit use of, or result in the person being denied access to, ordinary community facilities' (Emerson, 1995). There are three important aspects of this definition:

1. *Challenging behaviours are defined by their impact.* As such, they will

*Hester Adrian Research Centre, Manchester, UK

Clinical Psychology and People with Intellectual Disabilities. Edited by E. Emerson, C. Hatton, J. Bromley and A. Caine.
© 1998 John Wiley & Sons Ltd.

range widely in their form (topography) and, more importantly, the psychological and/or biological processes which underlie them. No one theoretical approach to intervention will be applicable across all forms of challenging behaviour.

2. *Challenging behaviour is a social construction.* They are behaviours which transgress social rules. Whether a behaviour is challenging will be based on complex interactions between what persons do, the setting in which they do it and how their behaviour is interpreted or given meaning. Violence is seen as more challenging if it is considered to be intentional and pre-meditated. As a result, it may in some circumstances be necessary to intervene by 'treating' the setting or by 'treating' the ways in which behaviour is construed by significant others.

3. *Challenging behaviours have wide-ranging personal and social consequences.* Challenging behaviours may directly impair the health and/or quality of life of the person, those who care for him/her and those who live or work in close proximity. However, the ways the community, carers, and services respond to people with challenging behaviours may prove significantly more detrimental than the immediate consequences of the actual behaviours themselves. These secondary responses include abuse, inappropriate treatment, exclusion, deprivation and systematic neglect. If our interventions are to be socially valid, they must be judged against their impact in: (a) reducing the frequency, duration or intensity of the person's challenging behaviour; **and** (b) ameliorating or preventing some of these broader physical and social consequences associated with challenging behaviour.

The epidemiology of challenging behaviours

Prevalence

Between 10% and 15% of people who are supported by intellectual disability services show behaviours which are considered to cause a serious management problem, or would do were it not for the implementation of specific controlling measures (e.g. avoidance of particular activities, use of medication) Figure 8.1 shows the prevalence of specific behaviours which were considered to currently or potentially cause a serious management problem among 393 people identified in the North West of England as showing challenging behaviour (Emerson et al., 1997a, b).

The figures in Figure 8.1 add up to more than 100% as people often show more than one form of challenging behaviour. Indeed, only 12% showed

Figure 8.1   Prevalence of specific forms of challenging behaviour among 393 people with learning disabilities

Behaviour	Shown by (%)	Behaviour	Shown by (%)
Non-compliance	54	Pulling others' hair	15
Hitting others	46	Biting self	14
Outbursts of temper	45	Pinching others	14
Repetitive 'pestering'	39	Hitting own body with hand	12
Destructive behaviours	35	Biting others	12
Verbal aggression	34	Scratching self	9
Repetitive screaming	28	Stripping in public	9
Over-activity	27	Hitting own body with objects	8
Hitting others with objects	24	Smearing faeces	7
Meanness or cruelty	22	Eating inedible objects	7
Running away	21	Pinching self	7
Inappropriate sexual behaviour	18	Stuffing fingers in body openings	5
Hitting own head with hand	17	Excessive drinking	4
Hitting own head against objects	17	Pulling own hair	4
Scratching others	16	Regurgitating food	4
Theft	16	Teeth grinding	3

just one form of challenging behaviour; 59% showed five or more and 19% showed ten or more forms.

Prevalence rates (and the probability of showing multiple forms of challenging behaviour) vary in relation to a number of 'risk' factors. Challenging behaviours are more common among:

❏ Boys and men.
❏ People between the ages of 15 and 35 years.
❏ People with more severe intellectual disabilities.
❏ People with additional sensory impairments, reduced mobility or specific impairment of communication.
❏ People with some specific syndromes (e.g. autism).

Natural history, incidence and chronicity

Very few studies have examined either the development or the course of challenging behaviour over time. The limited evidence which is available, however, suggests that severely challenging behaviours may develop in early childhood and be extremely persistent over time (Emerson, 1995; Kiernan et al., 1997).

Models

A large number of studies have been undertaken in an attempt to understand the processes underlying challenging behaviours (Emerson, 1995). The vast majority of this work has been conducted within either behavioural or neurobiological paradigms.

Behavioural models

The dominant behavioural approach has been to view challenging behaviour as an example of *operant behaviour*. That is, challenging behaviour is seen as functional and (in a general sense) adaptive. It can be thought of as a way through which the person exercises control over key aspects of his/her world. Environmental consequences which maintain behaviour are termed 'reinforcers'. Two types of relationship between behaviour and reinforcers are important in establishing and maintaining operant behaviour:

❑ *Positive* reinforcement refers to an increase in the rate of a behaviour as a result of the contingent *presentation* of a (positively) reinforcing event.
❑ *Negative* reinforcement refers to an increase in the rate of a behaviour as a result of the contingent *withdrawal* (or prevention of occurrence) of a (negatively) reinforcing event.

Of course, not all behaviour is shaped by environmental consequences. Some behaviours appear to be maintained by consequences internal to the person (e.g. masturbation may lead to orgasm, clenching your teeth may partially attenuate the pain from a sprained ankle). Such behaviours may be thought of as examples of operant behaviour maintained by a process of *automatic* or *perceptual reinforcement*, in which the reinforcing stimuli are private or internal to the person (Lovaas, Newson & Hickman, 1987; Vollmer, 1994). Again, these may be split into positive automatic reinforcement (behaviour leads to positive internal state, e.g. masturbation) and negative automatic reinforcement (behaviour reduces aversive internal state, e.g. clenching teeth).

Central to the behavioural approach are concepts of functional relationships, contextual control and dynamic systems of behaviour.

Functional relationships: Behaviour analysts are interested in discovering functional relationships between events. For example, they make no *a priori* assumptions about what particular stimuli (events) are likely to be reinforcing for a person in a particular context. Reinforcers are defined functionally (by what they do). This concern with functional relationships also extends to how behaviours are classified: behaviours which *result in the same environmental effects* (e.g. attracting the attention of carers) are classified as members of the same *response class*.

Contextual control: Contextual factors operate in two ways: they may *establish the motivational base* which underlies behaviour; or they may *provide information or cues* to the individual concerning the probability of particular behaviours being reinforced. The difference between these two classes of antecedent or contextual stimuli is crucial.

❏ The reinforcing or punishing power of events needs to be established by contextual factors. Food is only a positive reinforcer if (among other things) the person is denied free access to it and if he/she has not recently eaten. In a different context (e.g. during a stomach upset) food may act as a negative reinforcer or punisher. Personal, biological, historical and environmental *setting events* influence the motivational basis of behaviour by *establishing* the reinforcing and punishing potential of otherwise neutral stimuli.

❏ Aspects of contexts may also gain 'informational value'. *Discriminative stimuli* distinguish between situations in which reinforcement is more or less likely. So, for example, an 'out of order' notice on a lift door (discriminative stimulus) provides information about the probability of pressing the call button being reinforced by the appearance of the lift.

Behaviour as a dynamic system.   We have an enormous range of behaviours available to us, *most* of which will be under the control of different reinforcement contingencies. What we actually do is the product of a complex and dynamic behavioural system. This opens up possibilities of 'indirect' approaches to intervention, which aim to establish or increase behaviours that will replace challenging behaviour (Carr et al., 1994).

There is extensive evidence to support the idea that many examples of challenging behaviours are maintained by their environmental consequences (Emerson, 1995). Iwata et al. (1994), for example, reported the findings of detailed experimental assessments of the self-injurious behaviour of 152 people with intellectual disabilities. Their data indicated that the self-injury of 38% of people appeared to be maintained by *negative reinforcement*; 26% by *positive reinforcement*; 21% by *positive automatic reinforcement*; 5% by multiple controlling variables (e.g. positive and negative reinforcement); and only 10% showed undifferentiated or unpredictable patterns of responding (see also Derby et al., 1992).

Neurobiological models

Neurobiological theories have focused on the role of three classes of endogenous neurotransmitters in modulating behaviour: dopamine, serotonin (5-hydroxytryptamine) and the opioid peptides (in particular β-endorphin).

Dopamine. The dopaminergic system is closely involved in the regulation of motor activity. It contains two main groups of dopamine receptors (D1 and D2), each of which contains further subtypes. Evidence suggests that abnormalities in the D1 receptor sub-system may be implicated in the development and maintenance of at least some forms of self-injurious behaviour (cf. Schroeder & Tessel, 1994; Schroeder et al., 1995).

Serotonin. The serotoninergic system is closely linked with a number of processes including arousal, reactivity to aversive stimuli, appetite control, anxiety and depression. Some evidence suggests that there may be a link between serotonin and aggression, and, perhaps, serotonin and some forms of 'obsessional' self-injurious behaviour (Bodfish et al., 1995; Schroeder & Tessel., 1994; Thompson et al., 1994)

β-Endorphin. β-Endorphin is an opioid peptide neurotransmitter which is released in response to repeated trauma. It is closely related to morphine and has significant analgesic properties, is associated with an euphoric mood state and may lead to physical dependence. It has been suggested that self-injurious behaviour leads to the release of β-endorphin which, through its analgesic and euphoria-inducing properties, acts as an automatic reinforcer for the self-injury (e.g. Sandman & Hetrick, 1995; Thompson et al., 1995).

Summary

Evidence suggests that: (a) many examples of challenging behaviours shown by people with severe intellectual disabilities are maintained by behavioural processes; (b) neurobiological processes may be important in maintaining the challenging behaviours of at least some people (Carr & Smith, 1995; Emerson, 1995; Mace & Mauk, 1995). The evidence also highlights the complexity of challenging behaviour, in that the factors maintaining challenging behaviour:

❑ Are likely to be dissimilar across individuals, even for behaviours which have a similar form (e.g. head banging).
❑ May vary over time (cf. Guess & Carr, 1991; MacLean, Stone & Brown, 1994).

❏ May vary across different forms of challenging behaviour shown by the same individual (Derby et al., 1994; Emerson et al., 1995, 1996).

❏ May vary across settings or contexts (Emerson et al., 1995; Haring & Kennedy, 1990).

❏ May be complex in that the behaviour may be controlled by more than one reinforcement contingency (Day, Horner & O'Neill, 1994).

ASSESSMENT

There are a number of detailed guides to the assessment of challenging behaviour (e.g. Browder, 1991; Carr et al., 1994; Demchak & Bossert, 1996; Emerson, Barrett & Cummings, 1990; Meyer & Evans, 1989; O'Neill et al., 1990; Zarkowska & Clements, 1994). In this section we will summarise some of the key issues involved in the assessment process.

The aims of assessment

As we discussed in Chapter 7, the first step in any process of assessment is to clarify its purpose(s). Any intervention-linked assessment of challenging behaviour is likely to have four distinct aims. These are:

❏ Identify what it is that the person does which is challenging.

❏ Describe the impact of challenging behaviour upon the person's quality of life.

❏ Attempt to understand the process(es) underlying the person's challenging behaviour.

❏ Identify possible alternatives to replace challenging behaviour.

Identifying challenging behaviour

Challenging behaviours are often described by carers and care staff in very general terms. The first step in any process of assessment, therefore, is to clarify the 'how, what, where and when' of challenging behaviour.

What does the person do that is challenging?

Usually, the information needed to answer this question will come from interviews with people who are in close contact with the person (e.g. family members, care staff). It may also be useful, both as a prompt during interviewing and as a basis for evaluating change, to use a validated checklist of challenging behaviour (e.g. *Aberrant Behavior Checklist,*

Aman et al., 1985; 1996; *Behaviour Problems Inventory*, Rojahn et al., 1989; *Child Behavior Rating Form*, Aman et al., 1996). If the behaviour is very frequent or highly predictable it is also important to check out the accounts given by informants by spending time with the person him/ herself. The basic task is twofold:

❑ First, we need *detailed* descriptions of the *different forms* of challenging behaviour shown by the person (remember, most people who show challenging behaviour do so in several different ways). So, for example, recording that someone self-injures is too general. We need detailed descriptions of all the different ways in which the person injures him/herself (e.g. hitting self around the eyes with fist, bringing knee to chin, biting lip).
❑ Second, we need to know about the *sequence of behaviours* which lead up to an episode of challenging behaviour. Challenging behaviours rarely occur 'out of the blue'. More commonly they follow a sequence during which the person's behaviour escalates from more appropriate (e.g. turning away) to less appropriate (e.g. hitting out) ways of attempting to exercise control. Knowledge about sequences can be helpful in: (a) developing guidelines for managing challenging behaviour; and (b) identifying possible alternatives which could replace challenging behaviour.

When, where and how often does the person show challenging behaviour?

Again, preliminary information will come from interviews. This time, however, *it will nearly always be essential to collect additional information.* How that additional information is collected will depend upon the nature of the behaviour and the resources at your disposal. One of the main purposes of collecting this information will be to evaluate the impact of any intervention. As a result, it will be important to ensure that any additional recording you introduce is sufficiently 'user friendly' that its implementation could be sustained over quite long periods of time. This means:

❑ Keep things as simple as possible.
❑ Develop new systems in partnership with the people who will be collecting the information and (for care staff) their managers.
❑ Make sure that the information generated by any new recording system is regularly fed back to the people collecting it.

Low frequency/high impact behaviours. Some forms of challenging behaviour are relatively infrequent but have very serious consequences when they do occur (e.g. serious assault). In such cases, archival information is often available (e.g. from case notes, staff communication books, incident report forms). If so, check out the likely accuracy of this information with the people who actually fill in the records. Possible problems are:

❑ Inconsistent reporting between informants (e.g. some staff or shifts may be somewhat lax in filling in reports).

❑ Inconsistent reporting over time due to changes in the reporting system or administrative/managerial changes (e.g. managers or staff may have had a drive at a particular point in time to ensure that all incident reports were completed).

If archival information is unavailable (or of dubious reliability) it will be necessary to develop a new recording system. At a minimum it will need you to:

❑ Define what you will record as constituting an episode of challenging behaviour in such a way that different informants would be able to agree that an episode has or has not occurred (i.e. develop a tight operational definition of an episode of challenging behaviour).

❑ Decide on what other information you need (and it is viable) to collect.

For example, an incident sheet for monitoring low-frequency aggression could define an episode as 'any occasion in which Chris punches, bites, scratches or kicks another person or would have done if he had not been physically restrained by two or more members of staff'. Additional information may include: the time and date on which the episode occurred; the target of the attack; injuries sustained; and general activity at the time.

High-frequency behaviours. It will not be possible to monitor each instance of high-frequency challenging behaviours. Rarely will any useful information be available in existing records. As a result, it will nearly always be necessary to develop a new recording system. Recording/monitoring systems for high-frequency behaviours will need to sample occurrences of the behaviour.

❑ *Sampling by rate or intensity.* It is often possible to set a threshold (in terms of the intensity or rate of behaviour) which defines an 'episode'. So, for example, a recording system could monitor episodes of self-injurious head hitting which lead to bleeding (sampling by intensity) or episodes in which the person hit him/herself ten or more times in any given 30 minute block of time (sampling by rate). This approach is commonly taken when using scatter plots (Touchette, McDonald & Langer, 1985). These are particularly useful for collecting information

on the frequency, timing and contextual control of episodes of challenging behaviour. Carers simply note whether a (clearly defined) episode of challenging behaviour has occurred within a given interval. Intervals are usually set at 30 or 60 minutes (see Figure 8.2).
❑ *Sampling over context and/or time.* An alternative approach is to restrict recording to particular settings and/or times (e.g. over the lunchtime period every other week). The 'how and what' of recording will depend on the resources available (e.g. the use of dedicated observers to collect information, access to frequency counters or hand-held computers) and the nature of the behaviour. Options will include measuring: the rate of behaviours (frequency over a given period of time), the duration of behaviours (the percentage of time allocated to specific activities) and the intensity or impact of behaviours (see Murphy, 1986).

Describing the impact of challenging behaviour

In addition to describing the 'how, what, where and when' of challenging behaviour, it is also important to try to determine the impact that the person's challenging behaviour is having on his/her overall quality of life. This information is important for: (a) prioritising targets for intervention; (b) evaluating the social validity of interventions. Figure 8.3 gives some questions which may be useful.

Functional assessment: understanding the processes underlying challenging behaviour

Effective intervention is dependent on first identifying the processes underlying challenging behaviour. The assessment process typically follows a sequence in which preliminary information (often of dubious reliability and validity) is validated through comparison with the results of more rigorous assessment (Demchak & Bossert, 1996; Emerson, 1995; O'Neill et al., 1990). Carr et al. (1994) describe the process as one of describe, categorise and verify.

Describe

In the previous sections we discussed ways of describing the 'how, what, where and when' of the person's challenging behaviour and the general

Figure 8.2   Scatter Plot Recording Form

Week beginning:	9th December 1996							

Name:	Chris							
Behaviour:	Punching, kicking or biting other person or attempt to do so which required restraint by two or more people							

	Day							
Time	Mon	Tue	Wed	Thur	Fri	Sat	Sun	Total
7:00–7:30								0
7:30–8:00	X				X			2
8:00–8:30	X	X				X		3
8:30–9:00								0
9:00–9:30								0
9:30–10:00								0
10:00–10:30								0
10:30–11:00		X				X		2
11:00–11:30	X	X			X			3
11:30–12:00	X							1
12:00–12:30 etc...								0
TOTALS	2	3	2	0	2	2	0	11

impact such behaviour has upon their overall quality of life. In the descriptive phase of a functional assessment we are interested in describing the *immediate* social and environmental impact of the person's challenging behaviour. Through this, we are attempting to identify:

❏ The *reinforcement contingencies* which are maintaining the behaviour(s).
❏ The *setting events* or contextual factors which provide the motivational basis for challenging behaviour.

This descriptive information is often gathered through a combination of structured interview, rating scales and observation.

Structured interview.   Demchak and Bossert (1996) suggest ten simple questions which can be used as a basis for a structured interview (see Figure 8.4).

Rating scales.   There are a small number of rating scales which purport to identify the behavioural processes underlying challenging behaviour. Of these, the Motivation Assessment Scale (Durand & Crimmins, 1992) is probably the most commonly used. Unfortunately, while simple to use, such scales have dubious reliability and validity (Thompson & Emerson, 1995).

Figure 8.3   Identifying the personal and social impact of challenging behaviour

Injuries
Has the person's challenging behaviour resulted in direct injury to him/herself? To others?
If so, what is the most severe injury (to self and others) sustained in the last year? Six months? Month?
What level of injury is usually sustained during an episode of challenging behaviour?

Management
What medication is currently prescribed for the control of challenging behaviour?
Is . . . . (seclusion/PRN medication/physical restraint) ever used to manage episodes of challenging behaviour? How often has each been used over the last six months? Last month?

Participation
Is the person's participation in . . . . (domestic activities/social activities/ community-based activities) restricted because of his/her challenging behaviour? What specific activities are avoided?
Does the behaviour interfere with his/her learning or general development? In what way?

Relationships
What impact does the person's challenging behaviour have on his/her relation-ships with . . . . (his/her family/co-workers/co-tenants/care staff/members of the public)?
What is the emotional impact upon . . . . (his/her family/co-workers/co-tenants/care staff/members of the public) of the person's challenging behaviour?
What levels of stress/strain are . . . . (his/her family/co-workers/ co-tenants/ care staff/members of the public) experiencing?

Security
Is the person's home or job/school/day service in jeopardy because of his/her challenging behaviour?

Observation.   Wherever practicable, it is important to 'validate' the infor-mation collected through interview or rating scales by observation. For high-frequency behaviours this should always be possible. The aim of such observations is to describe the relationships between Antecedents, Behaviour and its Consequences. These A–B–C observations need to be con-ducted by *trained observers* who are familiar with the types of processes or relationships which may underlie challenging behaviour. Simply asking carers or care staff to complete the archetypal free-form A–B–C chart is of little or no value. Carr et al. (1994) suggests using index cards to record occurrences of challenging behaviour (see Figure 8.5).

Scatter plots can be used to identify the key times and situations in which to observe. Information should be collected on at least 10 episodes of *each form* of challenging behaviour shown by the person.

Figure 8.4 Structured interview to determine the immediate impact and contextual control of challenging behaviour

Ask each question separately for each form of challenging behaviour shown by the person

1. What are the activities or settings in which the behaviour typically occurs?
2. What typically happens when the behaviour occurs (i.e. what do you or others typically do)?
3. Are there particular events or activities that usually or often occur just before an instance of challenging behaviour? Please describe.
4. Are there particular events or activities that you usually avoid because they typically result in challenging behaviour? Please describe.
5. Are there particular events or activities that you encourage because they DO NOT result in challenging behaviour? Please describe.
6. What does . . . . appear to be communicating with their challenging behaviour? Please describe.
7. Does their challenging behaviour appear to be related to a specific medical condition, diet, sleep pattern, seizure activity, period of illness or pain? Please describe.
8. Does their challenging behaviour appear to be related to their mood or emotional state? Does this change following an episode of challenging behaviour? Please describe.
9. Does the behaviour appear to be influenced by environmental factors (noise, number of people in the room, lighting, music, temperature)? Please describe.
10. Does the behaviour appear to be influenced by events in other settings (e.g. relationships at home)? Please describe.

Modified from Demchak and Bossert (1996).

Categorise

Once sufficient information has been collected, *each episode of each form* of challenging behaviour should be reviewed to see if it is consistent with any of the four main behavioural processes which may underlie the person's challenging behaviour Figure 8.6 gives some questions which should help to identify possible 'categories' for particular episodes of behaviour.

(Amanda's challenging behaviour in Figure 8.5 would fall into the categories of positive social reinforcement (cafe) and negative reinforcement (psychology department). Remember that one behaviour can serve multiple functions).

Through the process of categorising episodes of challenging behaviours (e.g. by sorting the cards into piles or pinning them on a noticeboard in clusters) we want to answer several questions.

❏ Is it possible to assign the majority of episodes of each form of challenging behaviour to these categories?

❑ What appears to be the main function of each form of challenging behaviour? Does it also appear to serve other functions?
❑ If a specific behaviour serves several functions, is there anything about the context in which the behaviour occurs which predicts which function is operating?
❑ Do different forms of challenging behaviour appear to serve the same or different functions?

The answers to these questions will form a series of hypotheses about the function(s) of the challenging behaviour(s) shown by the person. As we have argued in Chapter 7, however, it is important that we test these hypotheses before proceeding to intervention.

Verify

There are two main approaches to checking out your hypotheses before proceeding to intervention.

Figure 8.5   Example of index card used for recording episodes of challenging behaviour during functional assessment

---

NAME: Amanda   OBSERVER: Eric   DATE: 9 December 1996

GENERAL CONTEXT: Psychology Department   TIME: 4:30 pm

INTERPERSONAL CONTEXT: Amanda was working in her room. Lawrence walked in with a large pile of files and placed them on her desk.

CHALLENGING BEHAVIOUR: Amanda began to moan quietly, rock backwards and forwards and bite her hand.

SOCIAL IMPACT: Lawrence looked concerned, picked up the files and walked out muttering to himself.

NAME: Amanda   OBSERVER: Eric   DATE: 9 December 1996

GENERAL CONTEXT: Cafe   TIME: 4:30 pm

INTERPERSONAL CONTEXT: Jo, Chris and Amanda are having a coffee. Chris and Jo are deep in conversation with each other.

CHALLENGING BEHAVIOUR: Amanda began to moan quietly, rock backwards and forwards and bite her hand.

SOCIAL IMPACT: Jo looked concerned, patted Amanda on the shoulder and included her in the conversation.

Modified from Carr et al. (1994).

Figure 8.6   Relationships between contextual factors, challenging behaviours and consequent events which may suggest particular behavioural processes

Socially-mediated positive reinforcement
Does the person's challenging behaviour sometimes result in them receiving more or different forms of contact with others (e.g. while the episode is being managed or while they are being 'calmed down') or having access to new activities?
Is the behaviour more likely when contact or activities are potentially available but not being provided, e.g. situations in which carers are around but are attending to others?
Is the behaviour less likely in situations involving high levels of contact or during preferred activities?
Is the behaviour more likely when contact or activities are terminated?

Socially-mediated negative reinforcement (escape or avoidance)
Do people respond to the behaviour by terminating interaction or activities?
Is the behaviour more likely in situations in which demands are placed upon the person or they are engaged in interactions or activities they appear to dislike?
Is the behaviour less likely when disliked interactions or activities are stopped?
Is the behaviour less likely in situations involving participation in preferred activities?
Is the behaviour more likely in those situations in which they *may* be asked to participate in interactions or activities they appear to dislike?

Positive automatic reinforcement
Is the behaviour more likely when there is little external stimulation?
Is the behavior less likely when the person is participating in a preferred activity?
Does the behaviour appear to have no effect upon subsequent events?

Negative automatic reinforcement (de-arousal)
Is the behaviour more likely when there is excessive external stimulation or when the individual is visibly excited or aroused?
Is the behavior less likely when the individual is calm or in a quiet, peaceful environment?
Does the behaviour appear to have no effect upon subsequent events?

Descriptive analysis involves very detailed naturalistic observation of the challenging behaviour(s) shown by the individual and events which are thought to be maintaining it. Statistical techniques such as lag sequential analysis can then be used to evaluate: (a) the effect of context on the probability of challenging behaviour occurring; and (b) the relationship in time between the occurrence of the behaviour and the presentation or withdrawal of possible reinforcers (Emerson et al., 1996). Figure 8.7, based on eight hours of observational data collected in a residential special school, illustrates the contextual control of a girl's self-injurious ear poking (it is much more likely to occur under conditions of instructional demands). These data suggest this form of her self-injury is maintained by negative social reinforcement (escape from instructional demands).

Figure 8.7   Conditional probability of Susan's ear poking under conditions of: teacher demand; other forms of teacher contact; teacher being in proximity but not interacting; and Susan being alone

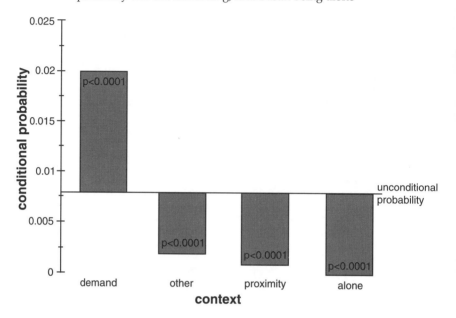

Experimental (functional) analysis involves undertaking a brief 'mini-experiment', during which aspects of the person's context which are related to the hypothesised maintaining processes are manipulated (e.g., Carr et al., 1994; Demchak & Bossert, 1996; Derby et al., 1994; Emerson, Barrett & Cummings, 1990; Iwata et al., 1982, 1994; O'Neill et al., 1990). Each session normally last 10 or 15 minutes, and in each block of 3–5 sessions different aspects of the person's social environment is briefly altered Figure 8.8 shows the results of such an analysis for another form of self-injury shown by Susan (she never engaged in ear poking during the experimental assessment). Again, the results are consistent with the notion that this form of her self-injury is maintained by negative social reinforcement (escape from instructional demands). As with descriptive analyses, such procedures can provide a compelling test of hypotheses which arise during a functional assessment but are demanding of time and resources and are really only applicable to relatively high-frequency behaviours.

Identifying possible alternatives to challenging behaviour

As discussed in Chapter 1, the aim of a constructional intervention is to replace challenging behaviour with other (more appropriate) behaviours.

The aim of intervention is never to simply reduce or eliminate challenging behaviour. One aim of the assessment process, therefore, is to identify possible alternatives to challenging behaviour. Some possible strategies are listed below.

❏ Look at the sequence of behaviours which lead up to challenging behaviour. Are there any earlier links in the chain which could be built on? For example, if the person often tries to 'wave away' unwanted demands before finally resorting to aggression, perhaps a manual sign based on waving could be used as a functionally equivalent replacement to challenging behaviour (see below).
❏ Ask carers and care staff what they think the person should do in the situations which are likely to lead to their challenging behaviour.
❏ Undertake a general assessment of the person's existing skills (see Chapter 7), preferences (see Lancioni, O'Reilly & Emerson, 1996) and, in particular, their methods of communication (see Chapter 13).

INTERVENTION

There are a number of detailed guides to intervention or the management of challenging behaviour (e.g. Carr et al., 1994; Meyer & Evans, 1989; Harris et al., 1996; Zarkowska & Clements, 1994). In this section we will summarise some of the key points involved in the intervention process.

All being well, the results of your functional assessment will have identified the function(s) served by the person's challenging behaviour. All you need to do now is design and implement an appropriate intervention!

Sometimes, of course, the results of assessment are not always straight forward. Challenging behaviours may be multiply controlled or may serve different functions at different times or in different contexts. As a result, it may be necessary to employ different interventions in different contexts. In fact, it will *nearly always* be necessary to develop a *multi-component intervention package* which combines a number of different approaches. Single interventions may appear in the research literature, but have no place in practice. Your job is to maximise the benefits of intervention (while controlling the personal and social costs involved). Maximising benefits is much more likely with multi-component strategies than with single interventions.

The possible components of an intervention package are to:

❏ Take account of the person's preferences.
❏ Change the context in which challenging behaviour takes place.
❏ Teach or support alternatives to challenging behaviour.

Figure 8.8   Rate of Susan's self-injurious hand-biting (SIB) during 10 minute
experimental sessions when: demands were placed upon her by
her teacher to complete an educational task; she was only given
attention by her teacher when she self-injured (contiugent
attention); she was given continuous non-instructional attention;
and she was alone

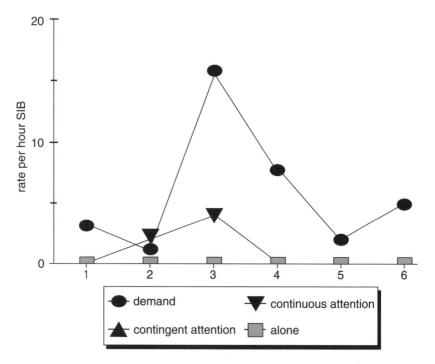

❏ Change the contingencies maintaining the person's challenging
behaviour.

Finally, we occasionally work with someone who defeats all our attempts
to understand why they are showing challenging behaviour. In the last
section of this chapter we will discuss the use of 'default technologies'
which can be applied in such situations and other courses of action
which may be appropriate.

Take account of the person's preferences

If the person's challenging behaviour is associated with particular activities, settings or events, one straightforward approach is simply to help
the person reschedule his/her life to eliminate or reduce exposure to

these situations. Why not respond to the person's wishes as 'expressed' through his/her challenging behaviour?

For example, Touchette et al. (1985) used a scatter plot to identify the settings associated with aggressive outbursts shown by a 14 year-old girl with autism and severe intellectual disabilities. The majority of episodes were associated with her attendance at pre-vocational and community living classes. 'Intervention' consisted of re-scheduling her weekly time table, in which preferred activities were substituted for these classes. As a result, her aggression rapidly reduced to near zero levels. Interestingly, it later proved possible to gradually reintroduce the problematic classes without eliciting further aggression (a process known as *stimulus fading*, see also Kennedy, 1994). Similarly, basing educational or vocational curricula on activities preferred by students is likely to result in reduced challenging behaviour and increased desirable behaviour (e.g. Foster-Johnson et al., 1994).

Such approaches have obvious attractions in that:

❏ They can result in rapid and marked reductions in the challenging behaviour.
❏ They may be relatively easy to sustain since it requires organisational change rather than day-to-day implementation by carers.
❏ They (in effect) empower service users.

Their possible disadvantages, however, are that:

❏ The settings or activities which elicit challenging behaviour may be important for the person's health and safety, development or quality of life (e.g. interaction with other people, requests to participate in an activity).
❏ It may be difficult to avoid the eliciting circumstances (e.g. the sight of dogs).

Change the context in which challenging behaviour takes place

It is not always necessary to intervene directly on the person's challenging behaviour. A wide range of approaches have been developed which intervene indirectly by altering aspects of the context in which challenging behaviour takes place (cf., Carr et al., 1990; Emerson, 1995).

As we discussed earlier, personal, historical and contextual *setting events* provide the motivational basis for challenging behaviour. So, for example, conditions of social deprivation may establish the reinforcing potential of *any* form of contact. Experience of repeated failure on educational tasks may establish them as aversive. Illness, overcrowding and high levels of background noise may lower the threshold at which particular activities become aversive. If we can intervene at the level of these setting events (e.g. by making sure tasks do not become aversive), it may be possible to simply make the person's challenging behaviour redundant.

Possible strategies include:

❏ Enriching the environment.
❏ Changing the nature of preceding activities.
❏ Changing the context of activities which elicit challenging behaviour.

Enriching the environment

Behavioural theory predicts that the rate of behaviours maintained by positive reinforcement (external or automatic) should reduce as the background level of reinforcement increases (McDowell, 1982). Indeed, a number of studies (often undertaken in institutional settings) have indicated that enriching impoverished environments (e.g. by increasing interaction or introducing materials) may lead to reduced rates of stereotypy and some forms of self-injury (e.g. Favell, McGimsey & Schell 1982; Horner, 1980; Mace, Yankanich & West 1989). Similarly, moving from impoverished institutional settings into the community is associated with reductions in stereotypic behaviour (Emerson & Hatton, 1994). Unfortunately, these effects are largely restricted to behaviours maintained by positive automatic reinforcement.

Changing the nature of preceding activities

The nature of preceding activities may have a significant impact on people's responses to ongoing events.

A small number of studies have linked idiosyncratic, temporally distant setting events (e.g. difficulty getting out of bed in the morning, the choice of route to school) with challenging behaviour later in the day (Kennedy and Itkonen, 1993; O'Reilly, 1995). Kennedy and Itkonen, (1993), for example, found that the route taken to college in the morning by a 20 year-old woman with severe and complex disabilities predicted the frequency of her aggressive and disruptive behaviours throughout the day. They instituted a 'travel program' which simply consisted of her travelling by her 'preferred' route. This resulted in marked reductions in challenging behaviour; gains which were maintained two-and-a-half months later. A detailed functional assessment which focused on identifying setting events (as well as the function of the person's challenging behaviour) should open up many opportunities for such approaches to intervention. For example, several studies have reported that *physical exercise* may result in reductions in self-injurious, aggressive and disruptive behaviours during subsequent activities (e.g. Baumeister & MacLean, 1984; Lancioni et al., 1984; McGimsey & Favell, 1998).

Finally, Mace et al. (1988) described the phenomenon of *behavioural momentum*, which may be useful in reducing challenging behaviours associated with non-compliance with specific requests. It involves: (a) identifying requests with which the person will happily comply (e.g. 'give me five'); and (2) preceding the problematic request (e.g. to take medication) with a *series* of these unthreatening requests (cf. Harchik & Putzier, 1990).

Changing the context of activities which elicit challenging behaviour

Tasks may become less aversive (and consequently less likely to elicit escape-maintained challenging behaviour) if:

❑ Frequent breaks are scheduled (Gaylord-Ross, Weeks & Lipner, 1980).
❑ Task variety is increased and repetition of tasks decreased (Winterling, Dunlop & O'Neil, 1987).
❑ The rate of positive reinforcers is increased in 'high-risk' situations (Carr & Newsom, 1985; Carr, Newsom & Binkolfs, 1980; Kennedy, 1994).

This latter strategy is known as *embedding* (Carr et al., 1994) and can have a powerful impact on challenging behaviour. For example, Carr, Newsom & Binkolfs (1976) conducted a functional assessment which indicated that the self-injurious head hitting shown by Tim, an eight-year-old boy with intellectual disabilities and autism, was elicited by adult requests. They then went on to show that relatively minor changes to the context in which the requests were made brought about dramatic changes in Tim's behaviour. When interaction consisted solely of request, his self-injury occurred at very high rates. However, when the time between *making the same requests* was filled with telling Tim a story, his self-injury immediately dropped to near zero levels. Relatively small changes in the situation (telling a story) appeared to be capable of totally disrupting his severe self-injury.

Summary

Approaches based on changing the context in which challenging behaviour occurs have a number of potential advantages:

❑ They can bring about extremely rapid and significant reductions in challenging behaviour.

❑ They may be relatively easy to implement and sustain over time as they place less reliance on altering the nature of carers' responses to episodes of challenging behaviour.

❑ They do not appear to have any negative 'side-effects' (e.g. user distress, emergence of other forms of challenging behaviour).

Teach or support alternatives to challenging behaviour

The single most significant development over the last decade in supporting people with challenging behaviour has been the emergence of interventions based on functional communication training or functional displacement (Carr & Durand, 1984; Carr et al., 1994; Durand & Carr, 1991, 1992). The aim of this approach is quite simple: to replace challenging behaviour by teaching/supporting the person to achieve the same ends through more appropriate means. So, for example, if a person's self-injury is maintained by escape from instructional demands, the aim of intervention would be to teach the person a more appropriate way of escaping (e.g. by asking for a break). Functional displacement does not aim to alter either the antecedents or the consequences of challenging behaviour. Instead, it seeks to introduce a new behaviour (or increase the rate of a pre-existing behaviour) which will tap in to the existing contingencies and displace the challenging behaviour.

Two studies illustrate the use of functional displacement to challenging behaviours shown by people with severe disabilities. Steege et al. (1990) taught two young children with severe multiple disabilities to press a micro-switch which activated a tape-recording to request a break from self-care activities. Use of this assistive device led to a significant reduction in their escape-motivated self-injury. Bird et al. (1989) taught two men with severe intellectual disabilities to either exchange a token for a short break or to use a manual sign for 'break'. This led to: (a) rapid reductions in their severe escape-maintained challenging behaviours; (b) an increase in spontaneous communication; and (c) both men spending *more* time on-task and actually requesting to work. This suggests that one general effect of the intervention may be to decrease the aversiveness of the tasks. This is consistent with the idea that *perceived control* over potentially aversive events is an important moderator of the level of stress people experience (cf. Bannerman et al., 1990).

Carr et al. (1994) provide detailed guidance on the implementation of intervention programmes based on functional communication training, including techniques for building rapport, selecting an alternative response, creating a context for communication, building tolerance for delay of reinforcement, generalisation and maintenance. The keys to success are that:

❏ The new replacement response must be truly equivalent to the challenging behaviour (i.e. serves *exactly* the same function).
❏ It must be a more 'efficient' response than the person's challenging behaviour.

By being more 'efficient' we mean that the new replacement response should require less effort than the person's challenging behaviour and should lead to more frequent, rapid and higher quality reinforcement (i.e. the 'pay-off' for the new replacement response should be greater than for the challenging behaviour). In order to maximise the impact of intervention, it is often necessary to *decrease* the efficiency of the challenging behaviour. That is, it will be important to combine functional communication training with more traditional reactive strategies (e.g. extinction, time-out) to weaken the challenging behaviour (Fisher et al., 1993; Wacker et al., 1990). If the challenging behaviour is multiply controlled by biological and behavioural factors (e.g. self-injury maintained by extrinsic reinforcement and β-endorphin release), this may involve the combined use of behavioural and psychopharmacological treatments.

Of course, we must not forget that challenging behaviour has a powerful influence on carers (Taylor & Carr, 1993, 1994). Often, the person with intellectual disabilities *does have* more appropriate behaviours at their disposal. The problem is that carers have, over time, come to preferentially respond only to their challenging behaviours. There is a very real risk that, without carefully planned approaches to maintenance, the response efficiency of the alternative behaviour will reduce (e.g. care staff not attending to socially appropriate requests for breaks or attention) and challenging behaviour will re-emerge. In many ways, teaching a functionally equivalent response to a service user may be considerably easier than ensuring that care staff continue to listen to and act upon alternative methods of communication (see Chapter 13).

Nevertheless, the available evidence does suggest that: (a) a range of challenging behaviours may be rapidly and substantially reduced by establishing and/or supporting functionally equivalent alternatives to challenging behaviour; (b) that the effects of such interventions may persist over time and generalise to new settings (Durand & Carr, 1991, 1992). This approach is attractive in that it is functionally-based, constructional and seeks to *tap into contingencies of reinforcement which are known to be highly effective in maintaining behaviour over time and across settings* (i.e. the contingencies maintaining challenging behaviour).

Change the contingencies maintaining the person's challenging behaviour

The approaches discussed so far have not involved any *direct* alteration of the contingencies maintaining the person's challenging behaviour. *Extinction* involves removing the contingencies responsible for maintaining the person's challenging behaviour. For example, if a person's aggression is maintained by carer attention, an extinction procedure would ensure that attention was no longer provided contingent upon the person's challenging behaviour. *Escape extinction* involves ensuring that negative reinforcers are *not withdrawn* contingent upon the person's challenging behaviour (e.g. challenging behaviour no longer leads to escape).

While extinction can be effective, its has a number of significant drawbacks:

❑ The rate, intensity and variability of the behaviour may *increase* during the initial stages of an extinction programme in an *extinction burst*.
❑ The programme needs to be implemented with great consistency (otherwise the procedure is equivalent to just reducing the rate of reinforcement for the person's challenging behaviour).
❑ The effects of extinction procedures may not generalise to new situations.
❑ Extinction may be associated with unwanted 'side-effects' (e.g. emergence of other challenging behaviours).

Given these problems, extinction procedures should not be used on their own. They are, however, often important components in treatment packages which seek to reduce the efficiency of challenging behaviour (see above).

Default technologies: or things to try when you haven't a clue what's going on

If your functional assessment fails to identify why the person is showing challenging behaviour, a number of alternatives should be considered. These will usually involve referral elsewhere and should include investigation of whether the person's challenging behaviour may be linked to:

❑ Undiagnosed medical illness (e.g. Peine et al. 1995).
❑ Undiagnosed psychiatric disorder (e.g. Bodfish et al., 1995; Mace & Mauk, 1995).
❑ Seizure activity (e.g. Gedye, 1989a, b).

❏ β-Endorphin release (Sandman & Hetrick, 1995; Thompson et al., 1995).

There are, however, two behavioural approaches which may be appropriate (given the severity of the person's challenging behaviour and the success of other investigations in detecting remediable causes).

Differential reinforcement

Differential reinforcement procedures intervene indirectly by increasing the rate of other behaviours. Procedures include: the *differential reinforcement of other behaviour* (DRO); and the *differential reinforcement of alternative* (DRA) or *incompatible* (DRI) *behaviour*. DRO, also known as omission training, is a non-constructional procedure involving the delivery of a reinforcement *contingent on the non-occurrence of the targeted challenging behaviour* during an interval of time or, more unusually, at a specific point in time (momentary DRO). In general, it would appear that such procedures may not be particularly effective in reducing severely challenging behaviours (Carr et al., 1990; Lancioni & Hoogeveen, 1990; O'Brien & Repp, 1990; Scotti et al., 1991). To maximise the chances of success, the differential reinforcement programme should ensure that:

❏ The alternative behaviour requires less effort than the person's challenging behaviour.
❏ The rate of reinforcement delivered contingent on the alternative behaviour is greater than the rate of reinforcement maintaining the challenging behaviour.
❏ Reinforcement is delivered immediately upon occurrence of the alternative behaviour.
❏ The reinforcers selected are more powerful than those maintaining the challenging behaviour, preferably through the use of empirical procedures to identify reinforcer selection.
❏ The alternative behaviours show a natural negative covariation with the challenging behaviour (e.g. Koegel & Frea, 1993; Parrish et al., 1986).

Punishment

Numerous studies have demonstrated that punishment procedures can produce socially significant reductions in severe challenging behaviours shown by people with severe intellectual disabilities (Emerson, 1995). Indeed, meta-analyses of the intervention literature indicate that punishment-based procedures are some of the most effective approaches available, both immediately and at follow-up (Scotti et al., 1991). In terms of the criteria which we suggest should underpin intervention, however, the use of punishment-based procedures is obviously problematic in that they are neither constructional nor functionally-based and that the procedures (if not the outcomes) are increasingly being seen as socially unacceptable. Forms of punishment which have been shown to be effective include:

❏ *Response cost*: withdrawing positive reinforcers contingent upon the occurrence of challenging behaviour.
❏ *Time-out*: withdrawing opportunity for positive reinforcement for a set period following the occurrence of a target behaviour.
❏ *Visual or facial screening*: the brief blocking of vision contingent upon the occurrence of challenging behaviour.
❏ *Positive punishment*: the presentation of an aversive stimulus contingent upon challenging behaviour. Aversive stimuli which have been employed to reduce challenging behaviour have ranged from the relatively innocuous (e.g. verbal reprimands), through brief response interruption and restraint (e.g. Azrin et al., 1988) to electric shock (e.g. Linscheid et al., 1990).

Obviously, such procedures should only be considered when: (a) alternative approaches have failed or are not feasible; (b) the costs of not intervening outweigh the costs and risks associated with the use of such procedures. They should only be implemented: (c) by qualified and experienced psychologists; (d) under the close supervision of an independent ethical committee; and (e) after formal consent has been received from the person him/herself or from someone who can act on his/her behalf.

SUMMARY: PERSON-CENTRED INTERVENTION

In the sections above, we have described a wide range of possible approaches to assessment and intervention. Central to the success of the whole process is understanding why this particular person is acting in this particular way in these particular settings. The person him/herself must remain at the very centre of the intervention process. Indeed, it appears that many of the more promising approaches to intervention involve supporting the user to take control over his/her life in ways which are more appropriate than displaying challenging behaviour. Functional communication training, for example, is very explicitly about retaining the users's control over what goes on around him/her.

Most of the procedures described in the sections above are, however, implemented by carers, care staff or professionals. The use of *self-manage-*

ment or *self-control* techniques by people with severe intellectual disabilities has received little attention (see Korinek, 1991, for a relatively recent review of self-management by people with mild/moderate intellectual disabilities). Two recent studies, however, suggest that these procedures may also be beneficial for people with more severe disabilities. Koegel and Koegel (1990) taught children with autism (age range 9–14 years; mental age 2 years to 5 years 11 months) to self-monitor their multiple forms of stereotypic behaviour. This resulted in marked reductions in stereotypy for three of the four children. More recently, Pierce and Schreibman (1994) examined the effects of a pictorial self-cueing and self-reinforcement on the independent performance of daily living skills. The participants were three children with autism (age range 6–8 years; mental age range 2 years 2 months to 3 years 10 months). Implementation of the self-management package was associated with an increase in independent performance and a decrease in stereotypy (see also Krantz et al., 1993; Stahmer & Schreibman, 1992). Hopefully over the next decade we will see examples of people with severe intellectual disabilities being supported in taking an increasingly active role in overcoming their challenging behaviour.

FURTHER READING

Carr, E.G., Levin, L., McConnachie, G., Carlson, J.I., Kemp, D.C., & Smith, C.E. (1994). *Communication-based Intervention for Problem Behavior: A User's Guide for Producing Positive Change*. Brookes: Baltimore, MD.

Demchak, M.A., & Bossert, K.W. (1996). *Assessing Problem Behaviours*. Washington, DC: American Association on Mental Retardation.

Emerson, E. (1995). *Challenging Behaviour: Analysis and Intervention in People with Learning Disabilities*. Cambridge University Press: Cambridge.

Koegel, L.K., Koegel, R.L., & Dunlap, G. (1996) *Positive Behavioral Support: Including People with Difficult Behavior in the Community*. Paul H. Brookes: Baltimore, MD.

Chapter 9

WORKING WITH OFFENDERS OR ALLEGED OFFENDERS WITH INTELLECTUAL DISABILITIES

Isabel C.H. Clare* and Glynis H. Murphy**

INTRODUCTION

Historically, interest in people with intellectual disabilities who have, or are alleged to have, committed criminal offences has often been limited to eugenically-based fears about the impact of the 'unfit' (Craft, 1984; Fennell, 1996). Recent years, however, have seen the beginnings of more constructive approaches to assessment, treatment and management for this group of people. Nevertheless, little practical guidance is available in the literature, perhaps reflecting uncertainty about whether the difficulties of offenders or alleged offenders can best be understood by reference to 'mainstream' forensic work or to the literature on intellectual disabilities.

Relationship between challenging behaviour, alleged offending and offending

Within 'mainstream' forensic practice, the term 'mentally disordered offender' is used very broadly to refer to people who are presumed to be breaking the law but have never been reported to the police, as well as to individuals convicted by a court (Vaughan & Badger, 1995). The word 'offender' is also widely used in relation to people with intellectual disabilities. Of course, much 'challenging behaviour' could constitute a criminal offence. However, in English law (i.e. the law in England and Wales), a crime is not defined simply by a behaviour or its consequence

*Lifespan Healthcare NHS Trust, and Department of Psychiatry, University of Cambridge, UK
**Tizard Centre University of Kent, at Canterbury, Canterbury, UK

Clinical Psychology and People with Intellectual Disabilities. Edited by E. Emerson, C. Hatton, J. Bromley and A. Caine.

(*actus reus*). Other key 'ingredients' must be present. One of the most important is a guilty 'state of mind' (*mens rea*) relating to the behaviour (such as intention, recklessness and so on; see Carson & Clare, 1997). Sometimes, it is clear that one or more of these ingredients is missing (e.g. because the person did not know that the act was illegal, or was not aware of the possibility that harm would result; see Carson, 1995).

The likelihood both of fulfilling the criteria for a crime and of being involved meaningfully in criminal justice procedures is much greater for people with *mild* intellectual disabilities, and it is this sub-group of people with problem behaviour who are most likely to come into contact with the criminal justice system. Ultimately, however, it is for a court, following a police investigation, to decide whether a person's behaviour is a crime and whether that person is an 'offender'. Until then, the offending is only *alleged*. Providers have a duty of care towards *all* service users and, whilst they need to protect the rights of alleged victims, they may place themselves at risk of being sued if they assume prematurely that a person is an offender and impose informal sanctions (Williams, 1995).

Service responses to offending and alleged offending

Despite many research studies and assertions, the extent to which people with intellectual disabilities are alleged or convicted offenders is unknown and the association with particular offences (such as arson and sexual offending) unclear. The problems reflect differing interpretations of an 'intellectual disability', together with some naivety about the operation of the criminal justice system, so that some researchers have imagined that the frequency of offending can be assessed by looking at criminal convictions (see Noble & Conley, 1992, for an excellent review of this area; Murphy & Holland, 1993).

What is known suggests that the response to alleged offending remains arbitrary. Where people are already living in health or social care provision for people with intellectual disabilities, whether in the community (Lyall, Holland & Collins, 1995; McNulty, Kissi-Deborah & Newsom-Davies, 1995) or in hospital (Thompson, 1997a), carers are reluctant to involve the police. This response seems to reflect a variety of factors, including a lack of relevant policies and practice guidelines to help staff identify and deal with alleged offences (Lyall, Holland & Collins, 1995; Thompson, Clare & Brown, 1997); a misguided belief—traditionally shared by the criminal justice system—that the person is already 'taken care of' (Carson, 1989); and assumptions by carers, which may be ill-founded (Sanders et al., 1997), that allegations by victims and other witnesses will not be taken seriously by the police and (in England and

Wales; Scotland has a different legal system) the Crown Prosecution Service. In contrast, people with mild intellectual disabilities who are not known to adult 'learning disability' services are at risk of coming into contact with the criminal justice system—and of being vulnerable within it—if it is alleged that they have committed an offence. The majority of people with intellectual disabilities merge into the general population after leaving school (Richardson et al., 1984) because, under ordinary circumstances, they need no further support, whilst others receive no services because they do not fulfil (often arbitrary) 'eligibility criteria' or have been excluded on the grounds that they are 'too difficult'. If members of this group are arrested and their intellectual disability is not identified by the police, the special provision introduced under the *Police and Criminal Evidence Act 1984* (England and Wales) and its accompanying guidelines (Codes of Practice, revised, Home Office, 1995) to protect young people (aged 16 years or less) and 'vulnerable' adult suspects cannot be implemented (Clare & Gudjonsson, 1995; Gudjonsson, 1992). This can lead, and has led, to miscarriages of justice (e.g. Gudjonsson, 1992). In at least some cases, perhaps because of their similarity in terms of intellectual and psychological disadvantages to alleged and convicted offenders in the general population (see Murphy, Harnett & Holland, 1995), they may proceed through the criminal justice system repeatedly before health and social services for people with intellectual disabilities become aware of, and accept responsibility for, meeting their needs.

In recent years, there have been a number of initiatives to provide a more consistent approach to people with complex needs (including 'mentally disordered offenders', see also Chapter 5). Briefly, these initiatives (Department of Health, 1993, 1996; Department of Health & Home Office, 1992; Home Office, 1990; Home Office & Department of Health, 1995) emphasise the need to:

❏ ... prosecute alleged offences where there is sufficient evidence and this is 'in the public interest' (e.g. there is a risk to the public, there is a pattern of allegedly escalating behaviour etc.; see Gunn, 1996, for a clear outline of the process of law). *Nowhere* is it suggested that alleged offending should not be reported to, and investigated by, the police. However, it is very important that the rights of the alleged offender should be protected: this will mean that s/he needs to have a solicitor with relevant experience, and someone who is independent (the 'Appropriate Adult') present during police procedures to assist him/her to understand what is happening (for practical guidance, see Hollins, Clare & Murphy, 1996; Hollins, Murphy & Clare, 1996; Mencap, 1997).

As far as possible, the outcome of this process should not be imprisonment. Instead, people with intellectual disabilities and/or mental health needs should be identified so that they can be provided with treatment and support:

❏ On a multi-agency basis. A variety of agencies may be involved in meeting a person's needs: e.g. health (including both the general practitioner and specialist health care providers), social care, criminal justice, and housing, alcohol and drug services. Some of these will be statutory, others will be independent and voluntary, and not all will have the same underlying philosophy. A case-management or key-worker role is often needed to ensure a consistent approach.
❏ In a range of services, providing different levels of supervision and support but, as far as possible, in community rather than in institutional settings. Where necessary, community services can be provided within a criminal justice framework (e.g. through a Probation Order with conditions, such as of treatment or residence) or through the *Mental Health Act 1983* (e.g. Section 37 Guardianship Order, Jones, 1996).
❏ In such a way as to maximise rehabilitation and the chances of sustaining an independent life.
❏ As near as possible to the person's home or family.
❏ Involving the person him/herself and carers as far as possible.

So far, however, most of the developments for offenders and alleged offenders with intellectual disabilities described in the literature have reflected a traditional forensic model, where the prototypical service-user is a person whose difficulties can be addressed within a hospital-based service (Cumella & Sansom, 1994; Day, 1988; Murphy et al., 1991). Instead, the emphasis needs to be on community-based services with access to hospital facilities (locally, as far as possible) when focused assessment and/or treatment is required under the *Mental Health Act 1983*.

What is known about offenders/alleged offenders with intellectual disabilities?

Little is known about the particular characteristics of offenders and alleged offenders with intellectual disabilities. The available literature, however, suggests that, in common with 'mainstream' offenders (see Gunn & Taylor, 1993), they will be young and, overwhelmingly, men (e.g. Borthwick-Duffy, 1994; Thompson, 1997b). The men, in particular, are likely to have been identified as having behavioural difficulties in childhood. Additionally, men, at least, are likely to have had childhood backgrounds characterised not only by chronic financial disadvantage but also by instability (Richardson, Koller & Katz, 1985). In many cases, this does not merely involve loss (such as the absence of a parent), but also placements (often multiple) away from their families of origin and extended families (Richardson, Koller & Katz, 1985). The disruption of sustaining relationships with adults in a 'parenting' role and the feelings of instability generated by unwanted separations are likely to have a particular effect on those with intellectual disabilities: studies consistently show that intellectual competence is a protective factor for children who experience chronic adversity (Garmezy & Masten, 1994).

In addition, like other people with intellectual disabilities, offenders and alleged offenders are at greater risk than their counterparts in the general population of limited opportunities for, and success in maintaining, friendships during childhood (Guralnick, 1997; Murphy, 1992). Some times, this is a result of social impairments, such as autism or Asperger's syndrome (Howlin, 1997). Such experiences increase the vulnerability to developing unusual styles of attachment, limiting the possibilities for supportive relationships in adulthood (Feeney & Noller, 1996). Not surprisingly, as adults, people with intellectual difficulties may also be more likely to experience mental health problems, including psychiatric disorders (Holland & Murphy, 1990; see also Chapter 12).

GENERAL PRINCIPLES OF ASSESSMENT AND TREATMENT OF THE PERSON AND MANAGEMENT OF FURTHER OFFENDING/ALLEGED OFFENDING

Assessment

The purpose of the assessment is to understand the behaviour and the context in which it occurs in order to minimise the risk of re-occurrence.

Background to assessment

Sometimes the outcome of a police investigation has implications for assessment and treatment (e.g. if a Probation Order with a condition of 'psychiatric treatment' or a Hospital Order under Section 37 of the *Mental Health Act 1983* is made—see Chapter 5). At other times there are no such implications, even when the person has accepted that he/ she has committed an offence (e.g. when a formal caution is given by the police). In any case, on many occasions, the outcome is indefinite (e.g. because the families of alleged child victims do not wish them to go to Court). In these circumstances, the person may need encouragement to participate in assessment and treatment since there will be no legal sanction if he/she does not participate. Often, alleged offenders are very reluctant to discuss their challenging behaviour. Perkins (1991) suggests that praise, persuasion, and an awareness that the therapist is able to detect evasion and side-stepping are likely to be helpful, and they may all be necessary at times. In addition, it may be possible to assist the person to acknowledge that there is some area in which 'help' might be useful, and to work from there towards the behaviour which constitutes the alleged offence. Even where the person is unwilling to accept any assistance, work can still be carried out with him/her and with carers to reduce the risk of re-offending by providing a framework for minimising the possibility of further allegations and ensuring a consistent response if they do occur.

Before carrying out any assessment, there are a number of issues which need to be addressed (see summary in Figure 9.1). Some particular matters are discussed in more detail below.

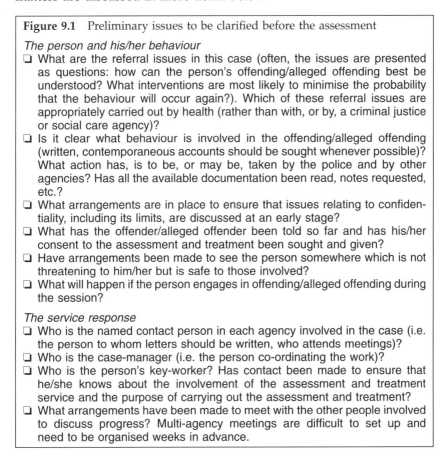

Figure 9.1   Preliminary issues to be clarified before the assessment

The person and his/her behaviour
❏ What are the referral issues in this case (often, the issues are presented as questions: how can the person's offending/alleged offending best be understood? What interventions are most likely to minimise the probability that the behaviour will occur again?). Which of these referral issues are appropriately carried out by health (rather than with, or by, a criminal justice or social care agency)?
❏ Is it clear what behaviour is involved in the offending/alleged offending (written, contemporaneous accounts should be sought whenever possible)? What action has, is to be, or may be, taken by the police and by other agencies? Has all the available documentation been read, notes requested, etc.?
❏ What arrangements are in place to ensure that issues relating to confidentiality, including its limits, are discussed at an early stage?
❏ What has the offender/alleged offender been told so far and has his/her consent to the assessment and treatment been sought and given?
❏ Have arrangements been made to see the person somewhere which is not threatening to him/her but is safe to those involved?
❏ What will happen if the person engages in offending/alleged offending during the session?

The service response
❏ Who is the named contact person in each agency involved in the case (i.e. the person to whom letters should be written, who attends meetings)?
❏ Who is the case-manager (i.e. the person co-ordinating the work)?
❏ Who is the person's key-worker? Has contact been made to ensure that he/she knows about the involvement of the assessment and treatment service and the purpose of carrying out the assessment and treatment?
❏ What arrangements have been made to meet with the other people involved to discuss progress? Multi-agency meetings are difficult to set up and need to be organised weeks in advance.

Ethical issues

For adults (i.e. those aged 18 years or more), consent to assessment and treatment *must* be sought from the person him/herself (see Chapter 5; Murphy & Clare, 1997); no one can 'give consent' on his/her behalf. If the person is *able* to consent but does not do so, then his/her decision must be respected. The most important exception relates to treatment for a mental disorder under the *Mental Health Act 1983* (see Chapter 5; Jones, 1996). However, if an adult is *unable* to consent (e.g. because of the severity of his/her intellectual impairment), then any intervention must be 'necessary' for the person's life, health and well- being and in his/ her 'best interests' (see British Medical Association & The Law Society, 1995; Murphy & Clare, 1997). Where a decision is made to carry out an intervention with a person who assessment suggests does not have the capacity to consent, the health care professional should consult with colleagues and others involved in the person's life, and both the decision and the discussions leading to it must be documented fully.

In practice, there is little direct psychological work that can be carried out without the individual's co-operation. Sometimes, though, the person is co-operative but divulges information, particularly about embarrassing material or further behaviour which may constitute an offence, which he/she asks not to be shared. Frequently, the person also asks that notes are not taken. He/she needs to be aware that confidentiality cannot be restricted to a single person and that those members of the multi-agency team who are directly involved in assessment, treatment and management will have access to all the information (as suggested by Department of Health & Home Office, 1992); it is unwise to keep information from other team members who have a 'need to know'. However, any further sharing should not be considered without taking into account the British Psychological Society's comprehensive guidelines for professional practice for clinical psychologists (British Psychological Society, 1995) and the ethical guidelines for forensic psychologists (British Psychological Society, 1997). The advice of other members of the team involved should also always be sought; if necessary, legal advice may be needed.

A written agreement (or videotape, if this is better suited to the person's abilities) should be made with the person so that he/she is clear about information sharing. A model is provided by the 'agreement of non-confidentiality' (Salter, 1998, p. 263), which can be adapted. Signed copies (or an equivalent, if another medium has been used) should be held by each of the agencies involved.

Areas of assessment

It has been suggested (Murphy, 1997a) that assessment involves three stages, not all of which need to be carried out together or by the same person:

❏ The initial investigation of the alleged incident (for the purposes of this chapter, we shall assume this has been completed).
❏ The assessment of the day and residential services (if any) the person currently receives (the principles here are similar to those widely used for people with intellectual disabilities (see, in particular, McGill & Toogood, 1994), and will not be discussed in detail here).
❏ The assessment of the individual.

In 'mainstream' forensic work, the dominant psychological approach to assessment is cognitive-behavioural. This is an adaptation of a basic behavioural model (described in Emerson, 1995, and Chapter 8). It includes the person's interpretations of his/her experiences (i.e. thoughts, feelings and beliefs) as part of the 'functional analysis' (Carr, 1994; Owens & Ashcroft, 1982) on which the formulation and subsequent treatment are based (see Kirk, 1989). In most areas of clinical practice, the research literature would be used as a basis for selecting topics relevant to the person's particular difficulty for use in the assessment. However, the literature relating to people with intellectual disabilities who have, or are alleged to have, committed offences is very limited (see below under specific types of offences). Taken together with the complexity of assessment and treatment, this means that the assessment needs to be very broad-based in order to produce information on the background of the person, his/her present functioning, and the behaviour which constitutes the offence/alleged offence.

The information needed is summarised in Figure 9.2. The material is obtained using the established methods of *self-report, reports from others, behavioural observations,* and *archival data.* However, there are some differences between work with people who have, or are alleged to have, committed offences, and other individuals with intellectual disabilities and challenging behaviour. First, since it is usual for people to have expressive language and relatively good comprehension (although these skills are very often over-estimated by carers), self-report measures such as interviews and questionnaires are used very frequently. It is clear that, when they are interviewed properly (Chapter 6; Bull, 1995), people with intellectual disabilities are perfectly well able to provide information about themselves and their experiences, thoughts and feelings (Atkinson, 1988). This is especially the case when concrete assistance is given (e.g. a choice of pictures of emotions: Benson, 1996; Murphy & Clare, 1991; Murphy, Estien & Clare, 1996). Nevertheless, as in all forensic work,

Figure 9.2   Information required for an assessment of alleged offending or offending

Background
❏ Developmental history, particularly:
  – 'Milestones'
  – Imaginative play, communication, social interaction
❏ Social history, particularly:
  – Periods away from biological family
  – Physical/sexual/emotional abuse
  – Bereavements
  – Past and present intimate and significant relationships
  – Friendships and social networks
❏ Medical and psychiatric history, particularly:
  – Periods in hospital for physical or mental health problems
  – Response to treatment in the community
❏ Forensic history, including allegations *but their status must be made clear.*
  – Witness statements wherever possible
  – Transcripts (and, if possible, tapes) of formal police interviews (often obtainable through the person's solicitor)
  – Level of violence used
  – Degree of planning
  – Responses to treatment and/or management

The person
❏ Mental health needs
❏ Cognitive skills, particularly:
  – Global intellectual ability
  – Executive functioning (i.e. the processes underlying goal-directed behaviour, Pennington & Ozonoff, 1996)
❏ Communication:
  – Understanding of single words, sentences and concepts (verbally and through other systems of communication)
  – Verbal and other means of expression
❏ Life skills—daily living skills; particular strengths; interests
❏ Other challenging behaviours (apart from the offending/alleged offending)
❏ Coping strategies
❏ Thoughts, feelings, beliefs about past experiences, the present and the future

This offence/alleged offence and any previous ones
❏ Antecedents, behaviour, consequences—both what happened and the person's thoughts, feelings and beliefs relating to each. To include:
  – Interests (excitement resulting from the behaviour; fantasies; planning and use of subterfuge)
  – Knowledge about the behaviour (whether it is against the law, its possible consequences for him/her)
  – Setting conditions (arguments with others, alcohol/drug intake, life events)
  – How the victim (if any) was selected (to include 'stalking' and 'grooming')

– Attitudes (beliefs about the impact of the behaviour on others; the extent to which victims 'deserved' the behaviour); whether the consequence was desired (e.g. in a physical assault which was interrupted by staff, was the person pleased to be stopped, or resentful that he/she did not succeed in injuring the victim?)

Also

❏ Details of times when the person felt like committing an offence but did not

particular care is needed in interviews. This is partly because the person may be very reluctant to admit to his/her part in what has or is alleged to have happened, and partly because, by the time the person is seen for assessment and treatment, he/she has often had to give an account of the same event(s) on many occasions (e.g. to the police, a solicitor, clinical psychologists and psychiatrists preparing reports for the Court). Since all interviews are social interactions, almost inevitably the account becomes 'shaped'. It is very important to try to counteract or at least minimise this process (see Bull, 1995, for very helpful guidance). Assisting the person to provide his/her account in a different way (such as through explaining drawings or other visual material related to the event) may help. Provided that the person consents, it can be useful to audiotape interviews, since this allows the interviewer to concentrate fully on the conversation (Rapley & Antaki, 1996). Similarly, it can be useful to have two interviewers so that each has more time to think about what he/she is saying.

In 'mainstream' forensic work, self-report measures relating to specific offences have been developed to supplement interview data. Unfortunately, with few exceptions, these are unsuitable for people with intellectual disabilities because they:

❏ Require reading skills the person may not have; if read out, they make very high demands on verbal memory. People with intellectual disabilities usually have poorer verbal memories than their counterparts in the general population (Clare & Gudjonsson, 1993).
❏ Use long sentences, unusual words or abstract concepts, or refer to experiences which are unlikely to be familiar to people with intellectual disabilities.
❏ Use four- or five-point rating scales which are too complex.

In any case, there are rarely norms for people with intellectual disabilities. Nevertheless, these self-report measures can still be used as a source of ideas about areas in which information needs to be obtained.

The balance of reports from others and of archival data is different from that usually encountered in work with people with challenging behaviour. Very heavy use is made of archival data. In part, this is so that a detailed history of offending and alleged offending can be obtained. There are a number of reasons why this is useful: (a) the extent of previous offending is a predictor of (poor) outcome; (b) since much of the behaviour of interest is infrequent (Dockrell et al., 1992), it is often difficult for the person him/herself to recall previous occasions on which it occurred; and (c) since it is not unusual, particularly in poorly-resourced and developed local services, for the person to experience multiple placement changes, current paid carers often have very limited information about the past. Whilst often not sufficiently recognised or acknowledged by health care providers, it is now accepted (Department of Health, 1996) that, where it is possible to contact them, families provide an invaluable long-term perspective on the person and his/her difficulties.

In contrast with assessments with people with more severe disabilities, behavioural observations are carried out infrequently with individuals who have, or are alleged to have, committed offences. In part, this is because the behaviours in question are often infrequent. Moreover, there are, of course, practical and ethical problems in setting up situations (such as experimental analogues) which might increase the possibility of offending, and any such strategies could only be implemented after careful consideration by the agencies involved. Nevertheless, given the uncertainty which often surrounds challenging behaviour, particularly when it takes place outside the home, such observations are often essential. Consistent with a cognitive-behavioural approach, it is important to learn about the person's thoughts and feelings during, or as soon as possible after, the experience.

Formulation

Formulation, the *provisional* summary which integrates the available information to provide (a) an understanding of the way in which the person's offending or alleged offending has developed and been maintained, and (b) the rationale for the interventions, is essential in order to clarify the issues for both the treatment provider and others involved (including the offender/alleged offender). In contrast with work on intellectual disabilities (e.g. Clare et al., 1992; Mattaini, 1995; Murphy, 1994), very little has been written about formulations in 'mainstream' forensic work. Flow-charts, rather than written formulations, appear to be particularly helpful because:

❏ A large amount of information, derived from complex assessments by different agencies with different perspectives, can be integrated, with the process of integration itself helping the team to develop a co-ordinated plan of intervention.

❑ They provide a clear focus for the intervention, keeping the team 'on track' during what is often a long and complicated, process.

❑ The expected impact of specific interventions in assisting the person is clear, allowing evaluation to be planned more easily.

❑ A visual format is more accessible to people with intellectual disabilities and their carers, encouraging a partnership.

Whilst the precise style of a formulation will depend on the theoretical backgrounds of the people involved, the style is generally likely to have historical information at the top, working downwards chronologically to the offending/alleged offending and its maintaining factors, with arrows implying causal and not just temporal connections. An example, summarising our understanding of Mr A.'s difficulties, is shown below in the case example (see Figure 9.3).

Treatment of the individual and management of further offending/alleged offending

The nature of the intervention will depend on the formulation. Almost always, successful interventions will involve a range of components: educational, psychological, pharmacological, supportive and practical. Some of the components will be general, and would be used by all kinds of people with all kinds of difficulties (e.g. coping strategies for dealing with feelings of distress, Lindsay, Neilson & Lawrenson, 1997); a few will be specific to the particular nature of the person's behaviour (see below). Whatever the particular combination, a successful intervention is likely to involve three main types of components:

❑ Lifestyle changes, based around O'Brien's (1987, cited in Emerson, 1992; see also Chapter 1) five accomplishments to improve the quality of life and combat feelings of helplessness.

❑ Direct treatment with the person, both on his/her own and often also in a group, to address the particular difficulties which contribute to the person's behaviour. Some of this treatment will involve methods used in mainstream 'forensic' work but it is likely to require adaptations so that it is:

(a) Simpler (e.g. using a single scene rather than a hierarchy in covert sensitisation (Maletzky, 1974, see Clare et al., 1992).

(b) More concrete, by providing photographs (Clare et al., 1992) or symbols.

(c) Presented visually rather than in text.

(d) Repeated, encouraging the person to use his/her own words.

Figure 9.3 Formulation of Mr A's difficulties, and summary of the interventions. The formulation is shown by the boxes and arrows; the italics show the interventions and their intended effect.

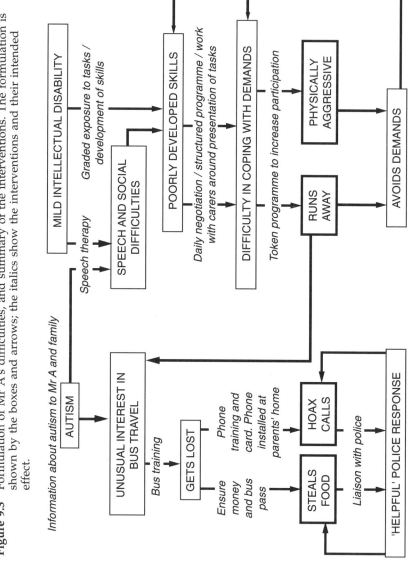

and also . . .

(e) Uses materials which are associated with being valued (e.g. a personal stereo for relaxation tapes; a pager rather than a 'cue card' to remind a person to carry out particular tasks).

(f) Is presented in a way which is associated with valued 'ordinary activities' and adult status (Murphy, Estien & Clare, 1996).

❏ Prevention and management of further offending/alleged offending. Whilst there is not enough space to discuss this component here (for details, see e.g. various chapters in Churchill et al., 1997), prevention and management require identification of the characteristics of the person and his/her victims, and of the situations in which further difficulties are most and least likely to occur; a strategy to minimise offending/alleged offending then has to be devised.

A framework for these overlapping and interlinking components is provided by the model for the organisation of proactive and reactive intervention strategies proposed by LaVigna, Willis & Donnellan (1989) and already widely used in work with people with intellectual disabilities.

In work with offenders and alleged offenders, there are two particular issues which need to be addressed: working with paid carers, and the impact on practitioners.

Working with paid carers

It is very frequently the case that paid carers will be resentful about the time and attention which the person receives as a result of his/her behaviour (see also McBrien & Candy, Chapter 15); families seem to be much more accepting (see Bromley, Chapter 14). There is no short-cut to listening to carers, acknowledging the difficulties they often face, and involving them as far as can be managed without breaching the person's right to confidentiality. In addition to working with the offender/alleged offender on his/her own and/or in a group, we encourage three-way sessions to enable the person to feed back to his/her key-worker. We have also found it helpful to:

❏ Explain repeatedly the rationale for working with the person. It is important to avoid unrealistic expectations ('You've seen the person for six weeks and he's no better') by providing information about the work which is being carried out and its (often) long-term nature.

❏ Ensure that victims and alleged victims (including carers) receive support and assistance from members of the team who are *not* working with the alleged offender (individually and/or as a group).

❏ Ensure that all carers in day-activity and residential placements understand through their managers (who, with the key-worker, should be members of the multi-agency team) precisely what has been agreed by all the agencies involved, to minimise the possibility that the behaviour will happen again and to respond if it is suspected or known to have taken place. These agreements should be in the form of written guidelines. Carers in direct contact with the person should be consulted during the drafting of these guidelines and the final version should be accessible to all carers, both physically and in terms of its language and content.

Impact on practitioners

Whilst in recent years there has been a major increase in the number of health care professionals wishing to work with offenders and alleged offenders with intellectual disabilities, the 'emotional' impact on practitioners is rarely discussed. Similarly, little attention has been given to the fact that those practitioners are mostly women, at least in the junior grades of clinical psychology (Nicolson, 1992) and other health care professions, who are mainly working with men. The health care practitioner (or carer) may develop strong conflicting feelings towards the person—anger at his/her behaviour (particularly when it victimises a vulnerable person), combined with pity and compassion as the frequently harrowing details of his/her life become known. These feelings can become intense because the work is very demanding and does not fit with standard working hours. In addition, the consequences of 'failure' can be very difficult—for the person him/herself as well as for any victims. Moreover, increasingly, therapeutic work has to be carried out in a context which is openly hostile to the treatment of convicted or alleged offenders, particularly within a community setting; for practitioners, the personal and professional costs of failure may therefore also be substantial (for further consideration of these issues, see e.g. Stanley, 1996; West, 1996).

In this area of work, it is particularly important to:

❏ Have good supervision, with opportunities to discuss personal issues raised by the person's behaviour (see also Chapter 1).
❏ Have opportunities to discuss the case with practitioners who are not directly involved. If this cannot be done anonymously, the person's consent must be sought;
❏ Liaise very closely with other members of the multi-agency team (co-working is very helpful; if this is not possible, ensure that at least a proportion of visits are carried out jointly).
❏ Ensure that documents and records are up-to-date and accessible, not only in the healthcare records but also in the records of other agencies

involved. Normally, we write a letter after every meeting with, or substantive telephone call to, each person involved with the offender/ alleged offender, summarising what has been discussed and agreed. Copies are sent to all other members of the multi-agency team involved to ensure that everyone is aware, and has the same understanding, of what has taken place.

❏ Be realistic about what can be achieved, particularly over a period of months rather than years.

WORKING WITH SPECIFIC OFFENCES

With the exception of some individual case studies and descriptions of group treatments, there are few published data on any aspect of assessment and treatment involving this group of persons; controlled or comparison studies are virtually unknown. Similarly, very few outcome data are available.

Sexual offending

Despite assertions (mainly based on Walker & McCabe's (1973) study of people detained in hospital under the *Mental Health Act, 1959*), there is very little evidence that people with intellectual disabilities commit a disproportionate number of sexual offences. However, as in the general population, there are people who engage in sexual activities with others who do not, or cannot, consent. Overwhelmingly, these perpetrators are men (Thompson & Brown, 1997).

In work with people who have, or are alleged to have, committed sex offences, it is important for treatment providers themselves to understand the legislation relating to sex, including those parts which are specific to people with intellectual disabilities. The relevant law is explained well in Gunn (1996). In addition, in carrying out assessment and treatment, clinical experience and the very extensive experience of many of those who practice in 'mainstream' forensic settings suggests that it is important to consider a wide range of issues (for more detail, see Maletzky, 1991; Salter, 1988: Morrison, Erooga & Beckett, 1994, in particular, provide an excellent account). It should be noted that virtually all this work derives from men who have, or are alleged to have, committed sexual offences; knowledge and experience of women is extremely limited.

At least the following should be addressed:

❏ *Attachment and intimacy* (for guidance about interventions, see Marshall et al., 1996), and *informal social networks* (see O'Connor, 1996).

❏ *Consent*: the materials devised for people with intellectual disabilities by McCarthy and Thompson (1998) are particularly useful.

❏ *Sexual knowledge* (Kempton, 1988; McCarthy & Thompson, 1998). Whilst it is rarely the case that men with mild intellectual disabilities engage in illegal sexual behaviour because of a lack of understanding of the technical aspects of sexual knowledge, the possibility needs to be excluded.

❏ *Consenting sexual experience.* Compared with students, men and women with mild intellectual disabilities are less likely to report a range of sexual experiences or experiences of closeness (McCabe & Cummins, 1996).

❏ *Sexual abuse.* Compared with students, men and women with mild intellectual abilities report *at least* as much sexual abuse (McCabe & Cummins, 1996). Since they have a more limited awareness of concepts relating to abuse (McCabe & Cummins, 1996), this is likely to be an underestimate of their experience.

❏ *The laws relating to sexual behaviour.* Even men with mild intellectual disabilities can be unsure about, for example, legal locations for sexual activity, reliable ways to judge age (Briggs, Hickey & Jones, 1996; Charman & Clare, 1992).

❏ *Sexual interests and fantasies* (the scales, such as Wilson's Sexual Fantasy Questionnaire, given in Salter, 1988, will need to be adapted).

❏ *Cognitive distortions* (again, the scales, such as Abel & Becker's Cognitions Scale, given in Salter, 1988, will need to be adapted) and victim empathy.

❏ *Social skills and assertiveness* (Beckett, 1994), focusing not only on behaviour but also on underlying skills (Dodge & Murphy, 1984; see Clare, 1993).

❏ *Denial and motivation to change* (see Beckett, 1994).

❏ *Ability to generalise from treatment sessions* (see O'Connor, 1996) and maintenance of treatment progress (see Beckett, 1994).

However, it must be stressed that, contrary to the approach sometimes adopted in 'mainstream' forensic work, the assessment of the individual is paramount (see Mr T. and Mr B.; Murphy, 1997b). As yet, there is no evidence that the established models of the development and process of sex offending (see Fisher, 1994) are applicable to people with intellectual disabilities. Similarly, there is also remarkably little evidence that methods which are well-established with sex offenders/alleged offenders in the general population, such as cognitive-behavioural group treatment, are effective. In working with alleged and actual sexual offences, there fore, practitioners need to be particularly aware of the need to use risk management at the same time as direct treatment (see Maletzky, 1991; Murphy, 1997b, c).

Fire-setting

It has now been shown that the belief that people with intellectual disabilities are disproportionately likely to set fires is unfounded (Gunn & Taylor, 1993). Rather, since fire-setters of all kinds are particularly likely to receive Hospital Orders under the *Mental Health Act 1983* and comprise 12% of those subject to an additional Restriction Order (Section 41 of the MHA, 1983), fire-setters with intellectual disabilities are over- represented in hospitals, especially secure hospitals.

Traditionally, there has been little interest in a psychological analysis of the possible motivation for fire-setting in adults or the provision of individual psychological treatment. Recently, two preliminary measures have been devised:

❑ *Fire Assessment Schedule* (FAS) (Murphy, 1990) a preliminary structured interview schedule to examine people's own views of the antecedents and consequences of their fire-setting. This comprises 32
   statements: 16, ordered randomly, relate to the frequency ('usually',
   'sometimes' or 'never') with which eight events, feelings or cognitions
   (excitement, anxiety, low social attention, low social approval from
   peers, presence of auditory hallucinations, depression, anger, and
   avoidance of demands/aversive events) are self-reported retrospectively as antecedents to fire-setting; the remaining 16 randomly
   ordered statements relate to the frequency with which these events,
   feelings or cognitions are self-reported as consequences. The schedule
   has reasonable test–retest reliability, which suggests that it may be
   useful as part of a fire-setting assessment, at least for those with good
   verbal skills who are able to label their emotions. It may be that
   the 'antecedents' part of the schedule will be more useful than the
   'consequences' part, since people seem to find it easier to report what
   happens prior to, rather than following, fire-setting (Murphy & Clare,
   1996). From initial studies, it appears that an individual's fire-setting
   often reflects a number of motivations; it may be simplistic to look
   for 'the' reason.
❑ *Fire Interest Rating Scale* (FIRS) (Murphy, 1990) fourteen descriptions
   of fire-related situations (e.g. watching a house burn down; watching
   an ordinary coal fire in a house), which the person is asked to rate
   (from 'very exciting, lovely, very nice' to 'most upsetting, absolutely
   horrible'). Interestingly, with the exception of the item about a coal-
   fire in a house (which the fire-setters rated as more exciting), there
   were no significant differences between the ratings of people with
   mild intellectual disabilities who had, or had not, engaged in fire-
   setting (Murphy & Clare, 1996). Nevertheless, in at least one sample
   of people who had been convicted of arson, there were a few indi-

viduals who obtained unusually high scores on the FIRS and who also identified the excitement of the fire as one of their motivations in the FAS (see above). This suggests that 'interest in fires' (so-called 'pyromania') may be important for some individuals, although, even for them, it may be only part of the motivation for setting fires.

Despite these advances in assessment, there remain few treatment studies. One example, based on a functional analysis, is described in Clare et al. (1992). As might be expected, much of the treatment (e.g. relaxation, coping strategies, assertiveness, social skills, day-activities and employment) did not relate *specifically* to the person's fire-setting but addressed psychological difficulties thought to increase his vulnerability to the behaviour. In contrast, other strategies (graded exposure to matches, contact with appropriate fires, covert sensitisation) were aimed specifically at his history of very serious fires. Almost nine years after leaving an in-patient service, there has been no recurrence of the fire-setting or hoax phone calls. The person now lives in his own flat and has been in paid employment.

Aggression

As there has been more emphasis on working *with* people with intellectual disabilities, self-management skills have developed increasing importance (see Cullen, 1993; Stenfert Kroese, Dagnan & Loumidis, 1997; Zarkowska & Clements, 1994, for very good practical accounts). Self-management has been particularly clearly described in accounts of anger-management.

Whilst the assessment of difficulties relating to anger in people with intellectual disabilities is most fully described in Black, Cullen & Novaco (1997), the most developed programme for anger-management training is probably that of Benson (an excellent practical description is given in Benson, 1992, summarised in Benson, 1994). The training normally takes place in a group format, with people with mild intellectual disabilities who are verbal and able to use a pictorial self-report inventory of the extent to which they are bothered by different situations (e.g. 'being blamed for something which is not your fault'; 'you start to tell someone a joke and you forget how it goes').

The programme has four components:

❑ *Identification of feelings*, using photographs, drawings, or videotapes of television programmes; and monitoring of mood (using anger diaries, see Benson, 1996; Murphy & Clare, 1991) between sessions, often carried out with carers. It is important that the person is allowed to

record his/her *own* feelings, rather than those which others think he/
she should have.

❏ *Relaxation training*, normally using a standard tension-release method
(see Clark, 1989; see also Chapters 10 and 12).

❏ *Self-instructional training*, largely through role-play of difficult situations which have arisen during the week, focusing on developing
'coping' statements and decreasing 'trouble' statements.

❏ *Problem-solving*, involving finding solutions for anticipated problems.
Compared with their counterparts who do not have any problems
relating to aggression, aggressive men with mild intellectual disabilities are more likely to generate aggressive solutions to problems
and to give an aggressive solution first (Fuchs & Benson, 1995). The
implication is that it is helpful for people to have a way of inhibiting
an angry response. They also need to practise alternative, more appropriate, responses. Normally, these tasks are carried out through role-
playing difficult situations.

Benson (1992), working with adults with intellectual disabilities who
attend an out-patient clinic, describes a 15-session programme. Our
clinical experience is that, even for people who are living in the community, this is far too short (26 weeks, followed by 'booster' sessions, is
more realistic).

Unfortunately, with the exception of three group studies (Benson,
Johnson Rice & Miranti, 1986; Cullen, 1993; Moore et al., 1997), and a
few case studies (described in Black, Cullen & Novaco, 1997), little is
known about the effectiveness of anger-management for people with
intellectual disabilities. Nevertheless, it is probably the intervention of
choice where it seems likely that the aggression is hostile rather than
operant (Geen, 1990), although the treatment provider needs to bear in
mind the possibility that both operant and broader cognitive-behavioural
techniques may be necessary (Murphy, 1993; Murphy, 1997d; see also
Chapters 10 and 12).

CASE EXAMPLE

Some of the points made in this chapter are illustrated by Mr A's history
and experiences. He comes from a financially disadvantaged but very
close family. In childhood, his mother noticed he was 'odd', particularly
in his lack of interest in his peers, resistance to changes in his routine,
and unusual interests, and sought professional advice. She was told that
he was just 'slow'.

Mr A was repeatedly expelled from schools because of his aggression and running away. Eventually, although he has mild intellectual disabilities, he was moved to a school for much more disabled children because it was more closely supervised. Later, as a young adult, he ran away from his day-centre. Mr A. was alleged to steal food from shops, but never charged by the police. He also made numerous hoax 999 calls, often from places miles from his home. He would wait at the phone box for the police. Since he looks and sounds unusual, he was easily identifiable as a vulnerable person. Normally, the police took him home.

For a while, Mr A's parents kept him at home and tried to help him live as an 'ordinary' adult. However, when he was asked to help in any way, he was aggressive and ran off. In desperation, his parents locked him in. He was referred to a specialist in-patient service for understanding of his:

❑ Running away.
❑ Physical aggression.
❑ Food stealing.
❑ Hoax telephone calls.

From detailed assessments, the formulation in Figure 9.3 was devised: it appeared that, in addition to his mild intellectual disability, Mr A was a person with autism. His skills were limited and he found it difficult to cope with any 'demands'. Instead, he would try to leave, if possible by taking a bus, since buses were a particular interest. If prevented, he would be aggressive. Either way, he avoided tasks, but this meant that his skills remained poor.

Although it appeared, from talking with him, that Mr A knew all about buses (time-tables, routes, etc.), behavioural observations showed that his practical knowledge was poor and he often got lost. It was presumed that he stole food because he was hungry. Certainly, the hoax calls to the police seemed to be a coping strategy to enable him to return home.

The italics in Figure 9.3 summarise the interventions carried out by the specialist service with members of his local service. Since Mr A was 'at risk' when he ran away, he was detained under the Mental Health Act (1983). However, he was given leave of absence each day, and then for increasingly long periods, so that work could be carried out with him in his area of origin. In terms of the framework developed by LaVigna, Willis & Donnellan (1989), the interventions included:

❑ *Ecological manipulations* (e.g. graded exposure to tasks; negotiation with him about what were reasonable expectations to help him feel more in control of his life; a structured programme with bus trips scheduled regularly).

❏ *Positive programming* (e.g. helping him use the telephone to ring his parents and other members of his family; skills training).
❏ *Direct treatment* (e.g. token programme, linked to outings to places of particular interest to encourage Mr A. to take part in the skills training).
❏ *Reactive strategies* (e.g. for his food stealing and hoax calls, helping the police in his area recognise that, whilst he was 'vulnerable' and would need the special provision for suspects under the *Police and Criminal Evidence Act 1984*, if he were arrested—see above—it was not appropriate to ignore his alleged offending).

After leaving the specialist service, Mr A went to live in a hostel in his area of origin, attended a local college, and remained in close contact with his family. For almost two years, there were no difficulties. There was no evidence of stealing, and running away and physical aggression were rare. Hoax calls were reported on only one occasion (when he had been out travelling on a bus but had no phone card). Consistent with the agreed strategy, he was charged by the police, went to court and was conditionally discharged; there was no repetition.

However, since he was 'doing well', Mr A was obliged to move to another hostel to meet the needs of the service; shortly after, he had to move again, once more because the service 'needed' his place. As might have been predicted, he became very aggressive. Subsequently, he was excluded from both his day and residential placements. Mr A was moved to an 'out-of-county' independent service. He reported that he was not happy, ran away constantly, and was known to have made dozens of hoax telephone calls to the emergency services. His key-worker at the time reported that she had deliberately chosen not to read anything about the work carried out in the specialist service because she thought it might influence her relationship with him. Attempts by his district of origin to obtain local support were unsuccessful. Eventually, the police charged Mr A with making hoax calls; he was convicted and, for a short period, imprisoned.

Mr A returned to the out-of-county service, with his district of origin providing health care support from a distance. He became more settled and moved from a large establishment to a group home within the same service. Still, five years after discharge from the specialist service, Mr A is living many miles from his local area and his contact with his family remains more limited than he, or they, would like.

This example illustrates that, even where a good understanding of a person's offending/alleged offending has been developed, and interventions introduced which appear to be effective, long-term success is far from assured. The provision of social care which recognises that offenders/alleged offenders are likely to remain vulnerable and need continuing support, even when they are doing well, is often crucial.

CONCLUSIONS

Work with people with intellectual disabilities who have, or are alleged to have, committed criminal offences remains in a preliminary form. There is some evidence that the models of multi-factorial, individualised, assessment, formulation and intervention, developed in other work with people with 'challenging behaviour', are useful for this population, although intervening in cognitions and emotions necessarily forms a larger part of the work. However, the outcome data are limited. At this stage, careful descriptions of single cases would be useful, based on clear relationships between assessment and treatment, with detailed accounts of the legal framework and multi-agency involvement which forms the context in which successful work is carried out and maintained, and with an acknowledgment of the need to balance the rights of alleged offenders and victims. Such descriptions are particularly needed for interventions carried out in the community.

FURTHER READING

Churchill, J., Brown, H., Craft, A., & Horrocks, C. (1997). *There Are No Easy Answers! The Provision of Continuing Care and Treatment to Adults with Learning Disabilities Who Sexually Abuse Others*. ARC/NAPSAC: Chesterfield.

Conley, R.W., Luckasson, R., & Bouthilet, G.N. (1992). *The Criminal Justice System and Mental Retardation: Defendants and Victims*. Paul Brookes: Baltimore, MD.

Cordess, C. & Cox, M. (1996). *Forensic Psychotherapy. Crime, Psychodynamics and the Offender Patient. Vol. I, Mainly Theory; Vol. II, Mainly Practice*. Jessica Kingsley: London.

ACKNOWLEDGEMENTS

We are grateful to 'Mr A' for giving his consent to the inclusion of the material about his experiences, and to his family for their support whilst we were seeking his consent. The work carried out with Mr A owes much to the contributions of Ms Rachel Archer, Dr Hedley Harnett, and Dr Tony Holland; we are grateful to all of them, and to Mr Peter McGill for assistance in refining our formulation.

Chapter 10

WORKING WITH ISSUES OF SEXUAL ABUSE

*Jude Moss**

INTRODUCTION

The attitudes and beliefs that society has about its intellectually disabled members have been reflected in, and in turn have supported, the denial and abuse of many of their human rights (see Chapters 1 and 4). Despite an increasingly powerful advocacy movement, it has taken many years for society's attitudinal 'selective deafness' to lift and to hear people with intellectual disabilities talking about the reality of abuse. Gradually we have been forced to 'think the unthinkable' (Brown & Craft, 1989).

Over time we have begun to recognise physically and emotionally abusive regimes of 'care'. Awareness of sexual abuse has been slower. This may reflect more subtle and pervasive beliefs about the sexual nature of people with intellectual disabilities, who are often treated as asexual, yet regarded as sexually dangerous.

Issues relating to definition

Defining what constitutes sexual abuse is complex. Definitions need to be relevant and helpful to those who use them. Brown, Turk & Stein (1994) defined sexual abuse as 'one-off assaults or sexual acts within an ongoing relationship in which the power differences are so great that they preclude the possibility of the person with learning difficulties freely giving their consent'. They outline the acts that might be involved, from non-contact abuse to vaginal or anal intercourse. They also note that, in order to decide whether a person gave consent, it is important to deter-

*Joint Service for People with Learning Disabilities, Manchester, UK

Clinical Psychology and People with Intellectual Disabilities. Edited by E. Emerson, C. Hatton, J. Bromley and A. Caine.
© 1998 John Wiley & Sons Ltd.

mine both his/her level of comprehension and whether he/she may have been under undue pressure as a result of authority, force, threat, trickery or manipulation (Brown, Turk & Stein, 1994).

Issues relating to prevalence and incidence

Determining how many people with intellectual disabilities have been subject to sexual abuse is difficult. Reported prevalence rates vary widely, reflecting, at least in part, the particular definition and methodology used. It is likely, however, that at least some of these reported rates significantly underestimate actual rates.

Prevalence

The majority of prevalence studies have attempted to determine the proportion of people with intellectual disabilities who have been sexually abused at some time in their lives. For instance, Hard and Plumb (cited in Brown, 1994) reported that, when interviewed, 83% of women and 32% of men attending a day centre stated that they had experienced sexual abuse. While studies which ask people with intellectual disabilities directly about abuse are undoubtably useful, they do rely on interviewees understanding what is being asked of them and being able and willing to recall and describe their experiences. This may be difficult for people with cognitive and communication difficulties (Brown, 1994). Other studies have estimated prevalence by different means. Cooke (1990), for example, undertook a postal survey of consultant psychiatrists who estimated that 4–5% of their intellectually disabled patients had been abused, sexual abuse being the most common form. Chamberlain et al. (1984) reported that 25% of a group of 87 young women with intellectual disabilities had a history of sexual exploitation. Finally, Elvick et al. (1990) found that more than 50% of the intellectually disabled women they studied showed strong evidence of a history of sexual abuse.

Incidence

Incidence studies have attempted to ascertain the number of new reports of sexual abuse that occur within a particular population within a specified time frame. In the Kent study (Turk & Brown, 1993), surveys were undertaken at two points in time (1989–1990 and 1991–1992) in one health authority. This is a particularly important study and the information gathered forms the basis of much current knowledge. The major findings are outlined below.

During the survey, 229 allegations of sexual abuse were recorded which, due to various levels at which reports get filtered out, probably greatly under-represented the true scale of the problem. Of these reports, 167 were strongly supported by corroborating evidence and were analysed in detail to give information on the victims, perpetrators and nature of the abuse. The proportion of male victims rose from a quarter in the first survey period to almost a half in the second. Adults of all ages and levels of disability were represented. In two-thirds of cases, penetration or attempted penetration was reported. Perpetrators were almost all male and were usually known and familiar to the victim, often in ongoing abusive relationships. Rarely was the perpetrator a total stranger; more usually perpetrators were family members, staff/volunteers and trusted adults within the community. For the largest number of victims, the perpetrator was another person with intellectual disabilities. Many of the perpetrators offended against more than one victim and most often the abuse took place within the homes of the victims or perpetrators or within a day service.

Explaining higher prevalence

Incidence and prevalence studies suggest that people with intellectual disabilities are at least as vulnerable to sexual abuse as other members of the population, and may be more so. Sobsey (1994) proposed an ecological model to explain this level of vulnerability. This emphasised the roles and interaction of macrosystems (cultural factors), exosystems (e.g. communities, institutions) and the microsystem of abuser–victim dyad. The characteristics of victim and abuser are considered below within the influences of their environmental and cultural context.

Characteristics of the victim

Vizard (1989) claimed that there were 'strong pointers in the direction of mental handicap itself being a risk factor for all forms of child abuse, including sexual abuse'. Although it is important that the factors which might increase the vulnerability of people with intellectual disabilities are recognised and addressed, this must not be misconstrued as 'blaming the victim'. A number of issues deserve consideration:

❑ *Communication*. People with intellectual disabilities are more likely to have communication problems (see Chapters 6 and 13). Even verbally skilled people may not have access to a vocabulary to describe their experience of abuse. Non-verbal methods of communication can be misunderstood, ignored or misattributed and labelled 'challenging behaviour'. People who may be isolated in terms of relationships are likely to be denied the opportunity to communicate, no matter how good their skills.

❑ *Dependence*. People who have intellectual disabilities are more likely to be dependent on other people for support. Relying on others for intimate and personal care may make them particularly vulnerable to sexual abuse.

❑ *Self-esteem*. We only protect the things we value. People with intellectual disabilities may have grown up in a culture that made it difficult for them to develop good self-esteem. They may not have been valued and may have been given powerful messages about being second-rate, 'damaged goods', having had their needs and identity ignored.

❑ *Comprehension and compliance*. Intellectually disabled people are often exposed to rules and experiences that differ from their non-disabled peers. They may learn to be compliant and may experience difficulty in comprehending the appropriateness of another's behaviour, particularly of those in powerful positions. Increased suggestibility may leave intellectually disabled people more susceptible to 'grooming' by perpetrators. Access may have been denied to education about sex, assertiveness and self-defence which would equip them with an appropriate vocabulary, information about boundaries and consent, and self-protection.

Characteristics of perpetrators

Perpetrators may actively seek out employment or contact with people with intellectual disabilities as potential victims because of the characteristics outlined above. This must be recognised in the way services employ, manage and dismiss staff, and support people with intellectual disabilities who sexually abuse. The relationship between sexuality and power is complex. It is likely that the internal inhibitory or excitatory factors that control the behaviour of perpetrators include aspects of the victim, such as their apparent lack of self-defence, the likelihood of being caught, and exposure to a culture in which there are other abuses of power. For intellectually disabled abusers there may also be difficulties in comprehending the appropriateness of sexual behaviour.

Characteristics of the environment

The cultural environment (macrosystem) in which people with intellectual disabilities live is characterised by certain beliefs and expectations that may increase their vulnerability to abuse. Thus, for example, to the extent that people with intellectual disabilities are considered not fully human, abuse may be seen as less damaging and less reprehensible. Similarly, a belief that intellectual impairments are protective against the impact of abuse may reduce inhibition of abusing among perpetrators. Beliefs that people with intellectual disabilities are either dangerous and should be segregated from society, or should themselves be protected by segregation from society, may increase exposure and vulnerability to abuse, given that sexual abuse is much more common in institutional than community settings (Sobsey, 1994).

How does sexual abuse affect people with learning disabilities?

There are a number of models that examine and explain the impact of childhood sexual abuse (see Christo, 1997, for a review). These can be helpful in considering and anticipating the effects of abuse on people with intellectual disabilities. There is only a limited amount of research available on intellectually disabled victims, but that which does exist counters the widespread belief that they are less affected by sexual abuse than other victims. Sobsey (1994), surveying the psychological sequelae of abuse, described withdrawal, behavioural difficulties and emotional distress to be common effects for intellectually disabled survivors. He noted that the absence of apparent emotional sequelae for many individuals related more to communication issues than actual lack of distress. Thus, it seems reasonable to assume that the effects of sexual abuse are similar for people with intellectual disabilities to those experienced by their non-disabled counterparts. However, there may be additional or slightly different manifestations, or effects may be compounded by other aspects of the person's disability.

The role of clinical psychology

Clinical psychologists may be able to address the issue of sexual abuse at a number of levels. In the context of Sobsey's model, intervention could be focused at:

❑ The macrosystem—addressing beliefs about people with intellectual disabilities by, for example, the behaviour we exhibit, supporting advocacy, publicising work.
❑ The exosystem—addressing the contexts in which people live. This might involve: developing policies and procedures that protect against abuse; guidance for staff about how activities and interactions should be undertaken; providing access to education about assertiveness and sexual rights; helping agencies that support survivors to develop their

services and make them accessible to people with intellectual disabilities.
❏ The microsystem—supporting individual survivors (and perpetrators) of abuse.

Although opportunities may exist at some or all of these levels, this chapter will focus primarily on work with individual survivors and their immediate support networks.

ASSESSMENT

In order to design appropriate interventions, a full assessment of the individual and the context within which he/she lives is vital. Certain issues may require an extension of the normal assessment process.

Information can be gathered in many ways and should establish:

❏ What each individual is like.
❏ Whether individuals are likely to be able to engage in a one-to-one therapeutic relationship, or whether intervention should focus on the context in which they live (this may be particularly relevant if the person has some form of autistic disorder).
❏ What their life is like.
❏ Their particular skills and difficulties.
❏ How they communicate about ideas and feelings (if they use words, what is their range of vocabulary? If they do not, do they respond to pictures, symbols, textures and objects? Do they understand or use any metaphors that can be useful in therapy?).
❏ To what degree they understand what has happened to them.
❏ Their beliefs and feelings about themselves, their sexuality and the abuse.
❏ How they have been affected and how these effects are manifested.
❏ What the most problematic aspects of the abuse are for the individual.
❏ Whether it is the individual or his/her carers seeking help.
❏ Other medical or behavioural issues that might impact on the process of therapy.

Factors relating to the context in which individuals live include:

❏ What their support networks are like.
❏ Beliefs about the individual and his/her response to the abuse.
❏ What support is already being offered or has been tried.
❏ What the most problematic aspects of the abuse are for the carers.

A clear assessment and analysis will outline the issues requiring intervention and allow a plan to be negotiated.

INTERVENTIONS

Intervening to support people with intellectual disabilities who have been abused is still in its infancy. As a result there is, as yet, little or no firm evidence regarding the efficacy of any particular approach. The following suggestions, therefore, have been drawn from clinical 'lore' and/or extrapolated from work with non-disabled survivors. The range of interventions that may prove useful can be split into:

❏ *Level 1 interventions*, which address the physical, emotional and social context in which people live.
❏ *Level 2 interventions*, which relate to the minority of people who need more specialised support to recover.

Level 1 interventions

Increase knowledge about abuse

Most carers and people with intellectual disabilities value being given information about the nature of abuse, its prevalence and effects. This helps carers to consider their practice, rectify inaccurate beliefs and contextualise policies and procedures. Carers may also feel more confident about recognising abuse and individual survivors are often relieved to realise that they are not alone.

Increase understanding of the impact of abuse

Media coverage has introduced most people to the notion of the deleterious effects of sexual abuse. Theoretical models that describe the impact of abuse are often complex and clinical psychologists can play a useful role in making this information accessible to people with intellectual disabilities and their carers.

A useful way of presenting information to carers and clients who have difficulty with complex and abstract issues has been developed by RESPOND from an original idea by Bray. The metaphor of a tree is easily understood by most people. The hidden roots of the tree symbolise abuse, providing energy for the physical and emotional manifestations. The roots are the least visible aspects. The most visible are the leaves of the tree, representing the multitude of behaviours and effects—the problems that carers may have heard of and report. The visibility of these behaviours can easily distract from recognition of the trunk and main branches, which represent core feelings—a smaller group of emotional consequences that are experienced by many survivors, including shame, guilt, rage and fear. These feelings are translated into the physical, psychological and behavioural manifestations of the leaves. If a branch is removed, energy is channelled elsewhere and new branches develop.

This metaphor can be used to describe a number of the important aspects of abuse. First, it can help carers recognise that victims tend to experience a range of effects. An individual's life experiences, relationships and beliefs will determine the overall structure of his/her 'tree'. Thus, the same event can be experienced very differently. One individual may experience a range of core feelings which result in a particular set of 'leaves'. Another may process it through entirely different structures into different behavioural effects. Second, in a context where few people support the individual survivor, they are likely to focus on addressing the most problematic or visible behaviours. The tree metaphor has value in acknowledging underlying feelings and explains why a whole range of interventions may not have helped a person get 'better' if those feelings have not been addressed.

Improving and facilitating communication

People who have limited verbal skills may express their feelings non-verbally. Sometimes, this behavioural expression may be challenging to others. As Fenwick (1994) suggests, 'One cannot help but wonder just how many people with "challenging behaviour" have been victims of sexual abuse at some time in their lives?'. It is therefore important, when working with people who do not have sophisticated speech, to help their carers 'hear' non-verbal communication. Time is rarely wasted in asking carers to consider how the individual communicates feelings, especially once they have recognised that there may be a range of emotional responses to abuse. Often carers understand the communication of physical needs, but have never had to articulate how they understand what the person is feeling. Discussing this can prove revealing for all involved and facilitate the process of communicating about emotions.

Increase understanding of the process of recovery

Clinical psychologists have a responsibility to help people to understand the process of recovery from abuse. A number of models and theories of recovery from trauma exist and it is important that carers and survivors access a model that is helpful for them. The following simple conceptualisation, based on that used by RESPOND, is often useful, as it describes a process that is not dependent on verbal or intellectual skills.

After a traumatic event a phase of numbness and disbelief is commonly followed by a period of distress, often characterised by tearfulness. Intense anger and rage, sometimes manifested by shouting, aggression or self-harm, may then occur. Gradually remembering and reminiscing allows for a process of realisation and for the person to understand the impact of the abuse. As memories are re-experienced and processed, the event is assimilated into their belief system and personal history. This gradually allows the person to move on.

Sharing a model of recovery is a vital aspect of an intervention for a number of reasons. It helps carers and survivors recognise that there is likely to be a process of recovery which may include a number of qualitatively different phases that may require different sorts of support. Without an understanding of the process, it is all too easy to perceive different feelings and behaviours as consecutive problems. This can cause increasing frustration for carers and perhaps a temptation to use stronger and stronger forms of control.

A model of recovery also suggests some of the important tasks of healing: being able to disclose and be believed; having the opportunity to describe the details of the abuse; expressing feelings and having the opportunity to think and talk about the abuse. It is often helpful to map the individual's behavioural communication relating to the various phases. When carers can appreciate current situations and anticipate the likelihood of future experiences, they can begin to think creatively and plan about how best to support the person.

It is important to explain that recovery does not necessarily progress smoothly, in any specific order or within any particular time frame. Each individual responds differently. Although some people experience recovery as clear phases, others experience feelings in a less 'ordered' fashion. Setbacks and 'stuckness' may also occur and require support. However, most people recognise the experience of recovery from trauma in their own lives, and this can facilitate a sense of solidarity between carers and the survivor. For the individual survivor it can provide a valuable sense of hope and expectation.

Prevention

The prevention of abuse should be addressed within a service through policy initiatives. However, it is important to empower each individual survivor to defend him/herself against further abuse. This may involve helping the individual and his/her carers to negotiate aspects of care such as privacy, confidentiality and how to allow the person maximum control, particularly in issues of personal care. All carers must be certain about how the person indicates 'No'. There is often value in improving a person's ability to communicate this clearly and to defend him/herself. Protection issues also include increasing opportunities for control and choice, self-advocacy and improving access to support networks.

Level 2 interventions: one-to-one therapy

Whereas most people will move naturally through the process of recovery if in a supportive environment, a minority will not and may benefit from one-to-one therapy. All interventions should be informed by an assessment which has described the individual, how he/she communicates, where he/she is in the process of recovery and outlined issues which are problematic for him/her and his/her carers. Assessment will often reveal difficulties that require a variety of interventions and it is important to reach a shared agreement about priorities. Interventions may be focused on helping a person to move through a particular aspect of recovery, may address particular effects or issues that have increased his/her vulnerability, or may aim to protect him/her from abuse in the future.

Historically, the range of therapeutic approaches used to support people with intellectual disabilities who are distressed, or whose behaviour has changed, is more limited than for other members of the population. The focus has often been on pharmacological and behavioural approaches, rather than on counselling or more emotionally-focused interventions. However, the fact that someone has an intellectual disability should not automatically lead to the rejection of the therapeutic approaches that non-disabled victims find helpful. Instead, these approaches can be adapted and redesigned to become more appropriate to the needs of survivors who have intellectual disabilities (e.g. Sinason, 1990). Such work can offer guidance and inform the clinical practice and stance of all practitioners, whatever their therapeutic orientation.

Issues to consider in one-to-one therapy

Issues which are important in therapy with non-intellectually disabled people do not lose their significance with disabled people. However, additional and slightly different issues may also require consideration.

Establishing the therapeutic relationship.   Many people with intellectual disabilities have little experience of relationships in which their emotional life is the focus. More often, their companions are either doing things to them or getting them to do things. Being asked about feelings can be unsettling and people may not know what is expected of them in response. As noted in Chapter 6, there are a number of important issues which need to be considered when interviewing a person with intellectual disabilities.

Expectations may have to be different than for non-disabled clients, where hour-long sessions once a week in a therapy room are a common arrangement. A gradual introduction to this model may overcome anxiety and allow people to accustom themselves to the experience—but more flexible arrangements can prove useful. A person with memory problems may need more regular sessions, someone who has concentration problems may need shorter sessions. For people who find it intolerable to sit in close proximity to another person, conversations may occur in other places, side by side, focusing on a shared activity.

Whatever the structure and location of meetings, it is always important that boundaries are clear (e.g. in terms of the therapist's role, time available, respect for individual privacy and needs). It is good practice to recognise the importance of consistency and stability (e.g. timing of sessions, venue). It may require creativity to make information accessible and careful thought should be given to helping the person understand the role of the relationship without the use of complex vocabulary. Careful assessment will indicate whether the person can think in terms of 'emotions', 'worries', 'bad feelings'.

Non-verbal communication. Working with people who do not use complex speech requires the use of other sources of information for communication. Everything that happens in the therapy room can provide important material, and the lack of verbal communication often makes it easier to interpret a person's feelings. Watching and listening to movement, facial expression and sound accesses a rich source of communication often overlooked in the more verbally-based therapies. Becoming aware of, and using, non-verbal communication helps overcome the anxiety that can be aroused by working with someone who does not speak, or whose speech is limited or perseverative.

The importance of silence. Recognition of the importance of non-verbal communication requires sensitivity in the use of silence in therapy. Silence is an important theme for survivors of abuse—keeping silent is often a powerful dynamic of abuse. It may be a rare and profound experience for people with intellectual disabilities to be in a situation of silence with the focus on their feelings. Silence may be uncomfortable for both the client and the therapist, but should be acknowledged as a powerful aspect of communication.

Touch. The issue of touch is often difficult for survivors of abuse and more so for people with intellectual disabilities, who may be touched more than most people on a day-to-day basis. This is an important consideration in therapy. There may be occasions where touch is useful and necessary, such as when a person is visually impaired. However, decisions to touch require careful consideration. It is easy to feel that the usual considerations are somehow less important for someone who is often touched by their carers. Therapists should always adopt a stance of respect—discussions about boundaries are nullified by unnecessary or thoughtless touch. Responses to touch from the client are also important. People with intellectual disabilities are sometimes not taught about boundaries in relationships and may have been encouraged to hug and touch other adults inappropriately to seek approval or reassurance. Responses must not communicate fear, disgust, that the person is unacceptable or that touch is desirable or necessary. This highly complex issue is usefully explored in supervision.

Sensitivity to issues of power. Power is a common theme in the content and nature of therapy. The therapist might usefully support the individual to examine power issues and imbalances in his/her life, particularly in relation to the abuse. Such issues may be discussed verbally, but can also be 'talked' about using pictures, objects and representations of size, strength and volume. In recognition of the power differential in the therapeutic relationship, it is important to ensure that the person in therapy has maximum control over sessions. This can include the person deciding where and when sessions occur, how they can be terminated and ensuring that the person has had the opportunity to give informed consent about the work. These apparently obvious issues are often overlooked when working with people who have intellectual disabilities.

Role singularity. Singularity of role is important when supporting a survivor of sexual abuse—dual roles are usually incompatible. For example, it requires two differing perspectives if one is to be involved in both an investigation of the accuracy of an abuse allegation and in seeing the survivor in a supportive capacity, yet this is not a rare expectation of a clinical psychologist's role. In a therapeutic relationship the objective is not to arrive at the truth, but to be giving clear messages that the individual is believed.

The role of pharmacology

Pharmacological support, such as the short-term use of anxiolytic medication, may have a role if based on careful assessment and functional analysis and if it is monitored and evaluated. People with intellectual disabilities have the same rights to medication and medical support following abuse as other people. However, it is vital that such approaches are not used simply because carers are unaware of alternatives.

Cognitive and behavioural strategies

Thoughtful use of cognitive and behavioural approaches can offer a sophisticated technology that, when based on functional analysis, can provide much support to survivors. The following strategies may be valuable.

Recalling and describing the abuse in detail using guided visualisation. Although this is traditionally a verbal technique, descriptions can often be successful using drawing or movement. Always progress from the general to the specific. For example, rather than immediately asking someone to draw a picture of his/her abuser, ask him/her first to draw other pictures such as the people he/she knows, people who were in the household and the house where abuse took place, before narrowing down to the details.

Expressing emotion.   Expressing emotion may be verbal or, when this is too challenging, maybe through noise, movement or pictures. The expression of rage is often particularly difficult and non-verbal methods may prove helpful, as may the use of masks or empty chair techniques.

Monitoring.   Monitoring of moods, thoughts and behaviours can take many forms. Although simplified written formats are useful, diaries can be kept in whatever format is most meaningful for the individual (e.g. pictorially, on audiotape, by putting objects into a box to represent each day).

Relaxation.   Many self-controlled relaxation techniques can be adapted for people with all levels of intellectual disability (see also Chapter 12). These range from simple breathing strategies to progressive muscular relaxation and autogenic techniques. All can be taught using a range of imitation, verbal or pictorial instructions and should be chosen according to the skills and needs of the individual. Ascertain which strategies the person already uses and increase access to other relaxing opportunities such as massage, hot baths and vigorous activity. Consider how the person will be offered options and how he/she can request them. Photographs, pictures or object cue systems can be helpful for people who cannot make a verbal request.

Distraction.   A range of distraction techniques can help people who are experiencing anxiety, flashbacks or intrusive thoughts. Choice of technique will be determined by the person's interests, cognitive abilities and the strategies he/she already uses. Techniques might include focusing on the environment, describing surroundings or engaging in an absorbing mental or physical activity.

Anger management.   Anger management strategies can be adapted to meet the needs and skills of the individual. It is vital that the person understands his/her right to feel anger and is helped to express this in meaningful and appropriate ways. Anger management strategies should be used to help the person feel in control in situations where he/she does not wish to express anger or where it would be dangerous to do so.

Graded desensitisation.   Graded desensitisation can be used to overcome anxiety provoked by abuse-related stimuli, and may help people tolerate being in a one-to-one situation.

Coping with flashbacks and nightmares.   Alongside relaxation and distraction, cognitive restructuring may enable the person to determine different outcomes to flashbacks and nightmares. This can be achieved using pictures and drawings as well as verbal approaches.

Recording the abuse.   Making a record of a person's experiences may be particularly important for people who have poor memory or concentration. It may involve the use of pictures, writing, audiotape or collections of objects. Choosing the right medium is important, giving the powerful message that the content is important and 'worth' preserving.

Using cognitive-behavioural interventions in ways that are meaningful to people with intellectual disabilities is both challenging and rewarding. Interventions must always be adapted to the level at which the person is functioning. It requires creativity and confidence to experiment with non-verbal approaches such as movement and drawing, but assessment should offer guidance about the media of objects, textures and smells that are meaningful for the individual. It is important to know preferences and skills at symbolic representation—some people use abstract representation, such as items of textured fabric, whereas others prefer photographs, drawing or dolls. The use of non-verbal materials such as pictures, videos and drawings can be valuable and a range of resources exist. Of particular value are the books *Jenny Speaks Out* and *Bob Tells All* by Hollins and Sinason (1992, 1993).

It may, on occasion, be important to involve other people in aspects of intervention. Confidentiality is a complex issue that always requires careful consideration. When information and opinion about the individual is shared too openly, it colludes with the notion that people with intellectual disabilities do not have the right to a private life. However, carers sometimes have a role in supporting people to remember and practise skills outside sessions or to help carry out aspects of monitoring. Carers are often concerned to know about progress in therapy and how best to support it. It is good practice to discuss this with the people concerned, to name the issues and reach agreement about what information will be shared.

SUPPORT AND SUPERVISION

Providing high quality support to people who have been abused requires good supervision. Although this can be difficult to arrange, receiving appropriate support is vital because working with intellectually disabled survivors raises many complex issues, both intellectually and emotionally. The importance of the therapist's reactions and responses is particularly significant when working with people whose communication is primarily non-verbal. Ways of achieving support might involve peer supervision with other therapists, working jointly with professionals from other services and contact with therapists who have specialised skills. Supervision is necessary to ensure that decisions are based on evidence and a well-considered appreciation of the individual, rather than by other beliefs. Supervision can also ensure that work is led by the needs of the individual and not the expectations and feelings of their carers or the therapist.

RECOMMENDED READING

Fenwick, A. (1994). Sexual abuse in adults with learning disabilities. Part 1: a review of the literature. *British Journal of Learning Disabilities*, **22**, 53–56.

Craft, A. (Ed.) (1994). *Practice Issues in Sexuality and Learning Disabilities*. Routledge: London.

Sobsey, D. (1994). *Violence and Abuse in the Lives of People with Disabilities— The End of Silent Acceptance?* Paul H. Brookes: Baltimore, MD.

APPENDIX: USEFUL SOURCES OF INFORMATION AND SUPPORT

NAPSAC (The National Association for the Protection from Sexual Abuse of Adults and Children). Information and a networking service to survivors and workers.

NAPSAC, Department of Learning Disabilities, University Hospital, Nottingham NG7 2UH.
Tel: 01159 709987

RESPOND. A psychotherapeutic service for people with intellectual disabilities who are perpetrators and/or survivors of sexual abuse. RESPOND also provide counselling and psychotherapy and consultancy education and training for professionals.

RESPOND, 3rd Floor, 24–32 Stephenson Way, London NW1 2HD.
Tel: 0171 383 0700

Chapter 11

WORKING WITH PARENTS WHO HAPPEN TO HAVE INTELLECTUAL DISABILITIES

*Sue McGaw**

INTRODUCTION

People with intellectual disabilities share the same needs as other adults, to form friendships, engage in sexual relationships and bear children. In fact, there are no legal impediments to prevent them from realising any of these ambitions, should they so wish. Nevertheless, there are many adults with intellectual disabilities who are still being discouraged from entering sexual relationships today because of the concerns of their families, carers or supporting professionals, who fear that such a relationship might result in an unwanted pregnancy. In itself, the pregnancy appears to be of less concern than the couple's ability to manage the complexities of parenthood long-term. Undoubtedly, it is the perceived risk of harm to the child's health, development and well-being which promotes most anxieties in others.

To some extent, the research literature does give credence to some of these concerns by reporting that many adults with intellectual disabilities are known to be unprepared and ill-informed on the topic of parenthood. Typically, prospective parents with an intellectual disability have limited knowledge, poor understanding and inadequate skills in parentcraft. They tend to be a doubly disadvantaged population and frequently suffer low incomes, sub-standard housing and social isolation, in addition to their intellectual disabilities. Nevertheless, it could be argued that these environmental and social disadvantages are also shared by the non-intellectually disabled parenting population, many of whom struggle to

*Trecare (NHS) Trust, Truro, UK

Clinical Psychology and People with Intellectual Disabilities. Edited by E. Emerson, C. Hatton, J. Bromley and A. Caine.

raise their children despite the hardships of poverty and deprivation. Unfortunately, parents with intellectual disabilities tend to be vulnerable to pejorative attitudes which deem them unfit for parenting and incapable of carrying full 'parental responsibility', solely on the basis of their IQ. Such judgements are, in fact, misplaced. The empirical evidence and proliferation of clinical reports disseminating from parenting programmes around the world indicates that *many* parents 'who happen to have an intellectual disability' *are capable* of providing adequate parenting, providing that they receive the appropriate training and support.

DEFINITION OF TERMS

Parents with intellectual disabilities

First, it is necessary to define what is meant by the term 'parents with intellectual disabilities' as different terms prevail, depending upon the country in which you live (see also Chapters 2 and 3). Currently, within the UK, the terms 'intellectual disability' or 'learning disability' are most commonly used ('learning difficulty' tends to apply to children with special educational needs) when someone's intellectual functioning falls two standard deviations below the mean (IQ of 70 or less) in conjunction with deficits in adaptive behaviour, as assessed during the developmental period (up to age 19 years). Other terms commonly used outside of the UK include 'mental retardation', 'developmental disability', 'cognitive disability' or 'cognitive limitations'. Regardless of the term adopted by professionals, it is important to remember that parents usually reject such classifications anyhow and view themselves, first and foremost, as parents rather than people with an academic label. Whilst a diagnostic approach establishes the level of intellectual functioning of parents, a functional approach to intervention and support is often what is needed.

Parental responsibilities

Clearly, parents with intellectual disabilities need to aspire to the same standards of child care as that expected of any other parent. However, a lack of clarity exists (even with the introduction of the 1989 Children Act, an important piece of legislation on child law) about what constitutes these standards (see Chapter 4). The notion of 'parental responsibilities' was introduced by the Children Act (to replace the traditional common law concept of 'parental rights') but it failed to specify these responsibilities in clear terms which are understandable to many parents, and especially those who happen to suffer an intellectual disability. Clarification of these terms was sought by the Scottish Law Commission (1992), when it was suggested in the *Report on Family Law*, that parental responsibilities should include, 'so far as it is practicable or in the interests of the child':

❑ To safeguard and promote the child's health, development and welfare.

❑ To provide, in a manner appropriate to the child's stage of develop ment, direction and guidance to the child.

❑ If not living with the child, to maintain personal relations and direct contact with the child on a regular basis.

❑ to act as the child's legal representative and, in that capacity, to admin ister in the interests of the child any property belonging to the child.

Whilst some parents may be helped by this definition, there will be numerous parents with intellectual disabilities who will remain confused. Their confusion will be compounded by personal experiences of abuse and neglect which many of them will have endured as children. Under standably, such parents will be hard-pressed to comprehend the term 'parental responsibilities' and 'standards of care' when these criteria were insufficiently met by their own parents during their childhood. Moreover, parents who have difficulty accessing the parenting literature (because of deficits in reading skills) will not be able to learn about alternative parenting styles in a way that non-intellectually disabled parents might do. As a consequence, such parents will rely heavily on support agencies to help them acquire the necessary knowledge and skills so that they can adopt a different parenting style to that which they may have experienced as a child. Clinicians need to be sensitive to the vulnerability of parents in this position. Interventions which adhere to 'good-enough' parenting can trigger feelings of anger, guilt and sadness in parents who grieve for the childhood which they might have had, and to which they were entitled. Professionals need the insight and skills to help parents deal with these issues.

EPIDEMIOLOGY

In the USA there are over 100 programmes, serving an estimated population of 1 million families with children, in which one or both parents have an 'intellectual disability' or 'mental retardation' classification. Only 2000 families within this population appear to get the specialised help that they require (Tymchuk, 1996; Woodruff, 1994). In contrast, the general parenting population (parents of dependent children) within the UK is estimated to be 12 million (Smith, 1996) and of this number it is estimated that as many as 250,000 of these parents may have an intellectual disability or borderline disability (McGaw, 1996). The national trend indicates (in the absence of a national survey to capture prevalence) that the number of families who are now being identified by support services is rapidly increasing. The emerging signs are that the demand on services by parents with intellectual disabilities is greater than was first anticipated by them. Currently, service purchasers and providers are raising a number of issues regarding:

❏ The potential demand for resources in the absence of a national survey or client register. This situation creates confusion across agencies about who to refer. In some instances, referrals are made on behalf of the whole family; in other instances they are made on behalf of the individual family members who have an identified or suspected intellectual disability.

❏ The type, range and combination of interventions to offer such families in the absence of research on long-term outcomes and the efficacy of service models.

❏ The funding of services and resources for families whose long-term needs span the health and social care divide.

RESEARCH

In the past, it was assumed that parents with intellectual disabilities were incapable of providing adequate care for their child and that they could not benefit from teaching programmes. Subsequent studies sought to substantiate or refute these assumptions using empirical research. In the main, this research has concentrated on three topics: (a) the vulnerability of children born to parents with intellectual disabilities; (b) parental competency; and (c) the efficacy of intervention programmes.

Vulnerability of children born to parents with intellectual disabilities

Epidemiological studies estimate that the majority of parents (at least 60%) will have offspring who function at a higher intellectual level than themselves, although this figure varies (Booth & Booth, 1997; Dowdney & Skuse, 1993). Some of these children will be of normal intelligence or superior intelligence, and will fare well as adolescents and adults provided that their families are given the necessary support that they require (Ciotti, 1989). However, for many parents who do not receive this specialist guidance and training, their children may be 'at risk' from abuse but most probably from unintentional neglect (arising from omission rather than commission). Many of these children will also be vulnerable to a developmental delay (especially in expressive language and cognitive skills). It is difficult to isolate poverty as a factor in their delay as there are few studies which have made comparisons with other similarly impoverished families (Tymchuk, Andron & Unger, 1987).

Parental competency

Conflicting findings have emerged from studies of parenting by people with intellectual disabilities conducted in the USA over the past 50 years. Some extensive support programmes report parenting breakdown, unsatisfactory physical care or poor behavioural management across a selection of families studied (Whitman & Accardo, 1987). In contrast, there have also been reports of good-enough parenting and adequate care from other studies (Espe-Sherwindt & Crable, 1993, Floor et al, 1975). Such disparities need to be treated cautiously, as the definition of 'success' appears different across programmes and variance may have resulted from differences in methodologies, changing criteria for parenting and sample selection.

Efficacy of intervention programmes

Reports of parenting training programmes for mothers and fathers who have an intellectual disability tend to focus on describing the curriculum of the parenting programmes, with some information on the teaching interventions used. In general, reports assert positive outcomes for families participating in the training but empirical evaluation across studies is often confounded by a lack of comparative data. Studies differ in their selected parent population (some concentrate on parents with intellectual disabilities, whilst others include parents with borderline intellectual disabilities); the teaching topic (Graves et al., 1990); age and vulnerability of children studied (Feldman et al., 1985); and programme settings which extend to homes, schools, community-based settings or a combination of these (Heighway, Kidd-Webster & Snodgrass, 1988; Whitman & Accardo, 1989).

In 1993, the New York State Commission reviewed eight programmes serving 41 families in New York State and concluded that:

> Measuring the success of the programmes in meeting the needs of parents with developmental disabilities and their children is difficult... the programmes differed significantly in the services that they provided and the resources that they had available, confounding evaluative comparisons

across programmes. Notwithstanding these significant limitations . . . parents themselves gave the programme high marks and generally matched the assessments of Commission staff who were impressed by the dedication of programme staff to the families, as well as their success in making many concrete and measurable positive changes in the lives of the parents and the children they served. However, whilst the parenting programmes received recognition for their short-term gains with families for most of the parents enrolled, parenting programmes helped them to compensate for their cognitive limitations, but they did not change them.

These findings mirror the present situation within the UK, where there exists a paucity of comparative data across programmes. The remainder of this chapter will offer practical guidance to clinicians regarding assessments and clinical interventions which are known to be helpful in supporting parents with intellectual disabilities and their children.

ASSESSING PARENTING

General intelligence

The research indicates that there is no direct correlation between parenting competency and IQ. However, parents whose IQ falls below 60 tend to experience more difficulties (particularly in their cognitive functioning and social skills) than similarly placed parents with intellectual disabilities whose general intelligence is estimated to be in excess of IQ 60. Frequently, it is reported that parents who function below this level become overwhelmed by the multiple demands of parenting. As a consequence, their children are more vulnerable to inadequate parenting and removal from their parent's care. All assessments need to be carried out sensitively and adjusted to the pace of the client (see also Chapter 7).

Typically, support agencies will ask clinical psychologists to provide detailed information regarding a parent's general intelligence, decision-making skills, discriminatory ability, logical sequencing skills, memory span and verbal or visual learning preference to guide them in their work. The Wechsler Adult Intelligence Scale—Revised is commonly used for the purpose of assessing parents' intellectual functioning, many of whom will present with a mild or borderline intellectual disability classification. This assessment helps to distinguish between those people with normal range abilities from those parents who have a moderate or severe intellectual disability. Similarly, the British Ability Scales, Non-reading Tests, SON (Snijders–Domen Non-Verbal Intelligence Tests), or Raven's Progressive Matrices are sometimes used instead of, or in conjunction with, the Wechsler Adult Intelligence Scale (WAIS) as a means of identifying specific skills or deficits.

Academic skills

It is essential to assess a parent's reading, writing and numeracy skills so that support agencies can pitch their teaching accordingly. Often, childcare information is conveyed on the back of packaging, in leaflets, prescriptions and letters, which many parents miss because they cannot read or understand the text (the average reading age for this population is about 7 years). Frequently, services will request information about a parent's reading age, listening comprehension, receptive and expressive language skills and numerical operations (simple addition, subtraction, multiplication and division). The WORD (Wechsler Objective Reading Dimensions), WOLD (Wechsler Objective Language Dimensions) and WOND (Wechsler Objective Numerical Dimensions) are just few of many assessments which can be used for this purpose. Whilst many of these assessments are designed to be used for children aged 6–16 years 11 months, they can be useful for assessing adults whose academic skills fall within this range of functioning.

Life skills

The influence of parents' life skills on parental competency (in particular their practical and social skills) is outlined in the Parental Skills Model (McGaw & Sturmey, 1994). Whilst standard assessments of adaptive behaviour such as the Vineland Scales of Adaptive Behaviour or the Comprehensive Test of Adaptive Behaviour provide useful general information about a person's independent living skills, they are limited in their usefulness. There is a need for instruments to assess a parent's life skills regarding their ability to establish and maintain routines and in areas of hygiene, symptom recognition, safety, emergency responses, etc., all of which are fundamental to child care. There are a number of check lists which are designed for this purpose but they have a functional rather than a diagnostic role and are not weighted. Most empirically-based assessments for use with parents with intellectual disabilities have not been standardised on a UK population. A Parenting Assessment is currently being developed by the Special Parenting Service to capture parents' life skills in relation to their functioning.

Family history

Whilst family histories, genograms and eco-maps are usually put together as part of the 'Orange Book Assessment' by social workers, clinicians need to ensure that social history reports, along with medical and educational information, are supplied by the relevant agencies. Joint and separate interviews need to be conducted with the parents, preferably within their own home. During this process parents often reveal important information about their own nurturing experiences and memories of childhood abuse/neglect, which may or may not affect their parenting. In some instances, there will be evidence of parental psychopathology which has a deleterious effect upon the child's health and development. In this instance, clinicians need to provide parents with the opportunity to receive therapy or counselling from specialists in the intellectual disabilities/mental health sectors (see also Chapters 10 and 11). Issues may arise as to whether such intervention will benefit the parent within the time-frame of the child's needs.

Support and resources

The best predictor of future parental competency for parents with intellectual disabilities is the quality and frequency of social and practical support available to them on a daily basis. Such support is usually provided by a partner, family member, friend or neighbour. Social support is helpful when it assists or prompts parents (frequency depends upon parent's needs) in their decision-making and maintenance of child-care routines. Hands-on practical support is needed by some parents to help them access resources such as transport, housing, paid employment, creches, playgrounds, health centres, day-care centres, advocacy services and professional services (especially the parenting and intellectual disabilities services). The Tymchuk Social Support Relationship Matrix (Tymchuk, 1996 and Service Use & Needs Survey (Feldman, 1996) are useful tools designed for this purpose.

CHILD CARE AND DEVELOPMENT

Child care is assessed by trained professionals (social workers, health visitors, paediatricians) on aspects of feeding, hygiene, warmth, safety, continuity of care and independence. Typically, a child's height, growth and weight will be monitored to ensure that they are thriving and growing at a rate appropriate to their birth size and weight. Judgements will be made about the quality of the parenting, based on the pattern of growth and gains made by a child during the perinatal period. Now adays, parents are able to keep their child's health records at home so that they become aware of their child's development and take responsibility for this. Health visitors are well-placed to interpret and simplify these records to parents with intellectual disabilities, who may find technical information involving growth centiles rather confusing.

Child development is assessed in particular by health visitors, psychiatrists, paediatricians, teachers and psychologists. Typically, clinical psychologists will take on the role of assessing a child's development (appropriate to their chronological age) and commenting on the quality of parent–child attachment, bonding, guidance and parental control. Usually, parents with intellectual disabilities have difficulty recognising the indicators of normal child development and have little understanding about their role in facilitating their child's learning. Commonly, parents perceive schools as the place where children learn to read and write and the home is where the child's primary needs (food, shelter, warmth, etc.) are met. Inevitably, problems will arise if parents do not become involved in stimulating their child's development (see Figure 11.1).

WORKING WITH PARENTS

Basic philosophy

Engaging parents with intellectual disabilities in support programmes can be problematic. Research indicates that parents will decline or with draw from professional services if:

❑ Services do not meet their needs.
❑ The language and resources used by professionals are inappropriate.
❑ They become 'over-serviced' by multiple professional input.
❑ Parents suspect or learn that their competency is being questioned covertly.
❑ Professionals are dishonest, disrespectful or negative in their attitude towards them.

Paradoxically, the offer of professional support can trigger anxieties in parents. Many such parents fear that their child will be taken away from them if they reveal that they are not coping. As a consequence, parents may attempt to disguise or hide their parenting difficulties from those who are offering to help them. Sadly, this is sometimes misinterpreted by some professionals as indicating parental resistance and poor motivation to engage with services. Conclusions are then drawn that such parents would be poor recipients of support programmes and the offer of support is withdrawn. In fact, parents will readily accept the support that is on offer to them if they are given reassurances that support agencies will enter into an honest, open relationship with them and that they will not be prejudged or 'talked about behind their backs', especially

Figure 11.1   Tamsin

Tamsin is a 28-year-old single mother with an IQ of 55 who has been known to the statutory agencies over a number of years. She has had four children removed from her care in the past, and, as a consequence, has no prior experience of raising a child beyond the age of two years. She has poor reading and writing skills and is mostly dependent upon friends, neighbours or professionals to help her read letters and bills. Whilst she enjoys caring for her fifth child, she recognises that he is a lot brighter and more capable than her in many ways. Nevertheless, she tends to let Terry (who is six years old) stay home from school at least three days a week, in part because she enjoys his company and it makes life easier for her. Inevitably, there is a downside. The school, educational welfare officer and social worker are extremely concerned about Terry's education and behaviour, which are deteriorating. In their opinion, it is not in Tamsin's interests to ensure that Terry attends school. She will feel less challenged by Terry if he becomes a poor achiever like herself.

Eventually, the family were referred to the clinical psychologist, who spent time building up a rapport with the family before organising a package of intervention and support:

(a) Tamsin received practical and financial assistance (including transport) to help her join a local literacy class. Initially, she was filled with anxiety about attending, but this lessened over time. Tamsin's self-esteem increased as she learned to read and write and she was then well-placed to help Terry in his school work. Another important outcome was that Tamsin became increasingly independent from other people and more in control of her life as she learned to read her mail and do things for herself.

(b) A training programme was offered to Tamsin on managing Terry's behaviour. However, these sessions only took place when Terry was at school. It was agreed that Tamsin would telephone the therapist beforehand to assure her that this was the case. During these sessions Tamsin learnt that all children misbehave and that it was normal for them to challenge their parents' authority at times. It was a sign they wanted to do things their way and to become independent of their parents. She was taught how to recognise the triggers to Terry's anti- social behaviour and how to avoid, manage and defuse a situation effectively, using one approach at a time and visual resources such as audio-tapes, videotapes and books.

(c) Tamsin was invited into the special parent's group which was about to commence on the theme of 'health and relaxation'. This had been selected by the other parents. The programme (facilitated by the two therapists) included visits to a college where they were shown how to make simple, cheap, healthy meals, a trip to the local health centre and 'fitness' studio (under guidance), and sessions with an aromatherapist and reflexologist. Initially, Tamsin was nervous and would have disengaged from the group if she had not been supported by the other parents. Thereafter, she enjoyed these new leisure experiences and her shyness diminished as she struck up new friendships within the group.

This case illustrates that professionals cannot make assumptions that all parents will or can teach their child academic skills, or that they will play with their child without some guidance, prompting or additional intervention. Usually, parents who do not engage children in this way are not deliberately neglectful, they are simply following the parenting behaviour of their own parents who, for whatever reason, did not teach them basic arithmetic, read stories or enter into play with them each day.

when there are concerns about the parenting. Parents benefit most from support which is pragmatic and positive in its delivery. Encouraging parents to self-refer to family/parenting services and to make their preferences known (regarding service input, staff, mode of teaching) is one way of facilitating this process.

Admission to programme

In order for services to provide intensive input to those families most in need there will be a requirement for services to formulate admission/discharge criteria. Typically these might specify that one or both parents have a classified intellectual disability of boderline intellectual disability *in addition* to one or more of the following being present:

❏ There is a significant lack of parental knowledge in areas of feeding, hygiene, warmth, healthcare, safety and child development.
❏ A significantly low HOME score (Caldwell & Bradley, 1984), which indicates poor stimulation within the home.
❏ History or potential risk of neglect and/or abuse for parents and/or children.
❏ The family is socially isolated.
❏ A history of psychiatric/substance abuse problems.

Home-based programmes

The research literature indicates that a combination of home-based programmes and centre-based programmes work best for families. Home-based programmes involve one-to-one contact with the family, which varies according to the specific needs of the parents and child. One family may need guidance from the clinical nurse specialist about weaning, whilst another may work with the occupational therapist in developing child care routines, another may talk with the psychologist about their child's development, while yet another parent may talk with a team member about concerns related to budgeting and benefits. Parents need guidance and teaching across a range of different topics. Most programmes include:

Feeding

It cannot be assumed that parents with intellectual disabilities know how to provide a balanced diet to their children or themselves. Frequently, parents require guidance on bottle- and breast-feeding, weaning, food

preparation and cooking skills. Often, parents are unaware of the importance of weaning and the need for infants to chew their food as a prerequi-
site to language development. Typically, parents may bypass weaning
altogether or they may shorten the complicated weaning stage in order
to introduce simpler 'adult' foods to their child.

Hygiene and warmth

Parents with intellectual disabilities do not always understand the need
to keep their offspring clean from germs through regular washing/
bathing and the sterilisation of equipment (teats, bottles, spoons). Also,
when their children suffer from flea bites, headlice, scabies, ringworm,
eczema, asthma and other complaints, their parents may struggle to treat
the condition, despite advice and medication from their GP, health visitor
or community nurse. Typically, such professionals provide parents with
complicated verbal or written instructions which they cannot read or
understand. Nevertheless, parents can benefit from intensive training on
symptom recognition (vomiting, breathing difficulties, constipation, etc.)
and first aid; however, this training needs to be generalised within the
home setting.

Safety

Safety presents as a significant risk for many children, especially those
under the age of five years (school limits the child's daily exposure to
risks within the home). All parents need training: (a) to recognise potentially dangerous or life-threatening situations; (b) to avoid or reduce the
risk of such dangers before there is a crisis; and (c) to learn to deal with
emergency situations such as choking, burns, house fires, etc., including
using the 999 procedure. Whilst parents can benefit from such training,
it cannot be assumed that such knowledge and skills will automatically
generalise to alternative settings or new situations. Generalisation may
be facilitated if parents are introduced to new knowledge and skills one
at a time. Once parents have mastered these skills to the point of 'over-
learning', variations of the skill can be taught across different settings.

Child development and stimulation

Parents and their children often benefit from guidance to engage in
structured and unstructured play with their children as part of a routine
or during child care activities such as dressing, washing or putting the
child to bed. Portage is an effective model to use, although it will need

adaptations if is to be used with parents with intellectual disabilities (McGaw, 1994).

Organisation and routines

Children like the predictability of family routines, which help them to feel secure. Commonly, parents with intellectual disabilities struggle with organisational tasks, which require them to prioritise, sequence and plan in advance. As a prelude to intervention, it is important to check whether parents are skilled in using diaries, calendars, watches and alarms before tackling the basics of planning, establishing routines and helping them to keep to schedules. Parents can benefit from teaching programmes that use a range of equipment and visual aids to promote these skills, such as *Baby Think It Over* (PSD Import Agency, undated). This is a realistically weighted, electronic doll which looks, cries and commands attention just like a real baby, and can be programmed to present the special needs of a premature or drug-dependent baby as well as the changing demands of healthy babies.

Supervision and discipline

Parents with intellectual disabilities often experience difficulties in establishing ground rules and instilling a sense of discipline within the home. The research indicates that children can be particularly challenging of their parents' decision-making and discipline, especially when they function at a higher intellectual level than their parents (sometimes referred to as the Huck Finn Syndrome; O'Neill, 1985). Both parents and children can benefit from guidance from parenting services and/or child guidance clinics which identify and strengthen parent–child boundaries, roles and responsibilities within the family unit (see also Chapter 14; Figure 11.2.

Centre-based programmes

Teaching programmes need to be flexible in their format, choosing set tings and delivery in order to suit the various needs of families. Centre-based programmes offer a useful adjunct to home-based teaching, and can be delivered across various settings such as family centres, churches,

Figure 11.2   Megan

Megan was referred to the Special Parenting Service by the social worker, who was concerned about the safety of two young children within the home. Both girls (aged five and three years) were being cared for in an erratic fashion by their young mother. They were allowed to wander outside the home onto a road unsupervised; they were constantly throwing objects around the house (often bouncing off visitors); they tampered with electrical wiring and had suffered minor burns from the coal fire on a number of occasions. Previously, there had been a baby in the home, who had been removed from Megan following an incident when the baby's leg was fractured, a possible non-accidental injury. First, a risk assessment was needed in order to: (a) identify the risks to which these children were being exposed; (b) identify the parent's strengths and needs; (c) reduce these risks immediately by offering an intensive teaching/support programme; and (d) address maintenance and generalisation of newly-learned skills. This programme was duly offered over a two-year period and was simple enough to achieve, except for the maintenance and generalisation of skills, which this mother did not seem capable of doing by herself, even when a skill had been over-learned.

Eventually, it was agreed with Megan that in order to facilitate this process a support network would be developed around her, involving her relatives, neighbours, family aides and the Special Parenting Service. Thereafter, Megan was constantly reminded about specific parenting skills and routines (which changed over time) by the support group, who called at the home frequently (on an individual basis) and who enquired about the programme and the application of skills. They were aware of the need to be positive in their feedback and to suggest alternative settings in which to apply the skills. Although this approach turned out to be extremely effective, it changed dramatically when Megan found a new partner, and he was on the spot to intervene if she forgot to use the skills appropriately or to apply these in naturally occurring, alternative situations. As Megan began to do this for herself, her partner's interventions reduced accordingly.

community centres and health centres. Groups tend to run for a limited period during the year and involve professional staff and small groups of infants (5–6) and their parents. Sessions can adopt a low-key, informal style that allows for addressing issues as they arise, rather than adherence to a 'curriculum'. Alternatively, semi-structured parenting programmes such as the LIFE programme (Learning Independence through Family Education), or those developed by the Special Parenting Service, tend to focus on specific topics of interest to parents and supporting agencies and cover:

❏ Self-esteem.
❏ Diet/health/relaxation.
❏ Anger management.
❏ Bereavement.
❏ Social skills and relationships.
❏ Independent living skills.

❑ Birth control.
❑ Behavioural management.
❑ Support networks.

However, as with parents generally, simply inviting parents to groups may not guarantee their attendance. Group organisers need to spend some time educating and preparing parents about group membership and what that entails. Some parents fear entering a social circle because they have difficulty communicating effectively and their natural response is to avoid such situations. In addition, some parents fear having to talk about past painful experiences and/or memories which relate to childhood abuse and/or neglect or about children who have been removed from their care. Nevertheless, there are many parents with intellectual disabilities who benefit greatly from group teaching and support (see also Chapter 14).

Support networks

Parents with intellectual disabilities often present with poor social skills which limit their ability to seek out, request and make choices about the services they need. Group sessions often address parents' self-esteem and confidence so that they become equipped to tackle new situations and access different resources. The group dynamic often facilitates this process by helping parents to talk about the obstacles which prevent them from taking the initiative and accessing resources of behalf of their family. Solutions or suggestions which come from the parents themselves tend to be the most useful vehicle for change. Programme facilitators can act as intermediaries by intervening or bridging between the group and community resources to optimise community networking.

COMPREHENSIVE SERVICES

Families benefit most from comprehensive services that acknowledge the multiple determinants affecting the physical and mental health of the child and family. These include unsafe and unhealthy environments, poor housing and transport, and poverty. Key elements of good practice identified for parents and children with intellectual/physical disabilities include:

❑ A named professional to meet with parents and their children if they request support or there is an identified need.
❑ Each family to have a named key-worker responsible for co-ordinating services and information.

❏ Core groups are formed involving families and professionals on a regular basis.
❏ Support and counselling to the family as a whole.
❏ Local agreements between health, social services and education about the funding and delivery of parent training and support.
❏ Services which are sufficiently responsive and flexible to meet urgent needs. A range of residential through to home-based support needs to be available; a 24-hour support service for parents in crisis or simply requiring guidance; readmission to intervention programmes rather than being placed on a waiting-list.
❏ Shared principles for providing continuing care.

CONCLUSION

There are encouraging signs that more and more services across the UK are now becoming involved with parents with intellectual disabilities, and that they are developing wide-ranging support programmes to meet the various needs of these families. However, clinicians often report that they feel ill-prepared for this task, despite their training and background across the children's services and intellectual disabilities sector. Clearly, this situation presents an interesting challenge to professionals, who feel obliged to assist such families as best they can but in the absence of a national strategy on professional training, policy standards and service guidelines. In response, professionals are turning to the research and models of good practice for guidance, some of which have been referred to in this article. Whatever the issues, it is clear that many adults who happen to have an intellectual disability will become parents and that professionals will continue to offer these families the support to which they are entitled, despite the difficulties.

FURTHER READING

Booth, T. & Booth, W. (1994). *Parenting Under Pressure*. Open University Press: Hilton Keynes.
Danish Ministry of Social Affairs (1996). *Parenting with Intellectual Disability Conference Papers*. Danish Ministry of Social Affairs: Copenhagen.
Hove, G. van, & Broekart, E. (1995). Independent living of persons with mental retardation in Flanders: a survey of research data. *European Journal of Mental Disability*, **2**, 38–46.
Llewellyn, G., McConnell, D., & Bye, R. (1995). *Parents with Intellectual Disability: Report to the Disability Services Sub-committee*. University of Sydney: Sydney.

O'Hara, J., & Sperlinger, A. (1997). *Adults with Learning Disabilities: A Practical Approach for Health Professionals*. Wiley: Chichester.

Chapter 12

WORKING WITH PEOPLE WITH MENTAL HEALTH PROBLEMS

Amanda Caine* and Chris Hatton**

INTRODUCTION

As with the population generally, mental health problems can have serious consequences for people with intellectual disabilities (Fletcher, 1988; Szymanski, 1994). The accurate assessment and effective treatment of mental health problems in people with intellectual disabilities is an essential component of any service aiming to improve the quality of life of its users. However, until recently mental health problems in people with intellectual disabilities have been largely neglected by professionals and researchers, resulting in the under-diagnosis of mental health problems (Charlot, Doucette & Hezzacappa, 1993; Patel, Goldberg & Moss, 1993) and inadequate services (Day, 1994; Patel, Goldberg & Moss, 1993). A number of reasons have been proposed for this situation, including:

❏ The separation of mental health and intellectual disability services, inhibiting integrated systems for the training of professionals and the assessment and treatment of mental health problems in people with intellectual disabilities (Campbell & Malone, 1991; Day, 1994).
❏ The difficulty of accurately assessing mental health problems in people with intellectual disabilities, partly because some people with intellectual disabilities are able to give little or no information about their mental state (Campbell & Malone, 1991; Moss, 1995).
❏ 'Diagnostic overshadowing' (Reiss, Levitan & McNally, 1982; Spengler, Strohmer & Prout, 1990), where carers and professionals often mistakenly attribute symptoms of mental illness as due to a person's intellectual disability. For example, poor self-care symptomatic of psy-

*Rochdale Healthcare NHS Trust, UK; **Hester Adrian Research Centre, Manchester, UK

Clinical Psychology and People with Intellectual Disabilities. Edited by E. Emerson, C. Hatton, J. Bromley and A. Caine.
© 1998 John Wiley & Sons Ltd.

chosis may be attributed to a person being incapable of self-care because of his/her intellectual disability.

❑ Differential diagnosis between mental illness and challenging behaviour. Much confusion surrounds the conditions under which a challenging behaviour should be considered as indicative of mental illness (Moss, 1995). This confusion is illustrated by the fact that many referrals to psychiatrists specialising in intellectual disability concern challenging behaviour rather than a specific mental health problem (Bouras & Drummond, 1992; Day, 1985).

❑ The absence of adequate referral systems to mental health services. In the UK, people in the general population tend to get referred to mental health services (through their GP) when they have problems fulfilling social roles (e.g. spouse, parent, employee) (Goldberg & Huxley, 1980). For people with intellectual disabilities, their life situations are such that they frequently do not have these social roles; therefore, the onset of a mental health problem may not be noticed.

Despite these obstacles, the importance of providing adequate services for this client group is becoming increasingly recognised amongst professionals in the UK (Bouras, 1994; Bouras et al., 1995). Before discussing clinical guidelines for the assessment and treatment of mental health problems in people with intellectual disabilities, a brief overview of the current state of knowledge concerning dual diagnosis will be provided.

WHAT DO WE KNOW ABOUT MENTAL ILLNESS AND INTELLECTUAL DISABILITY?

In this section we will briefly examine the current state of knowledge concerning two issues; classification and diagnosis; and the epidemiology of mental health problems in people with intellectual disabilities.

Issues in classification and diagnosis

Unsurprisingly, the issue of classifying mental health problems in people with intellectual disabilities is complex. As 'intellectual disability' is a social construction, so also is 'mental illness', a concept subject to considerable variation across time and cultures (Littlewood & Lipsedge, 1989; Porter, 1990; Scull, 1993). Consequently, diagnosing a psychiatric disorder in a person with intellectual disabilities is a complex business, with the reliability and validity of such diagnoses open to question.

Historically, diagnosing a person as having a psychiatric disorder has depended on the clinical judgement of a psychiatrist. However, research in general psychiatry has demonstrated that clinical judgement may be unreliable and subject to a number of biases which reduce the validity of a diagnosis (e.g. Ash, 1949; Sandifer, Hordern & Green, 1970; Termelin, 1968). The validity of clinical judgement is likely to be further reduced when an inexperienced or untrained psychiatrist attempts to gain information from a person with intellectual disabilities (Moss, 1995).

In general psychiatry, the reliability and validity of psychiatric diagnosis has been improved by the introduction of standardised classification systems of psychiatric disorders, the latest and most comprehensive of which are DSM-IV (American Psychiatric Association, 1994) and ICD-10 (World Health Organization, 1993). These systems operationalise each psychiatric disorder in terms of a set of specific criteria relating to the person's mental state or behaviour, which are then assessed using semi-structured interviews (World Health Organization, 1994).

While this approach has been shown to increase the reliability and validity of diagnoses, the validity of applying standard criteria to people with intellectual disabilities is problematic. First, there are questions concerning whether standard criteria will need to be modified for people with intellectual disabilities (Sturmey, 1993, Sturmey et al., 1991). For example, people with intellectual disabilities may display clear psychotic symptoms, but not display a sufficient range of symptoms to get a diagnosis of schizophrenia under standard criteria (Moss et al., 1996e). Second, mental health problems may express themselves in different ways in people with intellectual disabilities, particularly people with severe or profound disabilities, for example in behaviours often regarded as challenging (Moss, 1995). Where people have no way of accurately communicating their experiences or mental state, then gaining a valid diagnosis becomes even more questionable (Moss, 1995; Sturmey, Reed & Corbett, 1991).

Epidemiology

Given the complexity of issues concerning classification and diagnosis, it is not surprising that a wide variety of prevalence rates are reported for psychiatric disorders in people with intellectual disabilities (see Borthwick-Duffy, 1994; Campbell & Malone, 1991, for reviews). Indeed, studies are difficult to compare, as they use widely different methods of assessment that produce findings that do not routinely correspond to standard ICD or DSM criteria (Sturmey, Reed & Corbett, 1991; Sturmey, 1993).

While studies of the general population report that approximately 20%

of people have a major psychiatric disorder of some kind (i.e. excluding personality disorders; Bland, Orn & Newsman, 1988), prevalence studies of psychiatric disorders in people with intellectual disabilities report prevalence rates & between 10% and 80%, depending on definitions of disorders, methods of case identification and the population studied (Borthwick-Duffy, 1994; Campbell & Malone, 1991). Higher prevalence rates (40% upwards) are reported if behavioural disturbance is included as a psychiatric disorder (e.g. Gillberg et al., 1986), or if the population studied was referred for psychiatric evaluation (e.g. Bouras & Drum mond, 1992, Pary, 1993). Low prevalence rates (15% downwards) are reported by studies using case notes to identify psychiatric disorders (e.g. Borthwick-Duffy & Eyman, 1990; Reiss, 1990). Studies of general populations of people with intellectual disabilities using psychiatric evaluation to identify cases tend to report prevalence rates between these two extremes, usually between 25% and 40% (e.g. Iverson & Fox, 1989; Lund, 1985; Reiss, 1990).

It is unsurprising that the rate of psychiatric disorders may be higher in people with intellectual disabilities, given their likely life experiences and circumstances (e.g., birth trauma, institutionalisation, stigmatisation, unemployment, lack of friendships and intimate relationships), and their reduced capacity to cope with the demands of everyday life (Reiss & Benson, 1984; Szymanski, 1994). However, the distribution of psychiatric disorders in people with intellectual disabilities is also different to the general population (Jacobson, 1990; Moss, 1995). Reduced prevalence rates are reported for substance abuse, affective disorders (mania, depression and dysthymia) and neurotic disorders (phobia, panic and obsessive/compulsive disorder); higher rates are reported for psychoses and autism. Studies also report higher rates of psychiatric disorders in people with mild rather than severe intellectual disabilities (Borthwick-Duffy & Eyman, 1990; Bouras & Drummond, 1992, Jacobson, 1990), although this may partly reflect caution in diagnosing psychiatric disorders in people with very limited communication skills, or the increased likelihood of someone with borderline intellectual disability being labelled as such if they have a psychiatric problem.

As more people with intellectual disabilities survive into old age, dementia is becoming an increasingly important issue for services (Patel, Goldberg & Moss, 1993; Zigman et al., 1995), with prevalence rates for dementia at least twice as high in people with intellectual disabilities compared to the general population (Patel, Goldberg & Moss, 1993; Turner & Moss, 1996). People with intellectual disabilities and dementia are also more likely to have other psychiatric symptoms, such as depression (Moss & Patel, 1995). People with Down's syndrome are at particular risk of developing dementia (Zigman et al., 1995), with almost all people with Down's syndrome over 40 displaying the neuropathological signs of Alzheimer's disease (Wisniewski, Rabe & Wisniewski, 1987).

GUIDELINES FOR CLINICAL PRACTICE

In this section, we will provide some practical guidelines for assessing and treating mental health problems in people with intellectual disabilities. The aim is to arrive at an accurate formulation of the problem regarding the formation of current difficulties and their maintenance.

Assessment

As the above discussion should make clear, assessment of this client group is a complex process. This section will firstly outline some general principles of assessment for people with intellectual disabilities and mental health problems, followed by a discussion of the different assessment instruments available. One major consideration concerns the reason for referral; is the referred problem a problem for the individual or for others? People with intellectual disabilities are usually subject to greater control by other people than adults, generally, and interventions are often requested to increase compliance rather than address the person's distress. Therefore, the orientation of the assessment is extremely important and must be collaborative.

General issues in assessment

Assessment involves essentially the establishment of a therapeutic relationship, an understanding of the person's context and a formulation of the development of the person's current problems and how these are currently maintained.

Reiss (1994) and Bouras et al. (1995) provide some useful general guidance when assessing mental health problems in people with intellectual disabilities:

❏ Try to gain information from the person with intellectual disabilities and other informants. It is clear that people with mild and moderate intellectual disabilities can provide useful information concerning their own mental state, particularly concerning subjective experiences inaccessible to others (see also Chapter 6). Informants who know the person well are good sources of information concerning the person's behaviour, although information from several informants (e.g. day and night staff, parents) may be required to gain a full picture of the person's behaviour.

❏ Look for *patterns* of behaviour and/or experience indicative of a mental health problem. To get a diagnosis of a psychiatric disorder typically requires the person to have a constellation of symptoms characteristic of that disorder. This is important when trying to differ entially diagnose somebody as having a psychiatric problem rather than an isolated challenging behaviour.

❏ Look for *changes* in behaviour and/or experience indicative of a mental health problem. Psychiatric disorders typically have a recognisable time-course, involving periods of onset and possibly) remission, and this can be important in differential diagnosis. However, if a person is suffering from a psychiatric disorder that has gone unnoticed for some time, changes from usual may be rare. Similarly, the assessment of dementia in a person with intellectual disabilities represents a particular challenge, since normative baselines of cognitive func-tioning cannot be assumed and deterioration in such functioning may be difficult to detect. Current guidelines for best practice in dementia recommend the regular monitoring of the person's adaptive behaviour over time, and also looking for non-cognitive signs characteristic of dementia, such as wandering and irritability (Aylward et al., 1995).

❏ Make allowance for individual differences in the expression of symp-toms indicative of a psychiatric disorder. The level of intellectual disability is likely to have a substantial impact on how symptoms of distress are expressed, with people with more severe disabilities expressing distress in more behavioural rather than verbal ways. The life history and current circumstances of a person will also have an impact on how symptoms are expressed, particularly in terms of help-seeking. Finally, the culture, ethnicity and gender of a person can strongly influence both the expression of symptoms and the way that behaviours are interpreted by professionals.

❏ Consider alternative explanations for unusual behaviours and/or experiences. In any diagnostic procedure it is vital to eliminate alterna-tive explanations for unusual behaviours and/or experiences before making a diagnosis of a psychiatric disorder. Where people have limited communication skills, disturbed behaviours may be a result of distress from a physical illness. Similarly, people who lose their sight often have visual hallucinations for a period of time after their sight loss. Finally, it is worth considering whether any disturbed behaviours are the side-effects of medication.

❏ Admit limitations of knowledge. Sometimes, particularly with people with severe or profound intellectual disabilities, it may be impossible to assess a person's mental health status with any confidence. It is better to admit this than to provide a misdiagnosis on insufficient evidence.

Assessment instruments

Interviews

Standardised interviews for the assessment of mental health problems in people with intellectual disabilities are rare (Sturmey, Reed & Corbett, 1991; Sturmey, 1993), possibly due to the assumption that people with intellectual disabilities cannot give accurate information on their mental state.

Recently, however, a semi-structured clinical interview for people with intellectual disabilities has been developed, called the Psychiatric Assessment Schedule for Adults with a Developmental Disability (the PAS-ADD; Moss et al., 1993, 1996d; see also Chapter 6). This is based on the ICD-10 clinical interview (World Health Organization, 1994), with modified wording to maximise the likelihood of responses from people with intellectual disabilities. The interview is also designed to combine information from people with intellectual disabilities and a key informant, to maximise the information available (Moss et al., 1996b). The PAS-ADD has been shown to have good reliability and validity (Costello et al., 1997; Moss, Prosser pg 308 & Goldberg, 1996; Moss et al., 1993, 1996a), although it is unclear to what extent valid diagnoses are possible for people with severe or profound intellectual disabilities.

While it is clear that a semi-structured clinical interview yields reasonably accurate and reliable diagnoses, there are limitations when using this approach in routine practice. First, interviewers need extensive training in semi-structured interviewing techniques, as good interviewing skills are essential for gaining accurate information from people with intellectual disabilities. Second, semi-structured interviewing can be very time-consuming for both the interviewer and the interviewee. Third, translating scores on the interview into diagnoses is complex, requiring the use of a computer algorithm, rendering diagnosis difficult in many work settings.

Checklists

A more common approach to the assessment of mental health problems in people with intellectual disabilities has been the use of structured rating scales (see Sturmey, Reed & Corbett, 1991; Sturmey, 1993, for reviews). These rating scales have the practical advantages of being relatively short, easy to score, requiring little if any training, and designed to gain information exclusively from informants. Disadvantages in terms of accurate diagnosis are that they omit the experiences of people with intellectual disabilities, they are typically not scorable to standard DSM or ICD criteria (Sturmey, Reed & Corbett, 1991; Sturmey, 1993; Sturmey & Bertman 1994), and they often include items relating to challenging behaviour. Such scales often show good *sensitivity* (they are good at picking up general 'caseness'), but fail to show adequate specificity (they are bad at diagnosing specific types of psychiatric disorder). These rating scales are perhaps best viewed as screening instruments to indicate likely 'cases', who can then be assessed more fully using an interview method. They can also be useful for the routine monitoring of people with intellectual disabilities, to show up any changes in behaviour that may suggest the onset of a psychiatric disorder and to evaluate the impact of treatment programmes on psychiatric symptoms.

The most commonly used rating scales of this type include:

The Reiss Screen for Maladaptive Behavior (Reiss, 1988a, b). This is a 36-item instrument, providing a total score and scores on eight subscales: Aggressive Behaviour; Psychosis; Paranoia; Depression (behavioural signs); Depression (physical signs); Dependent Personality Disorder; Avoidant Disorder; and Autism. The Reiss Screen generally shows adequate psychometric properties and reasonable sensitivity (total scores can identify cases), but data concerning the validity of the individual scales is questionable (Sturmey & Bertman, 1994; Sturmey et al., 1996).

The Psychopathology Instrument for Mentally Retarded Adults—PIMRA (Matson, Kazdin & Senatore, 1984; Senatore, Matson & Kazdin, 1985). This is a 56-item instrument, providing a total score and scores on seven subscales: Schizophrenic Disorder; Affective Disorders; Psychosexual Disorder; Adjustment Disorder; Anxiety Disorders; Somatoform Disorders; and Personality Disorders and Inappropriate Mental Adjustment. Two versions of the PIMRA, self-report and informant, are available. The psychometric properties of the PIMRA are less robust than those of the Reiss Screen, and the sensitivity of total scores and the validity of the subscales have both been called into question (Sturmey, Reed & Corbett, 1991; Sturmey & Bertham, 1994).

The Diagnostic Assessment for the Severely Handicapped—DASH (Matson et al., 1991). This is an 83-item instrument designed to gain information on people with severe and profound intellectual disabilities, providing a total score and scores on 13 subscales: Anxiety; Depression; Mania; Pervasive Developmental Disability/Autism; Schizophrenia; Stereotypes/

Tics; Self-injurious Behaviour; Elimination Disorders; Eating Disorders; Sleep Disorders; Sexual Disorders; Organic Syndromes; and Impulse Control/Miscellaneous. To date there has been no independent evaluation of the psychometric properties or validity of the DASH.

The PAS-ADD Checklist and The Mini PAS-ADD (Moss et al., 1996c; Prosser et al., 1996). These instruments are designed to be compatible with the PAS-ADD discussed earlier. The PAS-ADD Checklist is a 29-item screening instrument designed to be completed by untrained carers and care staff, providing a total score and scores on three subscales: Affective/Neurotic Disorder; Organic Condition; Psychotic Disorder. The Mini PAS-ADD is a longer instrument designed to provide a comprehensive assessment of a person's mental health problems, and should be completed by professionals with some training. It provides scores on seven dimensions: Anxiety and Phobia; Depression; Expansive Mood; Obsessions and Compulsions; Psychoses; Dementia; and Autistic Features. Information on the psychometric properties and validity of these instruments is currently being collected.

In addition to these instruments, a number of instruments designed for the general population, such as the Beck Depression Inventory, the Zung Self-rating Depression and Anxiety Scales and the Schedule for Affective Disorders and Schizophrenia, have all been modified for use with people with intellectual disabilities, although evaluations of their reliability and validity are very sparse (see Sturmey, Reed & Corbett, 1991; Sturmey, 1993, for reviews).

Assessment will also involve consideration of the person's cognitive and developmental level of functioning. Clinicians have used developmental theory to structure psychotherapy and have obtained beneficial results (Dosen, 1990). An individual with a mild intellectual disability may have verbal skills ranging from highly functional to concrete and repetitive. An understanding of an individual's cognitive resources will guide the therapeutic intervention.

Establishing a therapeutic relationship

The assessment process will have involved the development of rapport and trust, which is essential for therapy to be effective. Clinicians should use initial sessions to develop a working therapeutic 'vocabulary'. People with intellectual disabilities often have impoverished emotional vocabularies (Bates, 1992). The therapist must pay attention to his/her own use of language, as this may need to be simplified. In addition, people with intellectual disabilities are used to not understanding much of what many people say, and are often in the less powerful position in relation ships. This is likely to be true in therapy and as a result it may be difficult for the person to interrupt the therapist or ask for clarification. Therefore, the use of repetition and asking the individual to summarise what has been said in his/her own words can be useful in order to check the individual's level of understanding (see also Chapter 6).

It is important to use the assessment to consider the person's perception of the problem and his/her motivation to change. It is more likely than with the general population that the person will have been brought to see you by someone else who considers that he/she has a problem. This will obviously affect his/her ability to co-operate with your intervention. It may be necessary to be more direct than when working with people of normal intelligence, in order to be understood. The first session is likely to involve a statement of the problem, e.g. 'The staff who support you say that you have been shouting at them'. Such honesty regarding the problem and the source of information can help to build trust. Therapists must, of course, be sensitive the effects of such directness. For clients who have sufficient verbal understanding, the work to be done must be clarified, stating the time of visits, number of visits and what will be expected. For clients with significant cognitive limitations, it is suggested (Hurley et al., 1996) that the structure of therapy can be conveyed through adherence to a standard protocol using repetitive routines and predictability.

INTERVENTION

Treatment approaches

The historical neglect of mental health issues in people with intellectual disabilities is reflected in a corresponding lack of interest in treatment issues. Traditionally, 'treatment' has been restricted to the indiscriminate use of psychopharmacy for the purpose of social control, with little matching of drug to diagnosis, monitoring of short-and long-term effects, or evaluation of treatment efficacy (Crabbe, 1994; Gualtieri, 1991).

A number of erroneous assumptions have led to the neglect of 'talking therapies' for people with intellectual disabilities. It has often been assumed that they are unable to generate verbal mediators which act as cues in regulating overt non-verbal behaviour and in a similar way they are unable to develop insight or recognise causes or consequences of their actions because of their level of intelligence (Hurley et al., 1996). More recently there has been a recognition that this is not so for many people with intellectual disabilities, and a range of treatments, including behavioural therapy and psychotherapy, have been described in the literature, although information on their efficacy is sparse (Benson, 1994; Gardner & Graeber, 1994; Hollins, Sinason & Thompson, 1994). Stenfert Kroese, Dagnan & Lonmidis (1997) suggest that the influence of normalisation (see Chapter 1) and the development of non-aversive behavioural approaches have made professionals more inclined to 'listen' (even if the client is non-verbal) in order to extract personal meaning and to create a collaborative relationship (where therapy goals are negotiated) rather than an authoritarian one.

As Stenfert Kroese, Dagnan & Lonmidis (1997) point out, Lovett (1985) stresses the importance of self-determination, especially through creating a collaborative relationship between therapist and client, when he wrote, 'I think that the relationship between the person helping and the person helped is often a critical variable. I think it is more than just "playing with words" to say that when we treat a person we are putting ourselves in a relationship that is very different (and for me less desirable) than when we work with a person on a challenging behaviour'. In his latest book, Lovett (1996) suggests, 'In the world of positive approaches, we work in collaboration and in a spirit of openness, honesty and equality' towards co-operation and personal growth, rather than control and behaviour change.

An examination of the lives of people with intellectual disabilities suggests that they will have had an increased exposure to experiences leading to mental health problems (e.g. loss, failure) compared to the general population, and therefore may be at increased risk of developing such problems. It seems that people with intellectual disabilities may develop mental health problems in the same way as other groups, and that models of aetiology and intervention developed with people without intellectual disabilities can be readily applied.

Some work has been done to see whether this holds true for depression. The findings of various studies (Nezu et al., 1995) suggest that people with intellectual disabilities become depressed for some of the same reasons that non-disabled people do and that cognitive models of depression hold true. Thus, they will be characterised by: (a) greater frequencies of negative automatic thoughts of self-statements; (b) higher levels of feelings of hopelessness; and (c) certain deficits in self-control or self-regulation.

A cognitive framework can therefore be used, varying the level of complexity and abstraction of the techniques to suit the client, to guide the formulation and overall strategy for therapy. Figure 12.1 shows some of the treatments that might be used in relation to particular problems.

Figure 12.1   Possible interventions for particular problems

Problem type	Possible interventions
Anxiety	Relaxation training
	Cognitive restructuring
	Problem solving
	Self-instructional training
	Medication
Depression	Self-reports
	Activity scheduling
	Medication
	Cognitive restructuring
Anger	Development of coping skills through inoculation procedure
	Cognitive restructuring
	Arousal reduction
	Behavioural skills training
Social Skills	Problem solving
	Role-play of problem situations
Phobia	Systematic desensitization
	Relaxation training
	Anxiety management

Thus, anxiety management training might involve teaching basic relaxation techniques, cognitive restructuring, problem solving and self-instructional training, depending on the formulation of the problem. The necessary modifications and issues that need to be considered in relation to people with intellectual disabilities will be described in the following sections.

Psychoactive medication

Psychopharmacy is the most common method of treatment for mental health problems in people with intellectual disabilities. In the UK, recent drug surveys have reported high rates of psychoactive drug prescription in hospitals (24–44% of people; Branford, 1994; Harvey & Cooray, 1993; Wressel, Tyrere & Bervey, 1990) and in community-based residential services (19–69%; Branford, 1994; Clarke et al., 1990; Fleming et al., 1996), although levels of drug prescription in family homes are somewhat lower (9–10%; Branford, 1994; Clarke et al., 1990).

The most common drugs prescribed to people with intellectual disability are anti-psychotics and anti-epileptics (Branford, 1994; Fleming et al., 1996); polypharmacy is also frequent (Fleming et al., 1996). Furthermore, the majority of people receiving psycho-active medication do not have a psychiatric diagnosis (Clarke et al., 1990; Fleming et al., 1996; Wressel,

Tyrere & Beruey, 1990), with the majority of psycho-active drugs being prescribed to control challenging behaviour (Clarke et al., 1990; Fleming et al., 1996).

Despite the widespread use of psycho-active medication, research on the effectiveness and long-term effects of such medication is relatively sparse. Most reviewers of the literature are forced to conclude that specific indications for various psychotropic drugs are lacking and that the evidence for efficacy in suppressing problem behaviours is at best weak and mixed (Emerson, 1995). In routine practice, drugs tend to be prescribed more for their general sedative qualities than to ameliorate specific psychiatric symptoms (Crabbe, 1994). Some research has demonstrated that behavioural responses of people with intellectual disabilities to drug treatment can be idiosyncratic or even paradoxical, compared to the general population (Crabbe, 1994), lessening the confidence with which drug treatments can be used. When medication is felt to be appropriate after multidisciplinary assessment, then 'the aim should be to ensure drugs are prescribed only for the condition(s) for which they have shown to be effective, in the correct dose, for the correct period of time' (Ghodse & Khan, 1988). Lepler, Hoods & Cotter-Mack (1993) recommend that:

❏ Psychotropic medication should be used for modifying behaviour only after less restrictive alternatives have been considered.
❏ The individual receiving psychotropic medication should be maintained on the minimum daily dosage necessary to modify behaviour.
❏ For each individual either receiving or being considered for psychotropic medication, there must be an interdisciplinary psychotropic drug review.

The previously described assessments may be useful in providing a baseline against which to assess the effect of the medication prescribed (i.e. is it having the desired effect without too many side-effects?). The consideration of side-effects is particularly important for people with intellectual disabilities, as they are less likely to complain and may have difficulty in identifying the particular symptom(s).

Behavioural approaches to intervention

There is considerable evidence demonstrating the effectiveness of behavioural techniques for ameliorating certain mental health problems in the general population (e.g. Marks, 1981). Such behavioural principles have been extensively and effectively applied to the management of challenging behaviours in people with intellectual disabilities (see

Chapter 8; Emerson, 1995). However, little attention has been paid to the use of behavioural techniques for the amelioration of specific mental health problems in people with intellectual disabilities, although some work has focused on anger management (Benson, 1994), enhancing people's coping skills (Gardner & Graeber, 1994) and treating phobias (e.g. Willis & Burgio, 1986). Some individual case studies have been reported which illustrate some useful ways of modifying behavioural techniques. A number of common interventions will be described.

Relaxation training

Abbreviated progressive relaxation.   Steen & Zurif (1977) taught an extremely self-injurious woman with a severe intellectual disability to relax. She was asked to focus on tension and relaxation only in her arms and the instructions were simplified to 'tighten up' and 'relax'. Physical help was given to help her to tense and relax her muscles and she was also reinforced for successful tension/release cycles. In all, 150 relaxation training sessions were given and following treatment the amount of self-injurious biting fell to low levels. Lindsay & Baty (1989) showed that progressive relaxation could be used in a group setting and that this could produce significant reductions in rated anxiety after a number of sessions. However, they found that some individuals became excited by the process and that this then caused a general rise in agitation in that particular group. This would suggest that attention needs to be paid to the selection of individuals for group treatment, perhaps by using individual sessions initially.

Behavioural relaxation training.   This technique, developed by Schilling & Poppen (1983), does not require the individual to understand the difference between tense muscles and relaxed muscles and is therefore conceptually simpler. The therapist models relaxed and unrelaxed behaviours and then asks the individual to imitate the relaxed position. Verbal prompts and manual guidance are used as needed.

Cue-controlled relaxation.   The essential aspect of this technique is that relaxation effects are linked to a cue stimulus (e.g. a word or music), so that eventually the subject will be able to relax to the cue word only, rather than a time-consuming relaxation procedure. In this way external cues can be used to help the person to control his/her arousal levels in particular situations likely to trigger such a response, which can be anticipated by carers.

Biofeedback techniques

The assessment of arousal methods using portable biofeedback equipment has been found to be useful, particularly when the individual does not show any clear verbal or behavioural manifestations of anxiety. It can also be useful in assessing whether epileptic activity is associated with particular behaviours. However, it is worth noting that different levels of arousal may or may not have clearly associated behaviours.

Monitoring and scheduling activities

The goal of behavioural strategies such as monitoring and scheduling activities and graded task assignment is to maximise engagement in mood-elevating activities in the treatment of depression. In order for someone with intellectual disabilities to self-monitor, it may be necessary to use different techniques to establish times of the day and to record activities (e.g. using symbols or pictures). This will give information about baseline levels of activity and the relation between mood and activity. This can then be used to schedule activities to increase people's activity levels. It may be necessary to break tasks down into small manageable steps, each of which is reinforced. Compliance with treatment regimes such as homework is a problem in all patient populations. Motivation of the individual and appropriateness of the assignment will determine success, as will ability to follow instructions and complete the task. Scheduling of activity can also be useful in conveying information to people with autistic characteristics, reducing their uncertainty and thus managing their arousal levels.

Response prevention

This technique can be used for the reduction of ritual behaviours which serve to heighten anxiety. This can be accompanied by distraction techniques, thus diverting the person from his/her rituals. However, explaining the rationale for this approach and gaining consent may be problematic.

In vivo and exposure methods

Graded exposure can be used to treat phobic responses. This may involve shorter and more frequent sessions. Care givers are likely to be involved in homework practice sessions. It may be necessary to identify the hierarchy with someone who knows the person well. It may be harder to identify the salient characteristics so that detailed observation is necessary. It may also be more difficult to manage the phobic response *in vivo*, e.g. flight, or to explain the usefulness of doing so. The rationale for systematic desensitisation is a complex one, as is the explanation of the role of avoidance in the development of a phobia.

Social skills training

The methods of training social skills vary from the shaping of target behaviours by means of simple reinforcement to more complex techniques. Benson (1994) suggested the following stages: instruction (defining the focus of training); modelling (demonstrating the appropriate behaviour); role playing (the supervised practice of behaviour); feedback (constructive criticism); reinforcement; and homework. Jones et al. (1997) suggest that interpersonal interactions are by their very nature both unpredictable and highly complex, while often containing ambiguous or contradictory social cues. Such complexity means that rules are not easy to make concrete and specific. For example, when is it appropriate to tell blue jokes? When you are with people you know well—but not with elderly aunts!

Psychotherapies

While psychotherapies of various kinds, including psychodynamic approaches (Freud, 1986) and cognitive therapeutic approaches (Hawton et al., 1989), are commonly used in the general population, particularly for affective disorders, they are very rarely used with people with intellectual disabilities (Dosen, 1993; Fletcher, 1993). Individual, group and family psychodynamic psychotherapies involving people with intellectual disabilities have been described (Hollins, Sinason & Thompson, 1994), although there is to date little evaluation of their effectiveness (Beail & Warden, 1996). Verbal communication is not considered essential by some psychodynamic psychotherapists. Other communication channels and the ability to create an emotional relationship form the basis of both group and individual psychotherapy (Sinason, 1990). It has been claimed that the expression of emotion through colour, gesture, and other non-verbal forms of communication has proved helpful. Similarly, the techniques of cognitive-behavioural therapy are not applied widely and have been subjected to little evaluation as to their effectiveness. Some issues relevant to all forms of therapy will be described, followed by a discussion of some of the ways in which cognitive-behavioural therapy has been adapted for people with intellectual disabilities.

Issues relevant to all forms of psychotherapy/counselling with people with intellectual disabilities

Developing the therapeutic relationship.   The therapeutic relationship is fundamental to all forms of psychotherapy and should be based on mutual trust and respect. The therapist needs to communicate such qualities as concern, acceptance, empathy and genuineness to the client as a basis for their relationship (Monfils & Menolascino, 1984). Establishing such a relationship may take longer with a person with an intellectual disability than with the general population, as many of them will have had lifelong experiences of rejection (Nezu et al., 1995) and may therefore find it difficult to develop trust within a relationship. It may be that the relationship needs to be developed through settings and activities other than the office. As a result, the therapist must take an active role in initiating and facilitating interaction and communicating the procedure and process of therapy at the appropriate level of intellectual and interpersonal development (Hurley, 1989, cited in Hurley et al., 1996; see also Chapter 6)

Boundaries.   Psychotherapists have suggested that individuals with intellectual disabilities display transference reactions that are more rapid, pronounced, and primitive than those seen in the general population (Hurley et al., 1996). Strong transference reactions, in fact, may make psychotherapy particularly effective with this group. However, they also make it necessary to clarify the therapeutic relationship in clear, concrete terms and to often review the limits of therapy. This is often helped by meeting in the same place at the same time of the week. Otherwise, there is a risk that the client may quickly see the therapist as a 'friend' or possible romantic partner. There will be a need to balance this against the above suggestion that more informal settings may be appropriate. Countertransference often takes the form of rescue fantasies or overprotection and should be discussed in supervision. Therapists must guard against becoming 'parents' or 'advocates' unless this is necessary and the relationship is re-negotiated (see also Chapter 10).

Cognitive-behavioural approaches

Evidence has accumulated that suggests that, for a number of reasons, interventions based on simple approaches to contingency management may not be effective, because they do not take full account of the factors underlying the maintenance of behaviour. Much of this evidence is concerned with the effects of language.

It is suggested that verbally formulated rules for responding, whether overt or covert, are major determinants of human behaviour (Davey & Cullen, 1988; Hayes, 1989; Lowe & Horne, 1985). The development of language in humans results in the emergence of rule-governed as opposed to contingency-shaped behaviour, which has a profound effect on behavioural relationships. The distinction can be described as follows: behaviour which is under the direct control of schedules of operant reinforcement or punishment is contingency-controlled: when individuals learn to describe their own behaviour and the particular contingencies in operation, then their behaviour is said to be mediated by verbal behaviour and to be rule-governed. The formulation of verbal rules may, under particular circumstances, render human behaviour insensitive to the immediate consequences that are central to the acquisition and maintenance of contingency-shaped behaviour. If a person creates a rule to explain the influences of their environment upon their own behaviour, then that internal rule may exert more of a controlling influence over the person's behaviour than the actual environmental contingencies in operation, although these internal processes will them selves be under the control of operant principles.

It seems that the ability of humans to symbolically represent environmental stimuli and their own behaviour has major effects on the organisation and control of behaviour. There seems to have been a growing interest in 'cognitive' procedures in working with people with intellectual disabilities, as elements of 'self-control' began to be incorporated into operant-based treatments. In general, the research and clinical literature concerning self-control in relation to people with intellectual disabilities is significantly delayed in comparison with that for other client groups. It is possible that this delay reflects a widespread attitude that those with intellectual disabilities are not capable of managing aspects of their own behaviour, and that the development of self-control is inconsistent with the external control integral to institutional management.

As for any individual, there is a need to consider whether a behavioural or cognitive-behavioural approach or a combination of the two is the most appropriate intervention.

Self-instructional training has been used widely in cognitive-behavioural therapy with children (Meichenbaum & Goodman 1971). This model suggests that control is developed through three stages: adults and others control the child's behaviour through overt direction; the child controls behaviour through speech; the child's speech becomes internalised. Some of the basic elements seem suitable for adaptation to people with intellectual disabilities. Meichenbaum has suggested that performance difficulties and social anxieties can be maintained by negative self-statements which people say to themselves before and during a sequence of interaction or behaviour. For example, if an individual goes into a social interaction with a thought, 'I can't think of anything to say', this thought will prevent him/her developing positive coping strategies in that situation.

It is not assumed that people are aware of their self-statements. Indeed, some may have not formed the thoughts linguistically but if asked about they can be elicited. It may be that individual self-statements become enmeshed into their emotions and do not reach the level of conscious thought. It could be that there is no thought or self-statement—people just feel bad and so do not engage in what is making them feel bad. However, the fact that mediated self-statements are possible means that they can either be inserted into the chain of responses if they are absent, or changed to more adaptive self-statements if they are present in the sequence of responding. In addition, positive coping self-statements can be used during therapy, whether or not the patient has experienced them beforehand. Patients are taught to use self-statements to guide them through a task, or help them cope with a stressful situation. The self-statements are ideally chosen by users, but if provided by the therapist should be meaningful for them and appropriate for their developmental level.

In the method described by Meichenbaum, the therapist first models the technique, then instructs the patients to use self-statements out loud, and then gradually encourages them to make the statements covert. It is important to keep the self-statements as simple and as natural as possible. Therefore, statements which individuals would use frequently might be the most powerful pieces of private speech to insert into a dialogue. Marshall (1989) used self-instructional training to increase the ability to complete an abstract task. The self-reinforcement which was inserted into the dialogue was, 'I'm doing brilliant'. Clear direct self-statements such as this produced improvements in performance after training and at six-week follow-up.

Cognitive restructuring involves identifying and recalling anxiety-provoking thoughts and reality-testing these fears. This may involve a level of complexity and abstraction that is too great for people with intellectual disabilities. Therefore, a simple procedure involving a combination of problem-solving and self-instructional training may be more use. For example, when approaching a task, a person may be encouraged to say, 'What do I have to do?' or 'Am I doing it?' (self-monitoring), 'How do I know when I've finished?' (self-evaluation) and once the task is finished to praise him/herself (self-reinforcement). Kendall & Wilcox (1980, cited in Stenfert Kroese, Dagnan & Loumidis, 1997) found that instructions of this kind, which could be used across a number of situations, produced better results than more restricted ones. Lindsay & Kasprowicz (1987) found that four out of five people in the group increased their assessed 'confidence' after training.

Problems of maintenance and generalisation might be reduced by increased flexibility. Assessment of problems is helped by other inform-ants, but this could be taken one step further if direct observation were carried out, and the patient asked to talk him/herself through stressful situations. Further information on 'hot' cognitions might be obtained by patients using a tape recorder between sessions, and there is scope for the creative use of audio-visual materials with people with poor literacy skills. It may be that shorter and more frequent sessions will maximise learning.

PROBLEM SOLVING

Some of the problems which are likely to arise during assessment/ intervention have already been addressed. One of the most likely prob-lems relates to carers assuming that all that a person does is explained by his/her handicap, and that people with intellectual disabilities do not feel a variety of emotions. Thus, people's behaviour is interpreted in terms of their intellectual disability rather than as an expression of their mood. It may therefore be necessary to work with carers to increase their understanding, as well as on an individual basis with the person with an intellectual disability. This is necessary as carers' beliefs are likely to affect the reliability of staff observations and their motivation to help the person to carry out homework assignments.

It may also be necessary to consider the effect on the therapist of a more drawn-out involvement which may involve some blurring of boundaries. This might result in over-involvement or premature disengagement by the therapist. Supervision is therefore of great importance, so that such issues can be addressed (see also Chapters 1 and 10).

It may also be difficult to co-ordinate services from different agencies and orientations, such as psychology and psychiatry (see also Chapter 15). It is easy to assume that other professionals will not make the same assumptions as carers concerning people with intellectual disabilities and their ability to experience emotion. It may be necessary to assume that they will share such misconceptions until proved wrong.

It is, therefore, necessary for us all to continue to work together to develop ways of working collaboratively with people with intellectual disabilities to address their emotional difficulties. We need to consider and evaluate the most effective models and interventions, while continuing to respect the person.

FURTHER READING

Bouras, N., Murray, B., Joyce, T., Kon, Y., & Holt, G. (1995). *Mental Health in Learning Disabilities: A Training Pack for Staff Working with People Who Have a Dual Diagnosis of Mental Health Needs and Learning Disabilities*. Pavilion Publishing: Brighton.

Lovett, H. (1985). *Cognitive Counselling and Persons with Special Needs*. Praeger: New York.

Lovett, H. (1996). *Learning to Listen: Positive Approaches and People with Difficult Behaviour*. Jessica Kingsley: London.

Stenfert Kroese, B., Dagnan, D., & Loumidis K. (1997) (eds). *Cognitive-Behavioural Therapy for People with Learning Disabilities*. Routledge: London.

Chapter 13

WORKING WITH PEOPLE WITH COMMUNICATION DIFFICULTIES

*Bob Remington**

INTRODUCTION

Communication skills of people with intellectual disabilities

The richness of our social and cultural lives depends on our ability to influence and be influenced by others through the use of language, spoken or written. For the most part, we take this marvellous ability to communicate almost entirely for granted. For most clinical psychologists, 'communication difficulties' are subtle problems in conveying emotional nuance or need—problems that may be resolved by a therapist possessing sufficient empathy, warmth, skill and patience. For those clinical psychologists who work with people with intellectual disabilities, however, difficulties in communication come about because the very mechanisms of normal communication have failed to develop normally. Individuals who have problems with speech and language cannot but be isolated from the educational, cultural and societal influences that allow most of us to make some sense of our lives.

Very many people with intellectual disabilities face extreme difficulties with communication. Indeed, as a first-order approximation, those with severe or profound intellectual disabilities fail to acquire fully effective speech. Around 80% of such individuals will be handicapped in this way (Garcia & DeHaven, 1974). In a recent study using reports from care givers, McLean, Brady & McLean (1996) provided a further analysis of the nature of the problem. Their work focused not on speech but on communicative function, a difference in emphasis which we will see has

*University of Southampton, UK

Clinical Psychology and People with Intellectual Disabilities. Edited by E. Emerson, C. Hatton, J. Bromley and A. Caine.

very considerable significance for work in this area. Care givers reported that 59% of the people they worked with showed limited evidence of symbolic communication, and a further 19% showed evidence of non-symbolic communicative intent. The most unfortunate 21% showed no evidence whatsoever of intentional communication.

The communicative categories used by McLean et al., need to be unpacked. By 'symbolic communication' they mean not only speech but also communication using manual signs, such as those used by the deaf, and iconic symbols (e.g. picture lexicons), both of which are now in common use by people with intellectual disabilities. Most of the children and adults in their sample who used words, signs or symbols were able to combine them into 'utterances' containing two or more elements, although the grammatical (syntactic) status of these combinatorial usages is uncertain. People who communicated non-symbolically used actions, gestures or other forms of deliberate interpersonal behavioural influence.

McLean et al.'s research illustrates clearly that language and communication are not the same thing. Human language involves the ability to transmit and receive messages via the medium of a shared symbolic code. Normally, the code is speech but, in principle at least, sign- and symbol-based languages are possible. Linguists specialise in understanding how humans process the perceptual motor units of a language (phonology), its word meanings (semantics), the structural properties of word combinations (syntax), and the ways in which linguistic cues influence behaviour (pragmatics). Applied psychologists place a major theoretical emphasis on pragmatics, in other words on communication. Intentional communication need not involve language as described above, because any deliberate action that has the function of social influence and control may be regarded as communicative. The contrast is with people whose reflexive responses, such as crying or making particular facial expressions, may provide cues for action to their care givers. Such communication is said to be unintentional if variations in a care giver's consequent actions fail to affect the likelihood of subsequent communication. In learning theory terms, non-intentional communication is reflexive, while intentional communication is operant in nature. Thus, speaking or signing for 'tea' is communicative if it reliably results in a cup of tea being provided—there is no need for a fully organised syntactic proposition. In fact, *any* behaviour whose reinforcement is mediated by another person can be regarded as verbal in this sense (Skinner, 1957). On this account, challenging behaviour (such as self-injury) that is characteristically, if unknowingly, reinforced would be seen as a form of verbal behaviour in these terms (Donellan et al., 1984; see also Chapter 8).

McLean et al. sampled communicative behaviour at a particular point in time. Much research in this area, however, uses longitudinal methodology, charting changes in language and communication over the developmental period. There is a great deal of evidence that people with intellectual disabilities suffer substantial distortion and delay in their language acquisition compared with the normal pattern (see Rondal, 1996, for examples of this approach in relation to Down's syndrome). For this reason, a basic understanding of the normal processes of language acquisition has some relevance to developing effective intervention. Those developmental perspectives that adopt a functional approach are particularly salient. Thus, before dealing with the practical aspects of clinical intervention, it is worth briefly outlining the various theoretical positions on the development of symbolic communication.

Theoretical accounts of language/communication development

Theories of language development differ in terms of the emphasis they place on the role of the environment. Broadly speaking, approaches that have a role for nurture are more concerned with pragmatics (and semantics), while those that hold to a nativist position argue that the critical feature of language requiring explanation is acquisition of syntax and, with it, linguistic productivity. This refers to the ability of language users to say and to understand propositions (sentences) which are completely novel to them. The basic nativist position (e.g. Chomsky, 1965; Lenneberg, 1967) is that humans are uniquely biologically adapted to 'grow' language when bathed in a normal verbal human culture during the developmental period. The view postulates a 'language acquisition device' (LAD) capable of picking out the local rules of human languages (French, Turkish, Chinese, etc.) and mapping them on to a more profound and invariant 'universal grammar', knowledge of which is inborn. This innate organisation of language learning accounts for the fact that despite a limited speech input (all the things we hear), almost all of us acquire the capacity to generate unbounded, syntactically competent, output (all the things we could say, do say and can understand).

The idea that the capacity for language is an evolved human specialisation, a 'language instinct' (Pinker, 1994), is attractive in many ways but it cannot be the whole story. Bruner (1983) and other social interactionists emphasise the importance of a child's care givers in the development of language, a 'language acquisition socialization system' (LASS) in Bruner's terms. For every LAD, there is a LASS! This social support system for language operates from birth. Reflexive behaviour is treated as if it were intentionally communicative; social turn-taking and joint attention are established long before an infant says its first word. For example, Bates, O'Conneil & Shore (1987) have identified patterns of infant behaviour that control the behaviour of care givers by functioning as requests (proto-imperatives) and attention-directing manoeuvres (proto-declaratives). Thus, the precursors of communication are shaped prior to the acquisition of effective speech. As single word utterances begin to emerge, conversational interactions continue to play a critical role. Moerk (1990) has analysed early patterns of care giver–child turn-taking, identifying important, regularly occurring dependencies between the behaviour of the interlocutors. These he claims are interpretable in terms of the three-term contingency that is the basis of operant con-ditioning and behaviour modification. Elsewhere, Moerk (1992) argues that language development can usefully be seen as a form of skill learning. Whatever the role of contingencies in early language develop-ment, there can be no doubt about the amount of time or effort children invest: Anderson (1990) estimates that 'easily 10,000 hours must have been spent practising speaking before a child is 6'.

It is almost impossible to imagine that the full complexity of language learning is the result of associative conditioning which needs no help from specialised mechanisms that are the product of human evolution. It is equally difficult to believe that the intense social interactions between infant and care giver have no role other than to provide an ambient language environment from which a LAD can extract the necessary information to produce mature language. However, when we come to consider how best to facilitate the communication of people with intellec-tual disabilities, the debate has less relevance. Despite having been exposed to a normal language environment, many have failed to develop normal language. Any failure of the evolved neural mechanisms which subserve language acquisition can only be remediated by structuring environmental input in a way that will allow communicative skills to be learned by whatever neural mechanisms are left—in other words, by effective teaching. A developmental perspective, with a focus on func-tion, may give us some useful clues as to how to proceed.

Overview of some key issues from research

The past two decades have seen an unprecedented increase in work on the remediation of communication difficulties. The literature is now quite extensive and wide-ranging. The list below indicates some of the many key questions that are being actively researched at present. All link back to the theoretical discussion above and all are relevant to the clinical practice section that follows.

- *Early intervention*. As developmental research makes clear, certain pre-requisites of effective vocal communication are socially learned long before functional speech. Given that, does prelinguistic intervention for children with intellectual disabilities enhance subsequent language acquisition? (e.g. Yoder & Warren, 1993)
- *Significant others*. Given that speech normally develops in the context of a LASS, what role can parents and peers play in establishing effective communication intervention in people with language disabilities? (Kaiser & Grey, 1993)
- *Form and function*. As language is normally acquired in the context of shared activities between child and care giver, should intervention focus on teaching communicative functions in everyday settings rather than teaching linguistic forms in clinical settings? (e.g. Carr, 1986)
- *Communication hypothesis*. Some forms of challenging behaviour are communicative in the sense that they are reinforced through the mediation of another person. In these circumstances, does intervention based on training effective symbolic communication in situations where such behaviour occurs reduce its incidence? (e.g. Carr & Durand, 1985; see also Chapter 8)
- *Augmentative and Alternative Communication*. What is the relationship between the development of oral speech and the use of sign- and symbol-based communication (e.g. Remington & Clarke, 1996)?
- *Building from basics*. How is it possible to build up flexible and 'spontaneous' communicative repertoires from a base of single word or single-sign utterances? (e.g. Goldstein, 1993). How is it possible to provide learners with effective information-eliciting strategies? (Guess, Sailor & Baer, 1978)

GUIDELINES FOR CLINICAL PRACTICE

Introduction

Working with people who have major communication difficulties can be one of the most satisfying areas of clinical practice in the field of intellectual disabilities. The changes that are achievable through well-designed intervention can develop a sense of control in people who were not previously effective agents in their social world. To get some sense of this, compare your feelings in a foreign country where you have even one or two words of the language with your sense of helplessness when you have no words at all. The goals of normalisation (see Chapter 1) in terms of effective community presence cannot be fully achieved without some basic level of effective symbolic communication.

Given the importance of developing communication skills, it would be handy if there was some simple, quick and foolproof way of developing them. In fact, during the present decade one such approach, 'facilitated communication', has been proposed—only to be discredited within a very few years of its first appearance. It is worth considering 'facilitated communication' briefly as a cautionary tale. The method sprang from the notion that people with apparently severe intellectual difficulties could be both fully language-competent in terms of receptive speech (understanding) and suffer from a motor problem, conceptualised as an inability to initiate action (cf. Parkinson's disease) that interfered with expressive speech production (talking). This led to the unlikely sugges-tion that perhaps such people could respond via a written medium, e.g. by keying statements into a computer, when a 'facilitator' gently guided their hands into movement without controlling the keys that were even-tually pressed. Initial results in uncontrolled conditions were startling. Previously mute individuals miraculously began to produce evidence of complex and subtle mental lives. Shortly afterwards, several 'communi-cators' used their new-found skills to accuse their care givers of abuse and cruelty—and the lawsuits began. A cool look at this work (e.g. Green, 1994; Hastings, 1996) reveals very little theoretical basis for believing that most communication difficulties are simply motor initiation problems, little evidence of the veracity of the accusations and virtually no good scientific evidence that the 'facilitated' communications are in fact auth-ored by the nominal communicators. Controlled studies have virtually uniformly shown that there is no reliable evidence for the efficacy of 'facilitated communication' in people with intellectual disabilities.

In one sense, a discussion of 'facilitated communication' is a diversion from the main theme of this chapter. But the very fact that it turned out to be a blind—and sometimes a very dark—alley makes an important point. In the field of communication intervention, there are no miracles on offer. To achieve meaningful change requires hard graft. The best work in this area requires a good working knowledge of the literature; careful planning; the collaborative support of care givers, peers and teachers; well-conducted assessment; conscientiously monitored inter-vention; proper evaluation and flexibility in the face of inevitable difficulties—in short, a great deal of work. In the context of clinical training, this means that it is wise not to attempt anything too ambitious for a small-scale research project or, indeed, a dissertation. Single-case experimental research methodology (Barlow & Hersen, 1984) can be used to ensure that well-focused, relatively low-key work is useful and can make a meaningful contribution to knowledge. As will become clear, longer-term and larger-scale work inevitably involves working closely with colleagues in other clinical professions, managers, and the family and friends of the individual(s) on whom the intervention is focused.

The sections that follow are designed to provide more detail on how to work with people with communication difficulties in relation to assessment and intervention.

Assessment

Since almost any intentional behaviour can be seen as communicative, the assessment of communication skills is by no means a simple matter. Attempts to simplify it typically involve the use of psychometric tests, designed to assess a person's (typically a child's) language in comparison with established (typically developmental) norms. For example, the Reynell Developmental Language Scales (Reynell, 1977) are designed to assess both expressive and receptive speech, essentially the complexity of what a child can say and understand, in relation to other normally-developing children. Similarly, the English Picture Vocabulary Test establishes understanding of word meanings in the same way. Such tests are useful as a rough guide to the kinds of difficulties a child—or even an adult—may be facing, and thus a basis for comparison between studies, but problems remain. First, developmentally referenced assessments may not be suitable for, or relevant to, adults with communication problems. Second, such assessments fail to provide the kind of information that is useful in constructing an intervention that will produce immediate benefits to the learner.

The clinical psychologist's focus on the pragmatics of language suggests a different kind of approach. The word 'pragmatics' derives from the Greek word for behaviour, and the way that behaviour is normally assessed is in relation to the context where it typically occurs. Communicative behaviour need be no exception to this general principle of applied behaviour analysis. Thus, in recent years the emphasis of assessment has switched from the measurement of individual differences to the measurement of an individual's interactions with his/her everyday environment. Such an approach is called ecological analysis.

Ecological analysis has three main and inter-related aims. First, it attempts to identify situations in which communication does, or could, take place. Here the similarities between the present approach and functional analysis are obvious. An ecological assessment can identify ways in which needs are normally communicated prior to intervention, e.g. by non-verbal vocalisation, gesture, physically 'leading' a member of staff or, in some cases, by engaging in challenging behaviour (see Chapter

8). The second aim of ecological analysis is to specify the appropriate content and mode of communication in everyday situations. For example, the effective communication skills needed in relation to leisure or work activities are different, but each can be identified through observation of current interaction patterns. Thus, an improvement in communication in a work setting may involve developing the ability to call for help; in leisure settings, improvement may require the initiation of social interactions. At the same time, it should be possible to establish whether intervention should involve teaching speech, sign or symbol use, depending on the individual's existing skills and the human and material support available in the environment where intervention is to take place. The final aim of ecological analysis is to locate these resources. For example, if it is deemed useful to teach requesting leisure items using manual signing, who is available to do this consistently during times set aside for leisure activities? Do they have the skills to do the teaching and, if not, can they be taught? With all this information to hand, it becomes possible to identify the most effective ways to teach particular communicative skills, i.e. to design an intervention programme.

By simply shadowing a person with intellectual disabilities throughout a normal day, a range of regularly-occurring situations where communicative skills are relevant can be identified. Such situations may take the form of regular social demands (e.g. to take part in designated activities) or previously unnoticed opportunities for interaction (e.g. to greet care staff). Meal-times may provide examples of both. For instance, in the context of a cafeteria, the ability to request the available food items is an essential communicative skill but, in addition, there are potential opportunities for teaching a person to request items that are usually provided without the need to ask (e.g. for the cutlery) or to comment on the food. At a more general level, there may be many potential sources of reinforcement that cannot be fully tapped without appropriate communication skills, e.g. interactions with other residents, trips away from the residence and participation in sports or other group activities. In developing intervention programmes for the long-term benefit of learners, it is particularly important to try to identify opportunities for communication that go beyond the present daily routine.

The above discussion emphasises the importance of establishing the functions of communication, such as requesting, rejecting, commenting, questioning and encouraging the behaviour of others. An ecological analysis pinpoints the particular functions relevant to specific situations. In addition, it suggests precise vocabulary elements necessary for effective communication in these situations and thus provides a basis for a more detailed individual baseline assessment of to-be-trained items. The relation between vocabulary and function again highlights an important difference between language (the abstract entity) and communication (the observable behaviour). Conventional language tests typically require items to be named or situations to be described. It should not, however, be assumed that vocabulary items which can be used in the service of the naming function will automatically generalize to other functions, such as requesting (LaMarre & Holland, 1985). From a functional perspective, requesting an object and naming an object by the use of the same word (e.g. 'Drink' used to mean 'Give me a drink' versus 'You've got a drink') are quite different acts (or, in Skinnerian terms, e.g. Skinner, 1957, different verbal operants). Similarly, what can be understood is not the same as what can be said—receptive and expressive vocabularies are by no means always identical.

Until now, we have implicitly assumed that assessment is based on the way that people with intellectual disabilities use speech. In fact, many people now make use of manual signs or symbol-based communication boards to supplement their speech skills. Assessment can focus on the use of each of these alternative communication modes which need not be mutually exclusive. Current interventionists are more likely to ask 'Which mode is right for this person in this situation?' than 'Is this person capable of speech or must we use something simpler?'. For example, someone who shows a little functional speech in some contexts may still benefit from a rapid and easily accomplished intervention using a symbol system, perhaps to indicate choices in regularly occurring situations such as meal times or leisure times. Symbol use is easy to teach and, in these contexts at least, can be reliably reinforced. A person with little or no speech may also be taught to use symbols in such situations for the same reason, but intervention through sign teaching may be more appropriate where comments or more opportunistic requests are likely to be reinforced.

Regardless of context, there are a number of arguments which favour both signs and symbol-based systems as alternatives to speech. These have been discussed in detail elsewhere (e.g. Remington & Clarke, 1996; Remington & Light, 1983) but briefly, they relate to the relative ease of learning and teaching alternative modes. For example, it is easier to shape expressive communication by moulding a hand into a manual sign or directing it at a particular symbol than it is to elicit an approximation to a speech sound. Similarly, the use of signs or symbols can be slowed down to facilitate learning. Under these circumstances, it should be easier to learn the often iconic relationship between sign or symbol and its referent than the arbitrary relationship between word and referent. It is also possible to compare the relative merits of signs and symbols on *a priori* grounds. Signs have the major advantages of portability and availability. Symbols depend on a communication board which may contain only a fraction of a person's potential communicative repertoire. On the other hand, pictographic symbols are more readily understood by untrained individuals with whom it may be useful to communicate, and are generally easier to teach.

The assessment of human and material resources is important to ensure that any intervention that is designed is sustainable (Ager, 1991). Sustainability refers to the fact that to be of maximum value, an intervention must produce long-term effects even after the major effort to bring about change has been withdrawn. For this to occur, it is necessary to identify individuals in the learner's environment who will continue to reinforce communicative behaviour appropriately. It is also important to consider whether the basis for this reinforcement (which often involves making resources available) will not be removed through budget cuts, staffing redeployments, changes in management philosophy, and so on.

Intervention

Like many interventions designed for people with intellectual disabilities, attempts to improve communication skills are grounded in the principles of behaviour analysis. Space constraints preclude detailing these general principles but excellent accounts are widely available (e.g. Grant & Evans, 1994). Any attempt to codify the major features of intervention to facilitate effective communication is almost certainly premature but, as a mnemonic, a checklist consisting of nine 'C's' (for Communication) may be helpful. As teachers, interventionists need to ensure they attend to Contingency, Consistency, Context, Clarity and Coordination. As scientist-practitioners, they must consider Charting and Control. Finally, as agents of sustainable change, they must not ignore Community and Continuity.

Teaching guidelines

Everything that has been learned from more than three decades of behavioural intervention, and much that is now known about the processes of normal early language acquisition, emphasises the importance of *contingency* in producing behavioural change. Whatever the communicative function being taught, it is essential to respond directly, immediately and enthusiastically to the behaviour of the learner. By the same token, the importance of *consistency* cannot be overstated. The learner's behaviour must be the most reliable way of securing the environmental consequences that will maintain it. When contingency and consistency are built into the design of an intervention and forms of communicative behaviour that need little effort to perform are selected, the interventionist can maximize the likelihood that the learner will acquire really effective levers on the social environment.

Ecological analysis virtually ensures that interventions will be based on the learner's living *context*. Rather than using sterile clinical environments for training sessions, behavioural intervention attempts, wherever possible, to make use of the opportunities afforded by the learner's habitual environment and daily routines. This approach is known as incidental teaching (Hart & Risley, 1975). By embedding communication training within the social milieu of people with intellectual disabilities, most of the steps between instruction and functional language use can be removed. Because it is possible to structure the course of any intervention without resorting to formal trial-by-trial procedures, most regularly-occurring events—grooming, food-related activity, shopping and many more—can provide excellent teaching opportunities. Such learning situations are high in spontaneity and involvement for both learner and teacher, and this provides its own intrinsic reinforcement. For example, a person who wants to eat a tasty snack must cook it first and may need some help. These simple needs provide many opportunities to teach how to request cooking implements and how to comment on the progress of the cooking. Far from forfeiting control over the teaching process itself, interventions that are woven into daily activities can remain highly structured, making use of the normal behaviour change techniques of imitation, prompting, shaping and reinforcement. The main difference between milieu-based and trial-by-trial-based training is that, in the former case, the teaching goal does not determine the purpose of the activity, whereas in the latter it does.

If there is trade-off between contextual relevance of intervention and the precision with which the teaching process can be reported, is a deal well worth making in terms of the empirical success of the approach. One aspect of any communication intervention programme that demands serious attention is the *clarity* with which its aims are specified. It is essential to ensure that targets are manageable and that teaching input is at a level to which the learner can be truly receptive. More often than not, this means attempting to produce small changes rather than large and dramatic ones. In the context of a well-carried-out assessment, a great deal can turn on teaching a person to use very few simple words or signs. Because effective intervention alters the capacity to communicate not just with an interventionist but with anyone who is a significant presence in his/her life, *coordination* of effort is vital. Ethical guidelines must be observed prior to intervention. All who may be involved should be advised of the aims and methods that will be used. Detailed project management reduces the possibility that the programme will founder as the result of some unanticipated organisational contingency which could have been planned around.

Scientist-practitioner guidelines

As with any other form of clinical intervention, work with people with communication difficulties should be approached as a research enterprise. As a minimum requirement, this involves *charting* the progress of the study, i.e. keeping a detailed record of each session so that the effects of intervention can be monitored. Beyond this, most interventions lend themselves to the use of single case research designs for the purposes of experimental *control*. This approach makes it possible to ensure that confident statements about the impact of communication-enhancing interventions can be defended (Remington, 1991).

Sustainability guidelines

Producing communicative change is, generally speaking, easier than maintaining it. Ensuring sustainability depends in part on constructing an effective intervention and in part on making sure that the context remains supportive of the intervention. A programme may ensure *continuity* by specifically designing generalization and maintenance as part of the planning process. There are a number of standard approaches to this; e.g. encouraging stimulus generalization by 'training loosely' (Stokes & Baer, 1977) and creating persistence by the introduction of intermittent reinforcement where appropriate. The second basis of sustainability is *community*. By getting cooperation, active involvement and support from other professionals, parents and caregivers, any communicative improvements will continue to function effectively long after the original interventionist has left.

An illustrative example

One problem with any set of guidelines is that they may seem somewhat arbitrary and distanced from the real business of intervention. As an antidote, it may be worthwhile to present one brief single-case study, which is a modified and simplified version of an experiment carried out by one of my own students (Hewitt, 1995). This study, in which Thomas—a child with severe intellectual disabilities—learned to use visual symbols to make appropriate requests, illustrates a number of the points discussed above.

Ecological analysis revealed that Thomas very much enjoyed laying the table for the morning snack-break at his school, and he did it on a daily basis. At each of six place settings he laid out a mat, a plate, and a cup appropriately as they were handed to him or were otherwise freely available. However, pre-tests revealed that he could not name these table items and did not request them verbally if they were not visible and in reach. This provided an excellent opportunity for communication training. The teaching procedure relied on the fact that a partially completed place setting created the circumstances (technically, a 'conditioned establishing operation'; Michael, 1993) in which access to the remaining item was necessary to complete the task. For example, when the mat and the plate had been placed, Thomas needed a cup, which the teacher had placed out of sight. Using the re-appearance of the cup as a reinforcer, Thomas was taught to select the pictographic symbol for cup from symbols for the three items of tableware placed in front of him. No artificial rewards were used—Thomas's appropriate symbol selection was ultimately reinforced by the opportunity to continue with a pattern of behaviour he found intrinsically enjoyable. Over a series of snack-breaks, Thomas was taught in a similar way to request all three table items using symbols.

This study illustrates a number of critical points about communication intervention. First, ecological analysis was used to identify an opportunity for training within a naturalistic setting. Second, the incidental training procedure was quite structured without being artificial. Third, because the requested table item was always out of sight, symbol use was spontaneous in that Thomas asked for what he wanted, even though he couldn't see it at the time he asked. Thus, the intervention had the potential for sustainability, since it did not involve any initiating action on the part of other care givers, who needed to do no more than respond to Thomas's request. Further, the fact that pictographic symbols were used meant that caregivers required no special expertise to understand his requests (c.f. manual signing).

Problem solving

A number of problems may arise in assessment and intervention for people with communication difficulties. Unfortunately, the number is so vast that it can scarcely be imagined. Thus, it is extremely difficult to attempt to formulate any specific 'if–then' advice and more general suggestions risk sounding merely platitudinous. This may, however, be a risk worth taking if it serves to reinforce some of the key considerations relating to any form of work with people with intellectual disabilities.

First, it is essential to be flexible in one's approach. When a procedure appears not to be working or to be causing distress, attempts to continue are almost always misguided. What is required is a reformulation. This is perhaps another way of saying that it is important to be data-led rather than bound to any particular theoretical analysis or methodological stricture. In the field of communication, in particular, it is important to keep watching and listening, not just to the individuals with whom you are working, but also to the many people with whom they interact on a daily basis. Sometimes care givers will be wrong, but more often than not they will have useful things to say to you. It is worth remembering that any intervention to improve communication has to make a difference to people other than the participants in your study before you can claim any success for it.

FURTHER READING

Grant, L., & Evans, A. (1994). *Principles of Behavior Analysis*. Harper Collins: New York.

Kaiser, A.P., & Gray, D.B. (1993). *Enhancing Children's Communication: Research Foundations for Intervention*. Paul H. Brookes: Baltimore, MD.

Reichle, J., York, J., & Sigafoos, J. (1991). *Implementing Augmentative and Alternative Communication: Strategies for Learners with Severe Disabilities*. Paul H. Brookes: Baltimore, MD.

PART IV

Consulting Skills

Chapter 14

WORKING WITH FAMILIES

Jo Bromley*

INTRODUCTION

A recent survey of a representative sample of people with intellectual disabilities in Wales (Evans et al., 1994) showed that 46% of people lived with their parents. This accounted for 77% of the sample who lived in private settings in the community. Although there has been an increasing move to provide independent living arrangements and sheltered housing for people with intellectual disabilities, it would therefore seem that care in the community, for many children and adults, means care provided by families. As such, it is inevitable that clinicians will find themselves working in family settings and with other family members at some time.

It has long been recognised that having some knowledge of the environment in which the referred client lives can be useful in formulating hypotheses and deciding whether certain interventions will be viable or acceptable. Functional analyses, for example, often take into consideration where and with whom clients spend their time (e.g. Donnellan et al 1988; see Chapters 1 and 8). From a behavioural perspective, therefore, there are clear advantages to interviewing families of clients with intellectual disabilities.

More recently, however, there has also been an upsurge of interest in the application of systemic ideas and principles in working with families where there is a member with an intellectual disability (see e.g. Turner, 1980; Vetere, 1993; Hennicke, 1993; Cobb & Gunn, 1994). One of the basic premises of family therapy is that the family acts as a self-regulating, interdependent 'system'. This system can be described as 'an entity whose parts interact, co-vary and evolve with each other in ways which maintain and protect existing patterns of living and adapt to change by

*South Manchester University Hospitals NHS Trust, UK

Clinical Psychology and People with Intellectual Disabilities. Edited by E. Emerson, C. Hatton, J. Bromley and A. Caine.

creating and promoting new patterns' (Burnham, 1994). The question practitioners may ask is what function a particular behaviour is serving for the whole family. The focus is firmly on examining how family beliefs and patterns of behaviour impact on the situation or behaviour that is being defined as problematic.

The aim of this chapter is to consider some of the issues a clinician may face in working with families where there is a member with intellectual disabilities, and to explore some of the challenges that this work may pose.

BREAKING THE NEWS

One of the earliest points of contact a clinician may have with families who have a member with an intellectual disability is shortly after that family have been given a diagnosis. Various studies have shown that families are often dissatisfied with the manner in which this is done (e.g. Quine & Pahl, 1986). Sloper and Turner (1993a) found that of a sample of 107 parents of children with physical and/or intellectual disabilities, 52% were dissatisfied or very dissatisfied with how the news was broken. Factors related to higher levels of satisfaction included whether professionals disclosing the news had seemed sympathetic, had appeared to understand parental concerns, and were direct and open to questions. Greater satisfaction was also achieved if parents were allowed to come back and ask questions later.

A number of documents have now been produced that illustrate good practice when breaking the news to parents that their child has some kind of disability (see Dale, 1996, for a review). These documents emphasise points such as seeing both parents together, giving enough time for a consultation, and having the child present and talking about him/her as a person of worth. Whilst clinical psychologists should not have to break the news directly, they may see a family shortly after the news has been given and should be sensitive to their needs at this point.

Being told that your child has an intellectual disability and, perhaps, some life-threatening disorder, is something parents do not prepare for (for a personal account of this experience, see Forrest, 1992). The process of adjusting to a child's disability has often been compared to the stages outlined in grief and bereavement work. Various research studies have suggested that shock is the first reaction that parents experience (see, for examples, the review produced by SCOVO, 1989).

Cunningham (1979; Cunningham & Davis, 1985) has suggested that families go through four stages;

❑ Shock.
❑ Reaction.
❑ Adaptation.
❑ Orientation.

In the shock phase, parents are described as being confused and disbelieving. In the reaction phase, they begin to accept the diagnosis and start to recognise that their lives will need to change and adapt. Common emotions at this point can include anger, sorrow, disappointment, guilt and failure. Parents may be horrified at their own responses; for example, the revulsion they may feel at their child's disability or thoughts that they wish their child were dead. An important role at this stage may be to voice some of the above reactions and facilitate discussion around parents' feelings or reactions.

In the adaptation phase, parents begin to ask about what can be done and how they can get help. Cunningham suggests that this signals a move forward, in that parents are seeking to gain a greater understanding of their child's condition and learn more about what they can do to support him/her. Whereas parents are still focused on the family at this point, by the orientation phase it is thought they are beginning to look outwards and start to develop routines for family life and make plans for the future.

Of course, not all families are told when their child is born that she/he has a disability. Sometimes parents or health visitors note that the child may have some difficulties when he/she is a toddler or young child. This can be an incredibly stressful time for families, particularly, for some carers, if a clear diagnosis cannot be given. As illustrated in Figure 14.1, supporting parents through the assessment process and helping them express some of their hopes and fears at this time can be a valuable role for a clinician.

Formulating parents' responses according to stage theories can, therefore, be helpful in that it can help clinicians understand family reactions or family needs. However, it should not be forgotten that stage models only provide general guidelines. As indicated by the case study in Figure 14.1, carers' responses are very individual and one carer may spend a lot longer in one stage than another. Parents' responses to their child's disability will depend greatly on their own belief families' views about disability. These beliefs will have originated from their own experiences, from their families' views about disability and from societal and cultural indicators. As noted in Chapter 4, Western society's views of disability have changed dramatically over the last century and it might therefore be expected that families might hold a number of different views on this issue. Families from other cultural groups may have different sets of

Figure 14.1 Case example 1

Mr and Mrs F had three children aged 11, 7 and 3. Their youngest child, E, was referred to the clinical psychology service as he was displaying pica. During the assessment, Mr and Mrs F expressed concern that E seemed to be quite socially withdrawn compared with their other children. They noted that he tended to prefer playing by himself and made little eye contact with others, particularly strangers. E's speech was delayed quite significantly and they were currently seeing a speech and language therapist. Mr and Mrs F noted that E's paediatrician had mentioned that E might have 'autistic tendencies' but were unsure what this meant for E and whether, if he received more speech and language input, E might develop to a cognitive level that was similar to other children his age.

Whilst the initial referral had therefore been for behaviour management advice with regards to the pica, the issue which turned out to be more important for Mr and Mrs F was whether their son had a global developmental delay and/or features of autism. To clarify this issue, a meeting was called for Mr and Mrs F and all the professionals involved and the paediatrician was able to explain his earlier comment. He noted that, although he thought E was too young for a definite diagnosis to be made, E did seem to be showing many behaviours that would fit on the autistic spectrum. It was then agreed that an educational assessment was warranted, along with further input from child psychiatry and clinical psychology.

This meeting had a profound impact on Mr and Mrs F and their feelings about the word 'autism', and the images they had of their son growing up were then explored in further clinical psychology sessions. Initially, Mr F was unable to accept the possibility that there might be any long-term difficulties with his son. He was guilty about feeling embarrassed by his son's behaviour and, since his daughters did not have any similar difficulties, his initial thought was that it must have been something he had passed on genetically. Mrs F did not react in quite the same way, as she said she had always felt something had been different about her youngest child. To some extent she said she was relieved that E was going to get extra help; however, she was clearly confused and upset when she thought of his future and she was worried that she had contributed to his difficulties by continuing to work when he was a young child.

Both parents initially reported feeling quite alienated from their son and both had fears about what might happen if they decided to have any more children; would they have the same difficulties; how would E cope? Gradually, however, both parents came to realise that neither of them were to blame for E's difficulties. They still experienced periods of upset but they began to be more active about exploring different nursery placements for E and became more interested in joining the local branch of the National Autistic Society. They were also more able to see past the diagnostic label they had been given to look at the strengths and weaknesses of their child. All of these might indicate a move to the orientation phase of Cunningham's model.

beliefs although, as Shah (1992) points out, it should not be assumed that every family from an ethnic minority has one view of disability born of their primary culture.

With stage theories, it is also often assumed that all families pass through each stage smoothly and consecutively and will eventually reach a point where they will have resolved any conflict or distress (Blacher, 1984). However, parents may move back and forth between stages and, whilst they may be able to look to the future and plan ahead, this does not mean they will have overcome feelings of loss. It is important to remember that responses and feelings such as grief and anger may well continue to re-emerge at later points in the family life cycle (Cunningham & Sloper, 1977).

LIFE CYCLE THEORY

The above issue is expanded by Vetere (1993), who notes that a family may re-experience a sense of grief and loss at later points in the child's life when they are forced to consider how different their child is from others without similar intellectual disabilities. Such times often correspond with changes in the family life cycle. In brief, life cycle theory (Carter & McGoldrick, 1980) states that there are different stages that families usually go through as they grow and develop. The first stage involves two people becoming partners, then there is the birth of their first child, the birth(s) of subsequent children, children starting school, passing through adolescence to adulthood, leaving school and leaving home, retirement, death of parents/grandparents and children forming relationships. Movement to each new stage can be difficult for many families to negotiate, particularly if family members are at incongruent stages of the life cycle (e.g. if older children in the family have their own children close to the age of their youngest sibling).

However, for families with a member with intellectual disabilities, each stage will have slightly different meanings and may lead to increased family stress or conflict (Vetere, 1993). When a child is ready to start school, for example, parents have to make the decision about whether they would like their child to be integrated into a mainstream school or attend a 'special' school. As the child with intellectual disabilities becomes a young adult, problems can arise if parents fail to renegotiate boundaries to give a young person more independence and allow him/her to take risks and have new experiences, or if they feel unable to let the person have a voice of his/her own (Konanc & Warren, 1984). For the person with intellectual disabilities, problems may arise at any point if he/she is prevented from completing different stages of the life cycle by other family members or by the state (e.g. if he/she wishes to form a partnership or have children). At such points, families may need extra support to help the person or themselves negotiate that particular stage.

Parker, Hill & Miller (1987) describe an interesting group approach for helping families, in which there is a young adult with intellectual disabilities available to discuss pertinent issues relating to the transition for that family member from child to adulthood.

How families cope at different stages of the life cycle will depend upon the stage each family member is at. If, for example, the child with intellectual disabilities is the youngest sibling and parents are older and have retired, there may be different pressures than in a family where the child with intellectual disabilities is the oldest sibling and parents are still expecting to care for younger children. The decision as to when the person with intellectual disabilities should leave home, usually to enter residential care, is often particularly difficult for families to make. Although parents are at the point in their life cycle when they would usually be focusing very much on their own lives, they are still involved in caring at a very high level for their offspring. This situation can be further complicated if they are also at the stage when they are caring for elderly relatives as well. Some studies (e.g. Selzer & Ryff, 1994, cited in Floyd et al., 1996) have shown that parents might enjoy caring for an adult with intellectual disabilities as they view their child as a companion, someone with whom they can still share their lives and maintain an important caring role. There may thus be a situation when an individual wishes to become more independent but is being hampered by his/her parents' caring role. When formulating any particular problem it can therefore be helpful to consider where the family is in its life cycle and what life cycle issues each member faces, and to ask oneself why this particular family might have presented for help right now. As with the concept of 'disability', each family member will have his/her own view on what is and what is not a 'normal' part of family life. However, life cycle theory can act as a useful framework within which to consider a family's difficulties and strengths (see Figure 14.2).

STRESS AND COPING

Although families with a member with intellectual disabilities do have certain issues to face which families without a member with intellectual disabilities do not, a common misconception is that all family members are more stressed as a consequence. However, there is evidence to suggest that many families cope very well with the extra pressures placed on them (Byrne, Cunningham & Sloper, 1988). Where once it was assumed that parents of children with intellectual disabilities, particularly mothers, would have very high stress levels compared to mothers of children without intellectual disabilities, it is now recognised that the amount of

Figure 14.2 Case example 2

N, a 16 year-old young man with moderate intellectual disabilities, was referred by his GP as his mother was concerned that he seemed to have become quite withdrawn. He attended the initial assessment with his mother, Ms D, who spoke for most of the interview. She noted that N had been spending a lot of time on his own in his room rather than with her in the lounge. She also said that he no longer seemed keen to go out for walks with the family and was reluctant to go to the local after school club, even though he used to enjoy it. Ms D noted that she was a single parent and had one daughter aged 26 and another son aged 18. N had been very close to his sister, who had just married and left home. Ms D said N's relationship with his brother was something of a 'love–hate' one, as although they had moments of being very close they also tended to fight, and his brother would tease N. This was something that angered his mother, however N's brother was about to go to university and she was hoping N's mood might improve when he was not around.

From a life cycle perspective, it could be hypothesised that N was actually feeling quite sad about his sister leaving and his brother's imminent departure. Perhaps their leaving highlighted his feelings of being 'different' and being left behind with his mother. This may have been the case with many young adults his age without a learning disability, although one could hypothesise that they could establish some independence from their parents and may be allowed out with their friends as and when they wished. Could the fact that his siblings were leaving lead N's mother to be more over-protective than usual and less able to allow N his own space to develop? Given N's age and his developmental stage, would it not be normal for him to be spending more time in his room away from his mother? Subsequent discussions with the family revealed that N had very few social contacts outside his family, although his brother and sister often had friends round. Another hypothesis was, therefore, that he was now at an age when he felt his disability more keenly and perhaps could be feeling quite depressed about his social life in comparison to his peers, as well as feeling low about his siblings leaving.

stress any family member might feel is individual and will change over time (Byrne & Cunningham, 1985). Undoubtedly some family members will be very distressed and experience high levels of stress at some times, but others seem to cope well.

What seems to make some families more vulnerable to stress than others? Vulnerability factors relating to the child include: severe levels of disability; extreme levels of activity; the existence of behaviour problems; poor sleep patterns; and the presence of physical health problems. Factors linked to the parents and family include: social isolation; economic difficulties; marital problems; lack of family closeness; and a high number of life events and the use of more passive coping strategies such as wishful thinking (i.e. wishing the situation was different) or avoidance.

Factors which seem to promote resilience to stress include: having a supportive social network; meeting parents who are in similar situations;

marital satisfaction; material wealth and resources; good health within the family; good communication between family members; ability to maintain a positive outlook; and the use of good problem-solving techniques and more active coping strategies, such as asking for help and support from services when it is needed (see e.g. Dale, 1996; Quine & Pahl, 1985; Sloper & Turner, 1993b).

When considering how best to conceptualise stress and coping in families with a member with intellectual disabilities many studies have explored the cognitive behavioural model described by Lazarus & Folkman (1984). According to this theory, when faced with a new situation, individuals will evaluate how important that event is to them and whether they have the resources to deal with it. The individual thus decides whether an event is potentially challenging (i.e. he/she has the resources to master it) or threatening (he/she does not have the resources and is in danger of losing something). Resources may mean financial back-up or degree of social support or professional assistance. Whether a particular event is considered threatening and stressful at any one time therefore depends on many factors. These include an individual's perception of the support he/she has both inside and outside the family, his/her attributions about the resources needed to cope, and the importance of the situation to him/her.

Various questionnaires have been designed to measure stress and coping, such as the Ways of Coping Questionnaire (Knussen et al., 1992) and it is important to consider family members' coping styles and attributions about certain events during your assessment and when you are formulating a case (see Cobb & Gunn, 1994). It may be that families need assistance to mobilise external support or to learn how to challenge attributions and appraisals of their own ability to cope that seem irrational or overly negative. High stress is often associated with depression, which has long been thought to be marked by negative biases in thinking (Beck et al., 1979). There may, therefore, be scope for some cognitive behavioural work with individual family members to help them identify unhelpful attributions and challenge more negative thought biases.

Floyd et al. (1996) describe a number of studies where cognitive behavioural techniques have been used to try and increase parents' access to social activities and social networks and challenge unrealistically negative attributions. For example, Nixon and Singer (1993) conducted a study with a group of parents with children with intellectual disabilities who showed high levels of self-blame and guilt. Parents were seen in a group format and cognitive behavioural techniques were used to challenge commonly held negative assumptions about their children and their roles as parents, with the result that levels of depression in parents and incidence of guilty and negative automatic thoughts decreased (see Nixon, 1992, cited in Floyd et al., 1996, for details of how to obtain a treatment manual). Changing attributions could be said to be similar to the systemic concept of 'reframing' (see Burnham, 1994).

Given that good problem-solving skills and the use of more active coping strategies seem to protect against stress, there may also be room to teach problem-solving skills and to focus parents on what they can do to tackle the problem situation (see Behaviour Management Technique for Parents).

SIBLINGS

Much of the above research into stress and coping has been criticised for focusing solely on how parents, particularly mothers, cope. More recently, however, some studies have focused on sibling reactions. Shulman (1988) identified three possible areas in which siblings of children with intellectual disabilities might experience disruption. The first is in the parent–child interaction, as parents may have to attend extra hospital appointments and may have less time for their non-disabled children. There may also be a time, when they first receive the news that their child has a disability, when parents are less emotionally available for their other children. The second area reflects family organisation, in that some families might change their routine to focus on the child with disabilities, thereby restricting activities and opportunities for their siblings. The third area is the role siblings may be given in the family. For example, parents' expectations of siblings' academic achievements may be raised to compensate for the change in their expectations regarding the child with intellectual disabilities. Alternatively, some siblings may also be expected to take on a more caring role than usual. A study by Cleveland and Miller (1997) indicated that a heavier burden of care does seem to fall on older sisters of children with intellectual disabilities.

Various studies have noted that siblings can express resentment and distress about having a member with an intellectual disability. Vevere (1993), for example, has noted that siblings can feel resentful if there is an expectation on them to look after their intellectually disabled sibling when their parents are no longer able to. However, not all siblings react adversely to having a brother or sister with an intellectual disability, and disruption of sibling–parent relationships is not necessarily a foregone conclusion. As with their parents, their reactions are likely to change over time and will probably vary depending on their interpretations and the family's beliefs, as well as the degree of support they receive from their parents and other agencies. Helpful books and videos are available from the National Autistic Society, for example, to help explain what autism or Asperger's syndrome are to siblings of children with these particular difficulties. MENCAP has other helpful publications for siblings of a child with intellectual disabilities.

THE FAMILY INTERVIEW

Who to invite?

Clearly, to assess some of the above issues there are going to be times when you want to interview different family members. One of the first points to consider is who to invite to a family session and when to invite them. If you have been seeing the person with intellectual disabilities as an individual client, it may be that this is negotiated with him/her. Alternatively, when you receive a referral for a client you may decide to invite the whole family to come to the initial session and work individually with the named client at a later point. A study by Goodyer (1986) suggests that some parents prefer non-disabled siblings not to be included in family sessions. However, as described above, meeting with siblings can reveal more about family functioning and highlight areas of potential difficulty and strength between them and the referred client. Basically, there are no hard and fast rules. For example, you may decide to start working with the client and his/her parents, and ask siblings to attend later in therapy when the family may be feeling more comfortable about the therapeutic process.

Including the person with intellectual disabilities

In keeping with the principles of social role valorization (see Chapter 1), it is important to ensure that the person with intellectual disabilities is included in family sessions. If the person can speak or sign, he/she then has an opportunity to comment on what he/she feels is happening within the family and can respond to comments others make. The therapist is also in a better position to observe how family members react to and communicate with this person. Does the person with intellectual disabilities have one particular advocate in the family? Do family members contradict each other in how they respond to the person with intellectual disabilities? Who interacts most/least with the referred person and who does he/she choose to interact with?

How to begin?

If you have never previously worked with a family where one member has an intellectual disability, it may be worth spending some time examining your own prejudices and beliefs about disability before you even see the family, so as to be aware of the impact these may have on your questioning in the session and subsequent formulation of the 'problem' (see Dale, 1996). It is also useful to review these prejudices if you find you have stopped being curious about a family's interactions, as it may be that you are making assumptions that are based on your own beliefs rather than on the family's (see Palazolli et al., 1980, for further information regarding maintaining curiosity).

When the family have arrived for their first session, as with any interview it is useful to begin with questions about whatever the family feel they have a problem with. This will elucidate whether family members do have the same ideas and recognise a similar problem, or whether their ideas are more diverse. If the 'problem' being described relates to the referred person's behaviour, a full behavioural assessment may be completed as usual. However, having all family members present does mean there is the chance to highlight any discrepancies in terms of how problematic behaviour is handled within the family, learn more about what functions that problem might be serving in the family, and discover family members' different beliefs and attributions about that problem.

As Floyd et al. (1996) point out, families with a member with intellectual disabilities may be very used to accessing services for that family member. However, like any other family, those with an intellectually disabled member will still have crisis points and may have to cope with separation, divorce or the reconstitution of two families as parents remarry. These issues may be particularly pertinent and the initial goal of therapy may be to help families identify what part of the 'problem' is to do with disability and what is to do with other external or environmental issues. Some families who are still adjusting to the news that their child has a disability might come hoping that this can be 'fixed'. In this case, it may be one of the first goals of therapy to address this and help the family look at exactly what difficulties they or their child are experiencing that together you might be able to modify.

Using geneograms

Geneograms can be a useful way of elucidating any recent life changes, gaining some perspective on family life cycle issues and assessing the degree of support a family might have available to them. The act of drawing up a geneogram is also one way to include the whole family, including the referred person. Commonly used symbols can be seen in Figure 14.3. Exact dates should be gained for significant life events such as marriages, births and deaths. It is helpful to draw out approximately three generations, although there are no hard and fast rules. Sometimes it can be useful to ask families if there is anyone else who is important to them or to the referred client who is not in their immediate family, such as a neighbour or close friend (see Burnham, 1994, for examples). It may also be helpful to review which other professionals are involved with the family you are seeing. If, for example, a community nurse has been working particularly closely with the family, it may be fruitful to invite her along to a session (as long as the family consent).

Using circular questions

When trying to elicit information about the family system, testing a hypothesis or when considering how to facilitate change, it is important to consider what kind of questions to ask the family. In the systemic literature, much emphasis has been given to the use of circular questions. The aim of using circular questions is to encourage family members to think beyond linear causation, raise their awareness of family relationships and consider alternative ways of acting for the future (see Tomm, 1985). By definition, a circular question has to refer to two or more entities that are external to the person being questioned.

Circular questions have been divided into various different categories (see Burnham, 1994, Mason, 1991; Tomm, 1985). These include questions relating to relationship differences, classification or ranking questions, questions focusing on one behavioural sequence, hypothetical or future questions and diachronic (now/then) questions. Examples of each are given in Figure 14.4. It is important to note that some questions can belong to more than one category. A question designed to produce change rather than just elicit information is sometimes referred to as a reflexive question. Examples can be found in Tomm (1987).

To understand a circular question, one clearly needs the ability to conceptualise family relationships in some way and it may be thought that this would preclude the use of such questions with people with intellectual disabilities. However, recent articles by Fiddell (1996) and Salmon (1996) indicate that circular questioning and other systemic techniques can be used effectively with people with intellectual disabilities. Questions may

Figure 14.3   Common symbols used in geneograms. From Burnham, 1994, with
permission

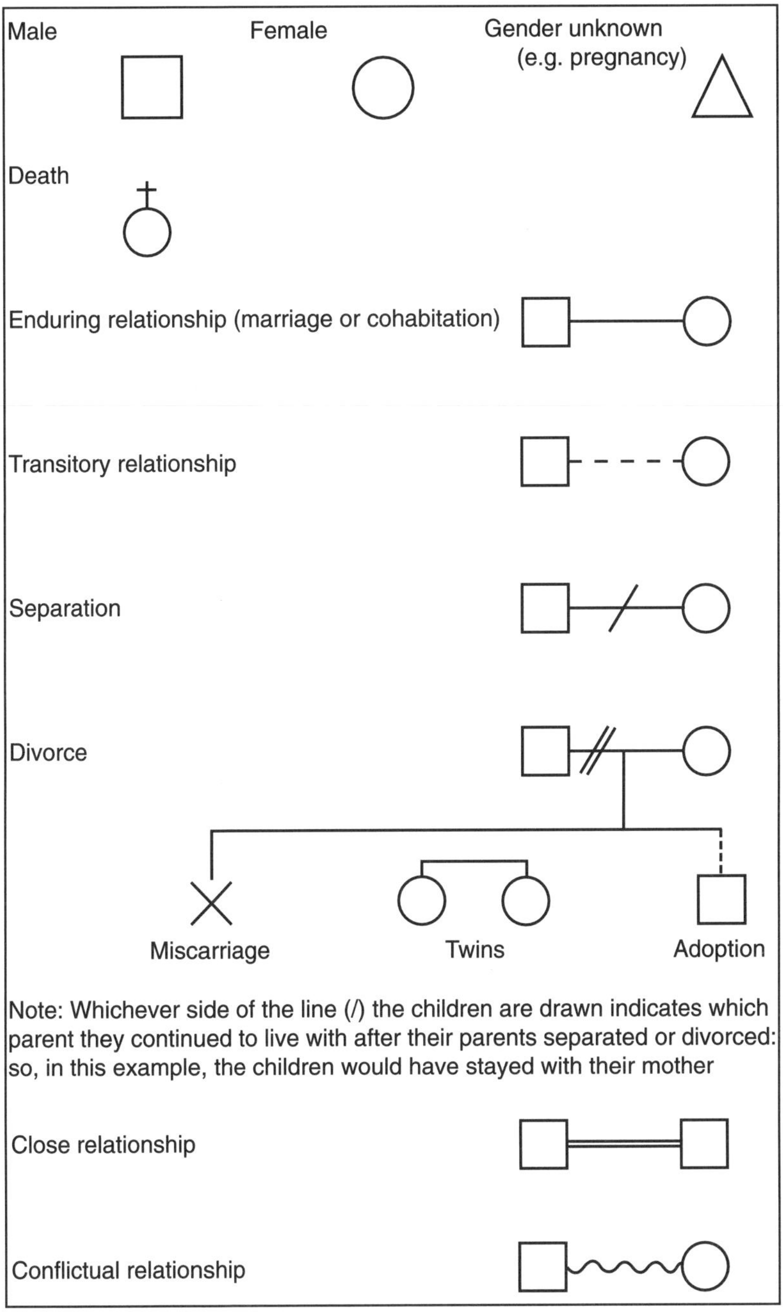

Male   Female   Gender unknown
(e.g. pregnancy)

Death

Enduring relationship (marriage or cohabitation)

Transitory relationship

Separation

Divorce

Miscarriage   Twins   Adoption

Note: Whichever side of the line (/) the children are drawn indicates which
parent they continued to live with after their parents separated or divorced:
so, in this example, the children would have stayed with their mother

Close relationship

Conflictual relationship

simply need adapting and more visual aids and markers may need to be included in the session. Fiddell refers to a comprehensive paper by Benson (1991), which explores the use of circular questions with children. When discussing relationship differences, Benson has tried using role plays to help elicit children's views about other family members (e.g. by encouraging children to use props like hats and scarve to act as if they are someone else in the family). Benson also suggests videoing the family and then using the video with them to explore different patterns of interaction and ask behavioural sequence questions.

With regard to classification questions, Benson discusses the use of pictures of smiling and frowning faces and asking children, 'Which one of these is most like what you and your brother have been like this week?' As discussed in Chapter 6, there is evidence that people with intellectual disabilities can use rating scales. Thus, there seems no reason why visual rating scales could not be used to back up classification or ranking questions in a session. Benson also discusses the use of pictures and cartoons to convey certain ideas. Again there seems no reason why similar ideas could not be used in family sessions where there is a person with an intellectual disability. The question 'If Nicola did not hit her head so much, what might happen in your house in the morning?' could be answered with words and pictures. People with intellectual disabilities are commonly talked over and about and it could be argued that circular questions might be seen to reinforce this practice if the question is not asked of all family members, and if attempts are not made to also hear the views of the person with disability. The challenge to the therapist is perhaps in seeing how inventive he/she can be.

Exploring relationships

Questioning families will reveal certain patterns of relationships and reflecting on these patterns might provide valuable insights into the 'problem' that the family brings. Minuchin (1974) was one of the first to talk about family enmeshment and disengagement. In an enmeshed family one might see extreme closeness, with enmeshed family members being unwilling to stand alone and act in an individual way. Disengagement represents under- rather than over-involvement in the family, with some members appearing distant to others. In enmeshed relationships, boundaries between the different roles of family members are likely to be blurred and diffuse, whereas in disengaged relationships they seem firm and inflexible.

As Burnham (1994) points out, it is rare that one sees a family that is totally characterised by enmeshment or disengagement, but one might

Figure 14.4 Examples of some circular questions

Question type	Focus	Examples
Relationship differences	Aim is to explore different relationship patterns within a family group	Who gets most upset when Shamila doesn't talk to them; your mum or your dad?
Classification/ ranking	Respondent is asked to rank items in some way	Who do you think gets most upset in your family?
		Who would you argue with most?
		Who is most likely to agree with Nick?
		If your brother isn't there; who's most likely to agree with Nick?
Behavioural sequence	Encourage families to reflect on what happens when a particular behaviour occurs. These are the types of questions that might be asked in a functional analysis	What does your mum do when Steve hits your brother?
		What does your stepdad do then?
		What does Steve do when your stepdad responds like that?
Hypothetical/ future	Can help the family acknowledge ideas they already have about the future and consider alternative ideas and possibilities	Let's suppose Hari finds a place where he does want to live, who will be the first to celebrate with him?
		How will you know when Louis is feeling less sad?
		If you thought Louis was never going to feel any better, what would your mum have to do to make sure he had some happy times?
Diachronic	Encourage families to look at time differences; compare the past, present and future	Do you think your sister was more aggressive towards you before Dad moved out or after?
		What was different about Sarah before she started high school compared to now?

see particular relationship dyads or triads within families which are characterised by one or the other pattern. One parent might become particularly enmeshed with his/her child with intellectual disabilities, for example, which might make it harder for that family to negotiate life cycle stages where the child might have to become more independent (e.g. on starting school or leaving home). Such an enmeshed relationship might also then impact on other siblings in the family, as noted earlier, and their relationships with their carer might be characterised more by disengagement. Similarly, one grandparent may develop a particularly close relationship with the person with intellectual disabilities and this might cause friction within a family.

When meeting a family it may be helpful to consider who seems allied to whom and what function that alliance might be serving. In diadic relationships, who seems to be 'in charge', and what does the alliance mean for other family members? If there is a particular triad in a family, what is the role for the third person? Is he/she a peacekeeper, a go-between, an ally for one person? The types of circular questions mentioned above can be useful tools in helping elicit relationship patterns and perhaps challenge established, inflexible patterns, to encourage the family to consider other possibilities and to set more appropriate boundaries.

In the above example, when the mother might have allied to the child with intellectual disabilities to the exclusion of other family relationships, one might ask; what was it like before (the child with intellectual disabilities) was born? Who did mum talk to most? What would happen if (the referred adolescent child) got a boy/girlfriend? Who would be most worried? Who would be most pleased?

Working with a team

Given that it is often difficult to observe all family interactions and concentrate on the discussion in hand, it may be helpful to utilise family therapy practices such as working with a co-therapist or supervising team. Not all services can accommodate this, but if working alone it might be helpful to tape the session to observe or listen to later, so that as well as the content of what has been said, the process (how it has been said, by whom) can also be explored. Does it seem, for example, that every time a question is addressed to the referred client, his/her sibling answers?

Unfortunately, as with many systemic concepts touched on here, there is not room in this chapter to explore teamwork in more detail. However, those interested should refer to Anderson (1987) or Parry and Doan (1994). Other systemic concepts, such as the use of stories and narratives, seem equally applicable to working with families with a member with an intellectual disability; however, a full discussion of these techniques is again beyond the scope of this chapter. Recommended reading in this area includes Roberts (1994).

BEHAVIOUR MANAGEMENT TECHNIQUES FOR PARENTS

At some stage in your interaction with the family, as well as exploring family relationships in a systemic way and considering parental attributions, there may well be some point where behavioural programmes are considered, particularly if the referred client is showing aspects of challenging behaviour (see Chapter 8). Various studies have confirmed that parents can be taught to use behavioural techniques successfully at home (see Baker, 1996, for a review) and may continue to use these techniques for some time (Harris, 1986), although care needs to be taken to discuss concepts such as generalisation.

Although training has tended to be done on an individual rather than group basis, groups have been found to be equally successful (Brightman et al., 1982) and are more cost-effective. Groups for parents with children with conduct disorders who do not have intellectual disabilities have currently produced much research interest (e.g. Webster-Stratton, 1991) and there would seem to be no reason why similar groups might not be useful for parents of children with intellectual disabilities and behaviour problems. Such groups might also provide a useful contact point for families and may help bolster support for families who are under stress.

WHEN TO END THERAPY

Often, one of the most difficult questions to answer is when involvement with a family should end. Life cycle changes are constant and mean that fresh dilemmas will be faced by families as time passes. In general, it should help if clear goals are set at the beginning of therapy with regards to what specific tasks or difficulties the family want help with. It will then be easier to take baseline measures, monitor change and establish when the tasks of therapy have been completed. Part of the therapeutic role may be to give families information about local self-help and support groups, as well as advocacy services. A useful contact in this area is MENCAP, who produce a comprehensive list of self-help booklets. Discussing issues such as how to end therapy and, indeed, how to use some of the techniques mentioned above, should also be something that is addressed in supervision.

FURTHER READING

Burnham, J. (1994). *Family Therapy.* Routledge: London.
Dale, N. (1996). *Working with Families of Children with Special Needs: Partnership and Practice.* Routledge: London.

Floyd, F.J., Singer, G.H.S., Powers, L.E., & Costigan, C.L. (1996). Families coping with mental retardation: assessment and therapy. In *Manual of Diagnosis and Professional Practice in Mental Retardation* (ed. J.W. Jacobson & J.A. Mulick). American Psychiatric Association: Washington, DC.

Vetere, A. (1993). Using family therapy services for people with learning disabilities. In *Using Family Therapy in the 1990s*, 2nd edn (ed. J. Carpenter & A. Treacher). Blackwell: Oxford.

Chapter 15

WORKING WITH ORGANISATIONS, OR: WHY WON'T THEY FOLLOW MY ADVICE?

Judith McBrien* and Sue Candy*

INTRODUCTION

Most of your career as a clinical psychologist specialising in work with people with intellectual disability (or any other dependent client group) will not be spent face-to-face delivering 'psychology' to the client. Rather, the majority will be spent working through third parties, asking them to collect assessment information, persuading them of the wisdom of your proposed intervention, providing them with advice and training. In this way, the lot of the clinical psychologist is to be 'an authority' rather than 'in authority', using persuasion rather than coercion. Contrast this with the position of, say, a head teacher or service manager who can insist that their advice is carried out. Whilst working as an authority can bring a sense of status and worth and earn the respect and gratitude of others, it may conversely prove a surprisingly frustrating and disempowering experience if mishandled.

To avoid such a fate, the clinical psychologist needs two skills in addition to his/her core skills *qua* psychologist; those of giving advice and of working with other advice givers (i.e. colleagues from other professions, as part of multi-disciplinary teams and wider service networks). These skills are essential for a successful psychologist who wishes to be influential with clients, carers and systems, but surprisingly, are not routinely taught on clinical training courses. Too often the clinical psychologist behaves as a 'one-man band' and fails to maximise his/her impact through joint approaches.

*Westbourne Unit, Scott Hospital, Plymouth, UK

Clinical Psychology and People with Intellectual Disabilities. Edited by E. Emerson, C. Hatton, J. Bromley and A. Caine.
© 1998 John Wiley & Sons Ltd.

This chapter commences with a brief description of the working environment, then discusses avoiding the pitfalls involved in giving advice, and when working with the recipients of your advice. It is assumed that the reader has at his/her fingertips a range of skills in conducting assessment, functional analysis and interventions.

THE WORKING ENVIRONMENT

Knowing the organisation is important when planning advice for an individual client and it will rarely be as simple as dealing with one provider. The same advice may apply across a number of settings but the intricacies of implementation may be very different in each one. An understanding of the ways in which such a plethora of providers and purchasers is linked is essential, in particular the NHS and Community Care Act 1990 and the ensuing local guidance, especially that governing the operation of care management.

Question: Do you know how care management works in your area?

People with intellectual disability are enmeshed in a web of caring agencies and individuals. For children and most adults, parents have a life-long role and stake in the care provided (see Chapter 14). In addition, the average adult with severe intellectual disabilities may be living in a staffed group home, attending two different day centres and occasionally spending time in a treatment unit. They may have different aspects of their healthcare delivered by any number of health professionals (generic and specialist). They will almost certainly have aspects of their lives organised by Social Services via a Care Manager. The purchasers of this range of care may include a health authority, a GP fundholder (in due course, Primary Care Groups or Trusts) and Social Services. The picture for children with intellectual difficulties is similar, with the all-important addition of education providers (special schools, mainstream schools, etc.).

The types of provider vary enormously. Residential, day care and support services may all be provided by the same organisation in which you work or, more commonly, by a number of different agencies, some of them independent providers in the voluntary or private sector, some statutory like Social Services, Education and the NHS (see Chapter 4). These providers will have varying levels of expertise and maturity as organisations, reflected in the quality of their staff, their management arrangements and their protocols. Different providers will also hold differing philosophies of care and treatment. Understanding your own position within this complex scheme is an essential first step in becoming a useful and influential practitioner.

Question: Do you know which organisations provide for adults and children in your area? Do you know the role and philosophy of each, especially your own employer?

GIVING ADVICE

This section assumes that you have made your assessments, developed an hypothesis and are ready to draw up a plan for intervention which you wish others to implement. The most soundly based advice is only good advice if it can be and is implemented. An important but often neglected step is to plan to increase advice compliance alongside the development of the actual intervention. Making a plan for implementation is as important as making a good assessment, functional analysis and plan of intervention. This section looks at some of the stages of doing this.

Presenting your rationale and plan

The aim in presenting your rationale is twofold—to gain agreement and to gain commitment to implementation. The recipients of your advice will need to reach a consensus that your rationale of the presenting problem is the right one or at least worth pursuing. An effective way to do this is to present the data from your baseline assessments and the options for intervention and then facilitate the care staff to identify the salient issues. This can be done through brainstorming at a staff meeting or with a smaller group of key workers and team manager/s. This will foster a joint responsibility for the success of the plan. The data should be presented in as creative a fashion as possible using videotapes or graphs of baseline information, role play, comparative case studies and so on, as appropriate.

Making the plan clear to all

Once agreement is reached on the nature of the intervention, it is important that everyone understands his/her role in implementation. Do not assume that gaining agreement means that everyone has a clear understanding of his/her role in the plan or that expectations are similar. Always check this out. This can be done informally or more formally through the use of an intervention agreement. This is a contract between the advice giver and the recipients of the advice (including the client as far as possible). It clarifies who will do what, when and for how long, what constitutes success or progress, when to seek further advice or a change and how the plan will be monitored and evaluated. Such a contract will clarify expectations for all stakeholders and avoid misperceptions or confusion as the plan unfolds. In some situations a contract may adversely affect rapport, so the use of such a formal approach should be carefully judged. A rule of thumb is that the more carers and settings there are, the more likely it is that an agreement of some sort will be useful.

Front-line staff, in particular, need the plan and its rationale explained at first hand. This can be time-consuming, especially when it involves a large staff group and a range of shift patterns, but it is time well spent. Without this expenditure of time you are at the mercy of the organisation's own communication system and the Chinese whispers that may involve.

If your plan necessitates expenditure by the recipients, it will help to be realistic about the level of resources available and to try to understand the organisation's constraints. When resources are required, especially if this is long-term, this must be presented to those who hold the budget as soon as possible in a way that is well argued and clear. If funding is not possible then your plan will need adjusting or even abandoning in favour of a different course of action.

The advice itself

The advice should be written down in a simple-to-follow way. You should avoid jargon or abbreviations which may not be understood by all. If the advice is genuinely lengthy and/or complex there should be a step-by-step summary to act as an *aide memoire*. Written instructions are not always sufficient to ensure compliance, as they may not be understood. Role-playing complex intervention programmes or videotaping someone carrying it out effectively is useful.

Follow-through

It is this stage of an intervention which is most often neglected, the psychologist moving on to new referrals and failing to provide adequate follow-up. Assuming an intervention has commenced and the carers are enthusiastic, remember that maintenance over time will be affected by your commitment to monitoring it, refining it and providing summarised feedback on progress. Initial advice compliance may be good, especially if the advice works immediately, but may then drift. Any records which you have asked staff to make should be regularly collected, analysed, summarised and fed back to the carers. Explain when carers should contact you during implementation. Keep other key stakeholders informed, for example the care manager. Hold follow-up reviews. Give positive feedback, including to managers, praising staff for compliance and enthusiasm. Keep monitoring. Identify when to let the recipients stop the programme or modify it. Listen to carers' views and any objections or practical difficulties which arise. Modify the plan to overcome these where possible. Keep setbacks and problems in perspective, referring back to the original baseline data and targets.

More can be achieved by a 10 minute telephone call at frequent intervals (even daily) in the early stages than by setting a review date a month ahead, by which time the intervention may already have faltered.

Good housekeeping

Keeping your own records in order and up-to-date is essential. There will be quality standards for this, set by your own organisation, which need to be followed. Make sure that all your contacts with the carers and client are recorded and dated, and that relevant others are copied in to your reports (e.g. care manager, GP), ensuring that the circulation list is clearly noted.

To cope with complaints against your practice and with potential or actual litigation, make sure that all your records and reports are observation-specific and do not stray into generalisations which go beyond the evidence. For example, write, 'I saw Mrs Jones pick up John Smith by the arm and shake him on Tuesday June 12th at 12.30 p.m.' rather than 'care staff in this home are aggressive towards clients'. If you feel it necessary to report third-party information, then note your source. For example, write, 'Mr Hopkins told me on Wednesday June 13th that he had seen Mrs Jones . . .' In writing a conclusion, you can say, for example, 'given the data collected there is some evidence that clients in this home are not being given adequate quantities of food. This is based on a limited number of direct observations. More data are needed to substantiate the suspicion'.

A final point on reports is to be careful about their distribution. Make it clear if the report is not to be copied on to others without your permission.

Problems in the psychologist

Some of the common pitfalls are lack of background information, on your part, about the setting or about previous interventions with the same client; a failure to listen to the carers' points of view; an over-theoretical approach which lacks practicality for the setting/s; an over-complex, and hence misunderstood, presentation of your advice; and failure to follow through.

Sometimes, when advice has not been followed, the psychologist looks to blame the setting, the staff or the management, rather than the quality of his/her own advice or the way it is delivered. This can lead to an array of problems, with the psychologist perceived as a 'hit and run' professional who does not really understand the day-to-day struggles faced by staff. The relationship suffers and it becomes harder to gain commitment and co-operation from the setting. This can make the psychologist adopt a 'take it or leave it' attitude to his/her own advice. At best this might result in an half-hearted attempt to follow the advice or, at worst, it would be sabotaged from the start.

Psychologists do not always enjoy a good reputation amongst colleagues. Osborne-Davis (1996) in a small survey of attitudes to clinical psychologists amongst nurses and occupational therapists in the same service, found that clinical psychologists continue to be a virtually unknown group in the eyes of other health care staff. Psychologists were perceived as 'remote' and 'aloof' and playing a 'minimal or no role in providing a service'. They were seen as occupying well-paid, well-resourced and privileged positions.

Unless psychologists can take steps to become real members of teams, recognising the contribution of other professionals, they will disappear from the National Health Service. The 'we know best' attitude coupled with the ability to walk away from a difficult case has long been tolerated, but this is rapidly changing in an NHS which is ever more accountable for both quality and costs.

WORKING WITH THE RECIPIENTS OF ADVICE

The previous section looked at how advice can be enhanced by attention to its delivery. This section looks at difficulties from which the recipients of your advice may be suffering which militate against advice being followed.

Difficulties within a provider team

In a group of carers, such as in a staffed residential home, a number of difficulties may present themselves. Some of these are outlined below. It is also worth remembering that sometimes staff are simply coping as best they can and the psychologist needs to be sensitive to identifying the problems in a way that facilitates change rather than demotivates staff. Detailed information on this area is to be found in the literature on organisational psychology.

Poor communication

Poor communication bedevils nearly all teams at some time, either between the managers and the staff or between the staff themselves. This is usually exacerbated by shift systems, especially those which have dedicated night staff. Most psychological interventions require consistent application by all staff and accurate record keeping and this means relying on good communication between carers.

Lack of staff

A team may be short-staffed for any number of reasons, resulting in burn-out for those who remain at work and a reduced capacity to implement new approaches.

Weak links

There may be one weak link in a team who is disaffected or incompetent and whose effect is to disrupt attempts at consistency in an intervention.

Lack of experience/knowledge

The staff in a team may be inexperienced in working with people with intellectual disabilities and may lack basic knowledge or information which you might have taken for granted. See the example of Joe (Figure 15.1).

Management style

There may be a management style in a home or day centre which is not conducive to the implementation of a new way of working with a client.

Figure 15.1   Joe

The local respite unit for children aged 5–15 years referred a 15 year-old boy with Down's syndrome. Joe lived at home with his parents and had been excluded from the unit because he was beyond their control. The parents and his severe learning difficulties (SLD) school experienced no difficulties, although he suffered frequent pain and could be moody and distressed. The respite unit had a large staff team (more than 20) who, with the exception of the manager, were all young women, newly recruited, many into their first jobs. They had no qualifications and no in-service training beyond induction. Moody adolescents are a very different proposition to endearing five year-olds. Staff were divided about their feelings for Joe. Some felt he should not attend and some were fond of him and felt he should. Staff inconsistency was high and previous psychological advice had been unsuccessful.

Approach taken   The manager was asked to identify a core group of staff who were fond of Joe. The psychologist worked solely with this group for the next few months to devise and implement a workable approach to Joe's behaviour. The manager's co-operation was crucial in that he had to alter the staffing rota to ensure that whenever Joe was in for respite, then staff from the core group were on duty. As the new approach was seen to work, other staff were gradually rota'd to work alongside members of the core group until each gained the confidence and skills necessary to work with Joe.

For example, a culture of fear and suspicion against a background of allegations and dismissals will not lend itself to frank discussion of a client's needs. A disorganised or *laissez-faire* management style is also counterproductive.

Attitudes, beliefs and theories

The staff team may hold, individually or collectively, beliefs about the client or about all people with intellectual disabilities which are in conflict with your own. They may have espoused a particular theory of behaviour or a particular 'therapy' or approach which would have to be dropped if your recommendations were to be followed. It is important to understand the underlying philosophy of a provider. For example, a group home which sees itself as a family will view client need and how to meet it differently from a home which has a philosophy of staff as support workers.

A common attitude which may well be voiced is one which says that 'these people cannot change—they just need tender loving care'. A variation on this is the attitude that 'this is their home—they must not be made to do anything they do not want to' (and therefore we must not keep records, change their behaviour, etc.).

> **Figure 15.2**   Group referral
>
> All the residents in a privately run residential home were referred to clinical psychology by Social Services for an assessment of their needs. Enquiry showed that the Social Services district who funded the home were overspent and had poured additional funding into the home for some years. The reason for the referral, whilst not unreasonable, was to gain information as to whether the fees paid to the home could be reduced whilst still meeting client need.
>
> *Approach taken* The reason for referral was discussed with the referrer, who was asked to make this explicit to the residential home, backed up in writing, before the referral was accepted. After discussion it was felt more appropriate that the local community nurse, linked to the home, should undertake the assessment task using the regular assessments for placing clients in residential care.

Hidden agendas

It may be that the staff team or their manager has an ulterior motive in referring a client to you. For example, it is not uncommon for a residential home to request an assessment to support an application for further funding, or to use your advice to have a client removed from a setting on the grounds that he/she is too difficult to manage or that his/her needs are not properly met in that setting (see the examples of the Group Referral, Figure 15.2 and Dan, Figure 15.3). Less common but still possible is an agenda that sets out to use your expertise to assist in building evidence against an incompetent or dangerous member of staff.

Difficulties between providers

A group of care staff, whilst in themselves well-organised, may be receiving advice contradictory to yours from another quarter, perhaps from another professional or organisation. Such advice may have been given in the past or may be occurring contemporaneously with yours. A particular problem may occur if different advice has been given by another Clinical Psychologist (see the example of Duncan, Figure 15.4).

Whose problem is it?

The client may have been referred because the care staff perceive that his behaviour or lack of it is a problem. Analysis may reveal, however, that this is not a problem to the client but presents difficulties for the staff. You may feel it unethical to change the client to suit the needs of the staff.

Figure 15.3 Dan

A man in his 40s, living in a large, private residential home and attending a nearby day centre, was referred to clinical psychology for stealing food and money. Whilst the couple who manage the home were seemingly keen to participate, the home was institutional, not well co-ordinated and had a low staffing ratio. At night Dan was socialising with and helping the cleaners in return for cigarettes. The Care Manager felt the home was not meeting his needs. However, the home was reluctant to lose another resident (few new clients were placed there) and Dan's sister was happy with his placement, especially as it was far enough away to prevent him from pestering his elderly mother for money.

Approach taken after discussion with the Care Manager, it was agreed to start by tackling Dan's stealing only within the day centre setting. Here there was a committed member of staff and a well-organised programme into which psychological advice could be slotted. Once a successful intervention was found, the plan was to approach the less well-organised residential home. Meanwhile, the Care Manager was able to continue the more complex task of trying to raise standards within the home generally. Subsequent reviews of Dan were attended by the psychologist, who was able to contribute further to the debate over whether or not the home was indeed meeting his needs.

Conversely, you may decide that a client definitely needs help with a particular behaviour or life style, but the staff team are content to allow the situation to continue. Again this raises an ethical dilemma. How do you bring pressure to bear in the interests of the client? (see the example of Diana, Figure 15.5).

Knowing your audience

As soon as you become involved in a setting or with staff whom you do not know, you will need to assess their strengths and weaknesses, in particular the skills and attitudes they possess, the available resources, the level of commitment and the nature of any constraints. It is important to do this at all levels, from the front line staff through to the manager(s).

How to assess staff's strengths and weaknesses? The extent to which care staff have completed baseline records and kept appointments with you is a guide to their *motivation* to follow advice. Further, the accuracy of such records and competence at filling them in are a guide to the care staff's *ability* to follow advice. A useful method to ascertain a staff team's capabilities is to seek the opinions of other members of the multi-disciplinary team who are familiar with working there.

Figure 15.4   Duncan

A 15 year-old autistic boy with profound learning difficulties was referred to clinical psychology because of aggression to others. He attended an SLD school, where he was taught in a class of eight by a teacher and classroom assistant. During assessment it was clear that the parents believed that the teacher did not understand or teach their son adequately. The school expressed confidence in the teacher, but the Speech and Language Therapist felt that the teacher was poor. The parents had close links with the Autistic Society and drew on their advice, which directly contradicted the psychologist's.

Approach taken there was little alternative here but to gather firm data on the problems by observation in class of the teaching content and style and the management methods and by listening to the parental views. This information was then presented at a series of meetings: parents with psychologist; psychologist with head teacher; psychologist with head teacher and class teacher; psychologist with Autistic Society representative; a meeting of all parties. It proved possible to iron out differences with the Autistic Society so that there was no further conflict of advice for the parents. The head teacher, recognising that the particular class teacher was failing, began a process of setting clear performance targets and requiring compliance with outside advice, but was not prepared to move the boy to another class (which the parents were requesting). It was not until the following school year that the boy moved to a different class and no further problems with aggression were experienced. Whilst meeting the reason for referral, the process of working in this way helped the parents to clarify what they desired for their son and helped the head teacher to tackle a sensitive staff management problem. It also brought about a better relationship between the psychologist and the local Autistic Society.

Minimise constraints

The most usual constraints and those that you should consider are: programmes with other clients in the same setting, staff holidays, other events due to take place (such as Christmas), staff burnout or turnover, inflexible staffing levels or rotas, and differences of opinion. Some constraints can be worked round and your intervention still remain viable. Others will require a different approach, such as staff training or reporting the difficulties to people who can effect more fundamental change. It may be that there is an issue to be dealt with but it may not be a priority, at this time, in comparison to other issues. Recognise that you may not be the right person or involved at the right time to be effective.

Attitudinal differences

Differences of opinion between stakeholders do present a challenge, as illustrated by some of the examples. Understanding why people act or express attitudes in certain ways will help you cope with your own feelings of frustration, annoyance or helplessness. Drawing on the full range of psychological theory and clinical practice and not just that relevant to people with intellectual disabilities is useful. The important message is not to work in isolation from other professionals, stakeholders, systems or rules, but to bring the stakeholders together early on to make differences explicit, seek agreement (compromising if necessary) and clarify roles.

Staff training

In order for staff to follow your advice it may be necessary to take a sideways step from meeting the needs of the referred client and set up some training. Staff training is most effective if delivered at the point when it addresses an immediate need for the staff group. Thus, providing training directly to support an individual intervention is likely to be a worthwhile use of your time.

There is an enormous array of quality training materials available off the shelf. Sources of information on training packages include the British Institute of Learning Disability and Pavilion Publishers. Do not assume that any training needs must be met by you. In most places the NHS Trust and/or Social Services will have local training officers (some generic and some dedicated to intellectual disability) and/or a local management development trainer. These people have a wealth of resources and expertise plus a remit to train staff. Skills and knowledge-based training founded in clinical psychology may appropriately fall to the clinical psychologist. Other topics may best be tackled with a colleague from another profession.

When to give up and when to blow the whistle

There will be times when, despite your best efforts, you are getting nowhere. You may reach a point when there is little or no compliance with your advice and apparently no constructive action left open to you. The important point here is not simply to walk away and discharge the client but to present a cogent report to the referrer and the stakeholders which highlights the needs and the obstacles. The objective is to alert the relevant people, who may be able to engineer change (having recourse to those 'in authority'). For example, you may recommend that the client's needs can only be served by a move from his/her residential home. In

---

Figure 15.5   Diana

During a personal relationships course, a woman with severe learning disability became distressed and disclosed that she had been told not to masturbate at home. Her key worker explained that Diana would masturbate in the lounge and that other residents were complaining. The psychologist suggested installing a lock on her bedroom door. This was against the home's policy. To overcome this, the psychologist suggested a sign which she could place on the outside of her door to signify that no one should enter. This idea was dismissed by the home.

Approach taken The home seemed unable to support the ethical solution to this problem and it was not possible for the psychologist to recommend or support a more aversive strategy. At this point the involvement of the Care Manager was invaluable. She was able to force the home to comply and facilitate privacy for the client. Whilst this solved the difficulties experienced by the client, and to a large extent the home itself, it did have a knock-on effect on the relationship between the psychologist and the home. The home began to feel suspicious of the psychologist's involvement and extra work had to be undertaken to mend the rift, which ultimately was successfully achieved.

---

such a case, a referral to the Social Services Care Manager is the best course of action. A risk assessment as part of your report can be helpful. Clarify in your reports the conditions which would need to obtain before psychological advice would be useful.

If you believe the risks to the client are significant and need to be acted upon, then you must make a report to the authority who can take action. To do this you will need to be familiar with the relevant legislation, e.g. the Registered Homes Act (1984), The Children Act (1989), The Mental Health Act (1983) (see also Chapters 4, 5 and 9). These are not only important for the safeguarding of clients when you perceive a risk but you can also use them to inform your interventions and to assist you in gaining compliance.

Similarly, it is important to be aware of the local policies of Social Services, Health and Education as they affect people with intellectual disability and the employees of these organisations. For example, many services now have policies for the protection of vulnerable adults. Make sure, especially, that you are fully conversant with the policies of your organisation.

It is very useful to understand the role of the various local and national inspection and monitoring systems. Every local authority has mechanisms in place for registering and inspecting residential care homes, as does the local Health Authority for Nursing Homes. They have the power to close a home or require them to improve their standards. Make informal links with such people and work with them.

You should also be aware of the local arrangements for purchasing different services and their associated contracts. Interventions or recommendations which require resourcing will need to come to the attention of the relevant purchaser. Contracts for services (whether set by Social Services or Health) can serve as a lever on the provider for improving the quality of care and for ensuring that interventions are implemented in a setting (see the example of Bill, Figure 15.6)

Always share your information—do not work in isolation. Talk over your concerns with your immediate supervisor/manager. Keep comprehensive notes. Strength lies in working with others. Do not let spurious ideas about confidentiality being paramount cloud your judgement of when to pass on information. A chilling account of the failure to pass on clinical information to others can be found in Blom-Cooper, Hally & Murphy (1994).

A multi-disciplinary team working in many different residential homes and day settings will, between them, build up a considerable body of knowledge on the strengths and weaknesses of different providers. It is important to share this knowledge and be able to feed it back to the relevant people in an objective and co-ordinated way. Keeping a 'concerns' file is one way of doing this. Such a method allows apparently isolated concerns noted by different professionals over a period of time to be put together and acted upon.

CONCLUSION

Clinical psychologists reading this book are likely to be in training, maintaining a faith in and enthusiasm for the profession and its capabili-

---

Figure 15.6   Bill

A young man with severe learning disability who lived in one of a chain of small, private residential homes was excluded from his home following an aggressive incident with a passer-by, which had been reported adversely in the press. The home had not followed the clinical psychologist's advice, which involved guidelines which highlighted the risk of such an incident and a recording system.

Approach taken The psychologist contacted Social Services, who set a new contract in collaboration with their registration officers, which stipulated that the home managers were to seek and follow the advice of the local health professionals and to keep adequate records. It had always been difficult to work collaboratively with this group of homes. The adverse press attention helped the manager of the organisation to realise how vulnerable their isolation made them. Consequently, they welcomed the changes to their contract and were receptive to the involvement of the psychologist. The psychologist used this to build a supportive relationship with the organisation.

ties—after all, it was hard enough to get onto the training course—and that is certainly worth holding onto. However, not everyone out there has such a rosy view of us. Clements and Rapley (1996) in a light-hearted but hard-hitting article, describe two alternatives for life as a psychologist. The less desirable alternative is to become one of the 'affluent, exotic and irrelevant'. This would mean spending your career feeling slightly hard-done-by, if superior and well-paid, and thus contributing to the eventual extinction of the profession. More useful, they recommend, is to adopt the role model of the 'psychologist as plumber'. The plumber comes when called, equipped with a range of useful skills. This means appreciating that clinical psychologists working in complex organisational structures with vulnerable, devalued people are only needed (and only likely to be hired at all) if the skills they offer, the way they offer them and their ability and commitment to work with a range of ordinary, down-to-earth people, dealing with some of the most intransigent problems in individuals, staff teams and organisations, are of the highest order. This approach can provide a truly rewarding experience of working life which is entirely achievable if some of the basic advice we suggest in this chapter is adopted.

FURTHER READING

Hawkins, P., & Shohet, R. (1989). *Supervision in the Helping Professions*. Oxford University Press: Oxford.
Morgan, G. (1986). *Images of Organisations*. Sage: London.

Chapter 16

WORKING WITH COMMUNITIES: HEALTH PROMOTION

Steve Turner* and Chris Hatton*

INTRODUCTION

In the 1990s health promotion became an increasingly important tool in government health policy. *The Health of the Nation* strategy, launched in 1992, aimed to improve the health and well-being of both the general population and of particularly vulnerable groups. It set national targets for lower mortality and morbidity from heart disease, cancer, accidents, mental health, and HIV, AIDS, and sexual ill-health, with an emphasis on 'health promotion as much as health care' (Department of Health, 1992). In 1997 the new Labour Government presented their own policy ideas through the consultative document *Our Healthier Nation* (Department of Health, 1997). But concern had been raised as to how such initiatives could help people with intellectual disabilities (North West Training and Development Team, 1993; Turner and Moss, 1996). *The Health of the Nation* policy acknowledged that two issues had to be addressed:

> First, some conditions or risks may apply in particular ways to them and may need special solutions . . . Secondly, care and special provision will be needed to ensure that health promotion messages and other information are adequately and conveniently made accessible to people in these groups (*The Health of the Nation*, p. 122: Department of Health, 1992d).

This chapter will be structured to address these two issues. The first part of the chapter will outline what we know about the health needs of people with intellectual disabilities and how they differ from the general population. The second part of the chapter will discuss what health

---

*Hester Adrian Research Centre, Manchester, UK

Clinical Psychology and People with Intellectual Disabilities. Edited by E. Emerson, C. Hatton, J. Bromley and A. Caine.
© 1998 John Wiley & Sons Ltd.

promotion is, how health promotion is applied to the general population, and how these applications may be implemented or altered for people with intellectual disabilities. The final part of the chapter will present a case study of health promotion with people with intellectual disabilities, focusing on behavioural programmes for reducing obesity and increasing fitness.

HEALTH NEEDS OF PEOPLE WITH INTELLECTUAL DISABILITIES

Before attempting to improve the health of people with intellectual disabilities, it is vital to understand what the major health and social care needs of this group are likely to be. This will ensure that health promotion efforts are targeted efficiently (i.e. important health issues and particular at-risk groups are prioritised) and effectively (i.e. health promotion strategies will result in socially significant improvements in health status). The major issues concerning the health of people with intellectual disabilities are addressed below.

Mortality

The age structure of the population, both with and without intellectual disabilities, is 'greying'. Mortality rates are still continuing to improve amongst people with intellectual disabilities, although life expectancy is much poorer for people with profound or severe intellectual disabilities. Differential survival of the fitter members of the population leads to an increasing proportion of healthy and high functioning individuals throughout most of the adult age span. In the 70s and beyond, however, there is an increasing prevalence of age-related conditions, as in the general population.

The most common cause of death is respiratory disease, which may be partly exacerbated by inadequate self-care. Death from cancer is, however, on the increase. This is undoubtedly due partly to greater life expectancy, but may also relate to changing lifestyles.

Recent improvements in infant survival of babies with Down's syndrome has had a significant impact on life expectancy. However, life expectancy continues to be lower than for people with intellectual disabilities as a whole, with very few living beyond 60. In people with Down's syndrome, the most common causes of death are respiratory infections and congenital heart disease.

Physical health

People with intellectual disabilities in general have *increased* health risks in the following areas:

❑ Infections, including hepatitis and tuberculosis.
❑ Vision and hearing problems—both congenital and due to infection, poor self-care, or self-injury.
❑ Poorer dental health and treatment.
❑ Incontinence.
❑ Obesity.

People with intellectual disabilities in general have *reduced* health risks in the following areas:

❑ Cardiovascular disease—the most common single cause of death in the general population.
❑ Most cancers, particularly cancers related to lifestyles such as smoking.
❑ Motor vehicle accident deaths, as few people with intellectual disabilities are drivers.

In addition to these general differences in health risks, there are also health risks associated with specific sub-groups. Specific health risks for people with Down's syndrome include: Alzheimer's disease; leukaemia; thyroid disease; immunological deficiencies; congenital heart disease; vision and hearing loss; and arthritis. Specific health risks for people with Fragile X syndrome include: abnormalities of palate, skeleton, endocrine system and connective tissue; miscarriage; scoliosis (spinal curvature); flat feet and laxity of joints; and ocular abnormalities.

Mental health

Although estimates of the prevalence of mental health problems in people with intellectual disabilities vary widely, it is becoming apparent that people with intellectual disabilities do experience the full range of mental health problems experienced by the general population. Indeed, recent studies suggest that mental health problems are at least as prevalent among people with intellectual disabilities as in the general population (see Chapter 12 for more details). Some mental health problems may have significant consequences for the person's physical health. For example, people with dementia show a range of chronic physical disorders, particularly those involving the central nervous system and gastro-intestinal functioning. Lifestyle factors may also be important. Day (1985), for example, argues that people with mild and moderate levels of intellectual disability living in the community are subjected to stress not only from the normal range of everyday problems, but also from the stigma and additional consequences of their intellectual disability.

Health and lifestyle

Obesity is up to twice as prevalent among people with intellectual disabilities as in the general population, and may affect as many as one in four (Turner & Moss, 1996; Welsh Office, 1996). The condition is a risk factor for a variety of conditions including cardiovascular, cancer and respiratory diseases. The level of obesity is particularly high among women.

Lack of fitness is an important risk factor for coronary heart disease and stroke. In addition, general strength and endurance have been shown to influence well-being. Poor levels of fitness limit capacity and may increase the likelihood of re-institutionalisation in later life. There is evidence that the majority of people with intellectual disabilities do no moderate or vigorous exercise (Turner, 1996; Welsh Office, 1996). Flynn and Hirst (1992) found that few young people with intellectual disabilities took part in sports compared with a matched sample of young people in the general population, and that much of their time was spent in passive activities.

Research on alcohol and tobacco consumption suggests that these risk factors are lower than in the general population. However, there is some evidence that these risk factors are greater among people with less severe disabilities, and those who are living independently or with their family. Poor diet has also been linked to independent living.

In relation to sexual health, a recent UK study (Thompson, 1994) reports a high rate of unsafe sexual practices among gay men with intellectual disabilities, and concludes that their passivity presents a barrier to the adoption of safe sex. Knowledge about risks to sexual health may be poor (Bell, Feraisos & Bryan, 1991). The growth in community involvement and lifestyle choices for people with intellectual disabilities has implications for risk and sexual health (Cambridge, 1994).

This last point is worth stressing. Patterns of health risks and lifestyle behaviours among people with intellectual disabilities are in a greater state of flux than in the general population as a result of changes in government policy. Recent evidence from surveys of people with intellectual disabilities in hospitals and community-based residential services suggests that, as people move to less restrictive settings where they have more control over their lives, they begin to adopt lifestyles similar to others in the local community. Thus, over time the pattern of risks to the mental and physical health of people with intellectual disabilities in less restrictive settings is likely to become more like that of the general population.

Service responses to health needs

The quality of primary care services has been criticised in relation to the detection of conditions, preventive care and prescription practices. Langan, Russell & Whitfield (1993) found that preventive medical procedures were not performed as frequently by GPs for people with intellectual disabilities as they were for other patients. Other studies report a large number of common medical problems which were not known to individuals' GPs and/or were not being managed (Cole, 1986; Howells, 1986; Wilson & Haire, 1990). There is a need to be aware of the impact of the ageing process, and the possibility of related secondary conditions such as nutritional and dental problems, as well as new health challenges such as HIV and AIDS. 'Polypharmacy', where a range of medications are prescribed and not necessarily adequately monitored, can be a danger.

Lack of communication skills on both sides may compound such problems. The primary care system heavily relies on a person's ability to recognise and report symptoms of ill-health. People with intellectual disabilities and their carers may not have the skills or knowledge necessary to do this, while primary health care professionals may not have the skills needed to overcome communication difficulties within a consultation, or be aware of the need to provide information about health promotion in an accessible form (see Chapter 6 on interviewing strategies).

Referral to psychiatric services is poorly targeted for people with intellectual disabilities. If the symptoms of the condition do not have a high profile it is likely that the individual will not come to the attention of medical services (see Chapter 12 on mental health problems for more details).

The special needs of families should be recognised. Research on the impact of the disclosure of a diagnosis of childhood disability highlights the need to take account of parents' feelings of incomprehension, anger and loss, and the importance of coping strategies and networks of social support (see also Chapter 14). Parents have a continuing need for information on health, developmental and service issues, particularly at times of transition like school entry, school leaving, and leaving the family home.

HEALTH PROMOTION WITH PEOPLE WITH INTELLECTUAL DISABILITIES

This second section of the chapter will focus on the UK context concerning health promotion for people with intellectual disabilities. A definition of health promotion will then be provided, followed by a discussion of its application with this group. Where appropriate, the role of the clinical psychologist in the health promotion process will be discussed.

The UK context

Improving the health of people with intellectual disabilities through health promotion has gained official recognition in the UK. For example, the Department of Health (1995d) is attempting to encourage purchasers to contract with health care providers for three types of service: health promotion, health surveillance and health care (see Chapter 4). The Department of Health also emphasises the need to involve carers, parents, and people with intellectual disabilities as well as health professionals, teachers and social services staff in health promotion. However, more specific guidance or legislation from the Department of Health has not been forthcoming. This lack of leadership at a national policy level has resulted in patchy health promotion services at a local level. A recent survey of 149 UK provider organisations (Turner, 1996) found that a high proportion offered some form of healthy lifestyle intervention or health promotion, although only one quarter had developed a health promotion policy specifically for people with intellectual disabilities. As with the general population, firm evidence concerning the effectiveness of health promotion strategies for this group is at best sparse.

The potential range of issues for health promotion to tackle in people with intellectual disabilities is huge; so much so that the Health Education Authority has produced a database and accompanying guide reviewing over 160 resources focusing on health, healthy lifestyles, and using health services for people with intellectual disabilities (Health Education Authority, 1995). As well as traditional areas of concern such as diet, fitness and weight control, psychological and social aspects of health are now also subjects of concern. Health promotion strategies focusing on sexuality, pregnancy, parenthood, abuse and bereavement are all becoming accepted as appropriate, as well as education relating to improving access to health services and information about health. However, there are still gaps in the range of health promotion activities offered to people with intellectual disabilities. Mental health and cancer (both *Health of the Nation* key areas), drug and alcohol misuse and smoking, all appear to be relatively neglected (Health Education Authority, 1995, Turner, 1996).

Health promotion—what is it?

Health promotion has been defined as activity which:

> ... seeks the development of community and individual measures which help people to develop lifestyles than can maintain and enhance their state of well-being (US Department of Health, Education and Welfare, 1978).

Health promotion is not to be confused with the more limited activity of health education, which aims at individual attitude and behaviour change, and often targets 'at risk' groups.

> Health promotion covers all aspects of those activities which seek to improve the health status of individuals and communities. It therefore includes both health education and all attempts to produce environmental and legislative change conducive to good public health. (Dennis et al., 1981)

Health promotion strategies

As the above definition makes clear, health promotion includes a bewildering variety of strategies, from working with individuals to passing legislation. To impose some structure on this variety, a typology of health promotion strategies for the general population (Beattie, 1991) is presented in Figure 16.1 This Figure shows four general types of health promotion strategy, varying along two dimensions; action with individuals versus collective action; and authoritative strategies versus negotiated strategies. The application of Beattie's typology to people with intellectual disabilities is presented in Figure 16.2.

The content of each sector of Figure 16.2 will now be examined in turn. Each class of health promotion strategy will be outlined, followed by a discussion of its application to people with intellectual disabilities. Where appropriate, the role of the clinical psychologist in implementation will also be discussed.

Beattie characterises the *health persuasion* strategy as being mainly based

Figure 16.1   Model of health promotion strategies

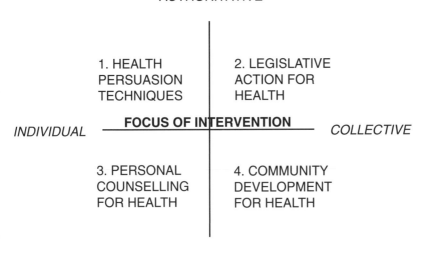

MODE OF INTERVENTION

AUTHORITATIVE

1. HEALTH PERSUASION TECHNIQUES	2. LEGISLATIVE ACTION FOR HEALTH

INDIVIDUAL ——— **FOCUS OF INTERVENTION** ——— *COLLECTIVE*

3. PERSONAL COUNSELLING FOR HEALTH	4. COMMUNITY DEVELOPMENT FOR HEALTH

NEGOTIATED

on mass media campaigns, underpinned by theoretical models such as the Health Belief Model (see Marteau, 1995; Ogden, 1996). This argues that health promotion must aim to bring about the adoption of preventive action by changing an individual's perception of: (a) their own susceptibility to the disease: (b) the threat of the disease: (c) the benefits of preventive action; (d) the barriers to or costs of preventive action (Rosenstock, 1972). Such strategies have been criticised as to their effectiveness with the general population, and have obvious limitations for targeting a relatively small population (less than 1 per 1000 of the general population) with limited literacy and cognitive ability. Consequently, this strategy of health promotion tends to be more local and individualised in work with people with intellectual disabilities, incorporating pictorial and electronic media to present health promotion material.

The type of role advocated for community intellectual disability nurses in the report of the Learning Disability Nursing Project (Department of Health, 1995b) may be described as following the 'health persuasion' strategy (Figure 16.3). It has also been argued that primary care teams could adopt such a strategy with carers and users in their practice (Langan, Russell & Whitfield, 1993), although care must be taken to avoid an excessively top-down approach to health persuasion, where the agenda is set unilaterally by provider or purchaser agencies

Figure 16.2   Health Promotion Strategies and People with Intellectual
    Disabilities

MODE OF INTERVENTION

AUTHORITATIVE

1. PERSUASION
HEALTH EDUCATION
Intellectual disability nurses,
group practice nurses

2. LEGISLATIVE
POLICIES ON
SMOKING, CATERING
Institutional, managerial

INDIVIDUAL **FOCUS OF INTERVENTION** *COLLECTIVE*

3. PERSONAL COUNSELLING
EMPOWERMENT
SELF-ADVOCACY
Nurse counsellors, psychologists

4. COMMUNITY DEVELOPMENT
GROUP EMPOWERMENT
People First, carers' groups,
group facilitators, outreach
workers

NEGOTIATED

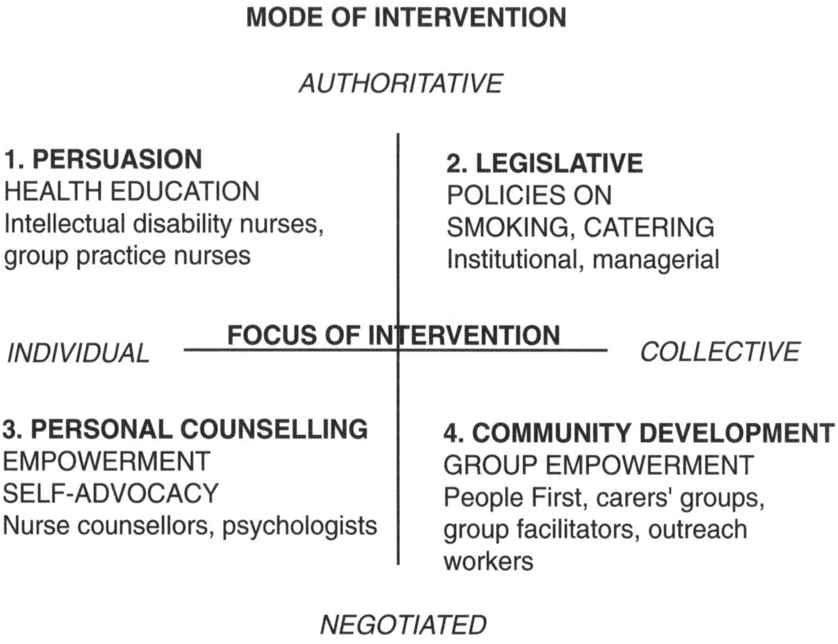

(Greenhaugh, 1994). It is also vital to use an approach that can be readily understood and acted upon by service users. Here, clinical psychologists have a role in designing appropriate information materials, and also advising other professionals on appropriate ways to disseminate information to people with intellectual disabilities, to maximise the retention of information and the choice of more healthy lifestyles (cf. Ley & Llewelyn, 1995; Ogden, 1996).

The second health promotion strategy identified by Beattie is based on *legislative action*. A famous example is the 1956 Clean Air Act, which led to marked improvements in morbidity and mortality from respiratory diseases. Clearly such legislation covers the entire population, and therefore people with intellectual disabilities may be in a position to share in health gains along with everyone else. Other legislative action may be less relevant. For example, laws aimed at reducing road traffic accidents may have little impact on a group with a low level of car use.

However, the relationship between users and providers of intellectual disability services affords the opportunity for regimes and policies to be established which, on a micro-societal level, perform a similar function

> **Figure 16.3**   Case study 1: the limits to health persuasion
>
> A social worker comments on the health promotion activities (weight and fitness, anti-smoking, healthy eating, and women's health groups) run in her local day centre:
>
> 'They are often successful, but perhaps the people who really need these groups have chosen not to participate in them. For example, the people who attend the gym are quite fit anyway. I find weight a difficult issue for people with intellectual disabilities, because often food is the main focus of their lives. Most have a good idea of how to eat more healthily but lack motivation. I would also think the psychological effects of food and health are quite difficult, especially as many people have always had restrictions put on them if they have lived in institutions or with parents most of their lives.
>
> The Centre does provide a lot of active leisure activities. However, outside of the centre evenings and weekends there is not much available with the correct support for people—motivation is still a problem, too. I think a lot more could be done, especially on an integrated basis with the correct support. I think this group of people are last on the list, and their health in all aspects isn't always taken seriously'.

to legislative action. Providers of residential or day care establishments may limit the availability of confectionery, prohibit alcohol, or influence diet through changing cooking practices. Historically, such benevolent policies were often prescriptive in character, but in recent years it has been the policy of both government and individual services to involve users and carers as much as possible in the framing and adoption of such initiatives (Department of Health, 1995c). However, tensions between collective action to improve health and individual choice will remain.

The third type of health promotion strategy, which Beattie calls *personal counselling for health*, is characterised by an in-depth examination of the client's interpretation of his/her social or personal situation. The counselling process leads to the identification of goals and a personal or group action plan which aims to achieve those goals. Such activity may be one-to-one or with a group which shares a common problem or concern. The strategy places a strong emphasis on personal autonomy and self-determination. Such an approach fits well with the philosophy of user involvement espoused by community care policies (Department of Health, 1995c), and could have wider benefits to a person than changes in physical health alone:

> Feelings of self-esteem or self-worth are not only important to mental health but are generally considered to be an important factor in making healthy choices. There are various factors influencing self-esteem but one of the most important is an individual's belief about control (Tones, 1992).

Criticisms directed at the personal counselling approach are that it holds

Figure 16.4   Case study 2: attitudes of young people and their parents towards smoking

The need for the in-depth study of attitudes which reinforce risk behaviour like smoking was made clear by a study undertaken with young people with moderate intellectual disabilities by Action on Smoking and Health (ASH) Scotland. Focus groups with young people and with their parents or carers revealed recognition of the risks in smoking, but low priority and commitment to change. The study concluded that smoking education was given a much lower priority amongst young people, their parents and teachers than issues with more immediate risk, like substance misuse or sexual health. There was a communication gap between health education taught at college and the family, with insufficient account being taken of the experience and influence of home life by teachers, and an assumption that health education was the responsibility of schools and colleges on the part of parents. Young smokers tended to downplay the long-term risks for themselves, while emphasising the social and psychological support gained from smoking. Non-smokers were found to be extremely tolerant to environmental smoke (Cairas, 1996).

dangers of invasion of privacy and intrusion into personal values, and that its emphasis on self-disclosure and goal planning is essentially based on middle-class values and attributes. Limited ability to articulate needs, and the tendency to acquiesce to suggestion (see Chapter 6), reinforce these dangers when adopting this approach with people with intellectual disabilities. The approach has also been criticised as essentially being one where subjects are encouraged to 'learn to cope' rather than addressing structural issues such as lack of access to facilities or life opportunities.

Clearly, clinical psychologists could have a major role to play in this aspect of health promotion, in working with both individuals or groups to formulate goals and action plans towards those goals, and to motivate users to maintain those action plans. The efficacy of behavioural and cognitive-behavioural approaches in attacking a wide range of health problems in the general population, from cardiac disorders through to disorders of the gut, have been well documented (Broome & Llewelyn, 1995; Ogden, 1996), and psychologists are well-placed to apply or adapt these techniques to people with intellectual disabilities. They may also be in a good position to monitor effectiveness—the extent to which attitudes and behaviour change as a result of health promotion activities.

The fourth of Beattie's strategy models is termed *community development for health*. He describes the strategy as recently developed, with origins in community-based social work and education, and in groups representing women, ethnic minorities, residents and other disadvantaged groups involved in direct voluntary action. The emphasis is on self-organisation and mutual support between group members. Common experiences and concerns are identified and discussed, options clarified, and a common agenda of action aimed at changing their circumstances pursued. However, Beattie warns that the community development for health approach may be assimilated by other priorities as a means of giving the agendas set by 'official' agencies better access to particular groups.

As the report of the Islington project makes clear (see Figure 16.5), the model of group empowerment makes the role of the outside professional health promotion worker particularly sensitive. It may involve identifying and bringing a group together, facilitating its activity, acting as advocate, secretariat and networker. Another example of this type of strategy comes from Greenhaugh's project in the Oxford region, which aimed to evaluate the needs for health information of people with intellectual disabilities and their problems in accessing such information (Greenhaugh, 1994). By working with a group of people with intellectual disabilities over time, it was hoped to identify ways of making health information more effective and acceptable, although achieving a balance between the multiple roles of the project worker and the continued self-determination of the group was problematic. Again, clinical psychologists, with their skills in group facilitation and multi-disciplinary working, could become involved in this aspect of health promotion.

As the examples described above have shown, the range of strategies characterised in Figure 16.2 are not discrete or mutually exclusive. For example, elements of health persuasion may exist within an ostensible self-determination approach, and the individual/collective dimension may be blurred when individuals in a group share few common attributes or needs.

Figure 16.5   Case study 3: individual and collective health promotion

The Access to Health Project in Islington, London, was funded by the Department of Health through a local voluntary organisation, and ran for three years to March 1997. It aimed to support people with intellectual disabilities in making choices and decisions about their lives. It developed a health advocacy model which emphasised the active involvement of the person referred to the Project. They were supported before seeking medical advice, accompanied to the consultation, and offered a de-briefing about what had happened. Carers and health staff were also supported by tackling problems in communication. In addition to this work with individuals, the Project developed a range of group work activities, and produced its own health promotion materials. It is argued that the Project has helped to change practice among providers, generate referrals and requests for health promotion, and has received positive feedback from service users. Diet, exercise, dental care, diabetes, childbirth, epilepsy and first aid were reported as areas of concern and interest (Elfreda Society, 1995).

> **Figure 16.6** Case study 4: assessing health needs and risks to health
>
> A prerequisite to effective health promotion with a group or community of people with intellectual disabilities is a careful assessment of current health problems, possible unmet needs, problems accessing services and aspects of lifestyle which increase the risk of ill-health. A intellectual disability service in the North West of England conducted a comprehensive survey of its service users' healthcare needs by getting information from main carers and care staff. The study found that the risk factors of obesity and physical inactivity were more prevalent in the study population than in the general population, while high alcohol consumption and smoking were less common. Younger people with lower levels of dependency were found to have more risk factors. Smoking, weight problems and other risk factors were linked to possible cardiovascular problems. The study indicated that people with intellectual disabilities and the population in general share similar risks to their health from lifestyle factors which are open to change. As a result of the survey, the intellectual disability service embarked on a series of strategy planning meetings to coordinate efforts to reduce risk factors and promote health among their service users (Turner & Dinnall, 1997).

Case study: behavioural approaches to reducing obesity and increasing physical fitness

In most areas of health promotion, there is little evidence concerning the efficacy of intervention programmes designed to improve the health of people with intellectual disabilities. However, the use of behavioural approaches to reduce obesity and/or increase physical fitness has a substantial literature—albeit almost exclusively from the USA. It is therefore possible to draw some conclusions on the effectiveness of health promotion techniques in this field. This literature will now be discussed in some detail in order to outline the range of behavioural approaches that can be used in promoting the health of people with intellectual disabilities, and to illustrate some of the difficulties and constraints in such work.

Obesity and lack of fitness are recognised risk factors for cardiovascular disease. Obesity has also been linked with some forms of cancer, renal disease, diabetes, hypertension, respiratory and other problems. Both risk factors are more prevalent among people with intellectual disabilities than in the general population. Apart from the direct health benefits, there is evidence that appropriate interventions could have a wider impact. Behavioural improvements may follow successful weight loss or fitness gain (Gabler-Halle, Halle & Chung, 1993; Neri & Sandman, 1992). For example, Neri and Sandman report that obesity is related to increased self-injurious behaviour. It has also been argued that acceptance by, and integration into, the wider community may be furthered by weight-loss programmes (Rimmer, Braddock & Fujiura, 1993).

There are a number of studies from the USA which report behavioural approaches to weight loss and fitness maintenance which have implications for the design of health promotion activities with people with intellectual disabilities. These techniques include:

❏ Self-monitoring of performance and results, which helps participants to relate changed habits to outcomes. Examples of self-monitoring include self-weighing, recording of food consumed, self-timing in exercise regimes, and internalisation of the adverse effects of relapse.

❏ The use of reward systems to reinforce achievement of programme goals. Studies have used token economies which build to the reward of a trip out or a special activity. Social reinforcement has also been used in this respect, although it is acknowledged that high levels of staff input are likely to be unsustainable in normal service settings (Pitetti & Tan, 1991).

❏ Limiting the influence of external eating cues. Availability of food may be reduced by limiting eating to a few specific settings, reducing portion size, slowing down the eating process, and substituting other pleasurable activities.

❏ Progressive replacement of external rewards (token economies, treats) by self-reinforcement. This may be made easier by the use of simple exercises and techniques which avoid the need for special equipment or close supervision, and by aiming for integration in mainstream exercise or dieting programmes (King & Mace, 1990; Lavay & McKenzie, 1991). Research suggests that supervision and reinforcement can be successfully faded, and self-monitoring established, even with subjects with severe intellectual disabilities (Ellis, Cress & Spellanan, 1992; Pitetti & Tan, 1991; Rogers-Wallgren, French & Ben-Ezra, 1992).

❏ Involvement of 'buddies', carers and parents in the motivation, monitoring and reinforcement process have been shown to be important (Fox, Rosenbery & Rotatori, 1985; Jackson & Thorbecke, 1982; McCarran & Andrasik, 1990). Page (1988) suggests that frequent follow-up contact, in conjunction with carer training, is critical for maintenance of weight loss. Interventions must therefore seek to maximise the commitment of subjects, carers and families to the goals of the programme.

❏ Generalisation of behaviour change to a variety of situations and settings beyond the training setting. This can be made less challenging by making the training setting as close as possible to the natural environment, e.g. by using actual foods and eating settings, or non-specialised fitness equipment. Training in maintenance skills should be an integral part of the programme, and these skills should be reinforced periodically following the end of the intervention (Burkhart, Fox & Rotatori, 1988; Phinney, 1992).

Evidence from US studies involving people with intellectual disabilities living in a variety of settings suggests that weight loss and fitness gain are achievable outcomes for this client group, and are likely to have a comparable impact on risk levels for cardiovascular and other disease as in the general population. The intervention should be designed to achieve gradual change in weight and/or fitness, using a combination of diet and exercise. There appears to be a consensus that, because of metabolic changes to the body during dieting, relatively slow losses of half to one pound per week are more sustainable (Rotatori, Switzky & Fox, 1981). The literature also suggests that neither exercise nor diet are effective alone for long-term maintenance of weight loss (Burkhart, Fox & Rotatori, 1988; Schurrer, Weltman & Brammell, 1985). Attention should be paid to the possibility that interventions may have other outcomes. These include health knowledge of users and carers, self-esteem, behavioural changes, illnesses and absenteeism, productivity, and aspects of the social life of subjects. Studies in the USA have increasingly recognised the above issues (e.g. Burkhart, Fox & Rotatori, 1988), and may provide the basis of a model for UK studies. In the weight-reduction field, several studies have used the behavioural programme developed by Rotatori and Fox (1981).

Interventions to improve weight and fitness are now commonly offered to people with intellectual disabilities. A recent survey of UK provider organisations (Turner, 1996) found that 77% of services provided weight reduction interventions for people with intellectual disabilities, and 50% offered fitness gain interventions. However, the two issues, although closely related, appear to be subject to rather different health promotion approaches. Weight loss interventions were typically targeted at individuals rather than groups, and tended to take place in segregated contexts. Only 11% of services reported interventions that involved groups in integrated settings, such as Weightwatchers groups. This is despite some evidence that weight loss interventions involving groups of service users in integrated settings were more often seen as successful, perhaps because they conform more closely to ideas of community presence and involvement. In contrast, fitness work was more commonly conducted with groups in integrated settings, and more likely to be offered by Social Services departments than by Health Service providers. However, fitness programmes were less often evaluated as to their effectiveness than other types of intervention. It is possible that fitness initiatives may have social as much as physiological aims, and thus be relatively informal, unstructured, and at a pitch that is unlikely to have any effect on cardiovascular fitness levels.

It appears that the lessons of the research literature reviewed above have yet to be applied to service provision. For example, one study of general practice found that while most GPs recognised that the family is the most important influence on weight loss in overweight patients, only one-third included them in their advice giving, and only 3% of GPs recommended behavioural programmes for weight loss, despite their documented efficacy (Cade & O'Connell, 1991).

The example of weight loss and fitness gain interventions highlight the relevance of the different health promotion strategies reviewed in this chapter. It also reinforces the need for psychologists to be involved in developing health–behaviour interventions which make use of the research on behavioural techniques described above. More generally, conclusions from the research literature as to the importance of the involvement of 'significant others', the use of non-specialised equipment, simple exercises and the development of exercise within leisure activities, including integrated activities, point to the negotiated, collective, self-empowerment model of health promotion. While some studies have concluded that fitness and weight programmes are more successful in more restrictive, i.e. institutional, settings, this is likely to be at the cost of individual choice, as diet, activities and programme participation may be more easily determined by professionals in such settings (Emery et al., 1985; Rimmer, Braddock & Fijiura, 1994).

CONCLUSION

This chapter has outlined the development of health promotion activity for people with intellectual disabilities in the context of the continuing shift from institutional to community care and the new emphasis on health promotion following the NHS reforms of the early 1990s. Despite the progress made towards this end, this chapter has touched on a number of challenges that remain. It may be useful to summarise these.

First, some topics remain relatively neglected and under-resourced. This may be because some areas like mental health, cancer, smoking, alcohol and substance abuse are seen as less relevant to this group, despite evidence that independent living may increase such risks. Linked to this point, there appears to be inconsistency in the priorities given to different topics from area to area, and provider to provider. Lack of an overall policy regarding health promotion for people with intellectual disabilities may be one reason for this (Turner, 1996), resulting in a situation where some issues of interest or concern to individual workers are taken up on an *ad hoc*, uncoordinated basis, while other remain ignored. No professional group or agency has clearly defined responsibility for this work.

Health promotion teams covering the needs of the whole population may lack the expertise and resources needed to properly serve people with intellectual disabilities. Specialists like dieticians may only have a limited input to intellectual disability services, responding to individual referrals rather than offering preventive services. Community intellectual disability teams, working with a clear remit and access to relevant professionals (psychologists, fitness experts, primary care team workers, dieticians) may be best placed to take on such a role. Clearly, psychologists could have a major contribution to make in promoting the health of people with intellectual disabilities.

Health promotion has been commonly perceived as being a process of problem-definition by professionals, resulting in action formulated by professionals, using means developed by professionals, with the aim of changing lay behaviour. This chapter has reviewed the variants of health promotion which challenge this model. It has described how there is increasing acceptance that the health promotion agenda should result from a dialogue with people with intellectual disabilities and their representatives (Whittaker, 1989). Furthermore Langan et al. (1993) and Greenhaugh (1994) have argued that any deficit of health-related knowledge is not wholly on the lay side of the professional–patient dyad. They conclude that there is a need for education *for* professionals like GPs, psychologists and psychiatrists on the health needs of people with intellectual disabilities, the risks associated with their lifestyles, and the problems they encounter in accessing services and information. Such a two-way dialogue is probably the best way of achieving an appropriate balance between promoting independence and protection from risk. However, the problems of stimulating and maintaining user and carer input to a health promotion strategy, and the development of related resources and techniques, should not be underestimated.

Such an approach is also likely to be the best safeguard against a narrow set of aims for health promotion. There are many examples of interventions in the weight and fitness field which have failed to lead to long-term gains because the intervention was dependent on high levels of staff input, and did not result in more varied or stimulating lifestyles for the people involved. The goals of health promotion should not be couched only in terms of freedom from disease or risk of disease, but in broader terms of quality of life outcomes. User and carer involvement should help guard against an excessively paternalistic approach which limits choice to a greater extent than would be acceptable to the general population. Perhaps the greatest challenge in promoting the health of people with intellectual disabilities is how to resolve the conflict between self-determination and the exercise of choice on the one hand, and on the other, the desire to influence the behaviour of people dependent on services over which they have little or no control.

FURTHER READING

Beattie, A. (1991). Knowledge and control in health promotion: a test case for social policy and social theory. In *The Sociology of the Health Service* (ed. J. Gabe, M. Calnan & M. Bury). Routledge: London.

Broome, A., & Llewelyn, S. (eds) (1995). *Health Psychology: Processes and Applications*, 2nd edn. Chapman & Hall: London.

Department of Health (1995). *The Health of the Nation: A Strategy for People with Learning Disabilities*. HMSO: London.

Gabler-Halle, D., Halle, J.H., & Chung, Y.B. (1993). The effects of aerobic exercise on psychological and behavioral variables of individuals with developmental delay: a critical review. *Research in Developmental Disabilities*, **14**, 359–386.

Turner, S., & Moss, S. (1996). The health needs of people with learning disabilities and the *Health of the Nation* strategy. *Journal of Intellectual Disability Research*, **40**, 438–450.

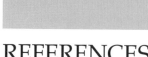

REFERENCES

Ager, A. (1991). Effecting sustainable change in client behaviour: the role of behavioural analysis of service environments. In *The Challenge of Severe Mental Handicap: A Behaviour Analytic Approach* (ed. B. Remington). Wiley: Chichester.

Allen, P. (1995). From the bottom up: ensuring quality with service users. In *Values and Visions: Changing Ideas in Services for People with Learning Difficulties* (ed. T. Philpot & L. Ward). Butterworth-Heinemann: Oxford.

Aman, M.G., Burrow, W.H., & Wolford, P.L. (1995). The Aberrant Behavior Checklist-Community: factor validity and effect of subject variables for adults in group homes. *American Journal on Mental Retardation*, **100**, 283–292.

Aman, M.G., Singh, N.N., Stewart, A.W., & Field, C.J. (1985). The Aberrant Behavior Checklist: a behavior rating scale for the assessment of treatment effects. *American Journal of Mental Deficiency*, **89**, 485–491.

Aman, M.G., Tassé, M.J., Rojahn, J., & Hammer, D. (1996). The Nisonger CBRF: a child behavior rating form for children with developmental disabilities. *Research in Developmental Disabilities*, **17**, 41–57.

American Psychiatric Association (1994). *Diagnostic and Statistical Manual of Mental Disorders* (4th edn): *DSM-IV*. American Psychiatric Association: Washington, DC.

Anderson, D.J., Lakin, K.C., Hill, B.K., & Chen, T.H. (1992). Social integration of older persons with mental retardation in residential facilities. *American Journal on Mental Retardation*, **96**, 488–501.

Anderson, J.R. (1990). *Cognitive Psychology and Its Implications*. W.H. Freeman: New York.

Anderson, T. (1987). The reflecting team: dialogue and meta-dialogue in clinical work. *Family Process*, **26**, 415–428.

Andrews, J. (1996). Identifying and providing for the mentally disabled in early modern London. In *From Idiocy to Mental Deficiency: Historical Perspectives on People with Learning Disabilities* (ed. D. Wright & A. Digby). Routledge: London.

Ash, P. (1949). The reliability of psychiatric diagnoses. *Journal of Abnormal and Social Psychology*, **44**, 272–276.

Atkinson, D. (1988). Research interviews with people with mental handicaps. *Mental Handicap Research*, **1**, 75–90.

Aylward, E.H., Burt, D.B., Thorpe, L.U., Lai, F., & Dalton, A.J. (1995). *Diagnosis of Dementia in Individuals with Intellectual Disability*. American Association on Mental Retardation: Washington, DC.

Azmi, S., Emerson, E., Caine, A., & Hatton, C. (1996a). *Improving Services for Asian People with Learning Disabilities and their Families*. Hester Adrian Research Centre, University of Manchester: Manchester.

Azmi, S., Hatton, C., Caine, A., & Emerson, E. (1996b). *Improving Services for Asian People with Learning Disabilities: The Views of Users and Carers*. Hester Adrian Research Centre, University of Manchester: Manchester.

Azrin, N.H., Besalal, V.A., Jamner, J.P., & Caputo, J.N. (1988). Comparative study of behavioral methods of treating severe self-injury. *Behavioral Residential Treatment*, **3**, 119–152.

Bailey, A., Philips, W., & Rutter, M. (1996). Autism: towards an integration of clinical, genetic, neuropsychological, and neurobiological perspectives. *Journal of Child Psychology and Psychiatry*, **37**, 89–126.

Baker, B.L. (1996). Parent training. In *Manual of Diagnosis and Professional Practice in Mental Retardation* (ed. J.W. Jacobson & J.A. Mulick). American Psychological Association: Washington, DC.

Bannerman, D.J., Sheldon, J.B., Sherman, J.A., & Harchik, A.E. (1990). Balancing the right to habilitation with the right to personal liberties: the rights of people with developmental disabilities to eat too many doughnuts and take a nap. *Journal of Applied Behavior Analysis*, **23**, 79–89.

Barlow, D.H., & Herson, M. (1984). *Single Case Experimental Designs: Strategies for Studying Behavior Change*, 2nd edn. Pergamon: New York.

Bates, E., O'Connell, B., & Shore, C. (1987). Language and communication in infancy. In *Handbook of Infant Development* (ed. J. Osofsky). Wiley: New York.

Bates, R. (1992). Psychotherapy with people with learning difficulties. In *Psychotherapy and Mental Handicap* (ed. A. Waitman & S. Conby-Hill). Sage: London.

Baumeister, A.A., & MacLean, W.E. (1984). Deceleration of self-injurious and stereotypic responding by exercise. *Applied Research in Mental Retardation*, **5**, 385–393.

Baumeister, A.A., & Sevin, J.A. (1990). Pharmacologic control of aberrant behavior in the mentally retarded: toward a more rational approach. *Neuroscience & Biobehavioral Reviews*, **14**, 253–262.

Beail, N., & Warden, S. (1996). Evaluation of a psychodynamic psychotherapy service for adults with intellectual disabilities. *Journal of Applied Research in Intellectual Disabilities*, **9**, 223–228

Beattie, A. (1991). Knowledge and control in health promotion: a test case for social policy and social theory. In *The Sociology of the Health Service* (ed. J. Gabe, M. Calnan & M. Bury). Routledge: London.

Beck, A.T., Rush, A.J., Shaw. B.F., & Emery, G. (1979). *Cognitive Therapy of Depression: A Treatment Manual*. Guilford Press: New York.

Beckett, R. (1994). Cognitive-behavioural treatment of sex offenders. In *Sexual Offending Against Children* (ed. T. Morrison, M. Erooga & R.C. Beckett). Routledge: London.

Bell, D., Feraisos, A.J., & Bryan, T. (1991). Intellectual disabled adolescents' knowledge about AIDS. *Intellectual Disabilities Research and Practice*, **6**, 104–111.

Benson, B.A. (1992). *Teaching Anger Management to Persons with Mental Retardation*. International Diagnostic Systems Inc: Worthington, OH.

Benson, B.A. (1994). Anger management training: a self-control programme for persons with mild mental retardation. In *Mental Health in Mental Retardation: Recent Advances and Practices* (ed. N. Bouras). Cambridge University Press: Cambridge.

Benson, B.A. (1996). Psychotherapy tools: a daily mood check form for use in outpatient services. *Habilitative Mental Healthcare Newsletter*, **15**, 92–95.

Benson, B.A., Johnson Rice, C., & Miranti, S.V. (1986). Effects of anger management training with mentally retarded adults in group treatment. *Journal of Consulting and Clinical Psychology*, **54**, 728–729.

Benson, M.J. (1991). Accessing children's perceptions of their family: circular questioning revisited. *Journal of Marital and Family Therapy*, **4**, 363–372.

Berg, J.M. (1985). Physical determinants of environmental origin. In *Mental*

Deficiency: The Changing Outlook (4th edn), (ed. A.M. Clarke, A.D.B. Clarke & J.M. Berg). Methuen: London.

Berney, T. (1997). Behavioural phenotypes. In *Seminars in the Psychiatry of Learning Disabilities* (ed. O. Russell). Gaskell: London.

Bersani, H.A., & Heifetz, L.J. (1985). Perceived stress and satisfaction of direct-care staff members in community residences for mentally retarded adults. *American Journal of Mental Deficiency*, **90**, 289–295.

Bird, F., Dores, P.A., Moniz, D., & Robinson, J. (1989). Reducing severe aggressive and self-injurious behaviors with functional communication training. *American Journal of Mental Retardation*, **94**, 37–48.

Blacher, J. (1984). Sequential stages of parental adjustment to the birth of a child with handicaps: fact or artifact? *Mental Retardation*, **22**, 55–68.

Black, L., Cullen, C., & Novaco, R.W. (1997). Anger asssessment for people with mild learning disabilities in secure settings. In *Cognitive-Behaviour Therapy for People with Learning Disabilities* (ed. B. Stenfert Kroese, D. Dagnan & K. Loumidis). Routledge: London.

Bland, R.C., Orn, H., & Newman, S.C. (1988). Lifetime prevalence of psychiatric disorders in Edmonton. *Acta Psychiatrica Scandinavia*, **77** (suppl 338), 24–32.

Blom-Cooper, L., Hally, H., & Murphy, E. (1995). *The Falling Shadow: One Patient's Mental Health Care, 1978–1993*. Duckworth: London.

Bodfish, J.W., Crawford, T.W., Powell, S.B., Parker, D.E., Golden, R.N., & Lewis M.H. (1995). Compulsions in adults with mental retardation: prevalence, phenomenology, and comorbidity with stereotypy and self-injury. *American Journal on Mental Retardation*, **100**, 183–192.

Booth, T., & Booth, W. (1997). *Exceptional Childhoods, Unexceptional Children*. York; Joseph Rowntree Foundation.

Borthwick-Duffy, S.A. (1994). Epidemiology and prevalence of psychopathology in people with mental retardation. *Journal of Consulting and Clinical Psychology*, **62**, 17–27.

Borthwick-Duffy, S.A. (1994). Prevalence of destructive behaviors: a study of aggression, self-injury, and property destruction. In *Destructive Behavior in Developmental Disabilities* (ed. T. Thompson & D.B. Gray). Sage: Thousand Oaks, CA.

Borthwick-Duffy, S.A. (1990). Who are the dually diagnosed? *American Journal of Mental Retardation*, **94**, 586–595.

Borthwick-Duffy, S.A., Eyman, R.K., & White, J.F. (1987). Client characteristics and residential placement patterns. *American Journal of Mental Deficiency*, **92**, 24–30.

Bouras, N. (ed.) (1994). *Mental Health in Mental Retardation: Recent Advances and Practices*. Cambridge University Press: Cambridge.

Bouras, N., & Drummond, C. (1992). Behaviour and psychiatric disorders of people with mental handicaps living in the community. *Journal of Intellectual Disability Research*, **36**, 349–357.

Bouras, N., Murray, B., Joyce, T., Kon, Y., & Holt, G. (1995). *Mental Health in Learning Disabilities: A Training Pack for Staff Working with People Who Have a Dual Diagnosis of Mental Health Needs and Learning Disabilities*. Pavilion Publishing: Brighton.

Bradley, V., & Knoll, J.A. (1995). Shifting paradigms in services for people with developmental disabilities. In *The Community Revolution in Rehabilitation Services* (ed. O.C. Karan & S. Greenspan). Andover: Andover, MA.

Branford, D. (1994). A study of prescribing for people with learning disabilities living in the community and in National Health Service care. *Journal of Intellectual Disability Research*, **38**, 577–586.

Briggs, D., Hickey, N., & Jones, J. (1996). Age recognition and learning-disabled offenders. *NOTA News* (The National Association for the Development of Work with Sex Offenders), **19**, 18–20.

Brightman, R.P., Baker, B.L., Clark, D.B., & Ambrose, S.A. (1982). Effectiveness of alternative parent training formats. *Journal of Behaviour Therapy and Psychiatry*, **13**, 113–117.

British Medical Association & the Law Society (1995). *Assessment of Mental Capacity: Guidance for Doctors and Lawyers*. British Medical Association: London.

British Psychological Society (BPS) (1995). *Professional Practice Guidelines 1995 (Division of Clinical Psychology)*. BPS Division of Clinical Psychology: Leicester.

British Psychological Society (BPS) (1997). *Ethical Guidelines on Forensic Psychology 1997 (Division of Criminological and Legal Psychology)*. BPS Division of Criminological and Legal Psychology: Leicester.

Bromley, J., & Emerson, E. (1995). Beliefs and emotional reactions of care staff working with people with challenging behaviour. *Journal of Intellectual Disability Research*, **39**, 341–352.

Bromley, J., Emerson, E., & Caine, A. (in press). The development of a self report measure to assess the location and intensity of pain in people with intellectual disabilities. *Journal of Intellectual Disability Research*.

Broome, A., & Llewelyn, S. (ed.) (1995). *Health Psychology: Processes and Applications* (2nd edn). Chapman and Hall: London.

Browder, D.M. (1991). *Assessment of Individuals with Severe Disabilities*. P.H. Brookes: Baltimore; MD

Brown, H. (1994). Establishing the incidence of abuse in services for people with learning disabilities. In *People with Learning Disabilities At Risk of Physical Or Sexual Abuse*. BILD Seminar Papers, No. 4. (eds. J. Harris & A. Craft). British Institute of Learning Disabilities: Clevedon.

Brown, H., & Craft, A. (ed.) (1989). *Thinking the Unthinkable—Papers on Sexual Abuse and People with Learning Difficulties*. FPA Education Unit: London.

Brown, H., & Smith, H. (ed.) (1992). *Normalization: A Reader for the Nineties*. Routledge: London.

Brown, H., Stein, J., & Turk, V. (1995). Report of a second two-year incidence survey on the reported sexual abuse of adults with learning disabilities: 1991 and 1992. *Mental Handicap Research*, **8**, 1–22.

Brown, H., Turk, V., & Stein, J. (1994) Findings: sexual abuse of adults with learning disabilities. *Social Care Research Findings*, **46**, 46–49.

Brown, S., & Wistow, G. (ed.) (1990). *The Roles and Task of Community Mental Handicap Teams*. Avebury: Aldershot.

Bruner, J.S. (1983). *Child's Talk: Learning to Use Language*. Norton: New York.

Bull, R.H.C. (1995). Interviewing people with communicative disabilities. In *Handbook of Psychology in Legal Contexts* (ed. R. Bull & D. Carson). Wiley: Chichester.

Burgio, L.D., Willis, K., & Burgio, K.L. (1986). Operantly-based treatment procedures for stair avoidance by a severely mentally retarded adult. *American Journal of Mental Deficiency*, **91**, 308–311.

Burkhart, J., Fox, R., & Rotatori, A. (1988). Obesity in the developmentally disabled. In *Behavioural Medicine with the Developmentally Disabled* (ed. D.C. Russo & J.H. Kennedy). Plenum: New York.

Burnham, J. (1994). *Family Therapy*. Routledge: London.

Byrne, E.A., & Cunningham, C.C. (1985). The effects of mentally handicapped children on families: a conceptual review. *Journal of Child Psychology and Psychiatry*, **26**, 847–864.

Byrne, E.A., Cunningham, C.C., & Sloper, P. (1988). *Families and Their Children with Down's Syndrome: One Feature in Common*. Routledge: London.

Cade, J., & O'Connell, S. (1991). Management of weight problems and obesity: knowledge, attitudes and current practice of General Practitioners. *British Journal of General Practice*, **41**, 147–50.

Cairns, G. (1996). *Educating Young People with Learning Difficulties about Smoking*. ASH Scotland, 8 Frederick Street, Edinburgh EH2 2HB.

Caldwell, B., & Bradley, R. (1984). *Home Observation for Measurement of the Environment*. University of Arkansas at Little Rock: Little Rock, AR.

Cambridge, P. (1994). A practice and policy agenda for HIV and learning difficulties. *British Journal of Learning Disabilities*, **22**, 134–139.

Campbell, M., & Malone, R.P. (1991). Mental retardation and psychiatric disorders. *Hospital and Community Psychiatry*, **42**, 374–379.

Carr, E.G. (1986). Behavioral approaches to language and communication. In *Current Issues in Autism, Volume 3: Communication problems in autism* (ed. E. Schopler & G. Mesibov). Plenum: New York.

Carr, E.G. (1994). Emerging themes in the functional analysis of problem behavior. *Journal of Applied Behavior Analysis*, **27**, 393–399.

Carr, E.G., & Durand, V.M. (1984). Reducing behavior problems through functional communication training. *Journal of Applied Behavior Analysis*, **18**, 111–126.

Carr, E.G., & Newsom, C.D. (1985). Demand-related tantrums: conceptualization and treatment. *Behavior Modification*, **9**, 403–426.

Carr, E.G., & Smith, C.E. (1995). Biological setting events for self-injury. *Mental Retardation & Developmental Disability Research Reviews*, **1**, 94–98.

Carr, E.G., Newsom, C.D., & Binkoff, J.A. (1976). Stimulus control of self-destructive behavior in a psychotic child. *Journal of Abnormal Child Psychology*, **4**, 139–153.

Carr, E.G., Newsom, C.D, & Binkoff, J.A. (1980). Escape as a factor in the aggressive behavior of two retarded children. *Journal of Applied Behavior Analysis*, **13**, 101–117.

Carr, E.G., Robinson, S., Taylor, J.C., & Carlson, J.I. (1990). *Positive Approaches to the Treatment of Severe Behavior Problems in Persons with Developmental Disabilities*. The Association for Persons with Severe Handicaps: Seattle, WA.

Carr, E.G., Levin, L., McConnachie, G., Carlson, J.I., Kemp, D.C., & Smith, C.E. (1994). *Communication-based Intervention for Problem Behavior: A User's Guide for Producing Positive Change*. P.H. Brookes: Baltimore, MD.

Carson, D. (1989). Prosecuting people with mental handicaps. *Criminal Law Review*, 87–94.

Carson, D. (1995). Editorial. *Mental Handicap Research (Journal of Applied Research in Intellectual Disabilities)*, **8**, 77–80.

Carson, D., & Clare, I.C.H. (1997). Boundaries with the criminal justice and other legal systems. In *There Are No Easy Answers! The Provision of Continuing Care and Treatment to Adults with Learning Disabilities who Sexually Abuse Others* (ed. J. Churchill, H. Brown, A. Craft & C. Horrocks). ARC/NAPSAC: Chesterfield.

Carter, E.A., & McGoldrick, M. (1980). *The Family Life Cycle: A Framework for Family Therapy*. Gardner: New York.

Carter, G., & Jancar, J. (1983). Mortality in the mentally handicapped: a 50 year survey at the Stoke Park group of hospitals (1930–1980). *Journal of Mental Deficiency Research*, **27**, 143–156.

Chamberlain, A., Raugh, J., Passer, A., McGrath, M. & Burket, R. (1984) Issues in fertility control for mentally retarded female adolescents: 1. Sexual activity, sexual abuse and contraception. *Paediatrics* **73**, 445–450.

Charlot, L.R., Doucette, A.C., & Mezzacappa, E. (1993). Affective symptoms of institutionalized adults with mental retardation. *American Journal on Mental Retardation*, **98**, 408–416.

Charman, T., & Clare, I.C.H. (1992). Education about the laws and social rules relating to sexual behaviour. *Mental Handicap*, **20**, 74–80.

Children Act (1989). HMSO: London.

Chomsky, N. (1965). *Aspects of the Theory of Syntax*. MIT Press: Cambridge, MA.

Christo, G. (1997) Child sexual abuse: psychological consequences *The Psychologist*, May, 205–209.

Churchill, J., Brown, H., Croft, A., & Horrocks, C. (1997). There Are No Easy Answers! The Provision of Continuing Care and Treatment to Adults with Learning Disabilities Who Sexually Abuse Others. ARC/NAPSAC: Chesterfield.

Ciotti, P. (1989). Growing up different: when the retarded become parents, perhaps their children know best how it works. *Los Angeles Times*, May 9.

Cipani, E., & Morrow, R.D. (1991). Educational assessment. In *Handbook of Mental Retardation* (ed. J.L. Matson & J.A. Mulick). Pergamon: New York.

Clare, I.C.H. (1993). Issues in the assessment and treatment of male sex offenders with mild learning disabilities. *Sexual and Marital Therapy*, **8**, 167–180.

Clare, I.C.H., & Gudjonsson, G.H. (1993). Interrogative suggestibility, confabulation, and acquiescence in people with mild learning disabilities (mental handicap): implications for reliability during police interrogations. *British Journal of Clinical Psychology*, **32**, 295–301.

Clare, I.C.H., & Gudjonsson, G.H. (1995). The vulnerability of suspects with intellectual disabilities during police interviews: a review and experimental study of decision-making. *Mental Handicap Research (Journal of Applied Research in Intellectual Disabilities)*, **8**, 110–128.

Clare, I.C.H., & Murphy, G.H. (1993). MIETS (Mental Impairment Evaluation & Treatment Service): a service option for people with mild mental handicap and challenging behaviour and/or psychiatric problems. *Mental Handicap Research*, **6**, 70–91.

Clare, I.C.H., Gudjonsson, G.H., & Harari, P.M. (in press). Understanding the current police caution (England and Wales). *Journal of Community and Applied Social Psychology*.

Clare, I.C.H, Murphy, G.H., Cox, D., & Chaplin, E.H. (1992). Assessment and treatment of fire-setting: a single-case investigation using a cognitive-behavioural model. *Criminal Behaviour and Mental Health*, **2**, 253–268.

Clark, D.M. (1989). Anxiety states: panic and generalized anxiety. In *Cognitive Behaviour Therapy for Psychiatric Problems* (ed. K. Hawton, P.M. Salkovskis, J. Kirk & D.M. Clark). Oxford University Press: Oxford.

Clarke, A.M. (1985). Polygenic and environmental interactions. In *Mental Deficiency: The Changing Outlook* (4th edn) (ed. A.M. Clarke, A.D.B. Clarke & J.M. Berg). Methuen: London.

Clarke, A.M., Clarke, A.D.B., & Berg, J.M. (ed.) (1985). *Mental Deficiency: The Changing Outlook* (4th edn). Methuen: London.

Clarke, D.J., Kelley, S., Thinn, K., & Corbett, J.A. (1990). Psychotropic drugs and mental retardation. 1: Disabilities and the prescription of drugs for behaviour and for epilepsy in three residential settings. *Journal of Mental Deficiency Research*, **34**, 385–395.

Clements, J. (1987). *Severe Learning Disability and Psychological Handicap.* Wiley: Chichester.

Clements, J., & Rapley, M. (1996). Go to the mirror! *Clinical Psychology Forum*, **89**, 4–7.

Cleveland, D.W., & Miller, N. (1977). Attitudes and life commitments of older siblings of mentally retarded adults. *Mental Retardation*, **15**, 38–41.

Cobb, H.C., & Gunn, W. (1994). Family interventions. In *Counselling and Psychotherapy with Persons with Mental Retardation and Borderline Intelligence* (ed. D.C. Strohmer & H.T. Prout). Clinical Psychology Publishing: Brandon.

Cole, O. (1986). Medical screening of adults at social recreation centres: whose responsibility? *Mental Handicap*, **14**, 54–56.

Connor, J.M., & Ferguson-Smith, M.A. (1993). *Essential Medical Genetics* (4th edn). Blackwell: Oxford.

Cooke, L. (1990). Abuse of mentally handicapped adults. *Psychiatric Bulletin* **14**, 608–609.

Cooper, J., & Vernon, S. (1996). *Disability and the Law.* Jessica Kingsley: London.

Costello, H., Moss, S., Prosser, H., & Hatton, C. (1997). Reliability of the ICD-10 version of the Psychiatric Assessment Schedule for Adults with Developmental Disability (PAS-ADD). *Social Psychiatry and Psychiatric Epidemiology*, **32**, 339–343.

Cox, C., & Pearson, M. (1995). *Made to Care: The Case for Residential and Village Communities for People with a Mental Handicap.* The Rannoch Trust: London.

Cox, P. (1996). *Girls, Deficiency and Delinquency. In From Idiocy to Mental Deficiency: Historical Perspectives on People with Learning Disabilities* (ed. D. Wright & A. Digby). Routledge: London.

Crabbe, H.F. (1994). Pharmacotherapy in mental retardation. In *Mental Health in Mental Retardation: Recent Advances and Practices* (ed. N. Bouras). Cambridge University Press: Cambridge.

Craft, M. (1984). Low intelligence, mental handicap and criminality. In *Mentally Abnormal Offenders* (ed. M. Craft & A. Craft). Baillière-Tindall: London.

Criminal Procedure (Insanity) Act (1964) (amended 1991, in force 1992). HMSO: London.

Crocker, A.C., Yankauer, A., & the Conference Steering Committee (1989). Basic issues. *Mental Retardation*, **23**, 227–232.

Cullen, C. (1993). The treatment of people with learning disabilities who offend. In *Clinical Approaches to the Mentally Disordered Offender* (ed. K. Howells & C.R. Hollin). Wiley: Chichester.

Cumella, S., & Sansom, D. (1994). A regional mental impairment service. *Mental Handicap Research*, **7**, 257–272.

Cummins, R.A., McCabe, M.P., Gullone, E., & Romeo, Y. (in press). The Comprehensive Quality of Life Scale: instrument development and psychometric evaluation on tertiary staff and students. *Educational and Psychological Measurement.*

Cunningham, C.C. (1979). Parent counselling. In *Tredgold's Mental Retardation* (12th edn) (ed. M. Craft). Tindall: London.

Cunningham, C.C., & Davis, J. (1985). *Working with Parents: Frameworks for Collaboration.* Open University Press: Milton Keynes.

Cunningham, C.C., & Sloper, P. (1977). Parents of Down's syndrome babies: their early needs. *Child: Care, Health and Development*, **3**, 325–347.

Dagnan, D., & Ruddick, L. (1995). The use of analogue scales and personal questionnaires for interviewing people with learning disabilities. *Clinical Psychology Forum*, **79**, 21–23.

Dale, N. (1996). *Working with Families of Children with Special Needs: Partnership and Practice*. Routledge: London.

Danish Ministry of Social Affairs (1996). *Parenting with Intellectual Disability Conference Papers*. Danish Ministry of Social Affairs: Copenhagen.

Davey, G., & Cullen, C. (1988). *Human Operant Conditioning and Behaviour Modification*. Wiley: New York.

Day, K. (1985). Psychiatric disorder in the middle-aged and elderly mentally handicapped. *British Journal of Psychiatry*, **147**, 660–667.

Day, K. (1988). A hospital-based treatment programme for male mentally handicapped offenders. *British Journal of Psychiatry*, **153**, 635–644.

Day, K. (1994). Psychiatric services in mental retardation: generic or specialised provision? In *Mental Health in Mental Retardation: Recent Advances and Practices* (ed. N. Bouras). Cambridge University Press: Cambridge.

Day, K., & Jancar, J. (1991). Mental handicap and the Royal Medico-Psychological Association: a historical association, 1841–1991. In *150 Years of British Psychiatry, 1841–1991* (ed. G.E. Berrios & H. Freeman). Gaskell: London.

Day, R.M., Horner, R.H., & O'Neill, R.E. (1994). Multiple functions of problem behaviors: assessment and intervention. *Journal of Applied Behavior Analysis*, **27**, 279–289.

Demchak, M.A., & Bossert, K.W. (1996). *Assessing Problem Behaviours*. American Association on Mental Retardation: Washington, DC.

Dennis, J., Draper, P., Holland, S., Snipster, P., Speller, V., & Sunter, J. (1981). Health promotion in the reorganised NHS. *The Health Services*, 26 November.

Department of Health (1971). *Better Services for the Mentally Handicapped*. HMSO: London.

Department of Health (1989). *Caring for People: Community Care in the Next Decade and Beyond*. HMSO: London.

Department of Health (1990). *NHS and Community Care Act*. HMSO: London.

Department of Health (1992a). *LAC(92) 15: Social Care for Adults with Learning Disabilities (Mental Handicap)*. Department of Health: London.

Department of Health (1992b). *LAC(92) 17. Health Authority Payments in Respect of Social Services Functions*. Department of Health: London.

Department of Health (1992c). *HSG(92)42: Health Services for People with Learning Disabilities (Mental Handicap)*. Department of Health: London.

Department of Health (1992d). *The Health of the Nation. A Strategy for Health in England (CM. 1986)*. HMSO: London.

Department of Health (1993). *Services for People with Learning Disabilities and Challenging Behaviour or Mental Health Needs* (Chair: Prof. J.L. Mansell). HMSO: London.

Department of Health (1995a). *A Guide to Joint Commissioning*. HMSO: London.

Department of Health (1995b). *It's Our Lives—Implementing Caring for People: Community Care for People with Learning Disabilities*. Department of Health: London.

Department of Health (1995c). *Learning Disability: Meeting Needs Through Targeting Skills*. Department of Health: London.

Department of Health (1995d). *The Health of the Nation: A Strategy for People with Learning Disabilities*. HMSO: London.

Department of Health (1995e). *Towards a Primary Care-Led NHS: An Accountability Framework for GP Fundholding*. Department of Health: London.

Department of Health (1996). *Building Bridges*. Department of Health: London.

Department of Health (1997). *Our Healthier Nation: A Contract for Health*. London: HMSO.

Department of Health & Home Office (1992). *Review of Health and Social Services for Mentally Disordered Offenders and Others Requiring Similar Services. Final Summary Report* (Chair: Dr J. Reed). HMSO: London.

Department of Health & Social Services Inspectorate (1991). *Case Management and Assessment: Manager's Guide.* HMSO: London.

Department of Health & Welsh Office (1993). *Mental Health Act 1983: Code of Practice.* HMSO: London.

Department of Health Statistics Office (1995). *Statistical Bulletin 95/6.* Department of Health: London.

Derby, K.M., Wacker, D.P., Sasso, G., Steege, M., Northup, J., Cigrand, K., & Asmus, J. (1992). Brief functional assessment techniques to evaluate aberrant behavior in an outpatient setting: a summary of 79 cases. *Journal of Applied Behavior Analysis,* **25**, 713–721.

Derby, K.M., Wacker, D.P., Peck, S., Sasso, G., DeRaad, A., Berg, W., Asmus, J., & Ulrich, S. (1994). Functional analysis of separate topographies of aberrant behavior. *Journal of Applied Behavior Analysis,* **27**, 267–278.

Didden, R., Duker, P.C., & Korzilius, H. (1997). Meta-analytic study on treatment effectiveness for problem behaviors with individuals who have mental retardation. *American Journal on Mental Retardation,* **101**, 387–399.

Digby, A. (1996) Contexts and perspectives. In *From Idiocy to Mental Deficiency: Historical Perspectives on People with Learning Disabilities* (ed. D. Wright & A. Digby). Routledge: London.

Division of Social Psychology (1995). *Professional Practice Guidelines.* British Psychological Society: Leicester.

Dockrell, J., Gaskell, G., Rehman, H., & Normand, C. (1992). Service provision for people with mild learning disability and challenging behaviours: the MIETS evaluation. In *Research to Practice? Implications of Research on the Challenging behaviour of People with Learning Disability* (ed. C. Kiernan). BILD Publications: Clevedon Avon.

Dodge, K.A., & Murphy, R.R. (1984). The assessment of social competence in adolescents. In *Adolescent Behavior Disorders: Foundations and Contemporary Concerns* (ed. P. Karoly & J.J. Steffan). Lexington Books: Lexington, MA.

Donnellan, A.M., La Vigna, G.W., Negri-Shoultz, N., & Fassbender, L.L. (1988). *Progress Without Punishment. Effective Approaches for Learners with Behaviour Problems.* Teachers College Press: New York.

Donnellan, A.M., Mirenda, P., Mesaros, R., & Fassbender, L. (1984). Analysing the communicative functions of aberrant behavior. *Journal of the Association for Persons with Severe Handicaps,* **9**, 201–212.

Dosen, A. (1990). Psychotherapeutic approaches in the treatment of depression in mentally retarded children. In *Depression in Mentally Retarded Children and Adults* (ed. A. Dosen & F.J. Menolascino). Logan: Leiden.

Dosen, A. (1993). Diagnosis and treatment of psychiatric and behavioural disorders in mentally retarded individuals: the state of the art. *Journal of Intellectual Disability Research,* **37** (Supplement 1), 1–7.

Dowdney, L., & Skuse, D. (1993). Parenting provided by adults with mental retardation. *Journal of Child Psychology & Psychiatry,* **34**, 25–47.

Dunckley, M.G., Piper, T.A., & Dickson, G. (1995). Toward a gene therapy for Duchenne muscular dystrophy. *Mental Retardation and Developmental Disabilities Research Reviews,* **1**, 71–78.

Dunn, J. (1996). The Emanuel Miller Memorial Lecture 1995. Children's relationships: bridging the divide between cognitive and social development. *Journal of Child Psychology and Psychiatry,* **37**, 507–518.

Durand, V.M., & Carr, E.G. (1991). Functional communication training to reduce challenging behavior: maintenance and application in new settings. *Journal of Applied Behavior Analysis*, **24**, 251–264.

Durand, V.M., & Carr, E.G. (1992). An analysis of maintenance following functional communication training. *Journal of Applied Behavior Analysis*, **25**, 777–794.

Durand, V.M., & Crimmins, D.B. (1992). *The Motivation Assessment Scale*. Monaco & Associates: Topeka, KS.

Durand, V.M., Crimmins, D., Caulfield, M., & Taylor, J. (1989). Reinforcer assessment, I: using problem behavior to select reinforcers. *Journal of the Association for Persons with Severe Handicaps*, **14**, 113–126.

Dykens, E.M. (1995). Measuring behavioral phenotypes: provocations from the 'new genetics'. *American Journal on Mental Retardation*, **99**, 522–532.

Edgerton, R.B. (1989). Retarded people of adult years. *Psychiatric Annals*, **19**, 205–209.

Education Act (1981). HMSO: London.

Education Act (1996). HMSO: London.

Education Act (Northern Ireland Order) (1996). HMSO: London.

Education Act Part III (1993). HMSO: London.

Education (Handicapped Children) Act (1970). HMSO: London.

Education Reform Act (1988). HMSO: London.

Education Reform Act (Northern Ireland Order) (1989). HMSO: London.

Education (Scotland) Act (1980). HMSO: London.

Education (Scotland) Act (1981). HMSO: London.

Elfreda Society (1995). *An Evaluation of the Access to Health Project* (executive summary). The Elfreda Society: London.

Ellis, D.N., Cress, P.J., & Spellman, C.R. (1992). Using timers and lap counters to promote self-management of independent exercise in adolescents with mental retardation. *Education and Training in Mental Retardation*, **27**, 51–59.

Elvick, S.L., Berkowitz, C.D., Nicholas, E., Lipman, J.L., & Inkelis, S.H. (1990) Sexual abuse in the developmentally disabled. Dilemmas of diagnosis. *Child Abuse and Neglect*, **14**, 497–502.

Emerson, E. (1992). What is normalisation? In *Normalisation. A Reader for the Nineties* (ed. H. Brown & H. Smith). Routledge: London.

Emerson, E. (1995). *Challenging Behaviour: Analysis and Intervention in People with Learning Disabilities*. Cambridge University Press: Cambridge.

Emerson, E. (1996). Early interventions, autism and challenging behaviour. *Tizard Learning Disability Review*, **1**, 36–38.

Emerson, E., & Hatton, C. (1994) *Moving Out: The Impact of Relocation from Hospital to Community on the Quality of Life of People with Learning Disabilities*. HMSO: London.

Emerson, E., & Hatton, C. (1996a). *Residential Provision for People with Learning Disabilities: An Analysis of the 1991 Census*. Hester Adrian Research Centre, University of Manchester: Manchester.

Emerson, E., & Hatton, C. (1996b). In practice: provocations from the 'new genetics'. *Tizard Learning Disability Review*, **1**, 31–33.

Emerson, E., & Hatton, C. (1997) Regional and local variations in residential provision for people with learning disabilities in England. *Tizard Learning Disability Review*, **2**, 43–46.

Emerson, E., Barrett, S., & Cummings, R. (1990). *Using Analogue Assessments*. Tizard Centre, University of Kent at Canterbury: Canterbury.

Emerson, E., Beasley, F., Offord, G., & Mansell, J. (1992). Specialised housing for people with seriously challenging behaviours. *Journal of Mental Deficiency Research*, **36**, 291–307.

Emerson, E., Forrest, J., Cambridge, P., & Mansell, J. (1996). Community support teams for people with learning disabilities and challenging behaviours: results of a national survey. *Journal of Mental Health*, **5**, 395–406.

Emerson, E., Reeves, D., Thompson, S., Henderson, D., & Robertson, J. (1996). Time-based lag sequential analysis in the functional assessment of severe challenging behaviour. *Journal of Intellectual Disability Research*, **40**, 260–274.

Emerson, E., Thompson, S., Reeves, D., Henderson, D., & Robertson, J. (1995). Descriptive analysis of multiple response topographies of challenging behavior. *Research in Developmental Disabilities*, **16**, 301–329.

Emerson, E., Alborz, A., Kiernan, C., Mason, H., Reeves, D., Swarbrick, R., & Mason, L. (1997a). *The HARC Challenging Behaviour Project Report 5: Treatment, Management and Service Utilisation*. Hester Adrian Research Centre, University of Manchester: Manchester.

Emerson, E., Alborz, A., Reeves, D., Mason, H., Swarbrick, R., Kiernan, C., & Mason, L. (1997b). *The HARC Challenging Behaviour Project Report 2: The Prevalence of Challenging Behaviour*. Hester Adrian Research Centre, University of Manchester: Manchester.

Emerson, E., Hatton, C., Bauer, I., Bjorgvinsdottir, S., Brak, W., Firkowska-Mankiewicz, A., Haroardottir, H., Kavaliunaite, A., Kebbon, L., Kristoffersen, E., Saloviita, T., Schippers, H., Timmons, B., Timcev, L., Tossebro, J., & Wiit, U. (1996). Patterns of institutionalisation in 15 European countries. *European Journal on Mental Disability*, **3**, 29–32.

Emery, C.L., Watson, J.L., Watson, P.J., Thompson, D.M., & Biderman, M.D. (1985). Variables related to body-weight status of mentally retarded adults. *American Journal of Mental Deficiency*, **90**, 34–39.

Espe-Sherwindt, M., & Crable, S. (1993). Parents with mental retardation: moving beyond the myths. *Topics in Early Childhood Special Education*, **13**.

Evans, G., Todd, S., Beyer, S., Felce, D., & Perry, J. (1994). Assessing the impact of the All Wales Mental Handicap Survey: a survey of four districts. *Journal of Intellectual Disability Research*, **38**, 109–133.

Evans, I.M. (1991). Testing and diagnosis: a review and evaluation. In *Critical Issues in the Lives of People with Severe Disabilities* (ed. L.H. Meyer, C.A. Peck & L. Brown). P.H. Brookes: Baltimore, MD.

Evans, I.M., & Meyer, L.M. (1985). *An Educative Approach to Behavior Problems*. P.H. Brookes: Baltimore, MD.

Farrell, P. (1997). The integration of children with severe learning difficulties: a review of the recent literature. *Journal of Applied Research in Intellectual Disabilities*, **10**, 1–14.

Favell, J.E., McGimsey, J.F., & Schell, R.M. (1982). Treatment of self-injury by providing alternate sensory activities. *Analysis and Intervention in Developmental Disabilities*, **2**, 83–104.

Fenwick, A. (1994). Sexual Abuse in Adults with Learning Disabilities—Part 1: A Review of the Literature. *British Journal of Learning Disabilities* **22**, 53–56.

Feeney, J., & Noller, P. (1996). *Adult Attachment*. Sage: Thousand Oaks, CA.

Felce, D. (1989). *Staffed Housing for Adults with Severe and Profound Handicaps: The Andover Project*. BIMH Publications: Kidderminster.

Felce, D. (1996). Changing residential services: from institutions to ordinary living. In *Changing Policy and Practice for People with Learning Disabilities* (ed. P. Mittler & V. Sinason). Cassell Education: London.

Felce, D., & Perry, J. (1995). Quality of life: its definition and measurement. *Research in Developmental Disabilities*, **16**, 51–74.

Feldman, M. (1996). *Courses for Parents with Intellectual Disabilities and their Children*. Parenting with Intellectual Disability Conference: Danish Ministry of Social Affairs.

Feldman, M., Case, L., Towns, F., & Betel. J. (1985). Parent education project I: the development and nurturance of children of mentally retarded parents. *American Journal of Mental Deficiency*, 90, 253–258.

Fennell, P. (1989). The Beverley Lewis Case: Was the law to blame? *New Law Journal*, **17**.

Fennell, P. (1996). *Treatment without Consent. Law, Psychiatry, and the Treatment of Mentally Disordered People since 1845*. Routledge: London.

Fernald, C.D. (1995). When in London . . . Differences in disability language preferences among English-speaking countries. *Mental Retardation*, 33, 99–103.

Fiddell, B. (1996). Making family therapy user friendly for learning disabled clients. *Context*, **26**, 11–13.

Fisher, D. (1994). Adult sex offenders: who are they? Why and how do they do it? In *Sexual Offending Against Children* (ed. T. Morrison, M. Erooga & R.C. Beckett). Routledge: London.

Fisher, W., Piazza, C., Cataldo, M., Harrell, R., Jefferson, G., & Conner, R. (1993). Functional communication training with and without extinction and punishment. *Journal of Applied Behavior Analysis*, **26**, 23–36.

Fleming, I., Caine, A., Ahmed, S., & Smith, S. (1996). Aspects of the use of psychoactive medication among people with intellectual disabilities who have been resettled from long stay hospitals into dispersed housing. *Journal of Applied Research in Intellectual Disabilities*, **9**, 194–205.

Flesch, R. (1948). A new readability yardstick. *Journal of Applied Psychology*, **32**, 221–233.

Fletcher, R.J. (1988). A county systems model: comprehensive services for the dually diagnosed. In *Mental Retardation and Mental Health: Classification, Diagnosis, Treatment, Services* (ed. J.A. Stark, F.J. Menolascino, M.H. Albarelli, & V.C. Gray). Springer-Verlag: New York.

Fletcher, R.J. (1993). Mental illness–mental retardation in the United States: policy and treatment challenges. *Journal of Intellectual Disability Research*, **37** (Supplement 1), 25–33.

Floor, L., Baxter, D., Rosen, M., & Zisfein, L. (1975). A survey of marriages among previously institutionalized retardates. *Mental Retardation*, **13**, 33–37.

Floyd, F.J., Singer, G.H.S., Powers, L.E., & Costigan, C.L. (1996). Families coping with mental retardation: assessment and therapy. In *Manual of Diagnosis and Professional Practice in Mental Retardation* (ed. J.W. Jacobson & J.A. Mulick). American Psychological Association: Washington, DC.

Flynn, M. (1989). *Independent Living for Adults with Mental Handicap: 'A Place Of My Own'*. Cassell: London.

Flynn, M., & Hirst, M. (1992). *This Year, Next Year, Sometime . . .? Learning Disability and Adulthood*. National Development Team/Social Policy Research Unit: London.

Flynn, M., Cotterill, L., Hayes, L., & Sloper, P. (1995). *A Break with Tradition: The Findings of a Survey of Respite Services for Adult Citizens with Learning Disabilities in England*. National Development Team: Manchester.

Forrest, L. (1992). Dream on. *Learning Together Magazine*, **2**, 4–8.

Foster-Johnson, L., Ferro, J., & Dunlap, G. (1994). Preferred curricular activities and reduced problem behaviors in students with intellectual disabilities. *Journal of Applied Behavior Analysis*, **27**, 493–504.

Fox, R.A., Rosenberg, R., & Rotatori, A.F. (1985). Parent involvement in a treatment program for obese retarded adults. *Journal of Behaviour Therapy and Experimental Psychiatry*, **16**, 45–48.

Freud, S. (1986). *The Essentials of Pscychoanalysis* (selected by A. Freud). Penguin: Harmondsworth.

Fryers, T. (1993). Epidemiological thinking in mental retardation: issues in taxonomy and population frequency. In *International Review of Research in Mental Retardation*, Volume 19 (ed. N.W. Bray). Academic Press: San Diego.

Fryers, T., & Russell, O. (1997). Applied epidemiology. In *Seminars in the Psychiatry of Learning Disabilities* (ed. O. Russell). Gaskell: London.

Fuchs, C., & Benson, B.A. (1995). Social information processing by aggressive and non-aggressive men with mental retardation. *American Journal on Mental Retardation*, **100**, 24–55.

Gable, R.A., & Warren, S.F. (1993). *Strategies for Teaching Students with Mild to Severe Mental Retardation*. Jessica Kingsley: London.

Gabler-Halle, D., Halle, J.H., & Chung, Y.B. (1993). The effects of aerobic exercise on psychological and behavioral variables of individuals with developmental delay: a critical review. *Research in Developmental Disabilities*, **14**, 359–86.

Garcia E.E., & DeHaven, E.D. (1974) Use of operant techniques in the establishment and generalization of language: a review and analysis. *American Journal of Mental Deficiency*, **79**, 169–178.

Gardner, W.I., & Graeber, J.L. (1994). Use of behavioural therapies to enhance personal competency: a multimodal diagnostic and intervention model. In *Mental Health in Mental Retardation: Recent Advances and Practices* (ed. N. Bouras). Cambridge University Press: Cambridge.

Garmezy, N., & Masten, A.S. (1994). Chronic adversities. In *Child and Adolescent Psychiatry: Modern Approaches (3rd edn)* (ed. M. Rutter, E. Taylor & L. Hersov). Blackwell: Oxford.

Gaylord-Ross, R., & Browder, D.M. (1991). Functional assessment. In *Critical Issues in the Lives of People with Severe Disabilities* (ed. L.H. Meyer, C.A. Peck & L. Brown). P.H. Brookes: Baltimore, MD.

Gaylord-Ross, R., Weeks, M., & Lipner, C. (1980). An analysis of antecedent, response and consequence events in the treatment of self-injurious behavior. *Education and Training of the Mentally Retarded*, **15**, 35–42.

Gedye, A. (1989a). Episodic rage and aggression attributed to frontal lobe seizures. *Journal of Mental Deficiency Research*, **33**, 369–379.

Gedye. A. (1989b). Extreme self-injury attributed to frontal lobe seizures. *American Journal on Mental Retardation*, **94**, 20–26.

Geen, R.G. (1990). *Human Aggression*. Open University Press: Milton Keynes.

General Assembly of the United Nations (1975). *Declaration of the Rights of Disabled Persons*. United Nations: New York.

General Assembly of the United Nations (1971). *Declaration of the Rights of Mentally Retarded Persons*. United Nations: New York.

General Assembly of the United Nations (1994). *The Standard Rules on the Equalization of Opportunities for Persons with Disabilities*. United Nations: New York.

Ghodse, H., & Khan, I. (1988). *Psychoactive Drugs: Improving Prescribing Practices*. World Health Organization: Geneva.

Gillberg, C., Persson, E., Grufman, M., & Themner, U. (1986). Psychiatric disorders in mildly and severely mentally retarded urban children and adolescents: epidemiological aspects. *British Journal of Psychiatry*, **149**, 68–74.

Gladstone, D. (1996). The changing dynamic of institutional care: the Western Counties Idiot Asylum, 1864–1914. In *From Idiocy to Mental Deficiency: Historical Perspectives on People with Learning Disabilities* (ed. D. Wright & A. Digby). Routledge: London.

Glover, N.M., & Glover, S.J. (1996). Ethical and legal issues regarding selective abortion of fetuses with Down's syndrome. *Mental Retardation*, 34, 207–214.

Goldberg, D.P., & Huxley, P. (1980). *Mental Illness in the Community: The Pathway to Psychiatric Care*. Tavistock: London.

Goldiamond, I. (1974). Toward a constructional approach to social problems: ethical and constitutional issues raised by applied behavior analysis. *Behaviorism*, 2, 1–84.

Goldstein, H. (1993). Structuring environmental input to facilitate generalized language learning by children with mental retardation. In *Enhancing Children's Communication: Research foundations for intervention* (ed. A.P. Kaiser & D.B. Gray). P.H. Brookes: Baltimore, MD.

Goldston, S.E. (1977). Defining primary prevention. In *The Issues: An Overview of Primary Prevention* (ed. G.W. Albee & J.M. Joffe). University Press of New England: Hanover, NH.

Goodey, C.F. (1996). The psychopolitics of learning and disability in seventeenth-century thought. In *From Idiocy to Mental Deficiency: Historical Perspectives on People with Learning Disabilities* (ed. D. Wright & A. Digby). Routledge: London.

Goodyer, I. (1986). Family therapy and the handicapped child. *Developmental Medicine and Child Neurology*, 28, 244–250.

Gostason, R., Wahlstrom, J., Johannisson, T., & Holmqvist, D. (1991). Chromosomal aberrations in the mildly mentally retarded. *Journal of Mental Deficiency Research*, 35, 240–246.

Grant, L., & Evans, A. (1994). *Principles of Behavior Analysis*. HarperCollins: New York.

Graves, B., Graves, D., Haynes, Y., Rice, G., & Whitman, B. (1990). Parents learning together II: selected modules from the curriculum. In *When a Parent is Mentally Retarded*. P.H. Brookes: Baltimore, MD.

Gray, G. (1996). Changing day services. In *Changing Policy and Practice for People with Learning Disabilities* (ed. P. Mittler & V. Sinason). Cassell Educational: London.

Green, G. (1994). The quality of the evidence. In *Facilitated Communication: The Clinical and Social Phenomenon* (ed. H.C. Shane). Singular Press: San Diego, CA.

Greenhaugh, L. (1994). *Well Aware: Improving Access to Health Information for People with Learning Disabilities*. NHS Executive, Anglia and Oxford Region: Oxford.

Gualtieri, C.T. (1991). A system for prevention and control. In *Mental Retardation: Developing Pharmacotherapies* (ed. J.J. Ratey). American Psychiatric Press: Washington, DC.

Gudjonsson, G.H. (1992). *The Psychology of Interrogations, Confessions and Testimony.* Wiley: Chichester.

Guess, D., & Carr, E.G. (1991). Emergence and maintenance of stereotypy and self-injury. *American Journal on Mental Retardation*, 96, 299–319.

Guess, D., Sailor, W., & Baer, D. (1978). *Functional Speech and Language Training*. H & H Enterprises: Kansas.

Gunn, J., & Taylor, P.J. (1993). *Forensic Psychiatry: Clinical, Legal and Ethical Issues.* Butterworth-Heinemann: London.

Gunn, M. (1994). The meaning of incapacity. *Medical Law Review*, 2, 8–29.

Gunn, M. (1996). *Sex and the Law* (4th edn). Family Planning Association: London.

Gunn, M. (1997). *De facto* detention. *Tizard Learning Disability Review*, 2, 11–17.

Guralnick, M.J. (1997). Peer social networks of young boys with developmental delays. *American Journal on Mental Retardation*, **101**, 595–612.

Hagerman, R., & Cronister, A. (ed.) (1991). *The Fragile X Syndrome: Diagnosis, Treatment and Research*. John Hopkins University Press: Baltimore, MD.

Happe, F. (1994). *Autism. An Introduction to Psychological Theory*. UCL Press: London.

Harchik, A.E., & Putzier, V.S. (1990). The use of high-probability requests to increase compliance with instructions to take medication. *Journal of the Association for Persons with Severe Handicaps*, **15**, 40–43.

Haring, T.G., & Kennedy, C.H. (1990). Contextual control of problem behaviors in students with severe disabilities. *Journal of Applied Behavior Analysis*, **23**, 235–243.

Harris, J., & Craft, A. (ed.) (1994). *People with Learning Disabilities at Risk of Physical or Sexual Abuse*. BILD Seminar Papers, No. 4. British Institute of Learning Disabilities: Clevedon.

Harris, J.C. (1992). Neurobiological factors in self-injurious behavior. In *Self-injurious Behavior: Analysis, Assessment and Treatment* (ed. J.K. Luiselli, J.L. Matson & N.N. Singh). Springer-Verlag: New York.

Harris, S.L. (1986). Parents as teachers: a four to seven year follow-up of parents of children with autism. *Child and Family Behaviour Therapy*, **8**, 39–47.

Hart, B., & Risley, T. (1975). Incidental teaching of language in the preschool. *Journal of Applied Behavior Analysis*, **8**, 411–420.

Hart, B., & Risley, T.R. (1995). *Meaningful Differences in the Everyday Experience of Young American Children*. P.H. Brookes: Baltimore, MD.

Harvey, R.J., & Cooray, S.E. (1993). Neuroleptic usage in a community mental handicap unit. *Psychiatric Bulletin*, **17**, 657–660.

Hastings, R.P. (1996). Does facilitated communication free imprisoned minds? *The Psychologist*, **9**, 19–24.

Hattersley, J. (1995). The survival of collaboration and co-operation. In *Services for People with Learning Disabilities* (ed. N. Malin). Routledge: London.

Hatton, C. (1996). A home of your own: Commentary. *Tizard Learning Disability Review*, **1**, 26–28.

Hatton, C., & Emerson, E. (1995). Services for adults with learning disabilities and sensory impairments: results of a national survey of local authorities. *British Journal of Learning Disabilities*, **23**, 11–17.

Hatton, C., & Emerson, E. (1996). *Residential Provision for People with Learning Disabilities: A Research Review*. Hester Adrian Research Centre, University of Manchester: Manchester.

Hatton, C., Emerson, E., & Kiernan, C. (1995) Trends and milestones: people in institutions in Europe. *Mental Retardation*, **33**, 132.

Hatton, C., Emerson, E., Robertson, J., Henderson, D., & Cooper, J. (1995). The quality and costs of residential services for adults with multiple disabilities: a comparative evaluation. *Research in Developmental Disabilities*, **16**, 439–460.

Hawton, K., Salkovskis, P.M., Kirk, J., & Clark, D.M. (1989). *Cognitive Behaviour Therapy for Psychiatric Problems: A Practical Guide*. Oxford University Press: Oxford.

Hay, D.F. (1994). Prosocial development. *Journal of Child Psychology and Psychiatry*, **35**, 29–72.

Hayes, S.C. (1989) *Rule Governed Behaviour: Cognition, Contingencies and Instructional Control*. Plenum: New York.

Heal, L.W., & Sigelman, C.K. (1995). Response bias in interviews with individuals with limited mental ability. *Journal of Intellectual Disability Research*, **39**, 331–340.

Health Education Authority (1995). *Health Related Resources for People with Learning Disabilities*. Health Education Authority: London.

Heighway, S., Kidd-Webster, S., & Snodgrass, P. (1988). Supporting parents with mental retardation. *Children Today*, **1988**, 24–27.

Hennicke, K. (1993). Systems therapy for persons with mental retardation. In *Mental Health Aspects of Mental Retardation: Progress in Assessment and Treatment* (ed. R.J. Fletcher & A. Dosen). Lexington: New York.

Henwood, M., & Wistow, G. (1994). *Monitoring Community Care: A Review*. Nuffield Institute for Health Community Care Division/Joseph Rowntree Foundation: Leeds.

Hewitt, J. (1995). Using Matrix Training Procedures to Develop Spontaneous and Functional Symbol Communication. Unpublished PhD Thesis, University of Southampton: Southampton.

Hill, B.K., & Bruininks, R.H. (1984). Maladaptive behavior of mentally retarded individuals in residential facilities. *American Journal of Mental Deficiency*, **88**, 380–387.

Hill, D.A., & Leary, M.R. (1993). *Movement Disturbances: A Clue to Hidden Competences in Persons Diagnosed with Autism and Other Developmental Disabilities*. DRI Press: Madison, WI.

Hodapp, R.M., & Dykens, E.M. (1994). Mental retardation's two cultures of behavioral research. *American Journal on Mental Retardation*, **98**, 675–687.

Holland, A.J. (1997). *De facto* detention: commentary. *Tizard Learning Disability Review*, **2**, 19–22.

Holland, A.J., & Murphy, G.H. (1990). Behavioural and psychiatric disorder in adults with mild learning difficulties. *International Review of Psychiatry*, **2**, 117–136.

Hollins, S., Clare, I.C.H., & Murphy, G.H. (1996). *You're Under Arrest*. Royal College of Psychiatrists & St George's Hospital Medical School: London.

Hollins, S., Murphy, G.H., & Clare, I.C.H. (1996). *You're On Trial*. Royal College of Psychiatrists & St George's Hospital Medical School: London.

Hollins, S., & Sinason, V. (1992). *Jenny Speaks Out*. The Sovereign Series, St George's Mental Health Library: London.

Hollins, S., & Sinason, V. (1993). *Bob Tells All*. The Sovereign Series, St George's Mental Health Library: London.

Hollins, S., Sinason, V., & Thompson, S. (1994). Individual, group and family psychotherapy. In *Mental Health in Mental Retardation: Recent Advances and Practices* (ed. N. Bouras). Cambridge University Press: Cambridge.

Home Office (1990). *Provision for Mentally Disordered Offenders*. Home Office Circular 66/90. Home Office: London.

Home Office (1995). *Provision for Mentally Disordered Offenders*. Home Office Circular 12/95. Home Office: London.

Home Office & Department of Health (1995). *Mentally Disordered Offenders. Interagency Working*. HMSO: London.

Horner, R.D. (1980). The effects of an environmental 'enrichment' program on the behavior of institutionalized profoundly retarded children. *Journal of Applied Behavior Analysis*, **13**, 473–491.

Horner, R.H. (1991). The future of applied behavior analysis for people with severe disabilities: commentary I. In *Critical Issues in the Lives of People with Severe Disabilities* (ed. L.H. Meyer, C.A. Peck & L. Brown). P.H. Brookes: Baltimore, MD.

Hove, G. van, & Broekart, E. (1995). Independent living of persons with mental retardation in Flanders: a survey of research data. *European Journal on Mental Disability*, **2**, 38–46.

Howard, J. (1996). A home of your own: moving from community residential services to supported living for people with learning disabilities. *Tizard Learning Disability Review*, **1**, 18–25.

Howells, G. (1986). Are the health care needs of mentally handicapped adults being met? *Journal of the Royal College of General Practitioners*, **36**, 449–453.

Howlin, P. (1997). *Autism. Preparing for Adulthood*. Routledge: London.

Hurley, A.D., Pfadt, A., Tomasulo, D., & Gardner, W.I. (1996). Counselling and psychotherapy. In *Manual of Diagnosis and Professional Practice in Mental Retardation* (ed. J.W. Jacobson & J.A. Mulick). American Psychological Association: Washington, DC.

Iverson, J.C., & Fox, R.A. (1989). Prevalence of psychopathology among mentally retarded adults. *Research in Developmental Disabilities*, **10**, 77–83.

Iwata, B.A., Dorsey, M.F., Slifer, K.J., Bauman, K.E., & Richman, G.S. (1982). Toward a functional analysis of self-injury. *Analysis and Intervention in Developmental Disabilities*, **2**, 3–20.

Iwata, B.A., Pace, G.M., Kissel, R.C., Nau, P.A., & Farber, J.M. (1990). The Self-Injury Trauma (SIT) Scale: a method for quantifying surface tissue damage caused by self-injurious behavior. *Journal of Applied Behavior Analysis*, **23**, 99–110.

Iwata, B.A., Pace, G.M., Dorsey, M.F., Zarcone, J.R., Vollmer, T.R., Smith, R.G., Rodgers, T.A., Lerman, D.C., Shore, B.A., Mazaleski, J.L., Goh, H-L., Cowdery, G.E., Kalsher, M.J., McCosh, K.C., & Willis, K.D. (1994). The functions of self-injurious behavior: an experimental–epidemiological study. *Journal of Applied Behavior Analysis*, **27**, 215–240.

Jackson, H., & Thorbecke, P. (1982). Treating obesity of mentally retarded adolescents and adults: an exploratory program. *American Journal of Mental Deficiency*, **87**, 303–308.

Jackson, M. (1996). Institutional provision for the feeble-minded in Edwardian England: Sandlebridge and the scientific morality of permanent care. In *From Idiocy to Mental Deficiency: Historical Perspectives on People with Learning Disabilities* (ed. D. Wright & A. Digby). Routledge: London.

Jacobson, J.W. (1990). Do some mental disorders occur less frequently among persons with mental retardation? *American Journal on Mental Retardation*, **94**, 596–602.

Jacobson, J.W., & Mulick, J.A. (1996). Psychometrics. In *Manual of Diagnosis and Professional Practice in Mental Retardation* (ed. J.W. Jacobson & J.A. Mulick). American Psychological Association: Washington, DC.

Jones, R. (1994). *Mental Health Act Manual* (4th edn). Sweet & Maxwell: London.

Jones, R. (1996). *Mental Health Act Manual* (5th edn). Sweet & Maxwell: London.

Jones, R.S.P., Miller, B., Williams, H., & Goldthorpe, J. (1997). Theoretical and practical issues in cognitive-behavioural approaches for people with learning disabilities. A radical behavioural perspective. In *Cognitive-Behavioural Therapy for People with Learning Disabilities* (ed. B. Stenfert Kroese, D. Dagnan & K. Loumidis). Routledge: London.

Kaiser, A.P., & Gray, D.B. (1993). *Enhancing Children's Communication: Research Foundations for Intervention*. P.H. Brookes: Baltimore, MD.

Kat, B.J.B. (1995). Psychology in health and social care settings: the new opportunities. In *Health Psychology: Processes and Applications* (2nd edn) (ed. A. Broome & S. Llewelyn). Chapman and Hall: London.

Kazdin, A.E., & Matson, J.L. (1981). Social validation in mental retardation. *Applied Research in Mental Retardation*, **2**, 39–53.

Kempton, R. (1988). *Life Horizons—Sex Education for People with Special Needs*. J. Stanfield: Santa Monica, CA.

Kennedy, C.H. (1994). Manipulating antecedent conditions to alter the stimulus control of problem behavior. *Journal of Applied Behavior Analysis*, **27**, 161–170.

Kennedy, C.H., & Itkonen, T. (1993). Effects of setting events on the problem behavior of students with severe disabilities. *Journal of Applied Behavior Analysis*, **26**, 321–327.

Kiernan, C., Reeves, D., Hatton, C., Alborz, A., Emerson, E., Mason, H., Swarbrick, R., & Mason, L. (1997). *The HARC Challenging Behaviour Project. Report 1: The Persistence of Challenging Behaviour*. Hester Adrian Research Centre, University of Manchester: Manchester.

King, D., & Mace, F.C. (1990). Acquisition and maintenance of exercise skills under normalised conditions by adults with moderate and severe mental retardation. *Mental Retardation*, **28**, 311–317.

King's Fund (1980). *An Ordinary Life: Comprehensive Locally-based Services for Mentally Handicapped People*. King's Fund Centre: London.

Kirk, J. (1989). Cognitive-behavioural assessment. In *Cognitive Behaviour Therapy for Psychiatric Problems* (ed. K. Hawton, P.M. Salkovskis, J. Kirk & D.M. Clark). Oxford University Press: Oxford.

Kitchen, W.H., Rickards, A.I., Doyle, L.W., Ford, G.W., Kelly, E.A., & Callahan, C. (1992). Improvement in outcome for very low birthweight children: apparent or real? *The Medical Journal of Australia*, **157**, 154–158.

Knussen, C., Sloper, P., Cunningham, C.C., & Turner, S. (1992). The use of The Ways of Coping Questionnaire (Revised) with parents of children with Down's syndrome. *Psychological Medicine*, **22**, 775–786.

Koegel, R.L., & Frea, W.D. (1993). Treatment of social behavior in autism through the modification of pivotal social skills. *Journal of Applied Behavior Analysis*, **26**, 369–377.

Koegel, R.L., & Koegel, L.K. (1990). Extended reductions in stereotypic behavior of students with autism through a self-management treatment package. *Journal of Applied Behavior Analysis*, **23**, 119–127.

Konanc, J.T., & Warren, N.J. (1984). Graduation: transitional crisis for mildly developmentally disabled adolescents and their families. *Family Relations Journal of Applied Family and Child Studies*, **33**, 135–142.

Korinek, L. (1991). Self management for the mentally retarded. In *Advances in Mental Retardation and Developmental Disabilities* (Volume 4) (ed. R.A. Gable). Jessica Kingsley: London.

Krantz, P.J., MacDuff, M.T., & McClannahan, L.E. (1993). Programming participation in family activities for children with autism: parents' use of photographic activity schedules. *Journal of Applied Behavior Analysis*, **26**, 137–138.

Kuo-Tai, T. (1988). Mentally retarded persons in the People's Republic of China: review of epidemiological studies and services. *American Journal on Mental Retardation*, **93**, 193–199.

LaMarre, J., & Holland, J.G. (1985). The functional independence of mands and tacts. *Journal of the Experimental Analysis of Behavior*, **43**, 5–19.

Lancioni, G.E., & Hoogeveen, F.R. (1990). Non-aversive and mildly aversive procedures for reducing problem behaviours in people with developmental disorders: a review. *Mental Handicap Research* **3**, 137–160.

Lancioni, G., O'Reilly, M., & Emerson, E. (1996). A review of choice research with people with severe and profound developmental disabilities. *Research in Developmental Disabilities*, **17**, 391–411.

Lancioni, G.E., Smeets, P.M., Ceccarani, P.S., Capodaglio, L., & Campanari, G. (1984). Effects of gross motor activities on the severe self-injurious tantrums of multihandicapped individuals. *Applied Research in Mental Retardation*, **5**, 471–482.

Langan, J., Russell, O., & Whitfield, M. (1993). *Community Care and the General Practitioner: Primary Health Care for People with Learning Disabilities*. Norah Fry Research Centre, University of Bristol: Bristol.

Lavay, B., & McKenzie, T.L. (1991). Development and evaluation of a systematic run/walk program for men with mental retardation. *Education and Training in Mental Retardation*, **26**, 333–341.

LaVigna, G.W., Willis, T.J., & Donnellan, A.M. (1989). The role of positive programming in behavioral treatment. In *The Treatment of Severe Behavior Disorders* (ed. E. Cipani). American Association on Mental Retardation: Washington, DC.

Lazarus, R.S., & Folkman, S. (1984). *Stress, Appraisal and Coping*. Springer: New York.

Lenneberg, E.H. (1967). *Biological Foundations of Language*. Wiley: New York.

Lepler, S., Hoods, A., & Cotter-Mack, A. (1993). Implementation of an interdisciplinary psychotropic drug review process for community-based facilities. *Mental Retardation*, **31**, 307–15.

Levine, H.G. (1985). Situational anxiety and everyday life experiences of mildly retarded adults. *American Journal of Mental Deficiency*, **90**, 27–33.

Ley, P., & Llewelyn, S. (1995). Improving patients' understanding, recall, satisfaction and compliance. In *Health Psychology: Process and Applications* (2nd edn) (ed. A. Broome & S. Llewelyn). Chapman and Hall: London.

Lindsay, W.R., & Baty, F.J. (1989). Group relaxation training with adults who are mentally handicapped. *Behavioural Psychotherapy*, **17**, 43–51.

Lindsay, W.R., & Kasprowicz, M. (1987). Challenging negative cognitions: developing confidence in adults by means of cognitive therapy. *Mental Handicap*, **15**, 159–62.

Lindsay, W., Neilson, C., & Lawrenson, H. (1997). Cognitive-behavioural therapy for anxiety in people with learning disabilities. In *Cognitive-Behavioural Therapy for People with Learning Disabilities* (ed. B. Stenfert Kroese, D. Dagnan & K. Loumidis). Routledge: London.

Linscheid, T.R., Iwata, B.A., Ricketts, R.W., Williams, D.E., & Griffin, J.C. (1990). Clinical evaluation of the Self-Injurious Behavior Inhibiting System (SIBIS). *Journal of Applied Behavior Analysis*, **23**, 53–78.

Littlewood, R., & Lipsedge, M. (1989). *Aliens and Alienists: Ethnic Minorities and Psychiatry* (2nd edn). Unwin Hyman: London.

Llewellyn, G., McConnell, D., & Bye, R. (1995). *Parents with Intellectual Disability: Report to the Disability Services Sub-Committee*. University of Sydney: Sydney.

Louhiala, P. (1995). Risk indicators of mental retardation: changes between 1967 and 1981. *Developmental and Child Neurology*, **37**, 631–636.

Lovaas, O.I., Newsom, C., & Hickman, C. (1987). Self-stimulatory behavior and perceptual reinforcement. *Journal of Applied Behavior Analysis*, **20**, 45–68.

Lovett, D.L., & Harris, M.B. (1987). Important skills for adults with mental retardation: the client's point of view. *Mental Retardation*, **25**, 351–356.

Lovett H. (1985). *Cognitive Counselling and Persons with Special Needs*. Praeger: New York.

Lovett, H. (1996). *Learning to Listen: Positive Approaches and People with Difficult Behaviour*. Jessica Kingsley: London.

Lowe, C.F., & Horne, P.J. (1985). On the generality of behavioural principles: human choice and the matching law. In *Behaviour Analysis and Contemporary Psychology* (ed. C.F. Lowe, M. Richelle, D.E. Blackman & C.M. Bradshaw). Lawrence Erlbaum: London.

Lowe, K., & de Paiva, S. (1991). *NIMROD: An Overview.* HMSO: London.

Luckasson, R., Coulter, D.L., Polloway, E.A., Reiss, S., Schalock, R.L., Snell, M.E., Spitalnik, D.M., & Stark, J.A. (1992). *Mental Retardation: Definition, Classification, and Systems of Supports* (9th edn). American Association on Mental Retardation: Washington, DC.

Lunacy Act (1890). HMSO: London.

Lund, J. (1985). The prevalence of psychiatric morbidity in mentally retarded adults. *Acta Psychiatrica Scandinavia,* **72**, 563–570.

Lyall, I., Holland, A.J., & Collins, S. (1995). Offending by adults with learning disabilities: identifying need in one health district. *Mental Handicap Research (Journal of Applied Research in Intellectual Disabilities),* 8, 99–109.

Mace, F.C., & Mauk, J.E. (1995). Bio-behavioral diagnosis and treatment of self-injury. *Mental Retardation & Developmental Disability Research Reviews,* 1, 104–110.

Mace, F.C., & Roberts, M.L. (1993). Factors affecting selection of behavioral interventions. In *Communicative Alternatives to Challenging Behavior* (ed. J. Reichle & D.P. Wacker). P.H. Brookes: Baltimore, MD.

Mace, F.C., Yankanich, M.A., & West, B. (1989). Toward a methodology of experimental analysis and treatment of aberrant classroom behaviors. *Special Services in the School,* 4, 71–88.

Mace, F.C., Hock, M.L., Lalli, J.S., West, B.J., Belfiore, P., Pinter, E., & Brown, B.D. (1988). Behavioral momentum in the treatment of non-compliance. *Journal of Applied Behavior Analysis* **21**, 123–141.

MacLean, W.E., Stone, W.L., & Brown, W.H. (1994). Developmental psychopathology of destructive behavior. In *Destructive Behavior in Developmental Disabilities: Diagnosis and Treatment,* pp. 68–79 (ed. T. Thompson & D.B. Gray). Sage: Thousand Oaks, CA.

Maletzky, B.M. (1974). 'Assisted' covert sensitisation in the treatment of exhibitionism. *Journal of Consulting and Clinical Psychology,* **42**, 34–40.

Maletzky, B.M. (1991). *Treating the Sexual Offender.* Sage: Newbury Park, CA.

Malin, N. (1995) (ed.). *Services for People with Learning Disabilities.* Routledge: London.

Mansell, J. (1994). Specialized group homes for persons with severe or profound mental retardation and serious problem behaviour in England. *Research in Developmental Disabilities,* **15**, 371–388.

Marks, I.M. (1981). *Cure and Care of Neurosis.* Wiley: New York.

Marshall, M. (1989). A comparison of self instruction training and modelling in the acquisition of an abstract task. Paper presented to the Annual Conference of the British Psychological Society, St Andrews, 1989.

Marshall, W.L., Bryce, P., Hudson, S.M., Ward, T., & Moth, B. (1996). The enhancement of intimacy and the reduction of loneliness among child molesters, *Journal of Family Violence,* **11**, 219–235.

Marteau, T.M. (1995). Health beliefs and attributions. In *Health Psychology: Processes and Applications* (2nd edn) (ed. A. Broome & S. Llewelyn). Chapman and Hall: London.

Martindale, A., McGrath, E., Hosking, G.P., & Buckley, R.A. (1988). Trends in the prevalence of severe mental handicap in Sheffield since 1960. *Community Medicine,* **10**, 331–340.

Marzillier, J., & Hall, J. (1992). *What is Clinical Psychology?* Oxford University Press: Oxford.

Mason, B. (1991). *Handing Over.* Karnac Books: London.

Matilainen, R., Airaksinen, E., Mononen, T., Launiala, K., & Kaariainen, R. (1995). A population-based study on the causes of mild and severe mental retardation. *Acta Paediatrica,* **84,** 261–266.

Matson, J.L., Kazdin, A.E., & Senatore, V. (1984). Psychometric properties of the Psychopathology Instrument for Mentally Retarded Adults. *Applied Research in Mental Retardation,* **5,** 881–889.

Matson, J.L., Gardner, W.I., Coe, D.A., & Sovner, R. (1991). A scale for evaluating emotional disorders in severely and profoundly mentally retarded persons: development of the Diagnostic Assessment for the Severely Handicapped (DASH) Scale. *British Journal of Psychiatry,* **159,** 404–409.

Mattaini, M.A. (1995). Contingency diagrams as teaching tools. *The Behavior Analyst,* **18,** 93–98.

McCabe, M.P., & Cummins, R.A. (1996). The sexual knowledge, experience, feelings and needs of people with mild intellectual disability. *Education and Training in Mental Retardation and Developmental Disabilities,* **31,** 13–21.

McCarran, M., & Andrasik, F. (1990). Behavioral weight-loss for multiply-handicapped adults: assessing caretaker involvement and measures of behavior change. *Addictive Behavior,* **15,** 13–20.

McCarthy, M., & Thompson, D. (1998). *Sex and the 3 Rs. Rights, Responsibilities and Risks* (2nd edn). Pavilion Publishing: Brighton.

McDowell, J.J. (1982). The importance of Herrnstein's mathematical statement of the law of effect for behavior therapy. *American Psychologist* **37,** 771–779.

McGaw, S. (1994). Raising the Parental Competency of Parents with Intellectual Disabilities. Unpublished PhD Thesis, University of Exeter: Exeter.

McGaw, S. (1996). Services for parents with intellectual disabilities. *Tizard Learning Disability Review,* **1,** 1.

McGaw, S., & Sturmey, P. (1994). Assessing parents with intellectual disabilities: the parental skills model. *Child Abuse Review,* **3,** 36–51.

McGee, J.J., Menolascino, F.J., Hobbs, D.C., & Menousek, P.E. (1987). *Gentle Teaching: A Non-aversive Approach to Helping Persons with Mental Retardation.* Human Sciences Press: New York.

McGill, P., & Toogood, S. (1994). Organizing community placements. In *Severe Learning Disabilities and Challenging Behaviours* (ed. E. Emerson, P. McGill & J. Mansell). Chapman and Hall: London.

McGimsey, J.F., & Favell, J.E. (1988). The effects of increased physical exercise on disruptive behavior in retarded persons. *Journal of Autism and Developmental Disorders,* **18,** 167–179.

McGrath, M., & Humphreys, S. (1988). *The All Wales CMHT Survey.* University College of North Wales: Bangor.

McGrother, C.W., Hauck, A., Burton, P.R., Raymond, N.T., & Thorp, C.F. (1993). More and better services for people with learning disabilities. *Journal of Public Health Medicine,* **15,** 263–271.

McLaren, J., & Bryson, S.E. (1987). Review of recent epidemiological studies of mental retardation: prevalence, associated disorders, and etiology. *American Journal of Mental Retardation,* **92,** 243–254.

McLean, L.K., Brady, N.C., & McLean, J.E. (1996). Reported communication abilities of individuals with severe mental retardation. *American Journal on Mental Retardation,* **100,** 580–591.

McNulty, C., Kissi-Deborah, R., & Newsom-Davies, I. (1995). Police involvement with clients having intellectual disabilities: a pilot study in South London. *Mental Handicap Research (Journal of Applied Research in Intellectual Disabilities)*, **8**, 129–136.

Meichenbaum, D., & Goodman, J. (1971). Training impulsive children to talk to themselves: a means of developing self-control. *Journal of Abnormal Psychology*, **77**, 115–126.

Meinhold, P.M., & Mulick, J.A. (1990). Risks, choices and behavioral treatment. *Behavioral Residential Treatment*, **5**, 29–44.

Mencap (1997). *How to Be an 'Appropriate Adult'*. Mencap National Centre: London Mental Deficiency Act (1913). HMSO: London.

Mental Health Act (1983). HMSO: London.

Mental Health Act 1983 Code of Practice (1993). HMSO: London.

Mental Health Act (1959). HMSO: London.

Mental Health Foundation (1996). *Building Expectations: Opportunities and Services for People with a Learning Disability. Report of the Mental Health Foundation Committee of Inquiry*. Mental Health Foundation: London.

Meyer, L., & Evans, I.M. (1989). *Non-aversive Intervention for Behavior Problems: A Manual for Home and Community*. Teachers College Press: New York.

Meyer, L.H., & Evans, I.M. (1993). Meaningful outcomes in behavioral intervention: evaluating positive approaches to the remediation of challenging behaviors. In *Communicative Alternatives to Challenging Behavior* (ed. J. Reichle & D.P. Wacker). P.H. Brookes: Baltimore, MD.

Meyer, L.H., & Janney, R. (1989). User-friendly measures of meaningful outcomes: evaluating behavioral interventions. *Journal of the Association for Persons with Severe Handicaps*, **14**, 262–270.

Michael, J. (1993). Establishing operations. *The Behavior Analyst*, **16**, 191–206.

Minuchin, S. (1974). *Families and Family Therapy*. Tavistock: London.

Mittler, P., & Sinason, V. (ed.) (1996). *Changing Policy and Practice for People with Learning Disabilities*. Cassell Education: London.

Moerk, E.L. (1990). Three-term contingency patterns in mother-child verbal interactions during first language acquisition. *Journal of the Experimental Analysis of Behavior*, **54**, 293–305.

Moerk, E.L. (1992). The clash of giants over terminological differences. *Behavior and Social Issues*, **2**, 1–26.

Monfils, N.S., & Menolascino, F.J. (1984). Modified individual and group treatment for the mentally retarded mentally ill. In *Handbook of Mental Illness in the Mentally Retarded* (ed. F.J. Menolascino & J. Stark). Plenum: New York.

Moore, E., Adams, R., Elsworth, J., & Lewis, J. (1997). An anger management group for people with a learning disability. *British Journal of Learning Disabilities*, **25**, 53–57.

Morgenstern, M., & Klass, E. (1991). Standard intelligence tests and related assessment techniques. In *Handbook of Mental Retardation* (ed. J.L. Matson & J.A. Mulick). Pergamon: New York.

Morrison, T., Erooga, M., & Beckett, R. (1994). *Sexual Offending Against Children*. Routledge: London.

Moss, S. (1995). Methodological issues in the diagnosis of psychiatric disorders in adults with learning disability. *Thornfield Journal*, **18**, 9–18.

Moss, S., & Patel, P. (1995). Psychiatric symptoms associated with dementia in older people with learning disability. *British Journal of Psychiatry*, **167**, 663–667.

Moss, S., & Turner, S. (1995). *The Health of People with Learning Disability*. Hester Adrian Research Centre, University of Manchester: Manchester.

Moss, S., Ibbotson, B., Prosser, H., & Goldberg, D. (1996a). Validity of the PAS-

ADD for detecting psychiatric symptoms in adults with learning disability (mental retardation). *Social Psychiatry and Psychiatric Epidemiology*, **31**, in press.

Moss, S., Prosser, H., Ibbotson, B., & Goldberg, D. (1996b). Respondent and informant accounts of psychiatric symptoms in a sample of patients with learning disability. *Journal of Intellectual Disability Research*, **40**, 457–465.

Moss, S.C., Prosser, H., Costello, H., Simpson, N., & Patel, P. (1996c). *PAS-ADD Checklist*. Hester Adrian Research Centre, University of Manchester: Manchester.

Moss, S., Goldberg, D., Patel, P., Prosser, H., Ibbotson, B., Simpson, N., & Rowe, S. (1996d). *The Psychiatric Assessment Schedule for Adults with a Developmental Disability: PAS-ADD*. Hester Adrian Research Centre, University of Manchester, and The Institute of Psychiatry: Manchester.

Moss, S., Prosser, H., & Goldberg, D. (1996e). Validity of the schizophrenia diagnosis of the psychiatric assessment schedule for adults with developmental disability (PAS-ADD). *British Journal of Psychiatry*, **168**, 359–367.

Moss, S., Patel, P., Prosser, H., Goldberg, D.P., Simpson, N., Rose, S., & Lucchino, R. (1993). Psychiatric morbidity in older people with moderate and severe learning disability (mental retardation). Part I: Development and relaibility of the patient interview (the PAS-ADD). *British Journal of Psychiatry*, **163**, 471–480.

Murphy, G.H. (1986). Direct observation as an assessment tool in functional analysis and treatment. In *Assessment in Mental Handicap* (ed. J. Hogg & N. Raynes). Croom Helm: London.

Murphy, G.H. (1990). Analysis of motivation and fire-related interests in people with a mild learning disability who set fires. Paper presented at the International Congress on Treatment of Mental Illness and Behavioural Disorders in Mentally Retarded People, Amsterdam.

Murphy, G.H. (1992). Community adjustment, social integration, work and social competence of people with intellectual disabilities or mental retardation. *Current Opinion in Psychiatry*, **5**, 831–835.

Murphy, G.H. (1993). The treatment of challenging behaviour in people with learning difficulties. In *Violence: Basic and Clinical Approaches* (ed. C. Thompson & P. Cowen). Butterworth-Heinemann: Oxford.

Murphy, G.H. (1994). Understanding challenging behaviour. In *Severe Learning Disabilities and Challenging Behaviours* (ed. E. Emerson, P. McGill & J. Mansell). Chapman and Hall: London.

Murphy, G.H. (1997a). Assessment: Establishing the clearest possible understanding of an offender. In *There Are No Easy Answers! The Provision of Continuing Care and Treatment to Adults with Learning Disabilities who Sexually Abuse Others* (ed. J. Churchill, H. Brown, A. Craft & C. Horrocks). ARC/NAPSAC: Chesterfield.

Murphy, G.H. (1997b). Assessing risk. In *There Are No Easy Answers! The Provision of Continuing Care and Treatment to Adults with Learning Disabilities who Sexually Abuse Others* (ed. J. Churchill, H. Brown, A. Craft & C. Horrocks). ARC/NAPSAC: Chesterfield.

Murphy, G.H. (1997c). Treatment and risk management. In *There Are No Easy Answers! The Provision of Continuing Care and Treatment to Adults with Learning Disabilities who Sexually Abuse Others* (ed. J. Churchill, H. Brown, A. Craft & C. Horrocks). ARC/NAPSAC: Chesterfield.

Murphy, G.H. (1997d). Understanding aggression in people with intellectual disabilities: lessons from other populations. *International Review of Research in Mental Retardation, Volume 21* (ed. N. Bray). Academic Press: New York.

Murphy, G.H., & Clare, I.C.H. (1991). MIETS: a service option for people with mild mental handicaps and challenging behaviour or psychiatric problems 2. Assessment, treatment, and outcome for service users and service effectiveness. *Mental Handicap Research*, **4**, 180–206.

Murphy, G.H., & Clare, I.C.H. (1995). Adults' capacity to make decisions affecting the person: psychologists' contribution. In *Handbook of Psychology in Legal Contexts* (ed. R. Bull & D. Carson). Wiley: Chichester.

Murphy, G.H., & Clare, I.C.H. (1996). Analysis of motivation in people with mild learning disabilities (mental handicap) who set fires. *Psychology, Crime & Law*, **2**, 153–164.

Murphy, G.H., & Clare, I.C.H. (1997). Consent issues. In *Adults with Learning Disabilities: A Practical Approach for Health Professionals* (ed. J. O'Hara & A.C. Sperlinger). Wiley: Chichester.

Murphy, G.H., & Holland, A.J. (1993). Challenging behaviour, psychiatric disorders and the law. In *Challenging Behaviour and Intellectual Disability: A Psychological Perspective* (ed. R.S.P. Jones & C. Eayrs). BILD Publications: Clevedon.

Murphy, G.H., Estien, D., & Clare, I.C.H. (1996). Services for people with mild intellectual disabilities and challenging behaviour: service-user views. *Journal of Applied Research in Intellectual Disabilities*, **9**, 256–283.

Murphy, G.H, Harnett, D.H., & Holland, A.J. (1995). A survey of intellectual disabilities amongst men on remand in prison. *Mental Handicap Research (Journal of Applied Research in Intellectual Disabilities)*, **8**, 81–98.

Murphy, G.H., Holland, A.J., Fowler, P., & Reep, J. (1991). MIETS: a service option for people with mild mental handicaps and challenging behaviour or psychiatric problems 1. Philosophy, service, and service users. *Mental Handicap Research*, **4**, 41–66.

National Assistance Act (1948). HMSO: London.

Neri, C.L., & Sandman, C.A. (1992). Relationship between diet and self-injurious behavior: a survey. *Journal of Developmental and Physical Disabilities*, **4**, 198–204.

Neugebauer, R. (1996). Mental handicap in medieval and early modern England: criteria, measurement and care. In *From Idiocy to Mental Deficiency: Historical Perspectives on People with Learning Disabilities* (ed. D. Wright & A. Digby). Routledge: London.

New York State Commission. (1993). *Parenting with Special Needs: Parents who Are Mentally Retarded and Their Children*. New York State Commission on Quality of Care for the Mentally Disabled: New York.

Nezu, C.M., Nezu, A.M., Rothenberg, J.L., Dellicarpini, L., & Groag, I. (1995). Depression in adults with mild mental retardation: are cognitive variables involved? *Cognitive Therapy and Research*, **19**, 227–239.

Nicolson, P. (1992). Gender issues in clinical psychology. In *Gender Issues in Clinical Psychology* (ed. J.M. Ussher & P. Nicolson). Routledge: London.

Nirje, B. (1969). The normalization principle and its human management implications. In *Changing Patterns In Residential Services for the Mentally Retarded* (ed. R.B. Kugel & W. Wolfensberger). Presidential Committee on Mental Retardation: Washington, DC.

Nixon, C.D., & Singer, G.H.S. (1993). Group cognitive behavioural treatment for excessive parental self blame and guilt. *American Journal of Mental Retardation*, **97**, 665–672.

Noble, J.H., & Conley, R.W. (1992). Toward an epidemiology of relevant attributes. In *The Criminal Justice System and Mental Retardation* (ed. R.W. Conley, R. Luckasson & G.N. Bouthilet). P.H. Brookes: Baltimore, MD.

North West Training & Development Team (1993). *A Strategy for the Nineties:*

Services for People with Learning Disabilities in Greater Manchester and Lancashire. North West Training & Development Team: Calderstones Hospital, Blackburn.

O'Brien, J. (1987). A guide to life style planning: using the Activities Catalogue to integrate services and natural support systems. In *The Activities Catalogue: An Alternative Curriculum for Youth and Adults with Severe Disabilities* (ed. B.W. Wilcox & G.T. Bellamy). P.H. Brookes: Baltimore, MD.

O'Brien, J., & Lovett, H. (1992). *Finding a Way Toward Everyday Lives: The Contribution of Person-centred Planning.* Pennsylvania Office of Mental Retardation: Harrisburg, PA.

O'Brien, J., & Tyne, A. (1981). *The Principle of Normalisation: A Foundation for Effective Services.* The Campaign for Mentally Handicapped People: London.

O'Brien, S., & Repp, A.C. (1990). Reinforcement-based reductive procedures: a review of 20 years of their use with persons with severe or profound mental retardation. *Journal of the Association for Persons with Severe Handicaps,* **15,** 148–159.

O'Connor, W. (1996). A problem-solving intervention for sex offenders with an intellectual disability. *Journal of Intellectual and Developmental Disability,* **21,** 219–235.

Ogden, J. (1996). *Health Psychology: A Textbook.* Open University Press: Milton Keynes.

O'Hara, J., & Sperlinger, A. (1997). *Adults with Learning Disabilities: A Practical Approach for Health Professionals.* Wiley: Chichester.

O'Neill, A.M. (1985). Normal and bright children of mentally retarded parents: the Huck Finn syndrome. *Child Psychiatry and Human Development,* **15,** 255–268.

O'Neill, R.E., Horner, R.H., Albin, R.W., Storey, K., & Sprague, J.R. (1990). *Functional Analysis of Problem Behavior: A Practical Assessment Guide.* Sycamore: Sycamore, IL.

O'Reilly, M. (1995). Functional analysis and treatment of escape-maintained aggression correlated with sleep deprivation. *Journal of Applied Behavior Analysis,* **28,** 225–226.

Orlik, C., Robinson, C., & Russell, D. (1991). *A Survey of Family Based Respite Care Schemes in the United Kingdom.* Norah Fry Research Centre, University of Bristol: Bristol.

Osborne-Davis, I. (1996). Awareness and attitudes of other health-care professionals towards clinical psychologists. *Clinical Psychology Forum,* **91.**

Owens, R.G., & Ashcroft, J.B. (1982). Functional analysis in applied psychology. *British Journal of Clinical Psychology,* **21,** 181–189.

Page, T. (1988). Clinical-research issues in the treatment of obesity in the developmentally disabled. In *Behavioral Medicine with the Developmentally Disabled* (ed. D. Russo & J. Kedesky). Plenum: New York.

Palazolli, S.N., Boscolo, L., Cecchin, G., & Prata, G. (1980). Hypothesising, circularity, neutrality: three guidelines for the conductor of the session. *Family Process,* **19.**

Parker, T., Hill, J.W., & Miller, G. (1987). Multiple family therapy: evaluating a group experience for mentally retarded adolescents and their families. *Family Therapy,* **14,** 43–51.

Parrish, J.M., Cataldo, M.F., Kolko, D.J., Neef, N.A., & Egel, A.L. (1986). Experimental analysis of response covariation among compliant and inappropriate behaviors. *Journal of Applied Behavior Analysis* **19,** 241–254.

Parrott, R., Emerson, E., Hatton, C., & Wolstenholme, J. (1997). *Future Demand for Residential Provision for People with Learning Disabilities.* Hester Adrian Research Centre, University of Manchester: Manchester.

Parry, A., & Doan, R.E. (1994). *Story Revisions. Narrative Therapy in the Postmodern World*. Guilford Press: New York.

Pary, R.J. (1993). Acute psychiatric hospital admissions of adults and elderly adults with mental retardation. *American Journal on Mental Retardation*, **98**, 434–436.

Patel, P., Goldberg, D., & Moss, S. (1993). Psychiatric morbidity in older people with moderate and severe learning disability (mental retardation). Part II: The prevalence study. *British Journal of Psychiatry*, **163**, 481–491.

Peine, H.A., Darvish, R., Adams, K., Blakelock, H., Jenson, W., & Osborne, J.G. (1995). Medical problems, maladaptive behaviors and the developmentally disabled. *Behavioral Interventions*, **10**, 119–140.

Pennington, B.F., & Ozonoff, S. (1996). Executive functions and developmental psychopathology. *Journal of Child Psychology and Psychiatry*, **37**, 51–88.

People First (1992). *Oi! It's My Assessment*. People First: London.

Perkins, D. (1991). Clinical work with sex offenders in secure settings. In *Clinical Approaches to Sex Offenders and their Victims* (ed. C.R. Hollin & K. Howells). Wiley: Chichester.

Perrin, B., & Nirje, B. (1985). Setting the record straight: a critique of some frequent misconceptions of the normalization principle. *Australian and New Zealand Journal of Developmental Disabilities*, **11**, 69–74.

Phinney, S. (1992). Exercise in the treatment of obesity. *Journal of the Florida Medical Association*, **79**, 400–402.

Pierce, K.L., & Schreibman, L. (1994). Teaching daily living skills to children with autism in unsupervised settings through pictorial self-management. *Journal of Applied Behavior Analysis*, **27**, 471–481.

Pinker, S. (1994). *The Language Instinct*. Penguin: Harmondsworth.

Pitetti, K.H., & Tan, D. (1991). Effects of a minimally supervised exercise program for mentally retarded adults. *Medicine and Science in Sports and Exercise*, **23**, 594–601.

Plomin, R., DeFries, J.C., McClearn, G.E., & Rutter, M. (1997). *Behavioral Genetics* (3rd edn). W.H. Freeman: New York.

Police and Criminal Evidence Act (PACE) (1984). HMSO: London.

Porter, R. (1990). *Mind-Forg'd Manacles: A History of Madness from the Restoration to the Regency*. Penguin: Harmondsworth.

Prosser, H., Moss, S.C., Costello, H., Simpson, N., & Patel, P. (1996). *The Mini PAS-ADD: A Preliminary Assessment Schedule for the Detection of Mental Health Needs in Adults with Learning Disabilities*. Hester Adrian Research Centre, University of Manchester: Manchester.

PSD Import Agency (undated). *Baby Think it Over*. 1A St Marks Road, Henley on Thames, Oxon RG9 1LD, UK.

Quine, L., & Pahl, J. (1985). Examining the causes of stress in families with severely mentally handicapped children. *British Journal of Social Work*, **15**, 501–517.

Quine, L., & Pahl, J. (1986). First diagnosis of severe mental handicap: characteristics of unsatisfactory encounters between doctors and patients. *Social Science and Medicine*, **22**, 53–62.

Race, D. (1995). Historical development of service provision. In *Services for People with Learning Disabilities* (ed. N. Malin). Routledge: London.

Ramcharan, P., Roberts, G., Grant, G., & Borland, J. (1997) (ed.). *Empowerment in Everyday Life: Learning Disability*. Jessica Kingsley: London.

Rapley, M., & Antaki, C. (1996). A conversation analysis of the 'acquiescence' of people with learning disabilities. *Journal of Community and Applied Social Psychology*, **6**, 207–227.

Registered Homes Act (1984). HMSO: London.

Reichle, J., York, J., & Sigafoos, J. (1991). *Implementing Augmentative and Alternative Communication: Strategies for Learners with Severe Disabilities*. P.H. Brookes: Baltimore, MD.

Reiss, S. (1988a). *Reiss Screen for Maladaptive Behavior*. IDS: Worthington, OH.

Reiss, S. (1988b). The development of a screening measure for psychopathology in people with mental retardation. In *Assessment of Behavior Problems in Persons with Mental Retardation Living in the Community* (ed. E. Dibble & D. Gray). National Institute of Mental Health: Rockville, MD.

Reiss, S. (1990). Prevalence of dual diagnosis in community-based day programs in the Chicago metropolitan area. *American Journal on Mental Retardation*, **94**, 578–585.

Reiss, S. (1994). Psychopathology in mental retardation. In *Mental Health in Mental Retardation* (ed. N. Bouras). Cambridge University Press: Cambridge.

Reiss, S., & Benson, B.A. (1984). Awareness of negative social conditions among mentally retarded, emotionally disturbed outpatients. *American Journal of Psychiatry*, **141**, 88–90.

Reiss, S., Levitan, G.W., & McNally, R.J. (1982). Emotionally disturbed mentally retarded people: an underserved population. *American Psychologist*, **37**, 361–367.

Remington, B. (1991). Why use single subject methods in AAC? In *Methodological Issues in Research in Augmentative and Alternative Communication: Proceedings of The First International ISAAC Research Symposium in Augmentative and Alternative Communication* (ed. J. Brodin & E. Bjorck-Akesson). Swedish Handicap Institute: Stockholm.

Remington, B., & Clarke, S. (1996). Alternative and augmentative systems of communication for children with Down's syndrome. In *Down's Syndrome: Psychological, Psychobiological and Socio-educational Perspectives* (ed. J. Rondal, J. Perera & L. Nadel). Whurr: London.

Remington, B., & Light, P. (1983). Some problems in the evaluation of research on non-oral communication systems. In *Advances in Mental Handicap Research Vol II: Aspects of Competence in Mentally Handicapped People* (ed. J. Hogg & P.J. Mittler). Wiley: Chichester.

Reynell, J. (1977). *Reynell Developmental Language Scales*. NFER: Windsor.

Reynolds, W.M., & Baker, J.A. (1988). Assessment of depression in persons with mental retardation. *American Journal of Mental Retardation*, **93**, 93–103.

Richardson, S.A., & Koller, H. (1985). Epidemiology. In *Mental Deficiency: The Changing Outlook* (4th edn) (ed. A.M. Clarke, A.D.B. Clarke & J.M. Berg). Methuen: London.

Richardson, S.A., Koller, H., & Katz, M. (1985). Continuities and change in behavior disturbance: a follow-up study of mildly retarded young people. *American Journal of Orthopsychiatry*, **55**, 220–229.

Richardson, S.A., Koller, H., Katz, M., & McLaren, J. (1984). Career paths through mental retardation services: an epidemiological perspective. *Applied Research in Mental Retardation*, **5**, 53–67.

Rimmer, J.H., Braddock, D., & Fujiura, G. (1994). Cardiovascular risk factor levels in adults with mental retardation. *American Journal on Mental Retardation*, **98**, 510–518.

Rimmer, J.H., Braddock, D., & Fujiura, G. (1993). Prevalence of obesity in adults with intellectual disabilities: implications for health promotion and disease prevention. *Mental Retardation*, **31**, 105–110.

Roberts, G., & Griffiths, A. (1993). *What Can We Do? The Legal Framework of Community Care Services for Adults with Learning Disabilities*. MENCAP/ National Development Team: Manchester.

Roberts, J. (1994). *Tales and Transformations. Stories in Families and Family Therapy.* W.W. Norton: New York.

Robinson, C. (1996). Breaks for disabled children. In *Developments in Short-term Care: Breaks and Opportunities* (ed. K. Stalker). Jessica Kingsley: London.

Rojahn, J., Polster, L.M., Mulick, J.A. & Wisniewski, J.J. (1989). Reliability of the Behavior Problems Inventory. *Journal of the Multihandicapped Person*, **2**, 283–293.

Rogers-Wallgren, J., French, R., & Ben-Ezra, V. (1992). Use of reinforcers to increase independence in physical fitness performance of profoundly mentally retarded youth. *Perception and Motor Skills*, **75**, 975–982.

Rondal, J.A. (1996). Oral language in Down's syndrome. In *Down's Syndrome: Psychological, Psychobiological and Socio-educational Perspectives* (eds. J. Rondal, J. Perera & L. Nadel). Whurr: London.

Rosenstock, I. (1972). The health belief model and preventive health behavior. *Health Education Monographs*, **2**, 254–86.

Rotatori, A., & Fox, R. (1981). *Behavioral Weight Reduction Program for Mentally Handicapped Persons: A Self-control Approach*. Pro Ed: Austin, TX.

Rotatori, A., Switzky, H.N., & Fox, R. (1981). Behavioral weight reduction procedures for obese mentally retarded individuals: a review. *Mental Retardation*, **19**, 157–61.

Rusch, R.G., Hall, J.C., & Griffin, H.C. (1986). Abuse provoking characteristics of institutionalized mentally retarded individuals. *American Journal of Mental Deficiency*, **90**, 618–624.

Rushton, P. (1996). Idiocy, the family and the community in early modern northeast England. In *From Idiocy to Mental Deficiency: Historical Perspectives on People with Learning Disabilities* (ed. D. Wright & A. Digby). Routledge: London.

Russell, P. (1996). Parents' voices: developing new approaches to family support and community development. In *Changing Policy and Practice for People with Learning Disabilities* (ed. P. Mittler & V. Sinason). Cassell Education: London.

Ryan, J. with Thomas, F. (1987). *The Politics of Mental Handicap* (2nd edn). Free Association Books: London.

Salmon, A. (1996). Family therapy and learning disabilities: a case discussion. *Context*, **29**, 42–45.

Salter, A. (1988). *Treating Child Sex Offenders and Victims*. Sage: Newbury Park, CA.

Sanders, A., Creaton, J., Bird, S., & Weber, L. (1997). *Witnesses with Learning Disabilities: Negotiating the Criminal Justice System*. Centre for Criminological Research, University of Oxford: Oxford.

Sanderson, H. (1995). Self-advocacy and inclusion. In *Values and Visions: Changing Ideas in Services for People with Learning Difficulties* (ed. T. Philpot & L. Ward). Butterworth-Heinemann: Oxford.

Sandifer, M.G., Hordern, A., & Green, L.M. (1970). The psychiatric interview: the impact of the first three minutes. *American Journal of Psychiatry*, **126**, 968–973.

Sandman, C.A., & Hetrick, W.P. (1995). Opiate mechanisms in self-injury. *Mental Retardation & Developmental Disability Research Reviews*, **1**, 130–136.

Schalock, R.L. (1996). *Quality of Life: Volume 1—Conceptualization and Measurement.* American Association on Mental Retardation: Washington, DC.

Scheerenberger, R.C. (1983). *A History of Mental Retardation*. P.H. Brookes: Baltimore, MD.

Schilling, D., & Poppen, R. (1983). Behavioural relaxation training and assessment. *Journal of Behaviour Therapy and Experimental Psychiatry*, **14**, 99–107.

Schroeder, S.R., & Tessel, R. (1994). Dopaminergic and serotonergic mechanisms in self-injury and aggression. In *Destructive Behavior in Developmental Disabilities: Diagnosis and Treatment* (ed. T. Thompson & D.B. Gray). Sage: Thousand Oaks, CA.

Schroeder, S.R., Hammock, R.G., Mulick, J.A., Rojahn, J., Walson, P., Fernald, W., Meinhold, P., & Shaphare, G. (1995). Clinical trials of D1 and D2 dopamine modulating drugs and self-injury in mental retardation and developmental disabilities. *Mental Retardation & Developmental Disability Research Reviews*, **1**, 120–129.

Schuman, H., & Presser, S. (1977). Question wording as an independent variable in survey analysis. *Sociological Methods and Research*, **6**, 151–170.

Schurrer, R., Weltman, A., & Brammell, H. (1985). Effects of physical training on cardiovascular fitness and behaviour patterns of mentally retarded adults. *American Journal of Mental Deficiency*, **90**, 167–170.

Schwartz, I.S., & Baer, D.M. (1991). Social validity assessments: is current practice state of the art? *Journal of Applied Behavior Analysis*, **24**, 189–204.

Scotti, J.R., Evans, I.M., Meyer, L.H., & Walker, P. (1991). A meta-analysis of behavioral research with problem behavior: treatment validity and standards of practice. *American Journal of Mental Retardation*, **93**, 233–256.

Scottish Law Commission (1992). *Report on Family Law*. Scottish Law Commission, Edinburgh.

SCOVO (1989). *Better Early Counselling in Wales*. Practical Steps to Better Practice. SCOVO: Cardiff.

Scull, A. (1993). *The Most Solitary of Afflictions: Madness and Society in Britain 1700–1900*. Yale University Press: New Haven, CT.

Secretary General, UN (1948). *Universal Declaration of Human Rights*. United Nations: New York.

Secretary General, UN (1976a). *International Covenant of Civil and Political Rights*. United Nations: New York.

Secretary General, UN (1976b). *International Covenant on Economic, Social and Cultural Rights*. United Nations: New York.

Senatore, V., Matson, J.L., & Kazdin, A.E. (1985). An inventory to assess psychopathology in mentally retarded adults. *American Journal of Mental Retardation*, **89**, 459–466.

Shah, R. (1992). *The Silent Minority: Children with Disabilities in Asian Families*. National Children's Bureau: London.

Shattock, P. (1995). Back to the future: an assessment of some of the unorthodox forms of biomedical intervention currently being applied to autism. In *Psychological Perspectives in Autism. A Collection of Papers from the Conference held at the University of Durham, April 5th–7th 1995*. Autism Research Unit: Sunderland.

Shaw, J.A., & Budd, E. (1982). Determinants of acquiescence and nay saying of mentally retarded persons. *American Journal of Mental Deficiency*, **87**, 108–110.

Shea, S.C. (1988). *Psychiatric Interviewing: The Art of Understanding*. Harcourt Brace Janovich: New York.

Shulman, S. (1988). The family of the severely handicapped child: the sibling perspective. *Journal of Family Therapy*, **10**, 125–134.

Sigelman, C., Budd, E.C., Spaniel, C., & Schoenrock, C. (1981). When in doubt say yes: acquiescence in interviews with mentally retarded persons, *Mental Retardation*, **19**, 53–58.

Sigelman, C., Budd, E., Winer, J., Schoenrock, C., & Martin, P. (1982). Evaluating alternative techniques of questioning mentally retarded persons. *American Journal of Mental Deficiency*, **86**, 511–518.

Sigelman, C., Schoenrock, C., Spaniel, C., Hromas, S., Winer, J., Budd, E., & Martin, P. (1980). Surveying mentally retarded persons: responsiveness and response validity in three samples. *American Journal of Mental Deficiency*, **84**, 479–484.

Simons, K. (1995). *My Home, My Life: Innovative approaches to housing and support for people with learning difficulties*. Values Into Action: London.

Sinason, V. (1990). Individual psychotherapy with severely and profoundly mentally handicapped patients. In *Treatment of Mental Illness and Behavioural Disorders in the Mentally Retarded* (ed. A. Dosen, A. Van Gannep & G. Zwanikken). Logan: Leiden.

Singh, N.N., & Repp, A.C. (1989). The behavioural and pharmacological management of problem behaviours in people with mental retardation. *Irish Journal of Psychology*, **9**, 264–285.

Skinner, B.F. (1957). *Verbal Behavior*. Appleton-Century-Crofts: New York.

Sloper, P., & Turner, S. (1993a). Determinants of parental satisfaction with disclosure of disability. *Developmental Medicine and Child Neurology*, **35**, 816–825.

Sloper, P., & Turner, S. (1993b). Risk and resistance factors in the adaptation phase of parents of children with severe physical disability. *Journal of Child Psychology and Psychiatry*, **34**, 167–188.

Smith, C. (1996). *Developing Parenting Programmes*. National Children's Bureau: London.

Sobsey, D. (1994). *Violence and Abuse in the Lives of People with Disabilities— The End of Silent Acceptance?* P.H. Brookes: Baltimore, MD.

Solnick, J.V., Rincover, A., & Peterson, C.R. (1977). Some determinants of the reinforcing and punishing effects of timeout. *Journal of Applied Behavior Analysis*, **10**, 415–424.

Sourkes, S. (1987). Siblings of the child with a life-threatening illness. *Journal of Children in Contemporary Society*, **19**, 159–184.

Spengler, P.M., Strohmer, D.C., & Prout, H.T. (1990). Testing the robustness of the diagnostic overshadowing bias. *American Journal on Mental Retardation*, **95**, 204–214.

Sprague, J.R., & Horner, R.H. (1992). Covariation within functional response classes: implications for treatment of severe problem behavior. *Journal of Applied Behavior Analysis*, **25**, 735–745.

Spreat, S., Lipinski, D., Hill, J., & Halpin, M.E. (1986). Safety indices associated with the use of contingent restraint procedures. *Applied Research in Mental Retardation*, **7**, 475–481.

Stahmer, A., & Schreibman, L. (1992). Teaching children with autism appropriate play in unsupervised settings using a self-management treatment package. *Journal of Applied Behavior Analysis* **25**, 447–459.

Stalker, K. (1996) (ed.). *Developments in Short-term Care: Breaks and Opportunities*. Jessica Kingsley: London.

Stalker, K., & Robinson, C. (1994). Parents' views of different respite care services. *Mental Handicap Research*, **7**, 97–117.

Stanley, A. (1996). The impact of the first therapeutic encounter: a trainees' view. In *Forensic Psychotherapy. Crime, Psychodynamics and the Offender Patient Vol. II: Mainly Practice* (ed. C. Cordess & M. Cox). Jessica Kingsley: London.

Steege, M.W., Wacker, D.P., Cigrand, K.C., Berg, W., Novak, C.G., Reimers, T.M., Sasso, G.M., & DeRaad, A. (1990). Use of negative reinforcement in the treatment of self-injurious behavior. *Journal of Applied Behavior Analysis*, **23**, 459–467.

Steele, J. (1993). Prenatal diagnosis and Down's syndrome: Part 2. Possible effects. *Mental Handicap Research*, **6**, 56–69.

Steen, P.I., & Zurif, G.E. (1977). The use of relaxation in the treatment of self-injurious behaviour. *Journal of Behaviour Therapy*, **8**, 738–741.

Stenfert Kroese, B., Dagnan, D., & Loumidis, K. (1997) (ed.). *Cognitive-Behavioural Therapy for People with Learning Disabilities*. Routledge: London.

Stern, J. (1985). Biochemical aspects. In *Mental Deficiency: The Changing Outlook (4th edn)*. (ed. A.M. Clarke, A.D.B. Clarke & J.M. Berg). Methuen: London.

Stokes, T.F., & Baer, D.M. (1977). An implicit technology of generalization. *Journal of Applied Behavior Analysis*, **7**, 599–610.

Strauss, D., & Eyman, R.K. (1996). Mortality of people with mental retardation in California with and without Down's syndrome, 1986–1991. *American Journal on Mental Retardation*, **100**, 643–653.

Sturmey, P. (1993). The use of DSM and ICD diagnostic criteria in people with mental retardation: a review of empirical studies. *The Journal of Nervous and Mental Disease*, **181**, 38–41.

Sturmey, P., & Bertman, L.J. (1994). Validity of the Reiss Screen for maladaptive behaviour. *American Journal on Mental Retardation*, **99**, 201–206.

Sturmey, P., Reed, J., & Corbett, J. (1991). Psychometric assessment of psychiatric disorders in people with learning difficulties (mental handicap): a review of measures. *Psychological Medicine*, **21**, 143–155.

Sturmey, P., Jamieson, J., Burcham, J., Shaw, B., & Bertman, L. (1996). The factor structure of the Reiss Screen for Maladaptive Behaviors in institutional and community populations. *Research in Developmental Disabilities*, **17**, 285–291.

Suen, H.K., & Ary, D. (1989). *Analyzing Quantitative Behavioral Observation Data*. Erlbaum: Hillsdale, NJ.

Szymanski, L.W. (1994). Mental retardation and mental health: concepts, aetiology and incidence. In *Mental Health in Mental Retardation: Recent Advances and Practices* (ed. N. Bouras). Cambridge University Press: Cambridge.

Tausig, M. (1985). Factors in family decision making about placement for developmentally disabled adults. *American Journal of Mental Deficiency*, **89**, 352–361.

Taylor, J.C., & Carr, E.G. (1993). Reciprocal social influences in the analysis and intervention of severe challenging behavior. In *Communicative Alternatives to Challenging Behavior* (ed. J. Reichle & D.P. Wacker). P.H. Brookes: Baltimore, MD.

Taylor, J.C., & Carr, E.G. (1994). Severe problem behaviors of children with developmental disabilities: reciprocal social influences. In *Destructive Behavior in Developmental Disabilities: Diagnosis and Treatment* (ed. T. Thompson & D.B. Gray). Sage: Thousand Oaks, CA.

Termelin, M.K. (1968). Suggestion effects in psychiatric diagnosis. *Journal of Nervous and Mental Disease*, **147**, 349–353.

Thompson, D. (1994). The sexual experience of men with learning disabilities having sex with men: issues for HIV protection. *Sexuality and Disability*, **12**, 221–242.

Thompson, D. (1997a). Profiling the sexually abusive behaviour of men with intellectual disabilities. *Journal of Applied Research in Intellectual Disabilities*, **10**, 125–139.

Thompson, D. (1997b). Men with intellectual disabilities who sexually abuse: A review of the literature. *Journal of Applied Research in Intellectual Disabilities*, **10**, 140–158.

Thompson, D., & Brown, H. (1997). Issues from the literature. In *There Are No Easy Answers! The Provision of Continuing Care and Treatment to Adults with*

Learning Disabilities who Sexually Abuse Others (ed. J. Churchill, H. Brown, A. Craft & C. Horrocks). ARC/NAPSAC: Chesterfield.

Thompson, D., Clare, I.C.H., & Brown, H. (1997). Not such an ordinary relationship: the role of women support staff in relation to men with learning disabilities who have difficult sexual behaviour. *Disability & Society*, **12**, 573–592.

Thompson, S., & Emerson, E. (1995). Inter-observer agreement on the Motivation Assessment Scale: another failure to replicate. *Mental Handicap Research*, **8**, 203–8.

Thompson, T., Egli, M., Symons, F., & Delaney, D. (1994). Neurobehavioral mechanisms of drug action in developmental disabilities. In *Destructive Behavior in Developmental Disabilities: Diagnosis and Treatment* (ed. T. Thompson & D.B. Gray). Sage: Thousand Oaks, CA.

Thompson, T., Symons, F., Delaney, D., & England, C. (1995). Self-injurious behavior as endogenous neurochemical self-administration. *Mental Retardation & Developmental Disability Research Reviews*, **1**, 137–148.

Thomson, M. (1996). Family, community, and state: the micro-politics of mental deficiency. In *From Idiocy to Mental Deficiency: Historical Perspectives on People with Learning Disabilities* (ed. D. Wright & A. Digby). Routledge: London.

Tomm, K. (1985). Circular questions. In *Applications of Systemic Family Therapy: The Milan Approach* (ed. D. Campbell & R. Draper). Academic Press: London.

Tomm, K. (1987). Interventive interviewing, Part II. Reflexive questioning as a means to enable self-healing. *Family Process*, **26**, 167–183.

Tones, K. (1992). Empowerment and health. *Journal of the Institute of Health Education*, **30**.

Touchette, P.E., McDonald, R.F., & Langer, S.N. (1985). A scatter plot for identifying stimulus control of problem behavior. *Journal of Applied Behavior Analysis*, **18**, 343–351.

Townsley, R., & Macadam, M. (1996). Involving people with learning difficulties in staff recruitment. *Social Care Research*, **91**. Joseph Rowntree Foundation: York.

Trent, J.W. (1995). *Inventing The Feeble Mind: A History of Mental Retardation in the United States*. University of California Press: Berkeley, CA.

Turk, V., & Brown, H. (1993). The sexual abuse of adults with learning disabilities: results of a two year incidence survey. *Mental Handicap Research* **6**, 193–216.

Turner, A.L. (1980). Therapy with families of a mentally retarded child. *Journal of Marital and Family Therapy*, **6**, 167–170.

Turner, S. (1996). Promoting healthy lifestyles for people with learning disabilities: a survey of provider organisations. *British Journal of Learning Disabilities*, **24**, 138–44.

Turner, S., & Dinnall, M. (1997). *The Health Needs of People Using Learning Disability Services in Tameside and Glossop*. Hester Adrian Research Centre, University of Manchester: Manchester.

Turner, S., & Moss, S. (1996). The health needs of people with learning disabilities and the Health of the Nation strategy. *Journal of Intellectual Disability Research*, **40**, 438–450.

Tymchuk, A. (1996). *The Development, Implementation and Preliminary Evaluation of a Cross-agency, Multi-site Self-healthcare and Safety Preparatory and Prevention Education Program for Parents with Intellectual Disabilities*. Parenting with Intellectual Disability Conference: Danish Ministry of Social Affairs.

Tymchuk, A., Andron, L., & Unger, O. (1987). Parents with mental handicaps and adequate child care—a review. *Mental Handicap*, **15**, 49–53.

United Nations (1971). *Declaration of the General and Specific Rights of the Mentally Retarded*. United Nations: New York.

US Department of Health, Education and Welfare (1978). *Disease Prevention and Health Promotion*. USD HEW: Washington, DC.

Van Houten, R., Axelrod, S., Bailey, J.S., Favell, J.E., Foxx, R.M., Iwata, B.A., & Lovaas, O.I. (1988). The right to effective behavioral treatment. *Journal of Applied Behavior Analysis*, **21**, 381–384.

Vaughan, P.J., & Badger, D. (1995). *Working with the Mentally Disordered Offender in the Community*. Chapman and Hall: London.

Vetere, A. (1993). Using family therapy services for people with learning disabilities. In *Using Family Therapy in the 1990s (2nd edn)* (ed J. Carpenter & A. Treacher). Blackwell: Oxford.

Vizard, E. (1989) Child sexual abuse and mental handicap: a child psychiatrist's perspective. In *Thinking the Unthinkable—Papers on Sexual Abuse and People with Learning Difficulties* (eds. H. Brown & A. Craft). FPA Education Unit: London.

Vollmer, T.R. (1994). The concept of automatic reinforcement: implications for behavioral research in developmental disabilities. *Research in Developmental Disabilities*, **15**, 187–207.

Wacker, D.P., Steege, J.N., Sasso, G., Berg, W., Reimers, T., Cooper, L., Cigrand, K., & Donn, L. (1990). A component analysis of functional communication training across three topographies of severe behavior problems. *Journal of Applied Behavior Analysis*, **23**, 417–429.

Walker, N., & McCabe, S. (1973). *Crime and Insanity in England*, (Volume 2). Edinburgh University Press: Edinburgh.

Ward, L. (1995). Equal citizens: current issues for people with learning difficulties and their allies. In *Values and Visions: Changing Ideas in Services for People with Learning Difficulties* (ed. T. Philpot & L. Ward). Butterworth-Heinemann: Oxford.

Webster-Stratton, C. (1991). Annotation: strategies for helping families with conduct disordered children. *Journal of Child Psychiatry and Psychology*, **32**, 1047–1062.

Weiss, N.R. (1992). *The Application of Aversive Procedures to Individuals with Developmental Disabilities: A Call to Action*. Weiss: Baltimore, MD.

Wellesley, D., Hockey, A., & Stanley, F. (1991). The aetiology of intellectual disability in Western Australia: a community-based study. *Developmental Medicine and Child Neurology*, **33**, 963–973.

Welsh Office (1996). *The Welsh Health and Community Care Survey*. Welsh Office: Cardiff.

Wertheimer, A. (1996). *Changing Days: Developing New Day Opportunities with People who Have Learning Difficulties*. King's Fund: London.

West, A. (1996). The risks of burnout. In *Forensic Psychotherapy. Crime, Psychodynamics and the Offender Patient. Vol. II. Mainly Practice* (ed. C. Cordess & M. Cox). Jessica Kingsley: London.

Whitman, B., & Accardo, P. (1987). Mentally retarded parents in the community: identification method and needs assessment survey. *American Journal of Mental Deficiency*, **91**, 636–638.

Whitman, B., & Accardo, P. (1989) (ed.). *When a Parent Is Mentally Retarded*. P.H. Brookes: Baltimore, MD.

Whittaker, A. (1989). *Supporting Self-advocacy*. King's Fund: London.

Whittaker, A. (1995). Partnership in practice: user participation in services for people with learning difficulties. In *Values and Visions: Changing Ideas in Services for People with Learning Difficulties* (ed. T. Philpot & L. Ward). Butterworth-Heinemann: Oxford.

Whittaker, A. (1996). Self-advocacy. In *Changing Policy and Practice for People with Learning Disabilities* (ed. P. Mittler & V. Sinason). Cassell Educational: London.

Widaman, K.F., & McGrew, K.S. (1996). The structure of adaptive behavior. In *Manual of Diagnosis and Professional Practice in Mental Retardation* (ed. J.W. Jacobson & J.A. Mulick). American Psychological Association: Washington, DC.

Williams, C. (1995). *Invisible Victims.* Jessica Kingsley: London.

Wilson, D., & Haire, A. (1990). Health care screening for people with mental handicap living in the community. *British Medical Journal,* 15 December, 1379–1381.

Winnett, R.A., & Winkler, R.C. (1972). Current behavior modification in the classroom: be still, be quiet, be docile. *Journal of Applied Behavior Analysis,* **5,** 499–504.

Winterling, V., Dunlap, G., & O'Neill, R.E. (1987). The influence of task variation on the aberrant behaviors of autistic students. *Education and Treatment of Children,* **10,** 105–119.

Wisniewski, H., Rabe, A., & Wisniewski, K.E. (1987). Neuropathology and dementia in people with Down's syndrome. In *Molecular Neuropathology of Aging (Banbury Report 27).* Cold Spring Harbor Laboratory: Cold Spring Harbor, NY.

Wolf, M.M. (1978). Social validity: the case for subjective measurement, or how applied behavior analysis is finding its heart. *Journal of Applied Behavior Analysis,* **11,** 203–214.

Wolfensberger, W. (1972). *The Principle of Normalization in Human Services.* National Institute of Mental Retardation: Toronto.

Wolfensberger, W. (1975). *The Origin and Nature of Our Institutional Models.* Human Policy Press: Syracuse.

Wolfensberger, W. (1980). The definition of normalisation: update, problems, disagreements and misunderstandings. In *Normalization, Social Integration and Community Services* (ed. R.J. Flynn & K.E. Nitsch). University Park Press: Baltimore, MD.

Wolfensberger, W. (1983). Social role valorization: a proposed new term for the principle of normalization. *Mental Retardation,* **21,** 234–239.

Wolfensberger, W., & Thomas, S. (1983). *PASSING: Program Analysis of Service Systems Implementation of Normalization Goals.* National Institute on Mental Retardation: Toronto.

Woodruff, M. (1994). *Building a Better System.* The Spokesman Review.

World Health Organization (1992). *ICD-10: International Statistical Classification of Diseases and Related Health Problems, 10th Revision.* WHO: Geneva.

World Health Organization (1993). *The Tenth Revision of the International Classification of Mental and Behavioural Disorders (ICD-10): Diagnostic Criteria for Research.* WHO: Geneva.

World Health Organization (1994). *Schedules for Clinical Assessment in Neuropsychiatry, Version 2.* World Health Organization: Geneva.

Wressel, S.E., Tyrere, S.P., & Berney, T.P. (1990). Reduction in anti-psychotic drug dosage in mentally handicapped patients. A hospital study. *British Journal of Psychiatry,* **157,** 101–106.

Wright, D. (1996). 'Childlike in his innocence': lay attitudes to 'idiots' and 'imbeciles' in Victorian England. In *From Idiocy to Mental Deficiency: Historical Perspectives on People with Learning Disabilities* (ed. D. Wright & A. Digby). Routledge: London.

Wright, D., & Digby, A. (ed.) (1996). *From Idiocy to Mental Deficiency: Historical Perspectives on People with Learning Disabilities*. Routledge: London.

Wright, L. (1995). Take it from us: training by people who know what they are talking about. In *Values and Visions: Changing Ideas in Services for People with Learning Difficulties* (ed. T. Philpot & L. Ward). Butterworth-Heinemann: Oxford.

Yaqoob, M., Bashir, A., Tareen, K., Gustavson, K-H., Nazir, R., Jalil, F., von Dobeln, U., & Ferngren, H. (1995). Severe mental retardation in 2–24 month-old children in Lahore, Pakistan: a prospective cohort study. *Acta Paediatrica*, **84**, 267–272.

Yoder, P.J., & Warren, S.F. (1993). Can developmentally delayed children's language development be enhanced? In *Enhancing Children's Communication: Research Foundations for Intervention* (ed. A.P. Kaiser & D.B. Gray). P.H. Brookes: Baltimore, MD.

Zarkowska, E., & Clements, J. (1994). *Severe Problem Behaviour: The STAR Approach*. Chapman and Hall: London.

Zigman, W.B., Schupf, N., Sersen, E., & Silverman, W. (1995). Prevalence of dementia in adults with and without Down's syndrome. *American Journal on Mental Retardation*, **100**, 403–412.

Zigman, W.B., Schupf, N., Zigman, A., & Silverman, W. (1993). Aging and Alzheimer's disease in people with mental retardation. In *International Review of Research in Mental Retardation* (Volume 19) (ed. N.W. Bray). Academic Press: New York.

INDEX

Entries refer to people with intellectual disabilities unless otherwise specified.

Index compiled by Sylvia Potter

The Wiley Series in

CLINICAL PSYCHOLOGY